THE EARLY REPUBLIC

*Primary Documents on Events
from 1799 to 1820*

Patricia L. Dooley

Debating Historical Issues in the Media of the Time
David A. Copeland, Series Editor

GREENWOOD PRESS

Library of Congress Cataloging-in-Publication Data

The early republic : primary documents on events from 1799 to 1820 / [compiled by]
Patricia L. Dooley.
    p. cm. – (Debating historical issues in the media of the time, ISSN 1542–8079)
  Includes bibliographical references (p.) and index.
  ISBN 0–313–32084–5 (alk. paper)
  1. United States—History—1783–1815—Sources. 2. United States—History—1783–1815
—Press coverage. I. Dooley, Patricia L. II. Series.
  E301.E15   2004
  973.4–dc22   2004020054

British Library Cataloguing in Publication Data is available.

Library of Congress Catalog Card Number: 2004020054
ISBN: 0–313–32084–5
ISSN: 1542–8079

First published in 2004

Greenwood Press, 88 Post Road West, Westport, CT 06881
An imprint of Greenwood Publishing Group, Inc.
www.greenwood.com

Printed in the United States of America

The paper used in this book complies with the
Permanent Paper Standard issued by the National
Information Standards Organization (Z39.48–1984).

10 9 8 7 6 5 4 3 2 1

Contents

Series Foreword   vii

Introduction: Newspapers in America's Early National Period   ix

Chronology of Events   xxi

Chapter 1: The Aftermath of George Washington's Death, 1799–1801   1

Chapter 2: The United States Capital Moves to the Potomac, 1800   21

Chapter 3: Thomas Jefferson's Election to the Presidency, 1800–1801   37

Chapter 4: Medical Treatment and *The Rush-Light*, 1800   53

Chapter 5: Gabriel's Slave Rebellion, 1800   65

Chapter 6: Jefferson's Patronage and the New Haven Remonstrance, 1801   85

Chapter 7: Thomas Jefferson's Mammoth Cheese and "Wall of Separation," 1802   97

Chapter 8: Nativism in the Age of Jefferson   109

Chapter 9: The Tripolitan War, 1801–1805   125

Chapter 10: The Louisiana Purchase, 1803   137

Chapter 11: *Marbury v. Madison,* 1801–1803   151

Chapter 12: Aaron Burr's Conspiracy and Arrest for Treason, 1805–1807   165

Chapter 13: The *Chesapeake–Leopard* Affair, 1807   177

Chapter 14: New Jersey's Repeal of Women's Suffrage, 1807   189

Contents

Chapter 15. The Embargo Act, 1807–1809   201

Chapter 16. The Launching of the Steamboat *Clermont,* 1807   213

Chapter 17. The Battle of Tippecanoe, November 7–8, 1811   225

Chapter 18. The Declaration of the War of 1812   243

Chapter 19. The Burning of Washington, D.C., August 24, 1814   261

Chapter 20. "Marats, Dantons, and Robespierres": The Hartford Convention, 1814–1815   279

Chapter 21. The Era of Good Feelings, 1817   295

Chapter 22. New York City's Wild Dogs, Mad Hogs, and Petty Criminals, 1816–1818   305

Chapter 23. The Establishment of the Second Bank of the United States, 1816   317

Chapter 24. The Financial Panic and Depression of 1819   325

Chapter 25. Poverty and Pauperism in the Early National Period, 1805–1819   337

Chapter 26. The Missouri Compromise, 1819–1820   349

Selected Bibliography   365

Index   367

Series Foreword

A s the eighteenth century was giving way to the nineteenth, the *Columbian Centinel* of Boston, quoting a wise judge on January 1, 1799, said, "Give to any set men the command of the press, and you give them the command of the country, for you give them the command of public opinion, which commands everything." One month later, Thomas Jefferson wrote to James Madison with a similar insight. "We are sensible," Jefferson said of the efforts it would take to put their party—the Republicans—in power, "The engine is the press."

Both writers were correct in their assessment of the role the press would play in American life in the years ahead. The press was already helping to shape the opinions and direction of America. It had been doing so for decades, but its influence would erupt following the Revolutionary War and continue into the 1920s and farther. From less than forty newspapers in 1783—each with circulations of around 500—the number of papers erupted in the United States. By 1860, newspaper circulation exceeded 1 million, and in 1898, Joseph Pulitzer's *World* alone had a daily circulation of 1.3 million. By the beginning of World War I, about 16,600 daily and weekly newspapers were published, and circulation figures passed 22.5 million copies per day with no slow down in circulation in sight. Magazines grew even more impressively. From around five at the end of the Revolution, journalism historian Frank Luther Mott counted 600 in 1860 and a phenomenal 3,300 by 1885. Some circulations surpassed 1 million, and the number of magazines continued to grow into the twentieth century.

The amazing growth of the press happened because the printed page of periodicals assumed a critical role in the United States. Newspapers and magazines became the place where Americans discussed and debated the issues that affected them. Newspapers, editors, and citizens took sides, and they used the press as the conduit for discussion. The Debating the Issues series offers a glimpse into how the press was used by Americans to shape and influence the major events and issues facing the nation during different periods of its development. Each volume is based on the documents, that is, the writings that appeared in the press of the time. Each volume presents articles, essays, and editorials that support opposing interests on the events and issues; and each provides readers with background and explanation of the events, issues, and, if possible, the people who wrote the articles that have been selected. Each volume also includes a chronology of events and a selected bibliography. The series is based on the Greenwood Press publication, *Debating the Issues in Colonial Newspapers*. Books in the Debating the Issues series cover the following periods: the Revolution and the young republic, the Federalist era, the antebellum period, the Civil War, Reconstruction, the progressive era, and World War I.

This volume on the Early Republic focuses on the events in the two pivotal decades that began the nineteenth century. The nation experienced its first "regime" change as the Republicans gained control of the White House and Congress from the Federalists. The nation closed the largest—and probably best—land acquisition in history with the Louisiana Purchase. The international situation of the period led to America's "second war of independence" in 1812. Slave revolts, fear of immigrants, and wars with Native Americans marked the era, too. The nation also faced disunion, and the issue was not slavery. The battle over that "peculiar institution" would come, however, but not before the nation experienced a time one newspaper editor called "the era of good feelings." In this period, the press drove politics, the economy, and even the call for war. Newspaper editors were fiercely partisan, and they and the political parties they supported fought through the printed page to direct the nation.

Introduction: Newspapers in America's Early National Period

O n New Year's Day, 1800, Americans were preoccupied with a multitude of weighty matters, and most of them were discussed in the country's 234 newspapers.[1] Among the topics of the day were the Federalist government's Alien and Sedition Act prosecutions, the nation's problems with France and England, and the approaching presidential election. Another big story was the December 14 death of George Washington, the people's beloved Revolutionary War hero and first president. Americans were bereft with grief, and the newspapers were filled with reports about his funeral and the many solemn events held across the country in his honor.

Since the American Revolution, a primary role of the newspaper was to provide the nation's citizens with news and commentary on politics and government. After all, it was the printers who churned out page after page of the rebellious propaganda that both ignited and helped the Patriots win the war against Great Britain. Afterward, newspaper proprietors sought to capitalize on their new reputations as crucial political communicators. In 1793, for example, Alexander Young and Samuel Etheridge reminded their potential subscribers of the importance of the newspaper:

At no period, since the discovery of printing, has there ever been so interesting an era as the present.... Newspapers originally fanned that favored flame of Liberty, which first was kindled on the Columbian Altar, and from thence with unexampled rapidity has spread to the furthest bourne of Europe, illuminating the universe of Man in its progress, and giving freedom to myriad of lives.[2]

The connection of the newspaper to the political and governmental realm became so firmly established that most newspapers were tied in one way or another to one of the nation's fledgling political parties. By the end of Thomas Jefferson's first presidency, in 1804, all but 56 of the nation's 329 newspapers supported either the Federalist or Jeffersonian Republican party.[3] To serve their politically opinionated customers, newspaper editors routinely provided them with election reports, political essays and letters, speeches, and transcripts of the proceedings of the U.S. Congress and state legislative bodies.

Some press historians call the early decades of the nineteenth century the black period of American journalism, because the newspapers were so filled with vindictive and inflammatory essays. These essays appalled many and at times even led to violence. Other historians remind us that the violence of the rhetoric included in early nineteenth-century newspapers must be considered in the context of the times.[4] But whether they liked newspapers or not, politicians used them liberally. On reaching the end of his second term as president in 1808, Thomas Jefferson swore he was so disgusted with the licentiousness of the country's newspapers that he would never read one again. In response, one of Jefferson's Federalist enemies reminded his readers that Jefferson had never been averse to using the newspapers for his own purposes. As the editor of Baltimore's *Federal Republican and Country Gazette* sarcastically put it, "Need we remind his Excellency of his covertly instigating and employing the infamous [Thomas] Paine, [James Thomson] Callender, and the still more execrable [William] Duane to traduce and calumniate the hero [George Washington] to whom we owe our liberties?"[5]

Along with the political communication in the newspapers, editors included a substantial amount of material on foreign relations, shipping and other business matters, religion, agriculture, science, literature, and art. In addition, the period's newspapers also contained content of a less serious nature. As New Year's Day, 1800, approached, for example, people wondered whether they should celebrate it as the first day of the new millennium or whether they should wait a year. Along these lines, Angier March, editor of the *Newburyport Herald and Commercial Gazette* in Massachusetts, entertained his readers with this story:

> A person was contending warmly at Paris that we were in the 19th century, and he employed all sorts of arguments to prove it. One of the company interrupted him…and said, "I am happy at meeting you, my friend; permit me to pay you a small debt of 18 francs which I borrowed of you the other day; here are 17 francs and 19 cents. But citizen, I lent you 18 francs, and there wants one cent. How ! have you not just proved that the year 1800 is the first year of the 19th century.—The franc being the century of the cen-

time, does it not follow that my 100th cent would be the first cent of the 19th franc; that in giving it you, I owe you but 18 francs, and you have not advanced me the first cent of the 19th franc?" The creditor not knowing what to reply, but wishing to shew himself steady in his principles, took the 17 francs, 99 cents, and gave a receipt for 18 francs.[6]

The *Herald*'s inclusion of this anecdote symbolizes the diverse roles newspapers served at the start of the nineteenth century. As the unknown author of this piece cleverly put it, newspaper editors satisfied the hunger of their readers by serving up more than politics:

> A NEWSPAPER is a bill of fare, containing a variety of dishes, suited to the different tastes and appetites of those who sit down at the entertainment. Politics are *beef steaks*, palatable to almost every one. Those who prefer them *rare done*, choose those from France.—Electioneering is *venison*. Congress news, is *stuffed meats*—Essays, humorous, speculative, moral and divine, are a *fine boiled dish*, where, by a happy commixture in the use of bread, meat and vegetables, a diet is obtained, nutritive, pleasant and healthy—Ship news is a *glass of grog at 'leven*—Poetry is *custard*—Marriages are *sweetmeats*—Ballads and love-ditties, *plum puddings*…and epigrams, are *seasoning spice* and *mustard*—Sometimes there comes along a Printer's Dun; that is *sour crout* or *cranberry tart*.[7]

While it's tempting to think of this "bill of fare" as merely a bit of charming self-promotion, it illustrates the realities of the period's newspaper industry. To stay in business, successful newspaper proprietors were hard-nosed businesspeople who paid ample attention to the growing needs of a literate public. And their formula worked: From 1800 to 1820, the number of newspapers published in the United States rose from 234 to more than 500.

Considering the difficulties inherent in the issuance of newspapers, such an increase was quite a feat. Newspapers were expensive enough that many Americans could not afford to buy them, and a lot of the day's news was spread orally or through the exchange of letters. Other problems faced by early nineteenth-century newspaper publishers were poor transportation, slow mail delivery, shortages of printing materials and other supplies, difficulties in attracting subscribers and sponsors, unpaid subscribers' bills, and the constant need for correspondents and other writers who would send material for publication. Nevertheless, newspapers were issued as soon as possible in the new communities that were forged out of the wilderness as people moved south and west from New England. Eventually, newspapers became so popular that they were issued in handwritten forms before the first printing presses arrived. Even though Horace Greeley's famous phrase "Go West, young man" had not yet been uttered, by the turn of the century, printers branched out from New England, the birthplace of America's press, to as far away as Georgia, Kentucky, Louisiana, Mississippi, Ohio, Tennessee, and West Virginia, and 21 newspapers had been started west of the mountains.[8]

In 1800, most newspapers were dailies, four-page weeklies, semi-weeklies, or tri-weeklies, printed with the same kind of equipment invented by Johannes Gutenberg in the fifteenth century. In appearance the newspapers looked as primitive as their eighteenth-century antecedents. Most of the front pages of America's newspapers were filled with ads and other notices of general interest, and although some political information was included there, the majority of it was printed inside on pages two and three. But despite their unassuming looks, the newspapers had much to do with the creation of the popular movement that made the West a new factor in American politics.

One center of noticeable growth in the newspaper business in 1800 was Washington, D.C., which that year replaced Philadelphia as the nation's permanent capital. During 1800, seven newspapers were started in Georgetown and Washington on the Potomac.[9] While several of them were short-lived, the *National Intelligencer* and its rival, the *Washington Federalist*, grew to be important conduits of news and political opinion in the early years of the century. The *National Intelligencer* was established just weeks before Congress met for the first time at Washington, D.C., in November 1800.[10] The founder of the *Intelligencer* was Samuel Harrison Smith, who moved to the Potomac from Philadelphia along with the federal government. Although historians have generally concluded that the *Intelligencer* was Thomas Jefferson's newspaper, there was no hint of that in Smith's first message to his readers. As he put it, the *Intelligencer* would be a national paper: "The design of the *National Intelligencer* is to diffuse correct information through the whole extent of the union." Smith reassured his readers that his paper would include "unperverted facts, and correct political ideas," and that there was a "strong necessity of having...at the seat of the General Government, a newspaper, that may claim the reputation of being useful."[11]

The fulfillment of this promise depended on the ability of Smith and his staff to attend all sessions of Congress, and at times this was a problem. In December 1800, when the presidential election was thrown into the House of Representatives by a deadlocked electoral college, 45 congressional members voted to exclude Smith's stenographers. In response, Smith published a lengthy diatribe from a local correspondent who objected to Congress's vote to close its proceedings. After a description of the course of events that led to the closure, "A Representative of the People" summed up his concerns:

> These facts elucidate the *manner* in which this business has been managed; but the *matter* itself is more important.

It involves the great question whether in a republican government those who make laws for the people have a right to conceal from the people the ground on which those laws are made. I affirm that they have not; and if they exercise such a power, it is usurped and not legitimate.[12]

In the wake of the Jeffersonian Republicans' triumph as they won the presidency and control of Congress in the election of 1800–1801, Smith continued publishing the *National Intelligencer* until 1810, when he retired and turned it over to Joseph Gales Jr. and William W. Seaton. Gales and Seaton turned the *Intelligencer* into a daily. Through much of the rest of its life, which extended until mid-century, it was generally considered the federal government's official newspaper because of its coverage of Congress and other news related to the nation's capital.

Rivaling the *Intelligencer* at Washington were popular Federalist newspapers such as the *Washington Federalist*, which was established on September 25, 1800, by William Alexander Rind. On every front, Rind and the nation's other Federalist editors questioned the principles and conduct of their Jeffersonian Republican opponents. Boston's *Columbian Centinel*, New York's *Evening Post*, Baltimore's *Federal Republican*, and a host of others both capitalized on and contributed to the contentious and acrimonious debates over the many important political and constitutional questions of the day.

Among this group, the *Columbian Centinel*, edited by Benjamin Russell since 1790 in the heart of Federalist territory, was always in the forefront of their battles against Thomas Jefferson's Republicans. Another strong Federalist voice was the *Evening Post*, started at New York City in 1801 by Alexander Hamilton under the editorship of William Coleman. And Baltimore's *Federal Republican*, established in 1808, was so critical of the Republican-run federal government that its presses and supplies were destroyed and its building was burned down by an angry mob after the War of 1812 broke out. Not until the demise of the old party of Washington and Hamilton in the election of 1816 would Federalists put down their pens; even then, there remained many vestiges of Federalism in the nation's newspapers.

While some of the material published in the newspapers was written by printers and editors, a great deal of it was sent by correspondents and other talented writers willing to see their words in print. But publishers had trouble getting enough material to fill the papers. To attract the interest of potential contributors, the editor of Lexington's *Kentucky Gazette* placed this artful notice in the May 15, 1800, issue of his paper:

If you wish to laugh a while,
Or if you only wish to smile,
Or if you wish to crack a joke,

Or if to make a witty stroke,
Pray put it in the News-Paper.

If you wish to serve the state,
Or useful tidings to relate,
Or if you wish advice to give,
To shew vain fools the way to live,
Pray do it in the News-Papers.

If politics you understand,
And useful thoughts you can command,
Or if a government you plan,
Or any thing to answer man,
Pray do it in the News-Papers.

If genius chance to be your lot,
Then value critics not a jot,
But aid the Press with something new;
And if the theme you should pursue,
Pray do it in the News-Paper.

The difficulties of filling the columns of their newspapers led editors to reprint material they found in other newspapers. Editors then complained about the unattributed copying of their newspapers' contents. *New-York Evening Post* editor William Coleman wrote about this in 1816:

> We have, in silence, witnessed the unhandsome practice of certain distant conductors of the public prints, in boldly appropriating to themselves the editorial articles of others, or of attributing them to those of their brother printers to whom they do not belong but for whom they happen to have a preference, as being their particular correspondents, or of crediting them to the New-York papers, at large: but though we have long seen this un-generous treatment in silence, those concerned are assured, we have not seen it with indifference. We for the present content ourselves, however, with the bare mention of the fact, and hope that no future repetition of conduct so injurious, and certainly, so unmerited, will render it necessary to be more particular.[13]

Adding to the confusion about who wrote what and where it was origi-nally published were the many writers who still adhered to the eighteenth-century practice of writing under pseudonyms. In a *New-York Evening Post* column on the Louisiana Purchase, for example, Alexander Hamilton wrote under the moniker "Pericles." Thomas Jefferson rarely wrote for the papers, but when he did, he wrote under an assumed name. One newspaper debate he couldn't resist contributing to was the squabble that broke out early in his first term over how he was handling his patronage. In a piece published in Boston's *Independent Chronicle*, Jefferson signed his essay with the name

"Fair Play." Added to these famous writers were the hundreds of more obscure individuals who also chose to write under pseudonyms. In this volume, for example, writers who contributed to debates on General Washington's death, the relocation of the nation's capitol to Washington, D.C., the presidential election of 1800–1801, and medicine in the new republic wrote under such names as "The Lay Preacher of Philadelphia," "Epaminondas," "Patriotism," "Burleigh," and "A Gentleman." Even though communicators who criticized the authorities were not prosecuted as frequently after the turn of the century as they were earlier, the habit of using assumed names when expressing strong opinions on one subject or another had not yet died out.

Between 1800 and 1820, newspaper editors stirred up public controversies that contributed to matters beyond ordinary state and national politics. William Coleman, for example, in addition to being one of the nation's most active political editors, was also one of America's most civic-minded citizens. While his peers tended to focus most of their attention on politics, Coleman was in the forefront of a small but growing number interested in how their town's or city's officials were (or were not) taking care of the towns and municipalities under their jurisdiction. In such a vein, Coleman launched vigorous campaigns designed to prod officials into keeping New York's streets clean and safe for its residents and many visitors. At other times, he called particular city officials to task for not performing as he thought they should. In 1807, he was sued by a city official for a humanitarian stance he took in reaction to a sad event. Coleman had accused New York City's almshouse superintendent, Philip R. Arcularius, of mistreating a homeless black woman about to give birth by refusing to give her shelter, thereby forcing her to have her baby in a vacant lot. In a courtroom speech on the duties of newspaper editors, Coleman's lawyer opined, "It is his [Coleman's] duty to keep a watchful eye over them [public officials], and to call the attention of the public to any of their acts, which in his opinion are neglectful or criminal."[14] The jury issued a verdict in favor of Coleman and, in response, Arcularius commissioned the printing of a pamphlet that included trial proceedings, speeches, and testimonies in an attempt to have the last word in the case.[15]

Another editor with an eye toward internal and civic improvements was Joseph Gales, who started Raleigh, North Carolina's *Register* in 1799. Among Gales's favorite causes were agricultural development, medical societies, public education, libraries, and improvements in the town's firefighting capabilities. After a devastating fire that destroyed 51 structures in a two-block area in one of Raleigh's most heavily populated neighborhoods, Gales complained the tragedy could have been avoided if the town had a fire engine and an adequate supply of water. He wrote, "Will not these

facts open the eyes of those who are opposed…[to such improvements as]
an unnecessary public tax?"[16]

Although the publication of such disputes may have helped newspapers
gain readers, attracting enough subscribers to make a profit was still, for the
most part, very difficult in the early nineteenth century. In 1811, the editor
of Lexington's *Kentucky Gazette* must have been in a cynical mood when he
published this piece of correspondence offering "several weighty reasons
why [people]…ought to be excused from taking the newspapers":

> There's no occasion for my taking the papers; I am in neighbor —'s store
> every day and see it as soon as it comes.
>
> There's no use in my taking the paper, for we can't have it a minute after
> it comes into the store; one or other catches it up so quick.
>
> I have no need to take the paper; I can always read it at the barber's.
>
> I need not take the papers; for I am so much among people, that I can
> hear all the news at the post-office, and see the arrivals in the Philadelphia
> papers, and that's all I want to know.
>
> It is no matter about *our* taking the paper; (a man once told the printer;)
> father generally goes to meeting every Sunday, and comes back by Mr.
> M—'s, as it is no more than three miles and a half out of his way, through
> the woods, and borrows his paper every week.
>
> I don't want the paper; there's a parcel left at the school house every
> week and the boys bring one home for us to read.
>
> We don't want the paper; there's one or two left at the house for the back
> neighbors that we read.
>
> I don't want the paper but a few minutes just to run over the foreign
> news, or see what congress or the legislature are about, or look at the ad-
> vertisements, and any body will lend one long enough for that, without
> taking it myself.[17]

If all these opportunities to get the newspaper without a subscription failed,
the less scrupulous among society could always simply steal them. Indeed,
paper stealing was more common during this era than newspaper proprietors could easily tolerate.

To launch new newspapers, printers sent out calls for subscribers in cir-
culars or advertisements. Often called prospectuses, such statements generally included details about the kinds of news and other information the
proposed periodical would print, whether its editor was allied with a particular political party, how often it would be issued, and so on. Sending out
prospectuses helped publishers assess whether they could be assured of
subscribers. It was important to know this, since the financial risk involved
in starting a newspaper was substantial, and for most proprietors, the newspaper business was anything but lucrative. As one editor from Trenton, New
Jersey, put it in the *True American,* "We do not believe there is any trade or
calling in the Union that involves those who pursue it in equal trouble and

expense with that of News-paper printing, & at the same time gives them such small profits and poor pay." Following that, he reprinted an editorial note clipped from a Kentucky newspaper on the costs incurred in its issuance:

> The cash expense for this paper...for the present year, amounted to $916– and the whole amount received for subscriptions, for the same time only $535.50. Leaving a balance of $380.50 for paper only, to be provided for from some other fund! But the paper is not the only expence–the wages of journeymen, board and cloathing of apprentices, house rent, fire wood, &c. are serious expenses, which, under existing circumstances, must involve innumerable difficulties.[18]

Such harsh financial realities meant the failure rate of newly established newspapers was high. Of the seven newspapers started at Washington, D.C., in 1800, for example, only the *National Intelligencer* and *Federal Republican* stayed in business for more than two years. Despite all these difficulties, newspapers were by this time considered so important by their publishers that they often persisted in their efforts to make a go of it. Benjamin True, for instance, established at least seven newspapers during his printing and publishing career. After starting out in 1795 at Hanover, New Hampshire, he moved to Boston, where he established six newspapers from 1804 to 1840. The prospectus he issued as he started the *Boston Courier* in 1805 sought to convince Americans of the importance of his work:

> The American press is now generally acknowledged to be an engine of great influence. Under the superintendence of skilled hands and judiciously conducted, it is calculated to disseminate useful information; to keep the public mind awake and active, to confirm and extend the love of freedom; to correct the mistakes of the ignorant, and the impositions of the crafty; to tear off the mask from corrupt and designing politicians; and finally, to promote union of spirit and action among the most distant members of an extended community.[19]

This book presents debates on issues discussed in America from 1799 to 1820. With a focus on a specific event or issue, each chapter includes writers who wished to share their views not only with those they opposed, but also with their friends and neighbors. Logically, a number of the chapters center on the more famous events and issues of the period. Among these are chapters on the ascendancy of Thomas Jefferson and his Republican Party to the presidency and their control of Congress in 1800–1801, the Louisiana Purchase of 1803, the infamous 1807 Embargo Act, the exploits of Aaron Burr, and the Missouri Compromise. But chapters on events or issues not as well known as these are also included. In this category are chapters on health and medicine, women's suffrage, pauperism and how to help the poor, nativism, slave rebellions, Native Americans, and conditions in America's slowly developing urban environments. These help underscore the point that the newspapers published in the first two decades of the nineteenth century were not entirely fixated on politics and building the nation. To portray newspapers in such a way would not only negate the richness of their offerings, but also deny the complexity of life in this period of American history. The newspaper material included in these chapters will, hopefully, contribute to the work being done today by students and historians who are studying the nation's social and cultural histories.

The chapters are roughly in chronological order, although some of them overlap. The organization of each chapter depends on the way the debate or issue was discussed in the newspapers. The topics are organized in a pro versus con format, and several chapters include sections with newspaper quotes that provide helpful background information. Twenty-six issues of concern in the early national period are included in this work. Each chapter concludes with questions for discussion.

NOTES

1. Carol Sue Humphrey, *The Press of the Young Republic* (Westport, Conn.: Greenwood Press, 1996), 71.

2. Alexander Young and Samuel Etheridge, *Massachusetts Mercury* (Boston), 1 January 1793.

3. Humphrey, *Press of the Young Republic*, 71.

4. Frank Luther Mott, in *American Journalism* (New York: Macmillan, 1962), derogatorily named the early decades of the nineteenth century the age of "Black Journalism." W. David Sloan, however, cautioned that this kind of rhetoric was common at the time. See his "Scurrility and the Party Press, 1789–1816," *American Journalism* 5 (1988): 98–112.

5. Alexander Contee Hanson, *Federal Republican and Country Gazette* (Baltimore, Md.), 3 August 1808.

6. Angier March, "The Nineteenth Century," *Newburyport Herald and Country Gazette* (Massachusetts), 13 May 1800.

7. Different versions of this were published in the period's newspapers, including the *Newburyport Herald and Country Gazette*, in Massachusetts, on 21 February 1800; the *New York Daily Advertiser*, 20 May 1819; and the 26 June 1819 issue of the *Carolina Centinel* at Fayetteville, North Carolina.

8. Michael Emery, Edwin Emery, and Nancy L. Roberts, *The Press and America* (New York: Allyn and Bacon, 2000), 80.

9. Clarence S. Brigham, *History and Bibliography of American Newspapers, 1690–1820*, vol. 1 (Worcester, Mass.: American Antiquarian Society, 1947).

10. William E. Ames, *A History of the National Intelligencer* (Chapel Hill: University of North Carolina Press, 1972).

11. Samuel Harrison Smith, *National Intelligencer* (District of Columbia), 3 November 1800.

12. "A Representative of the People," *National Intelligencer*, 19 December 1800.

13. William Coleman, *New-York Evening Post*, 28 August 1816.

14. Philip I. Arcularius, William Coleman, and William Sampson, *A Faithful Report of the Trial of the Cause of Philip R. Arcularius* (New York: Kirk for Dornin, 1807).

15. Ibid.

16. Joseph Gales, *Raleigh Register, and North-Carolina Gazette*, 15 June 1816.

17. Thomas Smith, *Kentucky Gazette*, 17 September 1811.

18. James J. Wilson, "Patronage of Printers," *True American* (Trenton, N.J.), 19 January 1807.

19. Benjamin True, prospectus for the *Boston Courier*, 13 June 1805.

Chronology of Events

1800	5.3 million people live in America, according to the federal census
1800	Treaty of Montefontaine ends undeclared war between the United States and France
1800	United States capital moves to Washington on the Potomac
1800	The *National Intelligencer* and *Federal Republican* are among seven newspapers established in the nation's new capital
1800–1801	Thomas Jefferson's election to the presidency starts the "Age of Jefferson"
1800	Outgoing President John Adams "packs the courts" and creates new positions for his Federalist friends in his famous "Midnight Appointments"
1801	Alexander Hamilton establishes the *New-York Evening Post* under the editorship of William Coleman
1801	America's first major camp meeting and the start of the Second Great Awakening
1801	Tripoli declares a war on the United States that lasts until 1805
1802	President Jefferson writes his famous "wall of separation" statement after receiving the mammoth cheese brought to him by a group of Baptists from Danbury, Massachusetts
1802	Excise duties, including controversial whiskey tax, repealed by Congress

1802	Naturalization Act of 1798, part of the Alien and Sedition Acts, nullified by Congress
1802	July 4 opening of America's first military academy in West Point, New York
1802	Congress lowers residency requirement to become a U.S. citizen to five years
1803	*Marbury v. Madison,* as decided by Supreme Court Chief Justice John Marshall, gives the power of judicial review to the court
1803	Libel trial of Harry Croswell ushers in more freedom of the press
1803	Ohio joins the union as the seventeenth state
1803	The Louisiana Purchase is negotiated in Paris, France, for the sum of $15 million
1803	Thomas Jefferson's Lewis and Clark expedition sets off down the Ohio River
1804	Impeachment proceedings against Supreme Court Justice Samuel Chase begin
1804	Adoption of the 12th Amendment to the U.S. Constitution
1804	Aaron Burr shoots and kills Alexander Hamilton in a duel
1805	Renewed hostilities between France and England lead to American shipping difficulties in the Atlantic Ocean
1806	Thomas Jefferson is inaugurated for his second term as president
1806	Noah Webster issues his *Compendious Dictionary of the English Language*
1806	Discovery of Pike's Peak by Zebulon Pike
1806	Congressional ban on all slave importation into the United States, which was to become effective in 1808
1806	First Non-Importation Act passed by Congress
1807	Robert Fulton's steamboat *Clermont* is launched
1807	*Chesapeake–Leopard* impressments incident
1807	Embargo Act enacted, leading to fierce protests in New England
1808	Thomas Jefferson refuses to run for a third term as president, naming James Madison as his successor
1809	Enforcement Act passed by Congress to halt smuggling
1809	New England conventions called to nullify the Embargo Act

1809	Non-Intercourse Act signed by President Jefferson reopens shipping with all countries except for France and England
1809	James Madison inaugurated as president
1809	Proclamation issued by President Madison, reinstituting trade with England
1809	Tecumseh Confederacy formed
1810	National third census totals more than 7 million people in America
1811	Hezekiah Niles starts his *Weekly Register* at Baltimore, which was published until 1849
1811	Battle of Tippecanoe, where General William Henry Harrison defeated the Shawnee
1812	James Madison inaugurated for his second term as president
1812	Louisiana enters the union as the eighteenth state
1812	United States declares war on Great Britain
1814	Great Britain invades the Potomac, burning the nation's capital on August 24
1814	On September 13, as the British attack Fort McHenry at Baltimore; Francis Scott Key writes the "Star-Spangled Banner"
1814	Hartford Convention and Treaty of Ghent
1815	Battle of New Orleans
1815	Library of Congress is established at the U.S. Capitol and arrangements are made for the purchase of Thomas Jefferson's library of 7,000 volumes
1815	Establishment of America's first peace societies in New York and Massachusetts
1815	First U.S. charter for railroad granted to John Stevens
1816	Indiana is admitted as a free state to become the union's nineteenth state
1816	Establishment of the Second Bank of the United States
1816	With the presidential election, the collapse of America's first party system
1816	Tariff Act passed by Congress perpetuates protective duties established in the War of 1812
1817	After his inauguration, newly elected President James Monroe's jubilee tour of the nation ushers in the Era of Good Feelings

1817	American Colonization Society is organized, with the purpose of returning freed slaves to Africa
1817	New York state legislature authorizes construction of the Erie Canal, which is completed in 1825
1817	Mississippi is admitted as a slave state to become the union's twentieth state
1818	Illinois is admitted as a free state to become the union's twenty-first state
1818	First Pension Act provides funds for Revolutionary War veterans
1818	Andrew Jackson begins his First Seminole War campaign in Florida
1818	Convention of 1818 settles borders between United States and Canada
1819	Adams-Onis Transcontinental Treaty cedes Florida to the United States
1819	Start of the nation's first major financial panic and depression
1819	*McCullough v. Maryland,* in which the U.S. Supreme Court rules that the states of the union cannot tax an agency of the United States
1819	Alabama is admitted as a free state to become the union's twenty-second state
1819–1820	Missouri Compromise results in admission of Maine as a free state (and as the union's twenty-third state) and Missouri as a slave state (and as the union's twenty-fourth state)

CHAPTER I

The Aftermath of George Washington's Death, 1799–1801

Toward midnight on Saturday, December 14, 1799, a gravely ill George Washington murmured, "I am just going. Have me decently buried; and don't let my body be put into the vault in less than three days after I am dead. Do you understand?" After his secretary, Mr. Lear, responded in the affirmative, the general murmured, " 'Tis well!" As he breathed his last, his wife said, " 'Tis well, all's now over; I shall soon follow him; I have no more trials to pass through."[1]

In fine health shortly before he died, the president was ill only a short time. He became wet and chilled the afternoon of Thursday, December 12, while out horseback riding in a sleet storm. Despite feeling sick with a sore throat and pain in his chest, he went riding again the next day. After retiring, he woke his wife at about 3 A.M. with the complaint that he was sick with an "ague" (chills, fever, and sweating) and was having difficulty swallowing and breathing. At about 7:30 A.M., George Rawlins, a local bloodletter, removed about 14 ounces of the president's blood. Shortly afterward, Dr. James Craik applied blisters of cantharides to Washington's throat and prescribed a mixture of molasses, vinegar, and butter. His physicians also ordered more bloodletting.

As his condition worsened, the president prepared to die. Toward evening, he said to his physician, "Doctor, I die hard, but I am not afraid to go. I believed, from my first attack, that I should not survive it. My breath cannot last long." A bit after 10 P.M., his breathing eased a bit, but this would be but a brief respite. At about 10:20 P.M., surrounded by his wife, secretary, several of his slaves, and his physicians, President Washington succumbed to his illness. After one of the physicians closed the president's eyelids and another stopped the bedroom clock, the body of the president was carried downstairs and laid on the dining room table.

Spreading "Sad Tidings." This etched and engraved print, titled "[George Washington] lived respected and fear'd—died lamented and rever'd," was published in 1800 in Philadelphia. It depicts a head-and-shoulder portrait of the president atop a funeral urn, which stands on a pedestal before an obelisk. The lines of verse on the bottom are "Columbia lamenting the loss of her son/ Who redeem'd her from slavery & liberty won/ While fame is directed by Justice to spread/ The sad tidings afar that Washington's dead." Courtesy of the Library of Congress.

This chapter begins by exploring the immediate aftermath of the president's death as it was reflected in the newspapers of the day. For years, Washington had been subjected to scathing criticism from his political enemies. But after word of the president's death, which was carried via special courier to President Adams, began to circulate, grief spread across the nation. On hearing the news, John Marshall told Congress, and plans for Washington's funeral commenced. Solemn bells tolled amid lavish public displays of grief, and for a few weeks America's citizens—even members of different political

groups—joined to pay their respects to their country's departed Revolutionary War hero and first president. The country's newspaper writers expressed
the nation's grief in the hundreds of reports, speeches, poems, funeral songs,
and essays that were published. Included here are examples taken from
Pennsylvania, New York, Maine, and Massachusetts newspapers.

But like all political leaders, George Washington was not revered by all,
a fact that is evident if you look carefully at the newspaper materials published after his death. After his retirement from the presidency, Washington
was increasingly criticized, especially by those who counted themselves
among the ranks of the burgeoning Jeffersonian Republican Party. When he
left the capital in Philadelphia on John Adams's inauguration in March 1797,
for example, Benjamin Franklin Bache included this comment in the *Aurora:*

> If ever there was a period of rejoicing, this is the moment—every heart, in
> unison with the freedom and happiness of the people, ought to beat high
> with exultation that the name of WASHINGTON from this day ceases to
> give currency to political inequity and to legalize corruption...[2]

But, as displayed in the *Aurora* obituary included here, when word of Washington's death reached Philadelphia, the anti-Federalist editor William
Duane kept in line with how Republican writers had treated Washington in
the years following the end of his presidential term: He praised Washington's accomplishments in the cause of liberty during the Revolutionary War
but ignored his later political activities.

Washington's death would not pass without provoking controversy, and
two of these controversies are highlighted here. The chapter's second group
of newspaper reports explores a debate over whether he died from the 80
ounces of blood removed during the bloodletting treatments administered
after he became ill (see chapter 4). Three entries involved in this controversy over the causes of Washington's death are included. A common treatment for both minor and serious conditions in the late eighteenth century,
bloodletting was under scrutiny. The purpose of bloodletting was to release
the "bad blood" that supposedly caused the illness. Bleeding was accomplished through the use of leeches or through cutting.

The first of these newspaper pieces was written by the president's attending physicians, James Craik and Elisha Dick. Their statement describes
the course of Washington's illness and the steps taken to try to save him.
Probably realizing they would be criticized for using bleeding and other
purging treatments in their treatment of the president, the pair of physicians
asked *Virginia Herald* publisher Timothy Green to publish their account.

The second entry in this section was published in response to Craik and
Dick's statement. In shock over Washington's death, William Cobbett, as
they had anticipated, blamed the physicians for the president's death in this

column published in his Philadelphia paper, *Porcupine's Gazette*. Cobbett had long violently opposed the kinds of medical treatments the former president had been subjected to.

Like Cobbett, the author of the final piece in this section also blamed Craik and Dick's treatment of the president for his death. The statement was written by Savannah, Georgia, physician John Brickell and was published in William Cobbett's *The Rush-Light*. The sole purpose of Cobbett's Philadelphia periodical, which lasted only five issues, was to destroy the reputation of bloodletting and other depletion methods, along with the reputations of physicians who practiced them.

A second controversy surrounding Washington's death concerned whether Washington's body should remain in its Mount Vernon vault or be moved to the nation's capital. Grief stricken, on December 18, the Sixth Congress petitioned Martha Washington to relinquish her husband's body to the nation, which would build a suitable place for his permanent interment.[3] The chapter's third section includes newspaper columns written by people on both sides of the issue. Like "Brutus" and Benjamin West in the *Washington Federalist*, some Americans believed a magnificent memorial tomb should be erected for President Washington in the new capital city. Others, including the authors of the two anonymous pieces published in the *National Intelligencer* and *Aurora*, disagreed. They considered the construction of elaborate tombs for the nation's heroes an unsuitable practice in a democratic republic. Not until 1848 would the construction of the Capital Mall's Washington Monument begin.[4]

A NATION GRIEVES

The Lay Preacher of Pennsylvania: "The Lay Preacher"

This Washington eulogy was by the "Lay Preacher of Pennsylvania," whose identity was unknown. His use of superlatives in reference to Washington was not surprising, considering the superlatives were published in the Gazette, *a newspaper that supported Federalist philosophies.*

Gazette of the United States (Philadelphia), 21 December 1799

It is an occurrence not less interesting, than extraordinary, that the departure of a single man should command the unaffected and indiscriminate lamentation of five millions of people. It is an event, the like of which the world has never witnessed, that the death of an individual should so touch a whole nation, that "the joy of the heart should cease, and the dance be turned into mourning."

The mighty monarch, whose throne is surrounded by armies numerous as the locusts of summer...goes down to the tomb, amid the execrations of oppressed subjects; or sleeps in the grave, as unheeded, as when slumbering on his bed of down. The prince, whose beneficence has whitened the plains of his country, "walks the way of nature"; and his subjects "mourn in black,"...

"His deeds exceed all speech." His fame is "written with a pen of iron with the point of a diamond." His counsel is "graven upon the table of our heart." His deeds, his fame and his counsel will endure, 'till "the great globe itself; yea, all which it inherit shall dissolve."

Anonymous: "Funeral of Gen. Washington"

Washington was buried a few days after his death in his family vault at Mount Vernon. In response, many newspapers published detailed descriptions of his funeral. Across the country, communities scheduled their own funeral services, complete with solemn parades and other somber activities.

Albany Gazette (New York), 30 December 1799

On Wednesday last the mortal part of Washington the great—the Father of his country and the friend of man, was consigned to the tomb with solemn honors and funeral pomp.

A multitude of persons assembled, from many miles around, at Mount Vernon, the choice abode and last residence of the illustrious chief. There were the groves—the spacious avenues, the beautiful and sublime scenes, the noble mansion—but, alas! The august inhabitant was now no more. That great soul was gone. His mortal part was there indeed; but ah! How affecting! How awful the spectacle of such worth and greatness, thus, to mortal eyes fallen!—Yes! Fallen! Fallen!

In the long and lofty Portico where oft the Hero walked in all his glory, now lay the shrouded corpse. The countenance still composed and serene, seemed to express the dignity of the spirit, which lately dwelt in that lifeless form. There those who paid the last sad honours to the benefactor of his country, took an impressive—a farewell view.

On the ornament, at head of the coffin, was inscribed surge *ad judicium*—about the middle of the coffin, *Glorio Deo*—and on the silver plate,

GENERAL
GEORGE WASHINGTON,
Departed this life, on the 14th December,
1799, Æt. 68.

Between three and four o'clock, the sound of artillery from a vessel in the river, firing minute guns, awoke afresh our solemn sorrow—the corpse was moved—a band of music with mournful melody melted the soul into all the tenderness of woe.

The procession was formed and moved on....

When the procession had arrived at the bottom of the elevated lawn, on the banks of the Potomac, where the family vault is placed, the cavalry halted, the infantry marched towards the Mount and formed their lines—the clergy, the Masonic Brothers and the citizens descended to the vault and the funeral service of the church was performed. The firing was repeated from the vessel in the river and sounds echoed from the woods and hills around.

Three general discharges by the infantry—the cavalry and 11 pieces of artillery, which lined the banks of the Potomak [*sic*] back of the vault, paid the last tribute to the entombed Commander in Chief of the Armies of the United States and to the venerable departed hero.

The sun was now setting. Alas! The son of glory was set forever. No; the name of Washington—the American President and General—will triumph over death—the unclouded brightness of his Glory will illuminate future ages.

Elezar Alley Jenks: "Agonizing Mortality! Washington, the Father of His Country, and the Admiration of the World, Is Dead!"

It took nearly two weeks for information about Washington's death to reach Portland, Maine. Immediately on receiving the word, normal business ceased in the town. People gathered to talk about the president's death, the town's bells were rung, and church services commenced.

Jenks' Portland Gazette (Maine), 30 December 1799

It is the inexpressibly grievous talk of this day, to announce to the people of Maine, the melancholy tidings of the Death of the illustriously Great and Good General GEORGE WASHINGTON; Who Died Suddenly, On Saturday, the 14th of December, 1799 at his Seat at Mount Vernon.... Selectmen, moved with the same sorrow which touched the hearts of all the grateful inhabitants of the town, judging they wished to manifest their respect to the memory of that justly esteemed man, recommended a suspension of business and amusements from one o'clock 'till the close of the day, ordered the bells to be tolled, and engaged the Rev. Dr. Deans, to deliver a Funeral Oration in the evening, on the solemn occasion.... The bustle of business gave way at once to the silence of sympathetic sorrow....

Anonymous: "The Lyre"

The following group of airs accompanied the recital of a funeral oration for General Washington at Philadelphia's New Theatre.

Newburyport Herald and Country Gazette (Massachusetts), 21 January 1800

AIR I.
Slowly strike the solemn bell,
Nature, found thy deepest knell;
Power of Music! touch the heart,
Nature there will do her part.
God of Melancholy, come!
Pensive o'er the Hero's tomb,
In saddest strains, his loss deplore,
With piercing cries rend ev'ry shore,
For Washington is now no more.

AIR II.
Glory, bring thy fairest wreath,
Place it on thy Hero's urn;
Mercy, in soft accents breathe,
"He never made this bosom mourn."
Ev'ry virtue here attend,
Bending o'er his sacred earth;
Gratitude, thy influence lend;
Make us feel his mighty worth.

AIR III.
Hold not back the sacred tear,
Give to him the sigh sincere,
Who living, liv'd for all.
Sorrow take the solemn hour!
Prostrate to thy melting pow'r,
Let humble mortals fall.
Come, sable goddess, take the soul
Devoted to thy dark controul;
Come take our hearts, and press them deep,
Angels may joy, but man must weep.

William Duane: "George Washington"

Democratic Republican Duane was able to give the departed president credit for helping win freedom against British tyrants. He makes no mention, however, of any of Washington's achievements after the revolution.

Aurora (Philadelphia), 19 December 1799

GEORGE WASHINGTON, commander in chief of the American armies, during the revolution, caused by the tyranny of Great Britain; in this distinguished character, his name will live to the latest posterity among the greatest men who have ornamented history, by the support of liberty and their country, against tyranny—As we can offer no higher Eulogism to the memory of a character elevated by fortune, talents, and the voice of his country to so high a station among the benefactors of mankind—we confine ourselves to that alone, recommending the principles for which he fought and so much honor to himself and his fellow citizens, and to the freedom of his country, to the careful and steadfast conservation of those who survive him.

A Medical Controversy

Drs. James Craik and Elisha Dick: "A Statement on Washington's Death"

This account of the last hours of Washington's life would be the only public description of the former president's death until more detailed eyewitness recollections were published many years later.

Virginia Herald (Fredericksburg), 31 December 1799

Presumed that some account of the late illness and death of General Washington, will be generally interesting, and particularly so to the professors and practitioners of medicine throughout America, we request you to publish the following statement.

Some time in the night of Friday the 13th instant, having been exposed to rain on the preceding day, General Washington was attacked with an inflammatory affection of the upper part of the wind-pipe, called in technical language, *cynache tracheatis.* The disease commenced with a violent ague, accompanied with some pain in the upper and fore part of the throat, a sense of stricture in the same part, a cough, and a difficult rather than a painful deglutition, which were soon succeeded by fever and a quick and laborious respiration. The necessity of blood-letting suggesting itself to the General, he procured a bleeder in the neighbourhood, who took from his arm, in the night, twelve or fourteen ounces of blood; he would not by any means be prevailed upon by the family to send for the attending physician till the following morning, who arrived at Mount Vernon at about eleven o'clock on Saturday. Discovering the case to be highly alarming, and foreseeing the fatal tendency of the disease, two consulting physicians were immediately sent for, who arrived, one at half after three, the other at four o'clock in the afternoon. In the interim were employed two copious bleedings; a blister was applied to the part affected, two moderate doses of calomel were given, and an injection was administered, which operated on the lower intestines— but all without any perceptible advantage; the respiration becoming still more difficult and distressing.—Upon the arrival of the remaining physicians, it was agreed, as there were yet no signs of accumulation in the bronchial vessels of the lungs, to try the result of another bleeding, when about thirty-two ounces of blood were drawn, without the smallest apparent alleviation of the disease. Vapours of vinegar and water were frequently inhaled, ten grains of calomel were given. Succeeded by repeated doses of emetic tartar, amounting, in all, to five or six grains, and with no other effect than a copious discharge from the bowels. The powers of life seemed now manifestly yielding to the force of the disorder. Blisters were applied to the extremities, together with a cataplasm of bran and vinegar to the throat. Speaking, which was painful from the beginning, now became almost impracticable; respiration grew more and more contracted and imperfect, till half after eleven o'clock on Saturday night, when, retaining the full possession of his intellect, he expired without a struggle....

William Cobbett: "To the Subscribers of This Gazette"

Following Drs. Craik and Dick's statement, William Cobbett, long a critic of bleeding and other depletion methods, published his own version of the last hours of President Washington. As noted by Cobbett in the second paragraph below, as Washington lay dying, it was ironic that Cobbett was being fined $5,000 in libel damages for calling the bleeding practices of contemporary physicians into question.

Porcupine's Gazette (Philadelphia), 13 January 1800

Thus we see, that, in the space of about *twenty hours* probably less, the patient was bled *four times* and took three doses of *Calomel,* that is, of *mercury in powder.* The bleeder, whom the general sent for, took 12 or 14 ounces of blood, suppose it to be only 12 ounces, messrs. Craik and Dick say that they next employed two *copious bleedings,* and after that a bleeding of about *thirty two ounces.* They do not tell us the weight of the "*copious bleedings,*" but if they were of thirty two ounces each (and there is not the least reason to suppose that they were less), there was taken in all 108 ounces, which is 9 pounds, and which makes in my measure, 9 pints, or one gallon and a pint!!!—Now, it is computed that *all the blood* in a man who is in the prime of his life and in the bloom of health, does not weigh more than about 15 pounds, and everyone knows that the quantity of blood decreases daily as old age comes on and yet these Physicians (if we believe their own report), took about 9 pounds of blood from General Washington, who was *sixty-eight* years of age, while, during the same space, they gave him *three doses of* CALOMEL, or *mercury in powder*.

Thus, on the fateful 14th of December, on the same day, in the same evening, nay, in the very same hours, that a Philadelphia court & jury were laying on me a ruinous fine for having reprobated the practice of Rush, GENERAL WASHINGTON *was expiring, while under the operation of that very practice!* On that day the victory of RUSH and DEATH was complete; but their triumph was but of short duration; for while I have continued on my course unchecked by the judgments, the seizures, the attachments of Rush, and the savage howlings of his "*dear fellow citizens*," General Washington has, I hope, broken the chains of the grim tyrant, Death, and soared into the realm of immortal glory.

John Brickell: "Observations on the Medical Treatment of General Washington, in His Last Illness; Addressed to his Physicians Messrs. Craik & Dick"

Not all physicians used bloodletting and other depletion methods to cure illness. Dr. John Brickell, from Atlanta, Georgia, was opposed to such practices, especially when used on the elderly.

The Rush-Light (Philadelphia), 28 February 1800

The life of this illustrious personage has been so eminently beneficial and ornamental to the world, that every man who has a just value for virtue, talents, or an attachment to civil liberty, must lament his death.

The loss to his country, at this critical period, is incalculable; it is irreparable: we shall never look upon his like again!

I have perused the account published by his physicians, of their medical treatment, and differ from them so entirely in my opinion of its propriety, that, with all due respect for their good intentions, I think it my duty to point out what appears to me a most fatal error in their plan: and although it is not in the power of science to restore his precious life, yet a discussion of this case may be productive of benefit to mankind.

I suppose myself addressing men of science, whose minds are so highly cultivated as to comprehend my reasoning on this subject; which I shall make as short and clear as possible.

When we examine the human blood by optical glasses, by chemistry, and by experimental philosophy, we find it full of nourishment in young people; but effete and poor in the aged.

When we examine by anatomical injections, the state of the vescular system, we find innumerable ramifications in the arteries through which the blood flows freely in young people; while many of their anastomoses are obliterated in the aged.

The blood of old people, therefore, being poorer, and the channels for conveying its nourishment fewer, is the reason that old people cannot bear bleeding so well as the young, and it likewise explains (what every man of science and experience must know) why a small bleeding has the same effect on an aged person, that a large bleeding has upon the young and robust.

These observations, founded on well established facts, demonstrate how guarded and circumspect we ought to be in the use of the lancet, when our patient is far advanced in life: and how actively we ought to employ our thoughts in devising other methods than profuse blood-letting in such a case.

From what the physicians have published and other documents, we have data sufficient to ascertain how far the maxims derivable from science, experience and judgment, have governed in the present instance.

The duration of this illness was 20 hours; from 3 a.m., till after 10 p.m.

A bleeder being sent for at the unusual hour of 3 a.m. we may suppose the operation was not performed until four o'clock; before eleven hours elapsed, he was bled again twice profusely; which must have been about eighteen ounces each time; and soon afterwards he was bled again to the amount of thirty two ounces.

Thus we see, by their own statement, that they drew from a man in the sixty ninth year of his age, the enormous quantity of eighty two ounces, or above two quarts, and an half of blood in about thirteen hours.

Very few of the most robust young men in the world could survive such a loss of blood; but the body of an aged person must be so exhausted, and all his powers so weakened by it as to make his death speedy and inevitable.

Here the effect followed the cause precisely: the physicians soon observed the powers of life yielding; a loss of speech; and that he expired without a struggle! The excessive bleeding *had left him no strength to struggle!!*

After what has been said it may be expected that I should point out my plan:—I will speak generally, without descending to criticise on the minor parts of the treatment, which, however, I do not admire.

They ought to have attacked the disease as near its seat as possible: the vein under the tongue might have been opened; the tonsils might have been scarified; the scarificator and cup might have been applied on or near the thyroid cartilege [*sic*]. One ounce of blood drawn in this way would relieve more than a quart drawn from the arm, and would not exhaust and enfeeble the body; in the same manner than an ounce of blood drawn at the temple, relieves an enflamed eye more than a quart drawn from the arm.

The neck might have been rubbed with warm laudanum and camphor; and a bag of warm fine salt laid on; but the unseasonable application of a blister would prevent this.

He ought to have been put into one, two, or three flannels; and instead of calomel, it would have been better to give him small draughts of hot whey, with a little laudanum, camphor, spiritous volatilis aromaticus, or spir-

itus nitri dulcis, occasionally, to remove the spasm which caused the dysp-
nea, and produce perspiration, which would relieve the lungs by turning the
course of the fluids toward the skin.

A Dispute Over Washington's Final Resting Place

Brutus: "For the *Washington Federalist*"

*In favor of the construction of a Washington memorial, the author of this
piece derided those who campaigned against the idea. It was reprinted as
far away as Portland, Maine.*

Washington Federalist (District of Columbia), 17 December 1800

"See nations slowly wise, and meanly just,
To buried merit raise the tardy bust."
                    Johnson's "Vanity of Human Wishes"

When the father of his country died, the lamentations of general sorrow
were loudly expressed, and re-echoed from one end of the country to the
other; the press teemed with elegy and panegyric; the forum, the pulpit and
the senate resounded with eulogy and pathetic declamations. During the
paroxism of grief, the representatives seemed willing to indulge people's
feelings, and decreed to erect honorable testimonies of a NATION's veneration and regret.

Washington has left us but twelve months, his remains lie yet green in
the earth; and sorrow has subsided, feeling has grown cold, and the remem-
brance of his services are fading in obscurity, like the objects of vision, when
the sun has sunk below the horizon. Thus stands the character of America,
if it may be drawn from the conduct of her delegates. A few, with liberal
spirit and enlarged views, wish to display the general will with magnificence
and grandeur suitable to the occasion; others, regardless of national dignity,
and not justly appreciating the exalted character, are wasting time in degrading calculations of petty economy while the rest hope to destroy every
efficient plan, by proposing to commit the memory, the fame, and the virtues
of Washington to the fragile temple of the human heart.

On an occasion like the present, three prominent objects of consideration naturally present themselves. To honor the illustrious dead, to evince a
people's gratitude, and to decorate the metropolis honored by his name
with specimens of the useful and the imitative arts. If, in the wisdom of antiquity it has been customary to honor the memory of the superlatively wise

and good, by some sensible memorial, of striking magnitude, and durable material; has the experience of mankind yet discovered the impropriety of the practice, or imputed folly, extravagance, or superstition to the principle? If a nation chooses by outward symbols to show its gratitude and veneration: ought not such representations to be obviously discriminated from others, by their superior grandeur and sublimity? And if it is honorable to encourage the elegant Arts, and congenial with the character of a refined and enlightened people to decorate with classic taste the capital of their empire, what fitter opportunity or noble subject can be offered to the hand of genius, than to exhibit Columbia's feeling for her departed Hero?

Benjamin West: "To His Excellency Rufus King"

Also in favor of building a monument for Washington, Benjamin West, an American artist residing in England, suggested that a tall pyramid-shaped monument be placed in a conspicuous place in the capital, that it be surrounded by trees, and that it be open to the public. The letter was addressed to Rufus King, America's minister in London.

Washington Federalist (District of Columbia), 17 December 1800

Observing the Resolutions passed by the United States of America, for removing the body of George Washington from the family vault to the City bearing his name, and their intention to raise an appropriate monument to his memory in that City, I thought the following observations, with the plan for a monument, from me as an American, and one not altogether obscure in the elegant arts, might be acceptable to those in that country, who are desirous of paying the last tribute to his memory, by a monumental record, placed in the Federal City.

The raising of monuments to departed virtue, has ever been an object of the first attention in all civilized countries, and no people ever had so proud an instance in doing this as the Americans, by raising one to true virtue and real worth, as that which presents itself to them in the character of General Washington, and that the placing of such records in public situations has ever been considered true policy, by all wise governments, for which the highways, squares and circuses for such records have been preferred, we have the highest authority from the Egyptians, Grecians, and Romans. That the raising of a monument to the memory of General Washington, I believe, is the wish of all the civilized world. I do therefore recommend, that the most durable form for such a monument be adopted, which is, that of the triangle or pyramid, and that its situation be the most conspicuous in the Federal City; its height one hundred and fifty feet, and its basis the same.

The place or square, where it is erected, to be planted with trees to give inviting shade, and to be open to the public: this will afford the parent or tutor an opportunity to inculcate the virtues of that great man, in the juvenile mind of their rising offspring. The inside of the pyramid has a conic cavity to save the expense of building, and at the same time gives as much strength as tho' solid; within that is built a rotundo, lighted from the top, in which is placed the pedestrian statue of the general in bronze, to be in height not less than seven feet, and round the rotundo eight bassorelievos in the same metal, four containing military, and four civil subjects. In place of the frize and dado round the rotundo, a groove to be cut to a considerable depth, and in the same manner round the eight bassorelievos. This will give a monumental simplicity, which belongs to its character, and the whole of the apartment to be the natural colour of the stone with which it is built; one of the four entrances into the rotundo to be closed, for the place where the remains of that great man should be deposited in a stone coffin, which should be elevated, and under it a proper inscription. The three entrances which lead into the rotundo, to have iron gates, to be opened on fixed days, for seeing the sepulchre. Such a monument would be an appropriate one, to the exalted character of George Washington, and worthy the United States of America to raise to his memory. It should stand pre-eminent in magnitude, as the character it records stood pre-eminent in virtue, as well as to give a taste to any monuments that may in future be erected—it will both adorn the City, and inspire the people with virtue from generation to generation, for some thousand years.

The better to elucidate the construction of such a monument, I send you the plan, section and elevation; they are geometrical, and laid down to a scale. The estimate of such a monument in erecting, the workmen in America will be able to ascertain, as the whole is to be of stone. The works of art, such as the statue and bassorelievos, their expense will be ascertained in Europe, agreeable to similar works.

Anonymous: "Occasional Letters, No. I. On the Mausoleum"

The movement to build a mausoleum in Washington did not have as many supporters as it would need to come to fruition in the early years of the new century. The author of this piece, published in Thomas Jefferson's newspaper, the National Intelligencer, *argued against the building of a monument for Washington. Jefferson and his supporters were against anything that smacked of monarchical pomp and circumstance. Thus, as this author stated, it would be unfitting for a republican nation to build such monu-*

ments to its leaders. But not only that, the author argued, the country could not afford to build such a monument.

National Intelligencer (District of Columbia), 1 January 1801

You ask my opinion of the mausoleum, proposed for general Washington—I think it unfortunate that it has been thought of. Mausoleums are frequent in despotic governments, in the Eastern World, but by no means appropriate to the great character, it is meant to honor here. They take their name from a superb tomb, built by Artemesia, queen of Caria, in memory of her husband MAUSOLUS, and saving only their superness and expense, are nothing more than common tombs, and *if one is erected in the city of Washington, it will probably, hereafter, become the Burying-place of eminent characters who may die here.*

For it is not to be supposed that we are never to have another President, worthy of funeral honors, or that party spirit will not hereafter decree that its favorite shall have equal honor, in being buried in the same tomb, *with the First President of the Nation.* He must know little of the history of mankind; and of the operations of their passions, in society, who does not see that the erection of a mausoleum, as is proposed, instead of being *appropriate,* to the contemplated object of it, will only be the commencement of a Burying-place, for other characters, as is universally the case where mausoleums have been erected in India, and other parts of Asia where they are frequent. In this view therefore there is nothing of taste, elegance, or honor, in a mausoleum *appropriate* to the hero and sage of our country. AUGUSTUS CAESAR, first emperor of the Romans, possessed the pacific virtues of a great prince. In his time there was a universal peace, and more public felicity than had ever been known before. The people felt their happiness, and justly ascribed it to the prudence of his conduct. His death was therefore universally lamented, and all possible honor done his memory. Among other things it was proposed, in the Roman Senate, that he would be DEIFIED, *for public adoration.* It was objected to as *impious,* and that if he had this honor it must be given to every succeeding emperor, however unworthy. It was said, in reply, there never would be another Augustus, and the public voice therefore would never DEIFY another. But every man who has read history, knows the same honor was decreed to a Nero, a Caligula, a Domitian, and other devourers of the species. Monsters who sported with the lives and feelings of men, and whose hideous characters and memories are execrated by all mankind.

But a mausoleum is objectionable, on the ground of its expense, and its natural tendency to beget disgust and disaffection to the government which votes it. An apprehension of an unnecessary increase of the National debt, and of great extravagance, in the expenditure of the public money, which has made it necessary to borrow, according to the information of the Secretary of the treasury, *two millions, five hundred and seventy-five thousand, one hundred and thirty-one dollars, and seventy-four cents,* on the loans authorized. July 16th, 1798, and May 7th, 1800, for the service of the first three quarters of the year 1800–has had a powerful effect, on the public mind, and has been the cause of the change of the administration.–The people of the United States, can never be reconciled to hiring money, at *eight per cent interest,* to be squandered away, without the least use or benefit. That government retains most the affections of the people at large, which seeks their happiness, without oppressing them with taxes for vain expenses and useless parade–Men who believe that the government is respectable and good, in proportion to its cost, its parade and expenditures, when supported by expressive taxation, calculate on no better principles than dishonest men, who are bankrupts, and never expect to pay, will buy goods to sell at auction, or sell for cash bills of exchange which [they] know will not be accepted, or who credit for goods, open shop, set up a riage, and live like a prince, on the property of others, (a short time however) and then sink without pity in contempt, distress and ruin. Two hundred thousand dollars, is the sum proposed to be expended–The probability however is, that if the mausoleum is begun, on the dimension proposed, by the House of Representatives, that it will eventually cost more than a million of dollars. The willingness of the people to pay the expense, be it more or less, will depend on their opinion of the propriety and usefulness of the expenditures. A very great proportion of them think of it, as historians have universally thought of the pyramids of Egypt, who have called them "*contemptible and ridiculous,*" "*Regum pecuniae atiosa ac stuttta ostentatio.*"–*A foolish and useless ostentation of wealth.* And Pliny has remarked that by a just punishment the memory of those who erected them is buried in oblivion. He says historians do not agree among themselves about the names of those who raised those, VAIN MONUMENTS– "*Inter eos non constat a quibus, factae sint justissimo cusu obliteratatis,* TANTAE VANITATIS *Auctoribus.*" But all the historians agree on this remarkable fact, which ought to be a warning against all similar folly;–"*That the public hatred, which the kinds of Egypt incurred, by laying the task of building those pyramids upon their subjects, occasioned their being buried, in some obscure place, to prevent their bodies, from being exposed to the fury and vengeance of the populace.*" Vid. Diod. Lib. 1. P. 40. "This, says an excellent historian, "teaches us what judgment we ought to pass on these kinds of edifices, and on those princes who considered as something grand, the raising by a multitude of hands, and by the help of money, immense structures, with the sole view of rendering their names immortal, and who did not scruple to destroy thousands of their subjects, to state their *vain glory.* They differed very much from the Romans, who sought to immortalize themselves, by works of a magnificent kind, but at the same time of public utility."

These quotations from history are in point against the proposed mausoleum, and the feelings of our country are also against it. How otherwise can we account for the opposition of almost one half of the House of Representatives, and the general and universal reprobation it has met with, so far as the sentiments of the people are known. Supposing that this grand pile of rocks, wanted (by the way) for the canal, the cellars, the wharves, and the public buildings of the city, and which cannot be purchased in the silent beds where nature has placed them, unless at an high price, should with vast labour and expense, be dragged from the banks of the Potomack [*sic*], and be placed *pyramid like* in some conspicuous square of the city, will not the first reflection of every visitant here, however he may love and revere the memory of its most illustrious founder, be like those of all persons who have viewed and spoken of the pyramids of Egypt! Will he not say, in spite of himself, how much better would it have been for our country, if the money expended in erecting this uncouth and useless pile of rocks, had been appropriated in the establishment and endowment of a NATIONAL HOSPITAL for the sick, wounded, or crippled seaman, or for the establishment and endowment of a NATIONAL UNIVERSITY in this city, so ardently wished for, and so repeatedly and strongly recommended by our beloved Washington in his address to congress—Will he not feel disagreeably and reprobate the mausoleum, as an ill-judged effort to show respect to a character exalted beyond the reach of obloquy or praise; not to be honoured by a pile of rocks however huge and massy, or however polished and ornamented. Will he not think that every attempt of this kind would be as useless and ridiculous, as lighting a candle in the full noon-day blaze of the sun, with a view of adding to its effulgence. No, so far from honouring the great name of Washington, it is dishonouring it. As if his virtues, his glory, and his fame, which have spread through the world a lustre, never to be tarnished or forgotten, and which will go down the long stream of time, with increasing honor and veneration, to the latest ages of posterity, stood the need of an odious tax, *to be gratefully remembered by his country.*

Was he my father, was he my friend, to whose memory I wished to have all possible honor shewn by his country. I would request no more than was proposed by the resolution of the two houses of Congress at the last session, "*That a Marble Monument be erected by the United States, in the City of Washington, and his remains deposited under it, and so designed as to commemorate the great events of his military and public life.* This should be neat, plain and simple, of no great expense, emblematical of the character of this great and illustrious man, who was wise and prudent, and on all occasions careful of the public money, in the expenditure of which, he often recommends the strictest frugality and economy. Or this monument should be an inscription, similar to that on the tomb of the Great Frederic of Prussia, containing a sentiment ten thousand times more sublime than any which would be excited by the most superb and expensive Mausoleum.

GEORGIUS WASHINGTON,
Hic Cinis,
Fama ubique.
GEORGE WASHINGTON.
His remains are here—His Tomb pervades the Universe—

There is something inimitably sublime in an inscription like this, for so great a character. It makes the globe a place which he has honored, and the universe a monument of his glory.

In a testimonial of respect like this, the whole nation will unite—they have united in it. Why then violate the public feelings, by attempting what the nation and the world will reprobate?

It is said, and it is generally believed, that the much loved and much respected family connexions of general Washington, aware of the uneasiness which might arise from an attempt to erect a mausoleum, are averse to the measure, and wish simply to have carried into effect *the joint resolution* of both houses of congress at the last session. To place his remains in the centre of the capital—in the heart and bosom of the nation, in the place whence the longitude of our country is reckoned, and where its laws are discussed and agreed to, would be expressive of our most affectionate regard, and by a natural association, would lead every legislator and every citizen often to contemplate those virtues which adorn the life of WASHINGTON THE GREAT, and to make them the models of their conduct.

There are my reflections on the subject of the mausoleum. Though written in great haste, I believe they are substantially correct.

I am, &c.

Anonymous: "Extract of a Letter from the City of Washington"

In a report about Congress in its new home in Washington, D.C., on the Potomac, the author of this letter reflected on the debate surrounding the proposed new tomb for General Washington. Of principal concern was the financing of the project, which had been estimated to cost $200,000.

Aurora (Philadelphia), 12 January 1801

They have at length entered upon business, and as a beginning they have voted away 200,000 dollars of the public money to erect an Egyptian pile to the memory of General Washington. Thus you see the toil and sweat of the husbandman, and the labourer, extracted by the representatives of freemen,...to establish a monument no way necessary, and which, if it can have any tendency, will be to take away from the just reputation of his revolutionary services.

QUESTIONS

1. Debates over where presidents ought to be buried and in what fashion don't arise today. Explain why you think Americans debated this issue in the early 1800s and why they probably wouldn't think of doing so today.
2. Contemporary medical experts generally confirm that George Washington would probably have died whether he was subjected to bloodletting or not. Why do you think some people still question the quality of the medical care Washington received from his physicians?
3. It would take until the mid-1800s for the Washington Monument to be built. Why do you think it took so many years for Americans to decide to do so?
4. President Washington's Mount Vernon funeral was an elaborate ceremony that was mimicked across the nation as people sought to honor the dead hero. Describe a more recent funeral of some public official or celebrity that rivaled Washington's funeral in scope and ceremonial fervor.
5. What were the primary arguments against the erection of a special tomb for General Washington given by the author of "Occasional Letters, No. I. On the Mausoleum"?
6. Eventually, most Americans would forget the controversies surrounding the life and career of George Washington and he would become one of the country's greatest heroes. Explain why you believe this happened and how.

NOTES

1. For an account of the death of George Washington as told by one of his slaves, Tobias Lear, see *The Papers of George Washington*, ed. Dorothy Twohig and Philander D. Chase, retirement series four (Charlottesville: University of Virginia Press, 1998–1999), 542–555.

2. Benjamin Franklin Bache, *Aurora*, 6 March 1797.

3. Congressional resolution presented by John Marshall to President Adams, *Annals of Congress*, 6th Cong., 1st sess., 203, 207–208.

4. Rubil Morales-Vázquez, "Imagining Washington: Monuments and Nation Building in the Early Capital," *Washington History* 12 (spring–summer 2000): 29.

CHAPTER 2

The United States Capital Moves to the Potomac, 1800

Today, we think of Washington, D.C., as a vital center of worldwide importance. But in 1800, when the government of the United States moved its headquarters to the banks of the Potomac River, few Americans imagined Washington would ever become an important place. Many painted less than unflattering portraits of Washington. Epithets for the town chosen by some of its early visitors included "City of Magnificent Distances," "Wilderness City," "Capital of Miserable Huts," and "A Mud-hole Equal to the Great Serbonian Bog." But the city of Washington did have its admirers. George Washington, who selected the capital's location (an honor granted to him by Congress years earlier), called the 68-square mile enclave "The Emporium of the West." Gouverneur Morris, a senator from New York, after arriving for the first time in Washington, called it "the best city in the world to live in—in the future."[1]

How the nation's capital came to be located on the great bog near the Potomac offers a cogent lesson in decision-making in the new republic.[2] In 1783, two developments led to a debate over whether the nation's capital (then located at Philadelphia) ought to be moved. First, the new government was having trouble paying its bills. When a group of unpaid soldiers invaded Philadelphia, demanding payment for services rendered in the Revolutionary War, Congress struggled to come up with the funds. The crisis ended without violence, but it precipitated a movement to build a federal city where the government's business could be conducted without fear of intimidation.

The second event that led to the relocation debate began when Congress considered where to erect a bronze equestrian statue of George Washington. After a resolution called for the statue to be located where a permanent seat of government was in place, regional jealousies emerged over where that would be. Some argued for two seats of government: one in

Washington, D.C., ca. 1800. This painting in the north wing of the U.S. Capitol illustrates the pastoral nature of the site when the federal government moved there in late 1800. At the time, this was the only finished part of the Capitol. Beyond it is a view westward toward the president's house and Georgetown. Courtesy of the Library of Congress.

the North and another in the South. General Washington considered the Potomac River an ideal location. Not only was it close to the geographic center of the republic, but it was also near the gateway to the Ohio Valley. Others argued for sites in New Jersey and Pennsylvania, among other places.

Arguments over where the new capital would be located continued for more than five years until, in 1790, the question was finally decided. Over dinner, Thomas Jefferson and Alexander Hamilton struck a deal that led to the selection of the Potomac site. At the heart of the compromise was disagreement over who would pay the debts incurred by the colonists during the American Revolution. Jefferson said he would support Hamilton's plan for the federal assumption of state debts if Hamilton would agree to locate the capital on the banks of the Potomac. When Congress ratified this pact, newly elected President George Washington was given the authority to pick the specific site in the area of the Potomac.

In 1791, Washington chose land for the capital near the village of Georgetown, which had been laid out in 1751 and incorporated in 1789. Development of the site began almost immediately, although it would long prove to be fraught with problems. General Washington appointed Andrew

Ellicott as the site's surveyor, and French architect Charles L'Enfant its designer. The Board of Capital Commissioners named the federal city Washington and the larger area it resided in the District of Columbia. In addition to the city of Washington, the capital district included the town of Alexandria (ceded by the state of Virginia), and Georgetown (ceded by Maryland). Early in 1792, construction started on a house for the president, and a few months later, a public auction of city lots took place. In 1794, construction of the nation's new Capitol building began.

In the months leading up to the government's move to the Potomac in 1800, the nation's newspaper editors were preoccupied with the upcoming presidential election, among other things, and paid scant attention to the relocation efforts.[3] In early June, Philadelphians bid the government farewell as President Adams and Congress left for Washington City. On the president's departure, Philadelphia editor William Duane, a Republican and one of Adams's most rabid critics, mixed a political message in with a farewell message he published in the June 7 issue of the *Aurora:*

> The President is gone—what! Gone? Yes!—dead?—mortally, no; politically, aye? But he has left town—How? In his coach and four with the blinds up— Ah! That's not a new thing, he has rode in the state coach with the blinds up for a long time.... Did the blues parade?—No, what! Not parade nor salute him whom the people delight to honor—the rock on which the storm beats— the chief who now commands? Did the republican militia parade?—No!

Washington's leaders welcomed President Adams with open arms on his arrival to their unpaved and only partially finished city. A crowd greeted Adams's carriage at the District line and escorted him to the city's Union Tavern. The president's newspaper in Philadelphia, *The Gazette of the United States,* told its readers, "The President of the United States arrived at Georgetown on Tuesday noon last where he was received with every demonstration of joy.... He was said to have made his entry into the city of Washington, the future seat of government of the union, on Wednesday last."[4]

Americans were curious about the new capital, and the newspapers kept them informed. The newspaper essays, poems, and reports selected for this chapter's first section provided Americans with descriptions of the new federal city, as well as with commentary on its living conditions. Writers who admired the new capital praised its potential as a great place for the country's new center of government. The author of the first of four laudatory reports, published in Albany, New York, clearly had an eye on the future potential of the city as a governmental and trade center. Other positive reports on the new federal city published in Portland, Maine, and New London, Connecticut, commented on the cultural amenities sprouting up in the new town.

The first section also includes several negative portraits of the new capital. The reputation of the place was besmirched by news of its bumpy and at times impassable muddy roads and of its insufferably hot and muggy summers and miserably cold and damp winters. During late fall 1800, reports of rampant fever, ague, and other illnesses circulated in the papers, and the capital's critics blamed the outbreaks on the bad weather. In a piece published in *Aurora*, William Duane sarcastically wrote of the many government officials who had taken ill during the new capital's first winter.

Another critic of the new city, noted poet and editor Philip Freneau, shared his thoughts on the federal city in a poem published in a South Carolina newspaper. Freneau deplored officialdom and never hesitated to attack it in print. In "Lines on the Federal City," Freneau hoped that the nation's common people would find a place alongside the "royalty" for whom the city was being built.[5]

The second section includes reports and essays on disputes about the capital that developed over the years following its relocation. As construction of the capital's facilities progressed, complaints about the extravagance of its buildings and furnishings were heard around the nation. The author of "The Red Chairs," for example, chastised government leaders for spending too much on the chairs to be used in the halls of Congress. Another dispute concerning the new capital related to how it should be governed. In the *National Intelligencer*, Epaminondas considered whether the District of Columbia should be treated like a new state, with the same powers and relationship to the federal government as the other states of the union. In opposition to this, some argued that the parts of the district ceded by Maryland and Virginia should remain under the jurisdiction of those state governments.

The final section includes two New Jersey newspaper pieces whose authors disagreed over whether Washington, D.C., ought to be abandoned for a new "permanent" seat of government. Disputes concerning whether the city on the Potomac should remain the nation's capital erupted from time to time in the early decades of the nineteenth century, including after it was burned by the British in August 1814 (see chapter 19).

OPPOSING VIEWS ON CONDITIONS IN THE NEW FEDERAL CITY

Anonymous: "Extract of a Letter from a Gentleman at the City of Washington, to His Friend in This City"

Many who wrote about the new capital complained about its climate, uncomfortable housing, muddy streets, and lack of cultural amenities. But not

*everyone agreed, and this author's essay serves as an example of a more fa-
vorable review of the new city and its benefits.*

Albany Gazette (New York), 15 December 1800

It is impossible for me to describe, or you to conceive the impression
which the first view of this metropolis of our vast empire made on my mind;
nature has bestowed here her best gifts—art has been much less advanta-
geously employed; the situation is the finest imaginable, whether considered
in relation to its commercial advantages, or the variety and grandeur of its
prospects; from the Capital, we behold both branches of the Potowmac [*sic*],
we mark their junction, and the eye embracing the whole of that noble river,
follows its majestic course as far as vision can extend—it may be then cast with
a single glance over the flourishing towns of Alexandria, and Georgetown and
a wide range of the surrounding country. The city is laid out fancifully
enough, and if the buildings already erected had been concentrated, it would
wear a rich and splendid appearance, but they are widely separated, the inter-
vening spaces are filled with a confused mixture of stumps, trees, huts, lime
kilns and brick yards. That *wing* of the Capitol which is finished for the accommodation of Congress, and which is about one hundred feet square, is in-
comparably the finest structure I ever saw; the President's house is also built
in a style altogether superb, but it is one mile and an half, and forty perches
from the Capitol, and all the public offices are at about the same distance.

Anonymous: "Washington City, Nov. 26"

*The nation's capital had moved from Philadelphia, a city with consider-
able social and cultural amenities. Thus, Washington's progress in establishing everything from schools to fancy balls was of interest to Americans.
This brief notice in a Connecticut newspaper reported on the new capital's
first dancing assembly. Its author framed the event, as well as the prospects
for the city, in a positive light.*

Connecticut Gazette (New London, Conn.),
10 December 1800

Last evening, the First Dancing Assembly for the season was held at Mr.
Stille's. The company, consisting of above one hundred ladies and gentlemen, among the latter of whom were several public characters, and members of the Federal Legislature, assembled at an early hour. The exhibition
was flattering to the expanding prospects of Washington; and the universal
spirit of good humour and gaiety which prevailed is the truest evidence of

the amicable sentiments which characterize in an eminent degree the citizens of the metropolis.

An Unnamed Gentleman at Georgetown: "City of Washington"

Rumors about the new capital being built in a wilderness circulated through America. This author attempted to correct these notions, predicting a bright future for the city and its inhabitants.

Jenks' Portland Gazette (Maine), 7 July 1801

I have taken frequent walks about Georgetown and the Federal City, and am very much pleased with both: the situation of the city is most charming; it is a fine open country, and delightful views; not covered with woods as I was informed in Philadelphia. There are a great number of very genteel and elegant houses. The President's house and the Capitol are noble buildings.—The country round and the river Potomac, when viewed from a hill just out of Georgetown, is a beautiful scene. I am certain, every person, not prejudiced against the removal of the seat of government, will on his arrival here, candidly confess, that every advantage is to be derived from this territory, and that Washington must inevitably soon become a flourishing and great city.

Anonymous: "Washington, Sept. 7"

In response to complaints about the lack of culture in Washington when compared to New York and Philadelphia, notices were spread throughout newspapers about the opening of theaters, museums, and other cultural establishments.

Jenks' Portland Gazette (Maine), 28 September 1801

The population of this city increases, and the improvements are progressing, with rapidity. The Navy Yard is in forwardness under the superintendance of Capt. Tingey. It is formed in the projection of a wharf, 800 feet into the Eastern Branch of the River—by which a dock will be made 1,000 feet in diameter. One half the range of Marine Barracks is erected. They will consist of a mass of brick buildings 600 feet in length, two stories high.—The maritime Warehouse is raised. It is three stories high—and 60 by 40 feet—an additional building for the same purpose is contemplated.—The elyptical Room at the Capitol for the Representatives, is 88 by 66 feet.—A turnpike road is making from Georgetown to the Capital, and a road on the New Jersey Avenue.—A company is incorporated for building a permanent bridge over the eastern branch of the river.—A handsome Market House is erecting by subscription.

William Duane: "Omens"

This brief report in the Aurora *commented on the effects the city's cold and damp weather had on certain city residents. These conditions, to make matters worse, led not just to discomfort, but also to sickness and death in some cases. Duane so hated the Federalists that the fact that the new capital was called the Federal City meant he would not support it under any circumstances.*

Aurora (Philadelphia), 14 November 1800

Mr. Adams is sick at Washington.

Oliver Wolcott has been almost suffocated.

Mr. Dexter has been thrown out of his carriage and much bruised.

And *Parson Abercrombie* is so ill with a *cold* that it is with difficulty he can breathe.

The former, we fear, has taken too great a dose of *Hamilton's Lozenges.*

The latter has been ill since the account of the New York election was received, and if some *British never-failing balsam* is not speedily administered, we fear he will not be long amongst us.

Philip Freneau, "Lines on the Federal City"

Poet Philip Freneau compared the fledgling capital city on the Potomac with Rome. In doing so, he sounded a lament for the common people, who he feared would not find a hospitable place in the new city being constructed for the nation's "royal race."

Charleston City Gazette (South Carolina), 18 December 1800

ALL human things must have their rise;
And Rome increas'd from pigmy size,
Till future ages saw her grown,
The mistress of the world then known.

So, bounding on Potawmac's flood,
Where forest-trees so lately stood,
An infant city grows apace,
Intended for a royal race.

Here Capitals of an awful height,
Already burst upon the site;

And palaces for embrio kings,
Display their fruits and spread their wings.

Not so are matters here design'd;
Here, places we only find;
And late must common people come,
In such a place to find a home;

Where Royalty, with vile grimace,
In Louis shews its scoundrel face;
And Antoinette a smile affords,
To Senators and would-be Lords.

Meantime, it will be fair and just,
Nor will our grandees fret, we trust,
If, while the poor at distance lurk,
Themselves do their own dirty work.

Rome's earliest citizens, they say,
Submitted to delusive sway,
In Romulus, who suck'd a bear,
Then went to Heaven, a royal star.

Pray Heaven, the case may be revers'd:
May they, who here inhabit first,
By some reforms that must be made,
And shaking off the royal trade,
Incline the late historian's pen,
To write, that "Here were honest men."

DISPUTES ON THE FINANCING AND GOVERNANCE OF THE NEW CAPITAL

Anonymous: "The Red Chairs"

According to the author of this letter, who was a writer from a northern paper, it was a travesty that each congressional chair cost $20, because the chairs' creators were scouring the globe for materials with which to make them.

Virginia Gazette & General Advertiser (Richmond, Va.), 26 December 1800

In England the members of the House of Commons are so simple in their manners, that they can sit upon benches. This practice was retained in most of the American States. Where then shall we find a precedent to justify, or reason to excuse the profligacy of expending twenty dollars to build a gaudy, sumptuous chair, for the seat of a Member of Congress? Does it comport with the plainness and simplicity which ought to pervade every branch of a Republican Government? Or does it quadrate with the state of our finances, when our national debt is increasing with gigantic strides (it will always increase in equal pace with corruption and extravagance) & when we are paying usurous interest for additional loans every year? Is it not extraordinary that a country extending two thousand miles in length, bounded on the two sides by the Atlantic and the Mississippi, cannot procure materials for that simple convenience a chair?

Surprising! But it has been thought necessary to send to the West-Indies for mahogany; to London for red morocco or goat skins, and to Birmingham for nails, to construct this intricate piece of furniture! Where is the surprising advantages of those gaudy fixtures in the Senate Chamber? We see that the members do not fly to their flittering feats with more ardour, nor with so much punctuality as do the Representatives, whose furniture is more plain; and where is the propriety of this distinction? Two words will account for the exotic qualities of the red chairs! British Influence! The British wish to promote extravagance with us, to destroy our republican system; They wish us to go to their islands for mahogany, for the same reason that we wish them to come for our lumber; if they can sell us manufactured goat skins, it promotes their manufacturing interest; So it is with the brass nails, &c.

Epaminondas: "Considerations on the Government of the Territory of Columbia"

One of the more difficult issues to resolve was how the people who resided in the District of Columbia would be governed. The following excerpt from a series of essays written by Epaminondas discussed the relationship of the territory of Columbia to the federal government.

National Intelligencer (District of Columbia), 26 December 1800

In order to come to a determination on these questions, it will be proper to ascertain with precision, how far it ought to be contemplated as a state; and in what respects it differs from a state.

It must be considered as somewhat analogous to a state, in being an association of men, for civil purposes, under a peculiar and singular authority.

The constitution of the United States has provided that the jurisdiction over this territory should be exclusively vested in the United States.

If therefore any part of it is suffered to remain under the jurisdiction of any one state in the union, it is not only infractive of the *spirit*, but of the *let-*

ter of the constitution. The policy which was in view in the making of this provision; than which none, considering the peculiar nature of our government, could have been more proper; will be entirely abandoned, and the provision in the constitution will become nugatory and useless.

This territory however differs from a state in this particular, that whereas the federal government is entitled, by the constitution, to exercise over a state, only the authority particularly delegated to it, on certain subjects, and leaves the state in undiminished possession of its sovereignty as to others; the territory of Columbia is placed by the constitution under the absolute and uncontrollable sovereignty of the United States, and possesses in itself none of the attributes of sovereignty.

In this situation, the people of the territory of Columbia do not cease to be a part of the people of the United States; & as such they are still entitled to the enjoyment of the same rights with the rest of the people of the United States, and to have some participation in the administration of their general government.

It is contrary to the genius of our constitutions, it is violating an original principle in republicanism, to deny that all who are governed by laws ought to participate in the formation of them.

The people of this territory therefore ought to be represented in the legislature of the United States; and to have a voice in the election of a President and Vice-President.

But shall they be represented in the House of Representatives only; or in the Senate also?

The Senate of the United States possesses a part of the legislative power; and it is certainly consonant to principle that those over whom that power is to operate should, if it can possibly be done, possess some voice in their transactions.

Would it be proper then to place the territory on an equal footing with a state and give it two senators; or ought a distinction be made?

As a distinction exists in fact between the territory and a state, it appears proper to recognize this distinction in giving it a representative in the Senate. As it cannot, if a distinction is made, lie on an equality with a state, and possess *two* votes; and as it cannot be represented at all with less than *one* vote; it would appear advisable to allow it *one vote,* and to assign it *one Senator.*

The Territory will then stand in the situation as it were of half a state; and when it is considered that its population may be one day equal to some of the smaller states, for instance Delaware; it would by no means appear inequitable to give it half the weight of such a state.

At present the population of the former seat of government is little different from the population of the state of Delaware; and if the permanent seat of government had been fixed there, and an equal extent of territory taken from one or two of the states in the union, the people thus losing their representation in the Senate as a part of the state, it would be highly unjust that sixty or seventy thousand people in one place should have two votes in the Senate, and that sixty or seventy thousand in another should be deprived of any.

With respect to its representation in the other house, there can exist but one opinion. It ought to be entitled to a representation in proportion to its population. While it continues however not to contain a population sufficient to entitle it to one member, a doubt may exist. In this interval it would be highly proper to place it on the footing of the Territories North West and South of the river Ohio; giving it one member who shall be entitled to deliberate, and receive pay, but not to vote.

Those who have observed the proceedings in relation to the territories North West and South of the river Ohio, must know the advantageous effect which even this right produces in the regulation of their affairs. The vote of one member in a large body is of little consequence; but his knowledge, when added to the general mass, his presence and abilities, produce the most powerful effects.... Under a system like this, the spirit of the Constitution appears to be preserved. The Territory stands in its natural and distinct situation. It is not a part of any state and is subjected to no extraneous legislation. The Federal Government is in exclusive possession of it, free from control and free from interference. The coterminous states regard it as no part of themselves; but as the common child of the Nation; the proud monument and great pilot of its union.

In the meantime the Territory itself sustains no disadvantages. It possesses in the administration of the federal government the full weight which its consequence and its talents may entitle it to; and no more. Its local concerns, concentrated within its own bosom, are not subjected to an unnatural association with two different governments; whose interests vary between themselves, and vary still more from those of the Territory.

It is impossible to point out with full force the evils of any other system. Those who advocate its remaining a part of the adjoining states, are not aware of the inconveniences to which this distracted situation must reduce its inhabitants; they are not aware of the consequences it may have in the future revolutions of our government. In the one case, it is to become a source of jealousy and contention; in the other, it is the cement of affection, the pledge of indissolubility. Every nation prides itself in its capital. A survey of the nations in Europe, if time admitted, would shew that in every country where a great and flourishing metropolis has existed, it advances in science, in arts, in consequence, in stability, with a progress which is in vain imitated elsewhere. The metropolis of the United States possesses advantages superior to any one place that can be selected on the old continent; and after having done so much towards placing our country on a basis that will excite the admiration and envy of Europe, why should we relax our exertions in this most important and decisive measure?

The inhabitants of this territory have totally changed their situation; when it has become a metropolis of the union, the views of those who come to reside in it are totally different from what they would have been had it remained in its former situation.

Whilst on the frontier of two counties, in two different states, its parts possessed a common interest with the people to which they were respectively allied; and a distinct interest between themselves. Now they possess a common interest with one another; and a distinct interest from the stocks, from which they have been taken. An entirely new direction is given to their views, habits, and necessities; and their mode of government ought to correspond with this new direction. Instead of diverting its exertions into two different channels; it ought to unite its efforts in a common current, for the attainment of common purposes. All its affairs ought to be administered in its own limits. It ought to have the same laws, the same justice, the same punishments. The Hamburgh merchant, or the Parisian manufacturer, who comes to reside in it, ought to find himself at home; and not be taken to the Chesapeake, or to James river, to be punished for his offences, or to seek redress for his wrongs.

ARGUMENTS OVER WHETHER TO MOVE THE CAPITAL AGAIN

James J. Wilson: "Receding the District of Columbia"

The question of whether the nation's capital should continue to be located in Washington arose from time to time in the early decades of the nineteenth century. In 1805, the U.S. House of Representatives considered this but refused to cede the District of Columbia, excluding the City of Washington, back to Virginia and Maryland and move the capital elsewhere. In response, the True American *weighed in with a strong call for the government to abandon the expensive and time-consuming process of building the capital and its surrounding areas.*

True American (Trenton, N.J.), 21 January 1805

It will be seen…that the house of representatives have been some days employed in an interesting discussion on the propriety of receding the district of Columbia (the city of Washington excepted) to the states of Virginia and Maryland; and that the question has been decided in the negative.

We cannot on this occasion but express our regret, not only that the territory contemplated has not been receded, but that any part of the district is retained. We should have been much better pleased had measures been taken for receding the whole territory, and for transferring the abode of government to some more auspicious spot. However desirable it may be to perpetuate the memory of Washington by a city bearing his name, and to have the residence of government permanently established; yet the experience of ten or twelve years has fully demonstrated the impracticability of rearing a city within the district of Columbia, either worthy of being the residence of our government.—Millions of public money have been already expended to improve this miserable spot, and to provide buildings for the accommodations of the President, Congress, heads of departments, &c. and yet the house of representatives has to occupy a library-room—the President's house looks not much better than an old barn, and neither the members of Congress, the officers of the various departments, nor private citizens, have accommodations that in any other place would be thought tolerable. Bills are now before Congress appropriating AN HUNDRED AND THIRTY THOUSAND DOLLARS more for furthering certain of the public buildings; and as such appropriations have not lately had a beginning, neither is it likely, if the government continues there, they will soon have an end.

The time consumed annually by Congress in legislating for this district, and the vast expence attending their fitting, is another weighty reason for abandoning this hopeless attempt to create a city where nature has determined there should be a desert.

Against removing the seat of government from Washington, we have heard it urged, that many persons have bought and improved, with the expectation that the government would remain there; and that, if it were removed, they would suffer disappointment and loss.

By way of answer we will ask, whether it is not better that comparatively a few individuals, (a considerable portion of whom are mere speculators) should sustain some disappointment and loss in their purchases and improvements, than that the United States should be annually sinking thousands, and hundreds of thousands of dollars—its government sacrificing much time and labor—and suffering great inconveniences, privations, and impositions?—Whether, in short, the public good and convenience ought not to be preferred, to private accommodation or cupidity?

But, it is said, vast sums of money have been expended by government in endeavors to improve Washington, and these will be sacrificed in case the city is abandoned.

We reply, that a great part of this money is already lost, it having been employed in building and demolishing, putting up and pulling down; and that it is better to give up what has already gone, than to squander millions more.

We do not hesitate here to avow the belief—a belief that we have long held, and which every letter we have received, and every person we have conversed with, from Washington, for years past, have tended to confirm—

that the city of Washington must one day, and that not now far distant, be abandoned by the government. Such a prodigious expense as this territory is to the nation—such a continual trouble as it is to Congress—ought not to be supported by the former, or undergone by the latter, without some benefits in return.—And if this abandonment is to take place at all, the sooner it does take place the better.

W. Helms: "Mr. James J. Wilson, Sir"

In response to True American *editor James J. Wilson's insinuation that defenders of the present capital's location sought to keep the seat of government there to honor George Washington, W. Helms responded to set the record straight. The government should remain in Washington so the people of the United States could have the matter settled for once and for all, thus avoiding the future expense of moving and re-establishing the seat of government once again.*

True American (Trenton, N.J.), 11 February 1805

To perpetuate the memory of Washington has but little weight with me in endeavoring to keep the seat of government at this place (he will not be forgot, was there not a single place in the United States bearing his name), but to have it permanently established, to prevent in future that warmth of argument that will ever arise when it is debated, to relieve the uneasiness the citizens of the district experience when held in suspense, to have suitable buildings for Congress to assemble in, and to prevent the expense, trouble, and loss of continually removing the public records.

QUESTIONS

1. Imagine that you are involved in the selection of a location for a county seat or a state or federal government's capital city. What benefits might come from the location of such offices in your vicinity? What disadvantages?
2. One of the biggest debates concerning early Washington, D.C., related to the power of the federal government to oversee a geographical locality—a concept called exclusive jurisdiction. What are the pros and cons of the federal government having power over its own city?
3. Can you think of any circumstance that might lead today's leaders to call for the removal of the seat of the federal government to another loca-

tion? If so, what places in America might be considered suitable and what objections would likely arise as to the selection and by whom?

4. In 1800, the nation's political parties did not pay much attention to the removal of the capital to Washington, D.C. Why not?

5. The essay titled "The Red Chairs" reveals its writer's reluctance to allow the government to spend large sums of money on its furnishings. Can you think of a more recent example of such a debate in relation to any government expenditure on the local, state, or federal levels?

NOTES

1. "Washington," *Encyclopædia Britannica* Premium Service, http://www.britannica.com/eb/article?eu = 115706.

2. Kenneth R. Bowling, *The Creation of Washington, D.C.: The Idea and Location of the American Capital* (Fairfax, Va.: George Mason University Press, 1991), 1–13.

3. Kenneth R. Bowling, "A Foreboding Shadow: Newspaper Celebration of the Federal Government's Arrival," *Washington History* 12 (spring–summer 2000), 5.

4. *The Gazette of the United States,* Philadelphia, Pa., 7 June 1800.

5. Judith R. Hiltner, *The Newspaper Verse of Philip Freneau: An Edition and Bibliographical Survey* (Troy, N.Y.: Whitston Publishing Company, 1986), 634.

CHAPTER 3

Thomas Jefferson's Election to the Presidency, 1800–1801

On March 4, 1801, the end of a long and bitter battle between Republicans and Federalists was marked by a peaceful ceremony in the chambers of the United States Senate. For the past year, the leaders of the two developing political parties had fought for the presidency. As the winner, Republican Thomas Jefferson took the oath of office and delivered his inaugural address in front of a crowd of nearly one thousand onlookers. Much was at stake, for Jefferson's election marked the first time the executive branch of the federal government was handed from one party to another, and some feared that the event would not pass without bloodshed. After Jefferson's speech, an observer wrote, "I have this morning witnessed one of the most interesting scenes a free people can ever witness. The changes of administration, which in every government and in every age have most generally been epochs of confusion, villainy and bloodshed, in this our happy country takes place without any species of distraction, or disorder."[1]

Such fears of disorder came out of the political culture of the times, which discouraged people from gathering together into parties. Americans thought political campaigning was mischievous and that gentlemen should not overtly seek public office. In contrast, by 1800, political parties and campaigning were becoming more prevalent in America, although those running for office remained behind the scenes, planning strategies and tempting newspaper editors with monetary compensation. Despite this, two groups whose members shared radically different visions of America supported candidates in the months leading up to the election. Three were Federalists: incumbent and Massachusetts native President John Adams; South Carolinian Charles Cotesworth Pinckney; and New Yorker John Jay. In the Democratic-Republican camp, the front-running candidates included

Thomas Jefferson, the former U.S. vice president from Virginia, and Aaron Burr from New York.[2]

Campaign rhetoric was plentiful and extremely vicious, with attacks on many fronts coming from both sides. Personal invective marred the campaign. Federalists accused Jefferson of being a dangerous radical and his followers of being wild men who would start a reign of terror comparable to that of the French Revolution. Republicans portrayed Adams as a tyrant conspiring to become king and accused Federalists of plotting to subvert human liberty. At times, the issues at the heart of the campaign came to the forefront. Prominent among them were the Federalist-imposed 1798 Alien and Sedition Acts, direct taxes for national defense, trade reductions with France, and the impressments of American seamen by the British (see chapters 9 and 14).

Federalist rhetoric was especially vitriolic, particularly when it focused on Jefferson's infidelity, religious beliefs, and affinity for the French. In a pamphlet titled "A Short Address to the Voters of Delaware," "A Christian Federalist" asked:

> Can serious and reflecting men look about them and doubt, that if Jefferson is elected, and the Jacobins get into authority, that those morals which protect our lives from the knife of the assassin—which guard the chastity of our wives and daughters from seduction and violence—defend our property from plunder and devastation, and shield our religion from contempt and profanation, will not be trampled upon and exploded.... Let these men get into power, put the reins of government into their hands, and what security have you against the occurrence of the scenes which have rendered France a cemetery, and moistened her soil with the tears and blood of her inhabitants.[3]

"A Christian Federalist" directed his comments to the members of the nation's electoral college, who selected the nation's presidents and vice presidents without a popular vote. Each state's electoral college members voted at home on December 3, and it took weeks for the votes to be counted. By late December, the final ballots were in: Thomas Jefferson and Aaron Burr each had 73 electoral votes; Adams, 65; Pinckney, 64; and Jay, 1. With no clear winner, the election was thrown into the Federalist-dominated U.S. House of Representatives. Finally, on February 17, after 36 House ballots, Jefferson was elected president, and Burr was elected vice president.

This chapter's "Jefferson's Opposition" section includes examples of pieces written by Americans who strongly opposed Thomas Jefferson's bid for the presidency. The author of the first piece, like many other Federalist writers during the campaign, sought to rouse his fellow party members from the stupor he thought they were in. Another Federalist tactic in the anti-Republican campaign was to appeal to the strong anti-French sentiments held by many Americans. In line with this, the author of the section's second essay disparaged the party's Republican opponents with anti-French slurs. The Portland, Maine, newspaper that printed it published "anti-Jacobin" material in nearly every issue. Likewise, the authors of the following *Connecticut Courant* and *Washington Federalist* essays brought their anti-French sentiments to the fore.

The section's "Burleigh" essay was part of a long series by this anonymous author. The *Courant* published his anonymous passionate statements throughout the campaign. At times, "Burleigh" invoked God's aide in the party's struggle. In one essay, he warned and challenged his readers, "Look at your houses, your parents, your wives and your children. Are you prepared to see your dwellings in flames, hoary hairs bathed in blood, female chastity violated, or children writing on the pike and the halberd?...Great God of compassion and justice, shield my country from destruction."[4]

While many of the anti-Republican newspaper writers assumed hysterical tones, they could also write with humor. This is illustrated in two of the pieces: Dick Vulcan's *Gazette of the United States* letter and the anonymous "Wonderful Egg" piece in the *Washington Federalist*.

The section's final piece from the *Washington Federalist* stoically announces Jefferson's election on the House of Representatives' 36th ballot.

The second section includes newspaper commentary that favored Jefferson's election to the presidency. It begins with a long *Kentucky Gazette* essay extolling the Virginian's virtues. Its author, John Bradford, came to Kentucky around 1779, and a few years later, without any schooling in printing, established the *Gazette,* the territory's first newspaper. The many misused and misspelled words in this worshipful sketch of Mr. Jefferson perhaps indicate the difficulty Bradford had in making the *Gazette* a respectable sheet. Bradford would become the patriarch in a whole clan of printers who would go on to make their mark across the West. His son Benjamin Bradford, for example, moved to Nashville, Tennessee, where he established several important newspapers.

The next two pieces address another common theme in the election—religion. William Duane, in the *Aurora,* wrote glowingly of Thomas Jefferson's support for religious toleration. Following this, Samuel Pleasants, in the *Virginia Argus,* complained about the imposition of religious tithes on Quakers, Baptists, and others by the heavily Federalist Congregationalists in several New England states. Thomas Jefferson, he reminded his readers, dismantled such a system of taxation in Virginia.

Several of the section's final articles commented favorably on the progress of the election as it began to be clear that the Federalists were losing. "The storm, which has so long raged in the political world, has at length subsided," wrote Samuel Harrison Smith of the *National Intelligencer*. And William Duane rejoiced with his *Aurora* readers that they had finally been rescued from the Federalists.

The chapter's final essay discussed the final stage of the campaign: the House of Representatives' election. According to Smith of the *Intelligencer,* it was clear that the people of the United States meant for Jefferson to be president and that Burr would not have their confidence if elected by the House.

JEFFERSON'S OPPOSITION

Patriotism: "Federalists!"

According to the author of this diatribe, Massachusetts Federalists needed to wake up or else lose to the Republicans. "Patriotism" called his party's merchants, farmers, ministers, and mechanics to action, along with those who could use their pens and printing presses in an intelligent campaign against their common "enemy."

Newburyport Herald and Country Gazette (Massachusetts), 1 April 1800

"YET a little sleep, a little slumber, a little folding of the hands to sleep," Is this your prayers? If not, it is your *practice*. So shall your destruction "come upon you, as an armed man."

When the adversaries of our Government and Independence are *active, organized,* & in the *field;* is it in character for you to be found in your *beds?* When their scouts are reconnoitering in every quarter; why *sit you still?* Believe and realize that *revolution* has not yet had its perfect work. The Republics in *Europe,* it is true, are all overturned; but the *American* fabric yet stands. Suffer the enemy, *by influencing your State elections,* to undermine the Federal Government, and the work is done. Your degradation complete. The train is laid, preparations are making, and the moment *hastening* to spring the mine.

Rouse then to action. Ye merchants, let not *private* emolument engross all your energies. Remember your country, and sacrifice a little at her shrine. Gentlemen of fortune, indulge not in glorious *ease,* when destruction is at the door. Worthy farmers, the stability of our country, *sleep not,* while the enemy are sowing tares. Mechanics and men of every description, awake, look about you, see your danger, be vigilant, be active, and make your escape. Be not *deceived.* Your destruction of a long time *slumbereth not.* Ministers of the altar, tremble for the ARK. Christianity is attacked, as a *debasing superstition.* Men of talents, who see the danger, employ your pens;—and, until the danger is overpast, let all Federal Printers prefer *judicious, weighty, patriotic* communications, to *juvenile* essays and *unimportant* advertisements. All, who love their COUNTRY more than private gain, will cheerfully acquiesce; and those who do not, though they may call themselves Federalists, are not true Patriots. "Oh, that my People were *wise,* that they would *consider!'*

Elezar Alley Jenks: "The Prosperity of the Community, so Far as it Depends on Political Measures, Is Always in Proportion to the Purity of Elections"

Elezar Alley Jenks, owner and editor of Jenks' Portland Gazette, *included essays and other items of an anti-Jacobin nature in nearly every edition of his paper during the campaign. Here he appealed to his fellow Federalists' sense of duty to their party.*

Jenks' Portland Gazette (Maine), 24 March 1800

It is time, Americans, to assume a determined spirit, a persevering energy; by which you cannot fail to rise superior to the artifice of your enemies, and foil forever their attempts to prostrate our government, and introduce anarchy and civil war.—With a view to accomplish their designs, our councils have been traduced, and our best men libeled and calumniated in a manner that must touch the feelings of every honest American.—Their views also, are extended to our state government. In two important states, jacobins have been chosen Governors; and in Massachusetts and Newhampshire to support the election of timid or doubtful characters in opposition to men of undoubted federalism and talents.—These considerations, it is not doubted, will operate forcibly at the election which is speedily to take place in this state. The privilege of free suffrage is great; but it will turn to our own destruction if not properly attended to. Citizens, be on your guard—for never was there greater occasion for unanimity and dissension, than at the present moment.

Burleigh: "Politics. No. 1—to the People of the United States"

"Burleigh" wrote for the Connecticut Courant *during the summer and fall of 1800, and his essays were widely reprinted in Federalist newspapers. In this, his first essay, he gave his readers a history lesson on the presidential campaigns held since the country was formed and attempted to convince them that victory would not be theirs if they continued in their "fatal sleep."*

Connecticut Courant (Hartford, Conn.), 23 June 1800

The season is rapidly approaching, when, by your constitutional agents, you will be called upon to elect a President of the United States. This will be the fourth time this high privilege has been exercised, since the adoption of our Federal Constitution. Twice there was no struggle, for Washington was the candidate; against him, who could have the hardihood to run the race of honor! At the third election, there was more difficulty. The all united spell of that great name which has scattered all intrigue, and effort, was dissolved, and the country was instantly divided into two parties, the one Federal, the other Democratic or Jacobinical. The contest was severe, but success followed the exertions of the Federalists. The disappointed party have not desponded by reason of their defeat but like all those whose object is mischief, they have pursued their plans since the last Presidential election, with ten fold vigour, and ingenuity. Faithful to themselves, and faithful to their cause, those who have no other spirit of union, no cordiality of heart, in any other pursuit, in this great work of destruction, move on with the firmness, the resolution, and the compactness of the celebrated Macedonian phalanx, while the Federalists, thinking or pretending to think that every thing will go on as it has done from the beginning, sit and fold their hands in a most astonishing security.

To rouse the Federal party from this fatal sleep, and when roused to stimulate them to counteract the baneful plots of the Jacobins, is the object of this address. That it is a subject worthy of attention, few will deny. If attended to thoroughly, I am perfectly persuaded it will rouse some, at least, to exertion. The exertions of some, will do some good; and perhaps, when the spark of patriotic fire shall once rekindle, it may spread from breast to breast, until the friends of government are all animated by its pure and fervent flame.

The Jacobins assert with the utmost confidence, that Mr. Jefferson's election is sure. If I tho't so, I should not hesitate to assert with equal confidence, that the destruction of the Federal Constitution is equally sure. I do not, however, believe that his election is sure. I am well convinced, that it may be prevented, if the friends of the government will act with as much union, as much zeal, and as much perseverance, as its enemies act. To induce this union, zeal, and perseverance, I shall proceed to support several propositions, which are of great weight and importance in the question to be decided—viz.

1. Mr. Jefferson has long felt a spirit of deadly hostility against the Federal Constitution and in conjunction with his party has been steadily plotting its destruction.
2. If he should be elected president, the Constitution will inevitably fall a sacrifice to Jacobinism.
3. The result will be dreadful to the people of the United States.

The consideration of these propositions will necessarily take up some time, as many facts and documents must be examined, and a review of the practices and conduct of the Jeffersonian (by this I mean the Jacobin party) must be had, in order to make the proper deductions.—Should the subject not grow interesting, before it is closed, the fault will be in the writer. It certainly furnishes materials for a discussion, not only interesting, but if the hearts of my countrymen are not harder than the nether-millstone, full of apprehension, full of terror.

And let it be deeply impressed on every mind, that there is a period of only a little more than *four months* remaining in which they can act with any chance of success. In that short period, they must overthrow the labour of years, planned by wisdom, and executed by skill and fidelity—skill and fidelity, exceeded by nothing but the wickedness, the dreadful depravity of the actors, or submit to all the evils, which follow a nation, without government, without law, without security, without peace or happiness.

Dick Vulcan: "Mr. Editor"

Anonymous writer Dick Vulcan somewhat humorously portrayed himself as a citizen recently brought out from underneath the spell of the Republican newspaper The Aurora *by his Federalist friends.*

Gazette of the United States (Philadelphia), 11 September 1800

I was a Democrat and was fully intent upon voting for Tom Paine, pshaw, I mean Tom Jefferson at the next election; but by the salutary counsel of my Friends…I have now become (I hope) a good Federalist…I have been accustomed to read the *Aurora* (by the advice of Duane) every morning…but…Mr. Worthy, the schoolmaster…said, "what, have you also degraded yourself so far as to become a subscriber for that infamous and abandoned paper; a paper constantly teeming with the greatest scurrility against every good man; from whose shaft of Malice even Washington was not exempted and which, not content, now seeks to undermine the throne of God himself?"

Anonymous: "The Wonderful Egg! Something New under the Sun"

This report revealed that humor was used at times in the campaign, although it's unclear whether it lightened the spirits of those who read the newspapers. Originally published in the Winchester Constellation, *it was clever enough to attract the attention of a* Federalist *editor.*

Washington Federalist (District of Columbia), 4 November 1800

A report has currently circulated that an Egg has been found near this town, the singularity of which deserves notice: On examining this Egg, the plainly legible words of *"Thomas Jefferson shall be the SAVIOUR of his country"* were discovered. One gentleman, it is said, scraped the letters with a knife, and cracked the shell, and to his astonishment found it to be a natural EGG. Even the hens declare war against the Presidency of Mr. Adams!

Anonymous: "For the *Washington Federalist*"

This piece was written when it had become clear that the deadlocked electoral college would result in the election being thrown into the House of Representatives. If the members of this body were bullied into selecting the wrong person, this author worried, the nation's future elections might be "drenched in blood."

Washington Federalist (District of Columbia), 16 January 1801

While the unrelenting opposers of the government were confident, that Mr. Jefferson would be placed in the chair of state, they abounded in professions of political moderation.

The hesitancy, which has been recently manifested, respecting the appointment of Mr. Jefferson in preference to Mr. Burr, has unmasked the hypocrisy of their professions. They have already exchanged their affected moderation for public menaces. Instead of a temperate examination of the merits or demerits of the two citizens, whom the electors have equally presented to the House of Representatives, an invitation to rebellion has been openly made.

It was thus that the Jacobins in France professed philanthropy, and prepared their poignards.

The presidential election now pending is but the second, since the retirement of the beloved, and now lamented, FATHER OF THE COUNTRY. It is the *first* that has occurred, since the time when the news of his decease covered all America with mourning. If this election is to be controlled by menaces, must not the next be determined by arms?

In the face of Jacobinical menaces, the Representatives in Congress are called, by the constitution, to discharge an important public duty. They are called to decide, between the merits and demerits of the candidates, as in their judgment and conscience, they shall believe to be best for their country. Whatever menaces may be employed to stagger their decision, if they desert their duty in the moment of high responsibility (no disrespect is intended by the supposition—the honorable guardians of the public weal will not be guilty of such desertion,—but were the event possible) what ought not to be apprehended by the friends of domestic peace, and national union?

If the jacobinical menaces should be attended with that purposed effect, the principle of determining the appointment of President by force, will be virtually established. And what powers of language are adequate to depict all the possible consequences of so fatal a precedent?

The attempts to control the public councils by a system of terror should, therefore, be faced, with a bold and impressive serenity. They should be met with unshaken fortitude, by all who would preserve this our natal country from being eventually drenched in blood.

William Alexander Rind: "Mr. Jefferson"

This brief report on the results of the 36th ballot in the House of Representatives told the news that many in the Federalist camp dreaded. In protest, the editor printed the image of an eagle upside down below these words.

Washington Federalist (District of Columbia), 17 February 1801

The House of Representatives met at twelve o'clock to day and proceeded to ballot for President of the United States.

On examining the ballot boxes it appeared that Mr. Jefferson had a majority of all the States, and he was therefore declared to be elected to the Presidential chair.

May he discharge its duties in such a manner as to merit and receive the blessings of all good men, and without reddening the cheek of the American Patriot with blushes for his country ! ! !

PRO-JEFFERSON COMMENTARY

John Bradford: "Character of Thomas Jefferson"

John Bradford, along with many other Kentuckians and westerners, was a great admirer of Jefferson's philosophical and political stances, especially Jefferson's advocacy of freedom for citizens from the controls of a strong central government.

Kentucky Gazette (Lexington), 29 May 1800

THE superior distinction which Mr. Jefferson has acquired, in the political world, was founded upon the alliance of virtue and fortune. Great events give birth to great talents. It is not difficult to say, however, that had the revolution in America, never taken place, he would have arisen to considerable fame, in the republics of letters and philosophy. The advantages of an excellent education, habits of application and study, were circumstances, that gave to his mind, an inclination for philosophical and literary pursuits.—His notes on the state of Virginia, a work though incomplete, and considered merely as bearing the features of its title, is however not without considerable merit.— It discovers a mind at once sagacious and inquisitive and capable by the gradual means of experiment and rational deduction, of unfolding the sublimest principles of truth.—But the same great event which has immortalized the genius of American patriotism, and drawn from obscurity, the most brilliant talents in the field and the cabinet, paid an equal tribute to the virtues of Mr. Jefferson, and gave him distinction in the first rank of statesmen,—At the first shock of that convulsion, which eventually separated the continent of America, from Great Britain, the philosophical apparatus fell from his hand. Governed by that genuine patriotism which sacrifices private interest to public felicity, he exchanged rural ease and retirement for the battle of active life, the amusements of the laboratory, for the more interesting duties of the cabinet.—In this situation, Mr. Jefferson appears to have been designed by fortune and accident, to combine with the solidity the durability of a reputation. His advancement was gradual; and every step of it, was marked by a display of talents that was equally honorable to himself and competent to the difficulties occasioned by the precipitancy of events....

The political principles of Mr. Jefferson, are drawn from an expanded intellect, that consults the oracles of nature and reason, as its only guides.— Born at a period, when the whole universe is convulsed, by the conflicting passions of mankind, his study to reconcile the jarring elements and to extract felicity and order from misery and confusion.—Experience and observation have pointed out to him the wrecks of ambition and the despotism of error and prejudice. They have conveyed his mind, through the various regions of society, familiarized it with the melancholy exhibitions of lost dignity, of injured innocence, of polluted virtue, and left it in the awful contemplation of scenes at which, his humanity shudders.—It is no wonder, therefore that his opinions are the pious innovations of the philosopher, who wishes to repair the injuries which an unjust policy has occasioned in the world; that he cherishes them as a peculiar tribute to his own feelings, which the understanding confirms and the heart ratifies. Upon this liberal plan of philanthropy, Mr. Jefferson is the true citizen of the world. Like Cato he feels an attachment for his country, but like Socrates, his affections embrace the universe....

It is said that Mr. Jefferson is a philosopher; that consequently he possesses a peculiar cast of mind that unfits him for the duties of a statesman. Let this obligation rest in the bosom of the illiberal parasite of power, who sits at the foot-stool of despotism and dreads the influence of a single qualification that might soften the afflictions of a nation. For my part, I perceive not the incompatibility complained of....

Disdaining the character of the courtier, where pufilanimity and flattery are the steps by which, the obsequious arise to fame and distinction, Mr. Jefferson has filled the highest office of governments, by his own intrinsic merit. The simplicity of his manners and the reservedness of his tempers are the characteristics of a vigorous mind, which grasps at higher objects, than the mere arts of pleasing.—Yet there is no man, in private life, more amenable, none more dignified, and none, whose manners, possess, in a higher degree, the incomparable felicity of inspiring the combined emotions of attachment and respect. He has contemplated men and things in different lights, in which they are, and in which they should be. His reflections on this subject, are the sources of his humanity and forbearance; qualifications which travel, business and books, have matured into practice, and gives to his mind a degree of philosophical tranquility, infinitely superior, to those of his contemporaries. Let not this placidity of temper, be mistaken for coldness and apprehension. He does not possess an understanding, incapable of being inspired with intrepidity, when great objects demand its energy. The American declaration of independence, his negociations in favor of the most subtle cabinets in Europe, and his communications with the intriguing ministers of France and England, while secretary of state, will remain the durable memorials, of a great mind, at once capable of combining the various qualifications of energy, deliberate coolness and penetration.

William Duane: "Tolerance"

Questions about religion came up often in the campaign, especially in regard to Jefferson, whose beliefs were regularly maligned by Federalists who saw their influence on the wane.

The Aurora (Philadelphia), 9 September 1800

Toleration in religion, complete and perfect, was not known, except among the Hindus, in any part of the earth before our revolution. In Pennsylvania, a few years before the revolution...even here in this city of brotherhood...*Papist* was a term of reproach as constant as *Democrat* or *Jacobin* in the mouth of good federalists two years ago!...In the state of Virginia before the war, a Quaker on going into that state *a third time* was liable to the punishment of death! A Roman Catholic clergyman dared not to go even once within its boundary to exercise even an office of charity!

Our revolution has obliterated these impious institutions. [T]he New England states alone support intolerance. In Virginia, Mr. *Jefferson* has been the author and mover of those laws which put down the national church there and abolished *tythes* [taxes]. This is a sin for which those who deal in tythes will never forgive him; this is Mr. *Jefferson's* crime in their eyes...[T]he Roman Catholics are now building a Church in Norfolk, Virginia...From this happy state of toleration, the furious zealots for the British government would bring us back to our former condition...

Samuel Pleasants: "Mr. Adams and Mr. Jefferson's Religious Services Compared"

Here, in stark contrast to many of the day's campaign writers, the editor of the Argus *got right to the point in this comparison of the conduct of Jefferson and of Adams in relation to religion.*

The Virginia Argus (Richmond), 24 October 1800

The religion of these two public men is much talked of. The states of Massachusetts and Connecticut afford at this time, frequent examples of persons being *forced* to pay taxes to support Mr. Adams's church though the payers be *Baptists, Quakers,* & others of different religious principles, practice and discipline from Mr. Adams's church. The same was the case about fifteen years ago in Virginia, where Mr. Jefferson's church then forced all others to pay to their support. Mr. Jefferson set himself strongly against this practice, declaring it *cruel* and *impolitic* toward our fellow citizens, & *impious* towards our Almighty creator.—Mr. Adams ought to have thought and acted *like Mr. Jefferson,* but *he did not.* The consequence is, that great *religious oppression* yet exists in Massachusetts, by the remissness of Mr. Adams, who had a principal hand in forming their State constitution; and religious oppression is abolished in Virginia, *by the piety* and *exertions* of Mr. Jefferson, who introduced the law, which gives to *all* men of *all* churches and denominations, *perfect religious liberty* and *the rights of conscience.*

Samuel Harrison Smith: "The Storm...Has Subsided"

The new federal city's staunchly Republican National Intelligencer *had only just been established on October 31 when this piece was published.*

Many of Jefferson's critics claimed that that the paper was established and overseen by him. Here, the paper's first editor rejoiced over the shift of power to the Republicans, although it wasn't yet known which Republican candidate would sit in the president's chair.

National Intelligencer (District of Columbia), 15 December 1800

The storm, which has so long raged in the political world, has at length subsided. Parties have tried their strength, and victory has crowned with success, in the Presidential election, the efforts of the REPUBLICANS.

To *Republicans* it must be a cause of sincere felicitation that their country has surmounted, without any other agitation than that of the public sentiment, the choice of their first magistrate. The example is auspicious to the destinies of the world. For while other nations, the victims of monarchical or aristocratical error, on similar occasions, invariably appeal to the sword, America presents the august spectacle of a nation, enlightened and jealous of its rights, discharging with dignity the most interesting duty which republican institutions enjoin.

On such a result as this, every true American, every lover of his country, will reflect with increasing satisfaction. Beholding in the system of representation, founded on an extensive right of suffrage, the source as well as the palladium of his political rights, he will rejoice to behold the confirmation of experience imparting new stability to the structure. And while he mourns over the tottering ruins of European states, he will, with proud philanthropy, present his own system to the old world as a cure for all her evils.

William Duane: "People of America"

On behalf of his party, William Duane expressed considerable relief that one of the election's Republican candidates would likely advance to the high office, and that a second Republican candidate would serve as vice president.

The Aurora (Philadelphia), 16 December 1800

Our Country and our form of government are rescued
From the talons of Monarchists.
In spite of intrigue,
In spite of terror,
In spite of unconstitutional laws,
In spite of British influence,
In spite of the Standing Army,

In spite of the Sedition Law...
The public voice of America and of virtue Prevails...

Aristides: "No. II. On the Election of President"

Aristides wrote three pieces for the Intelligencer. *In No. I, Aristides foresaw that Jefferson and Burr would have an equal number of votes and that the election would be thrown into the House of Representatives. By the time the second piece was published, the tie had been confirmed, and the campaign had switched to its second phase. Clearly in favor of Jefferson, Aristides considered the possibility of a Burr win.*

National Intelligencer (District of Columbia), 5 January 1801
From the remarks I have made, it must be manifest to every unprejudiced mind, that Mr. Burr, if elected President by Congress, would not possess the confidence of the people. Not that I think his talents or integrity unworthy of the proudest distinctions that republicanism can confer. I am ready to acknowledge that his reputation has not only survived, but in all probability will ultimately survive the loud clamours of party resentment. But being selected by the people for the Vice Presidency, and not the Presidency, in the exercise of the duties of the first station he would enjoy their entire confidence, while in the exercise of the duties of the last place, he would entirely be destitute of that band of union, which, in a republican government, can only proceed from the decided preference of the people, expressed in a constitutional form. It is in vain to say that the House of Representatives would express this national preference. The assertion is not true. Not a citizen of America is so ignorant as not to know that every vote given to Mr. Jefferson was as President, and every vote given to Mr. Burr was as Vice President... .

QUESTIONS

1. Why do you think the founders of the nation did not establish direct popular vote as the method for selection of the country's presidents?
2. Besides newspapers, what other communication channels existed in early America for the acquisition of information about politics and politicians?
3. Compare the events of the 1800–1801 presidential election to those surrounding the 2000 presidential election.

4. Presidential candidates' religious beliefs rarely come up in contemporary presidential campaigns. Why was this so different in 1800?
5. Americans today generally accept the role that parties play in the country's political process, although we at times still find them unsatisfying. Explain.
6. Why do you think early Americans worried that violence might erupt if President John Adams were not re-elected to the presidency?

NOTES

1. Mrs. Samuel H. Smith to Susan B. Smith, 4 March 1801, in *The First Forty Years of Washington Society, Portrayed by the Family Letters of Mrs. Samuel Harrison Smith*, ed. Gaillard Hunt (New York: F. Ungar, 1906), 25–26.

2. Page Smith, *The Shaping of America: A People's History of the Young Republic*, vol. 3 (New York: McGraw-Hill, 1980), 285–308.

3. "A Christian Federalist," "A Short Address to the Voters of Delaware," Kent County, 21 September 1800, 1.

4. "No. 8. to the People of the United States," *Connecticut Courant*, 29 September 1800.

CHAPTER 4

Medical Treatment and
The Rush-Light, 1800

By contemporary standards, public health conditions in the early decades of nineteenth-century America were terrible. Up to about 1822, yellow-fever epidemics swept the nation's seaports, spreading fear among the population. Smallpox was still enough of a threat that the discovery of a new treatment for it late in the eighteenth century was of immense importance. Regardless of one's age or level of financial security, the field of medical science and treatment was in such a primitive state in the early 1800s that even minor illnesses or injuries could lead to death or lifelong disabilities. Indeed, Americans had little trust in the medical profession and were always on the lookout for quackery. As a result, editors included a variety of medical information in their newspapers. Essays and reports on illnesses and their treatments were common. Advertisements for drugs, which their sellers claimed would relieve people's sufferings, were also printed in newspapers. And when epidemics broke out, newspaper editors raised questions about how diseases were transmitted, who was to blame for starting particular epidemics, how to prevent and treat diseases, and what medical and governmental authorities should do in public health emergencies.[1]

American medicine was in what historians call its heroic era in the early national period. Physicians' understanding of sickness and health to some extent still reflected the ancient Greek idea that the body had four fluids—blood, black bile, yellow bile, and phlegm—and that illness was caused by excess amounts of them. The cures of heroic medical practitioners consisted of bloodletting, vomiting, blistering, and purging, all of which depleted the body of such excess fluids. Yellow fever, consumption, dropsy, hydrocephalus, apoplexy, and gout were among the diseases and conditions treated in these ways. Depletion methods were even used to treat madness and other diseases of the mind.[2]

The first section in this chapter includes three newspaper pieces related to the depletion methods often prescribed by physicians. The first two essays relate to bloodletting, and the third to biliousness. Bloodletting was one of the most controversial of the depletion methods and was used by physicians desperate to find effective treatments in the midst of the frequent epidemics that hit the nation. The procedure involved the removal of a prescribed amount of a person's blood, usually through a vein, but at times by leeches. Started by the Egyptians, bloodletting would reach its peak of popularity early in the nineteenth century.

A few people began to wonder whether bloodletting and other common treatments of the period were more harmful than helpful, and they found the period's newspapers and magazines to be effective vehicles for spreading their concerns. Editor Joseph Gales, for example, in an endorsement of a medical society for North Carolina, argued that standards were needed to suppress "the fatal and criminal practices of Quacks and Empyrics."[3] One of bloodletting's staunchest critics was journalist William Cobbett, owner and operator of the *Porcupine's Gazette*. On September 19, 1797, under the title "Medical Puffing," Cobbett published this statement in the *Gazette:*

> Those who are in the habit of looking over the Gazettes, which come in from the different parts of the country, must have observed, and with no small degree of indignation, the arts that our remorseless Bleeder is making use of to puff off his preposterous practice. He has, unfortunately, his partisans in almost every quarter of the country. To these he writes letters, and in return gets letters from them: he extols their practice, and they extol his; and there is scarcely a page of any newspaper that I see, which has the good fortune to escape the poison of their prescriptions.—Blood, blood! Still they cry more blood!—In every sentence they menace our poor veins. Their language is as frightful to the ears of the alarmed multitude, as is the raven's croak to those of the sickly flock.

Cobbett's "remorseless Bleeder" was Dr. Benjamin Rush, a well-known Philadelphia physician who was one of the period's most famous proponents of heroic medicine and its system of depletions.[4] In his search for a cure for yellow fever in the midst of the terrible epidemics of 1793–1794, Rush had increasingly turned to bloodletting and the use of calomel, which he called the "Sampson of the Materia Medica."[5] As negative views of his treatments spread, Rush defended the practice in "A Defence of Bloodletting as a Remedy for Certain Diseases," a tract published in 1798. According to Rush, Americans distrusted bleeding as a treatment because the English also disliked the practice:

> In contemplating the prejudice against blood-letting, which formerly prevailed so generally in our country, I have been led to describe them to a cause wholly political. We are descended chiefly from Great Britain, and

have been for many years under the influence of English habits upon all subjects. Some of these habits, so far as they relate to government, have been partly changed; but in dress, arts, manufacturers, manners, and science, we are still governed by our early associations. Britain and France have been for many centuries, hereditary enemies. The hostility of the former to the latter nation, extends to every thing that belongs to their character. It discovers itself, in an eminent degree, in diet and medicine. Do the French love soups? The English prefer solid flesh. Do the French love their meats well cooked? The English prefer their meats to be half-roasted. Do the French sip coffee after dinner? The English spend their afternoons in drinking Port and Madera wines. Do the French physicians prescribe purges and glysters to cleanse the bowels? The English physicians prescribe vomits for the same purpose. Above all, do the French physicians advise bleeding in fevers? The English physician forbid it in most fevers, and substitute sweating.... Here then we discover the source of the former prejudices and errors of our country men, upon the subject of blood-letting. They are of British origin. They have been inculcated in British universities, and in British books; and they accord as all with our climate and state of society, as the Dutch foot stoves did with the temperate climate of the Cape of Good Hope.[6]

Rush's defense of bloodletting only spurred Cobbett further in his efforts to discredit Rush and his practice. Writing under the name Peter Porcupine in *Porcupine's Gazette*, Cobbett's anti-Rush commentary became so scathing—he essentially accused him of murder—that Rush sued Cobbett for libel in 1797. After a lengthy trial, Cobbett lost his case in 1800 and was ordered to pay Rush $5,000. This was such a heavy blow that Cobbett, now bankrupt, made plans to return to his native Great Britain. Before leaving, he launched a short-lived periodical called *The Rush-Light*. Introduced on February 28, 1800, *The Rush-Light* continued to disparage Rush and the rest of the physicians who used depletion methods. Several pieces from *The Rush-Light* are included here. The first of these, "A Bitter Pill for the Rushites," commented on the death of George Washington, because Cobbett believed Washington's death was caused by bleeding (see chapter 1).

The author of the third newspaper article published in this section warned readers not to consume gamboges in an effort to rid themselves of an excess amount of bile. Gamboges are brownish and orange-colored resins harvested from Southeast Asian trees. When the resins are combined, they form a yellow pigment. Physicians often prescribed gamboges to treat biliousness, an uncomfortable condition earmarked by nausea, abdominal discomfort, headache, and constipation. In addition, the author sought to set the record straight on bile: He contends that many people incorrectly assumed that biliousness occurred when bile entered the stomach. Instead, he argued, biliousness was caused by an excessive secretion of bile from the liver into the small intestine.

The second group of newspaper reports and letters focuses on two of early America's most terrible scourges: yellow fever and small-pox. These diseases led to so many deaths that people eagerly sought news about their treatments and possible cures. In 1796, Edward Jenner discovered the vaccine that would save millions of people from small-pox, and within a few years, the news spread to America. Dr. Benjamin Waterhouse is given credit for introducing the vaccine to Americans. On July 8, 1800, Waterhouse inoculated his 5-year-old son and other family members with pure kine-pox vaccine acquired from England. Dr. J. M. Mann, in his report, brought the news to the readers of the Albany *New York Gazette*.

Like small-pox, yellow-fever epidemics led to many comments and reports in newspapers. Editors like New York City's Noah Webster at times took part in debates that arose over where yellow-fever epidemics came from, how they spread, and how to prevent them. In 1795, Webster wrote an open letter to the physicians of Philadelphia, New York, Baltimore, Norfolk, and New Haven, asking them to send him information that would help determine if yellow fever was of domestic origin. This involvement of newspaper editors in the search for answers about the scourge of yellow fever continued into the early decades of the nineteenth century. This section's letter from the *Philadelphia Gazette* and column from the *New-York Evening Post* serve as interesting examples. We know today that yellow fever is a virus spread by mosquitoes, but in the early decades of the nineteenth century, physicians and scientists were still struggling with whether or not it was contagious and how to stop it from spreading. The writer of the 1802 commentary argued that the frequent use of olive and other oils in bathing and cooking might help prevent the disease. The *New York Evening-Post* column, published in 1816, reported that public health officials had taken steps to deal with the illness by imposing quarantines.

"Quacks," the first selection in the final section, was written and published by *New-York Evening Post* editor William Coleman in 1816. This piece reflected people's fears about dangers posed by poorly trained physicians and by unschooled individuals posing as physicians. Until the end of the second decade of the nineteenth century, the business of dispensing medicines and performing medical treatments was unregulated. While some early nineteenth-century Americans considered their physicians to be learned individuals, others failed to regard them with the kind of respect they are generally afforded today. Many years would pass before the dispensing of medical advice became the bailiwick of licensed physicians.

The section's second entry, published in an 1820 issue of the District of Columbia's *National Intelligencer*, reports on good news—that the medical profession was launching important reforms in the field of pharmacology. No longer, it was hoped, would sick people become victims of pharmacists who improperly mixed medicines.

The Early Republic

Recent Titles in
Debating Historical Issues in the Media of the Time

The Antebellum Era: Primary Documents on Events from 1820 to 1860
David A. Copeland

The Revolutionary Era: Primary Documents on Events from 1776 to 1800
Carol Sue Humphrey

The Reconstruction Era: Primary Documents on Events from 1865 to 1877
Donna L. Dickerson

The Progressive Era: Primary Documents on Events from 1890 to 1914
Elizabeth V. Burt

The Civil War: Primary Documents on Events from 1860 to 1865
Ford Risley

THE EARLY REPUBLIC

GREENWOOD PRESS
Westport, Connecticut • London

1801, a position he held until he died on June 6. The dictionary did not mention Mr. Dallas, Kittera's replacement.

Jenks' Portland Gazette (Maine), 10 August 1801

IF there be any sensibility in the grave, how must the great Washington be agonized by the treatment which the objects of his favor and his confidence now receive. Whenever the French party denounce those who were appointed to office by Washington, who, in times of war, fought under the illustrious Hero, and in times of peace supported his wife and virtuous administration—they are directly dismissed the service. Instances of the intolerance of the present administration are too numerous to admit of recapitulation: One, however, has occurred in Pennsylvania which will long be remembered. Mr. Kittera, of Lancaster, had for many years been a member of the federal House of Representatives:—He here advocated with zeal and with talents all the measures of Washington (between whom and himself there existed a sincere and uninterrupted friendship) and he assisted in the establishment of that system of measures, projected by Mr. Adams, and the adoption of which by Congress, preserved us from the fangs of France, and issued in the prosperity we everywhere witness. At the close of the session of Congress, Mr. Kittera was appointed Attorney for the district of Pennsylvania; in the room of Mr. Ingersol, who had resigned—not who was dismissed—Mr. Kittera accepted the appointment, broke up his establishment at Lancaster, brought his wife and children to Philadelphia, where he took a suitable house for a year, and as soon as all this had been incurred, Mr. Kittera was turned out of his office, which was given to a Mr. Dallas, who comes from one of the West India islands, and wrote many pieces for the *Aurora,* advocating the election of Mr. Jefferson. The sensibility of Mr. Kittera was deeply affected by this undeserved treatment.—His health, which never had been robust, immediately declined; in spite of the exertions of his friends, the presidential contumely preyed upon his spirits, he took to his bed, and after a short illness, he died. The day before poor Kittera departed for the land of forgetfulness, his Physician enquired of him if some pain, of which he complained, was sharp—He answered, "Tis dreadfully acute,—like Mr. Jefferson it cuts to the very quick."

Justice: "For the Centinel"

The debate over Jefferson's patronage continued through the years of his two terms. "Justice" opined in this essay that only a ruling class bent on absolute control would continue to throw qualified individuals out of positions whose duties they admirably fulfilled. The dispute that brought forth this statement began when the Amherst, New Hampshire, postmaster was removed from his position to make way for a Republican.

Columbian Centinel (Boston), 20 August 1803

Every man who is acquainted with this transaction; every man of common sense, or feelings, must see that this act, like many others, must reflect indelible disgrace upon administration—must demonstrate that they are, like *Macbeth,* resolved to effect "by the worst means the worst."

We would ask (says a writer upon the late general *removals*) what notion of private individual benefit, and fair rotation, if such a thing could be supposed to exist, can be put into competition with the injury arising to the country, from its offices being converted into means of undue influence? And whether the country can be said to be represented where such powerful instruments of terror on the one hand, and seduction on the other, are not only left in the hands of a party, but permitted to be violently strained in wrenching the constitution from its appointed posture, and accumulating despotic power in the hands of any one man or set of men? Those who look upon this as trifling cannot look deeper than the surface of things. We do not hesitate to say, that if there was a chief magistrate who possessed genius and boldness equal to, and combined with, the power with which party craft and popular delusion have vested our present President, and along with that the ambition to rule, five years at farthest would make the United States a despotic monarchy, under some name or other, perhaps consulate. We do not accuse Mr. *Jefferson* of any design of that kind: But we venture to assert that the mass of power, founded on popular delusion, now accumulating in his party, will, if ever it shall pass, into the hands of a crafty, bold, and ambitious man, produce the subjugation of *America.* The Republic of *Florence* sunk under the despotism of a family (the *Medicis*) whose virtues and brilliant endowments had undesignedly collected round them an undue accumulation of popularity: and we need go no further for an example of what we say than the late revolution in *France*—where the wicked popularity-catching, and arts of *Mirabeau* and his set, and afterwards of the *Brissotine* faction, laid the foundation of those horrible temporary tyrannies which have at last ended in the firm established despotism of *Bonaparte.*

Americans, look to it in time!

IN FAVOR OF JEFFERSON'S REMOVAL
OF FEDERALISTS

William Duane: "A Great Outcry"

President Jefferson was not a hypocrite, according to Duane, for turning Federalists out of office after saying "We are all republicans: we are all federalists" in his inaugural address.

Aurora (Philadelphia), 5 June 1801

A great outcry has been made against the President of the United States, for removing from office persons whose fitness to hold offices was at least questionable. The *Washington Federalist* charges him with hypocrisy, asserts that the aristocrats (or as they choose to denominate themselves, the federalists) were led to believe that all their partisans would be retained in the places for which the wisdom and moderation (both so well known) of Mr. Adams had selected them. The tory editors in this city, charged the democrats with being enemies to the President, after his inaugural speech; the *Centinel* published that speech, leaving out the whole paragraph in which religion was mentioned; the *Palladium* asserted that it was a jumble of professions that meant nothing; and the republicans one and all considered this same speech as containing an elegant and concise exposition of those principles, which had been maintained by them through a reign of persecution and terror, of folly and of federalism. If Mr. Jefferson has departed from his professions in that speech, the republicans will be the first to oppose him. But he has not departed from them, he has not manifested even an intention to depart from them. The only charge that has or can be made against this object of continued unremitting federal abuse, is that he has removed men from office, the authors, abettors, and tools of weak and wicked persecutions; men who have prostituted their official powers and influence, for the purpose of electionary corruption, and some of whom have been so villainous as to abuse their official duties so far as to pack juries even on trials of life and death. Is the removal of such men to be considered as dereliction of principle?

David Denniston and James Cheetham: "Removals from Office"

In New York, some Republicans thought Jefferson wasn't moving fast enough to remove Adams's appointments. Under the kind of pressure evident in this newspaper essay, and out of his growing realization that his earlier conciliatory overtures would now cause Federalists to soften in their stances against him, Jefferson began to modify his patronage policies.

American Citizen (New York City), 5 June 1801

It was ardently desired and confidently expected by the Republicans of New-York...that by this time one half at least of the Tories now in office in the United States, would have been removed; and its not being done has occasioned, we solemnly and reluctantly confess, very serious apprehensions and doubts in the public mind, which are every day increasing.... It is rational to suppose that those who removed John Adams from office, because of his manifold transgressions of the constitution, and his pointed hostility to liberty...would naturally expect the removal of lesser culprits in office. If this should not be the case, for what, in the name of God, have we been contending? Merely for the removal of John Adams, that Mr. Jefferson might occupy the place which he shamefully left?

David Denniston and James Cheetham: "Connecticut Policy"

As soon as word spread that Elizur Goodrich was being removed from his post as New Haven tax collector, Federalists cried out against what they considered presidential hypocrisy. Here is but one of the many strong Republican responses.

American Citizen (New York City), 13 June 1801

The few removals of federal offices which Mr. Jefferson has made...has drawn from federal pens volumes of obloquy. It has been represented as intolerance wicked in itself, and prejudicial to the union of our citizens. The removal of Elizur Goodrich, the only solitary instance of supercedence in Connecticut, has been a theme for the most rancorous federal virulence; and such has been the pointed and passionate violence of some of the friends of order in N. Haven, that it has nearly produced an insurrection— They view it as a crime of the worst kind to appoint a Republican to office, and conceive it as an exercise of tyranny and injustice, which would warrant open rebellion against the government. They really conceive that laws are made to rule the people *generally,* but that *offices* were instituted *entirely* and *exclusively* for *themselves....* It was this system which imparted to the administration of J. Adams a power so Herculean as rendered it difficult for the republicans with all their energy, to make an impression on their phalanxes, and overturn their power. But thank God it was effected. It would impart strength to any party. And if pursued by Mr. Jefferson, according to the Spirit of the Constitution, it will render Republicanism omnipotent.

Abijah Adams and Ebenezer Rhoades: "Men of Probity and Integrity"

Republican writers were as dramatic in their descriptions of their opponents as were Federalists. With the "hydra of aristocracy gasping in the agonies of death," the nation's citizenry would be safer with Republicans in charge. The view advanced here on patronage is that Jefferson was consti-

tutionally, and even morally, bound to remove Federalists from their posts and fill them with Republicans.

Independent Chronicle (Boston), 13 July 1801

The constitution of our country is now administered in its primitive purity; our citizens are no longer loaded with reproach for being republicans; the appointment of tories to offices of trusts and profit now ceases; and that acrimony of sentiment, which distinguished the late administration, is no longer cherished among our citizens: but on the contrary, placid confidence resumes her domain, and social enjoyments enlivens our individual happiness. But this is not all. View the hydra of aristocracy gasping in the agonies of death; see the pernicious policy which dictated the sedition law appearing in all its odious colours; behold the reign of terror entombed; and a standing army no longer exciting fear and tumult. In the appointments of the new administration, we find men of probity and integrity selected; men whose abilities render them proper persons to be entrusted; men, who never, like a Hamilton advocated monarchy—but men who will discharge their various duties with conscious fidelity. Mr. Jefferson has displaced some of the offices appointed by his predecessor, and federal vengeance has hurled its weapons against him—but in doing which, he has attended to the nation. Did the republicans place him at the head of the government to continue in office men whose sentiments were at variance with the fundamental principles of our constitution? Did they expect that he would continue men in office who were odious to the people? Certainly not. He is sworn to support the constitution, and to promote its welfare;—therefore he is bound by every moral obligation to discharge men whose hostilities to our system of government were as clear as the light of the noon day. On events so interesting and salutary to our independence, where is the republican that exclaims not, in the gratitude of his heart—Hail Columbia, happy land!

Jabez Parkhurst and Samuel Pennington: "Extra"

Based on Jefferson's inaugural promises, Federalists were sorely disappointed when many Federalists lost their positions and were replaced by Republicans. Federalist newspapers were filled with essays accusing Jefferson of hypocrisy. This essay refuted that claim.

Centinel of Freedom (Newark, N.J.), 28 July 1801

It is hoped that the different federal Editors and federal scribblers, will no longer be deceiving their readers with the cries of political intolerance, on account of the removal of some of their partizans from office—that they will not by distorted construction of detached sentences in Mr. Jefferson's inaugural speech, attempt to palm a belief on the public mind that he is a deceiver, whose practices are at variance with his professions—the falsehood of these assertions we conceive to be amply proved by his conduct, as well as his reply to the remonstrance of the merchants of New-Haven.

Anonymous: "An Equal Distribution"

As expressed here, Republican satisfaction with the president's letter to the New Haven merchants was high. Why should they expect less than the Federalists had during their day?

Aurora (Philadelphia), 10 August 1801

An equal distribution of the offices at his disposal, between the contending parties which divide the country, is the object of the President. Can reasonable OPPOSITIONISTS expect or hope for more? Can liberal and enlightened republicans be disposed to give less?...the PEOPLE will be highly pleased with this wise, liberal, and magnanimous policy of the President.

Elisha Babcock: "Unmerited Abuse"

Republicans were appalled, as indicated here, by the amount of Federalist abuse heaped on the president over how he was handling his patronage. Editor Babcock explained that, since President Adams had excluded Republicans from his administration, Republicans ought to expect at least an equal number of government positions because Jefferson was in office.

American Mercury (Hartford, Conn.), 13 August 1801

That Mr. Jefferson has received, from the Federalists and British adherents, more unmerited abuse within the last three months, than his predecessors received from the Republicans, since the adoption of the Constitution, is a truth, which can never be doubted by any person who has noticed the publications devoted to the cause of Aristocracy in the United States. His reply to the New Haven remonstrance has been animadverted upon in a manner extremely indecent, in a style that yields an additional portion of disgrace to his enemies....

If it be a fact that the late President, and "his constitutional advisers," did act upon the uncharitable principle of excluding, to the utmost of their power, every Republican from office—and that they for four years did effectually act upon this principle, nor one of their partisans has the assurance to deny—if the majority have been interdicted "from the right and blessings of self government," are they when in the possession of means to neglect them, and wait for "accident to raise them to their just share"? At this present day, more than three fourths of the offices pertaining to the general government, are in the hands of men whose principles are at variance with republicanism; the friends of our government are entitled at least to an equal share; "correctives" are both just and necessary; and that class of men who cannot "harmonize in society, unless they have every thing in their own hands," are the least entitled to confidence;—in vain will they attempt "to present an imposing phalanx"; it is daily becoming more evidence that they have already imposed too much on the country.

Fair Play: "For the Chronicle—Federalism Returning to Reason, Tho' Not to Good Manners"

Jefferson had pledged never to write for newspapers. But after reading a piece related to patronage in the Federalist New-York Evening Post, *he wrote this explanation of his policy under the pseudonym "Fair Play."*

Independent Chronicle (Boston), 27 June 1803

Hither to I have spoken of the Federalists as if they were a homogeneous body. But this is not the truth—under the name, lurks the heretical sect of Monarchists. Afraid to wear their own name, they creep under the mantle of Federalism, and the Federalists, like sheep, permit the fox to take shelter among them, when pursued by the dogs. These men have no right to office; if any Monarchist is in office anywhere, and be known to the President, the oath he has taken to support the Constitution, imperiously requires the instantaneous dismissal of such officers; and I should hold the President highly criminal if he permitted such to remain. To appoint a Monarchist to conduct the affairs of a Republic, is like appointing an Athiest to the Priesthood. But as to real Federalists, I take them to my bosom as brothers; I view them as honest men, friends to the present Constitution. Our difference has been about measures only, which now having passed away should no longer divide us.

QUESTIONS

1. Why do you think the nation's founders frowned on the extension of patronage powers to newly elected presidents, governors, or other elected leaders?

2. Can you think of any situation that should stop a political friend of a new government leader from being appointed to a government position?

3. Describe the overall role you think newspapers played in this contentious issue in Jefferson's presidential administration.

4. It would take the federal government until 1971 to pass a law that stated that postmasters should not be political appointments. Why do you think this took so long?

5. What advantages would newspaper publishers have if they also served as postmasters in early America?

6. Compare the viciousness of several of the writers included in this chapter to those who write for the journalistic media today. In the first section, for example, Angier March wrote as if he and his compatriot Federalists were going to die at the hands of the advancing Republicans. Can you think of any examples of journalism you've heard lately that is similarly inflammatory in tone?

7. Why would President Jefferson only write for the newspapers under an assumed name?

NOTES

1. Inaugural Addresses of the Presidents of the United States. (Washington, D.C.: U.S. G.P.O.: Supt. of Docs., 1989); Bartleby.com. 2001. www.Bartleby .com/124/.

2. Noble E. Cunningham, *The Jeffersonian Republicans in Power: Party Operations, 1801–1809* (Chapel Hill: University of North Carolina Press, 1963), 19.

3. See, for example, an extra edition published in the 27 July 1801 issue of Boston's *Independent Chronicle* and in the 3 August 1801 issue of *Jenks' Portland Gazette* (Maine).

4. Richard Kielbowicz, *News in the Mail: Post Office and Public Information, 1700–1860* (Westport, Conn.: Greenwood Press, 1989).

CHAPTER 7

Thomas Jefferson's Mammoth Cheese and "Wall of Separation," 1802

On New Year's Day, 1802, Thomas Jefferson received a most unusual gift. With outstretched arms at the door of his house in the nation's capital, the president received a Cheshire cheese of huge proportions. Delivered all the way from western Massachusetts on a wagon led by six horses, the 1,235-pound cheese was 4 feet wide, 13 feet across and 17 inches tall. Brought by Baptist preacher Elder John Leland, it attracted considerable attention during its monthlong journey. As crowds gathered along the road, Federalist editors busily churned out commentary lampooning the cheese and its presidential recipient. Dubbed the "Mammoth Cheese," this was not only one of the oddest gifts ever received by any president, but it was also one of the most significant ones because of what it inspired. The day after the cheese was delivered, the president issued a statement that included his position on the proper relationship between church and state. Called the "Wall of Separation" letter, it is considered to be one of the most significant statements ever made by a president on religion and government.[1]

Jefferson's religious convictions led his Federalist critics to vilify him in the 1800–1801 presidential campaign (see chapter 3). But Jefferson wasn't hated for his religious convictions by everyone, and among his admirers were various communities of New England Baptists who had also been marginalized as religious outsiders. The mammoth cheese was sent by a group of fervent Baptists from Cheshire, Massachusetts, who greatly appreciated the president for his support of religious freedom. Along with the cheese, the group sent a letter with the salutation "The Greatest Cheese in America—For the Greatest Man in America."

Several days before the cheese was presented to the president, he received a letter from another group of Baptists from Connecticut. The Danbury Baptists Association had written the president in October, complaining about their treatment at the hands of their community's Congregationalist-Federalists, who forced them to pay taxes based on their religious affiliations. Oddly, the letter's delivery was delayed until December 30, just two days before the cheese arrived at the president's house. Here is what the Danbury Baptists wrote to the President:

> Our Sentiments are uniformly on the side of Religious Liberty—That Religion is at all times and places a matter between God and Individuals—That no man ought to suffer in Name, person or effects on account of his religious Opinions—That the legitimate Power of civil Government extends no further than to punish the man who *works ill to his neighbour.* But Sir, our constitution of government is not specific. Our ancient charter together with the Laws made coincident therewith were adopted as the Basis of our government, At the time of our revolution; and such had been our Laws & usages, & such still are; that Religion is consider'd as the first object of Legislation; & therefore what religious privileges we enjoy (as a minor part of the State) we enjoy as favors granted, and not as inalienable rights: and these favors we receive at the expence of such degrading acknowledgements, as are inconsistent with the rights of fre[e]men. It is not to be wondered at therefore; if those, who seek after *power & gain* under the pretence of *government & Religion* should reproach their fellow men— should reproach their chief Magistrate, as an enemy of religion Law & good order because he will not, dares not assume the prerogative of Jehovah and make Laws to govern the Kingdom of Christ.
>
> Sir, we are sensible that the President of the United States is not the national legislator, & also sensible that the national government cannot destroy the Laws of each State; but our hopes are strong that the sentiments of our beloved President, which have had such genial Effect already, like the radiant beams of the Sun, will shine & prevail through all these states and all the world till Hierarchy and tyranny be destroyed from the Earth. Sir, when we reflect on your past services, and see a glow of philanthropy and good will shining forth in a course of more than thirty years we have reason to believe that America's God has raised you up to fill the chair of State out of that good will which he bears to the Millions which you preside over. May God strengthen you for the arduous task which providence & the voice of the people have call'd you to sustain and support you in your Administration against all the predetermin'd opposition of those who wish to rise to wealth & importance on the poverty and subjection of the people.[2]

The president wasted no time in his drafting of a response, which he had delivered the day after the cheese arrived. According to historian C. A. Browne, "The presentation of a mammoth cheese to President Jefferson at the White House was a spectacular affair."[3] On receiving the gift from Leland, the president stated that he considered it of such great importance that he would place the event "upon the archives of the Nation, and that he would ever esteem it as one of the happiest occasions of his life."[4] Here is part of the letter that includes his famous statement on separation of church and state:

> Believing with you that religion is a matter which lies solely between Man & his God, that he owes account to none other for his faith or his worship, that the legitimate powers of government reach actions only, & not opinions, I contemplate with sovereign reverence that act of the whole American people which declared that *their* legislature should "make no law respecting an establishment of religion, or prohibiting the free exercise thereof," thus building a wall of separation between Church & State.

The story of the mammoth cheese and how the president came to write and distribute his "Wall of Separation" letter illustrates the growing importance the printing press played in the dissemination of religious communication in America. North America's first printing press was set up at Harvard in 1638, and its first book—*The Bay Psalm Book*—was religious in nature. While few printing presses were established in America in the 150 years after the first press arrived in Massachusetts, the number of presses increased after the American Revolution. Along with the new printing presses came a continued emphasis on the publication of religious materials, including sermons, doctrinal tracts, poetry, hymnals and catechisms, magazines, and newspapers. At times, as in the case of the mammoth cheese event, politics and religion intersected. Many newspapers printed not only the President's letter, but also those of the Danbury Baptists and the Cheshire ladies who sent him the cheese. Federalist editors especially couldn't resist lampooning the cheese along with the president who received it.

This chapter's first section contains examples of pro-Jefferson commentary on the cheese and the president's religious beliefs. The first piece was published in mid-November 1801, in a Pittsfield, Massachusetts, newspaper titled *The Sun*. Its author, Phinehas Allen, humorously stated that the cheese had received as much publicity as Elizur Goodrich's loss of his tax collector position to a Republican (see chapter 6). The second entry in this section is the letter sent with the cheese by the Danbury Baptists Association. The third entry is a brief note on the cheese published many months after it was delivered to the president.

The chapter's second section offers stunning examples of how the literary imaginations of Federalist writers were inspired by the mammoth cheese. The first anonymous entry, published in the *Hampshire Gazette*, makes fun of Elder John Leland and the Cheshire Baptists in their efforts to honor the president with the giant cheese. The second piece is an excerpt from a Carrier's Address published by the *New-York Evening Post* on New Year's Day, 1802. Carrier's Addresses were single-sheet poems distributed by newspapers' carriers or newsboys. The poems, often anonymous, described the events of the year—local, regional, and national—and requested a gratuity for the faithful carrier. At times, the addresses made predictions about future events. The address reprinted here was published the day before the cheese was delivered to the president.

The third anti-Jefferson entry, published in a Boston newspaper, is a report on the cheese's arrival in Washington. It includes a Federalist version of the letter sent by the Cheshire cheesemakers to the president with their gift.

The last entry in the chapter's second section, another poem, was published by Philadelphia editor and writer Joseph Dennie in his literary and political journal *The Port Folio*. Here, the poet makes the cheese a metaphor for Jefferson's agony over his lack of religious scruples.

FAVORABLE COMMENTARY ON THE CHEESE AND JEFFERSON'S RELIGIOUS BELIEFS

Phinehas Allen: "On the 'Cheese Plot'"

According to this author, the cheese rivaled the New Haven Merchants' Remonstrance incident (see chapter 6) in its incitement of Jefferson's Federalist critics. This writer commented on the objections of Federalists to the cheese.

The Sun (Pittsfield, Mass.), 16 November 1801
One of the principal subjects of *Federal* Complaint against President JEFFERSON seems to be the "*Mammoth Cheese,*"...made by a number of the Ladies of Cheshire, to be presented to the President, as a mark of respect, and for the encouragement of the staple production of that grazing town. The intended PRESENT, and the appointment of ABRAHAM BISHOP'S Father, Collector of New Haven, in the place of Mr. Goodrich, have probably drawn forth more *federal* objections against the New Administration, than any other two measures. The Cheshire Cheese has not yet been seriously represented to be in itself a violation of the Constitution; but presenting it to the President is thought to be inconsistent with the monopoly of a *federal* market, and consequently a crime nearly related to that of taking *their daily bread away from meritorious federal officers;* and it is an alarming principle of disorganization and modern philosophy, that, upon every change of Admin-

istration, subordinate office holders and marketers must be deprived of their Bread and Cheese!

Danbury Baptists Association: "The Cheshire Present"

As Leland and Brown prepared to transport the cheese to the nation's capital, five prominent Cheshire citizens penned a letter addressed to the president. The group expressed its devotion to the president, as well as their views on the federal constitution. After the letter was delivered, its text was reprinted in a number of newspapers.

Mercury & New-England Palladium (Boston), 22 January 1802

"The greatest Cheese in America—for the greatest Man in America."

SIR,

NOTWITHSTANDING we live remote from the national government, and in an extreme part of our own State, yet we humbly claim the right of judging for ourselves.

Our attachment to the National Constitution is strong and indissoluble. We consider it a description of those Powers which the people have submitted to their Magistrates, to be exercised for definite purposes, and not a charter of favors granted by a sovereign to his subjects.

Among its beautiful features—the right of free suffrage to correct abuses, the prohibition of religious tests to prevent all hierarchy, and the means of amendment which it contains within itself to remove defects as fast as they are discovered, appear the most prominent.

Such being the sentiments which we entertain, our joy must have been exquisite on your appointment to the first office in the nation.

The trust is great, the task arduous. But we believe the supreme Ruler of the Universe who raises up men to achievements has raised up a *Jefferson* at this critical day to defend *Republicanism* and to baffle the arts of *Aristocracy*. We wish to prove the love we bear to our President, not by words alone but in *deed and in truth*. With this address we send you a cheese by the hands of Messrs John Leland and Darius Brown, as a token of the esteem we bear to our chief Magistrate and of the sense we entertain of the singular blessings that have been derived from the numerous services you have rendered to mankind in general and more especially to this favored nation, over which you preside. It is not the last stone of the Bastile, nor is it an ar-

ticle of great pecuniary worth, but as a freewill offering we hope it
will be favorably received.

The cheese was produced by the personal labor of *Freeborn Farmers*
with the voluntary and cheerful aid of their wives and daughters without the assistance of a single slave. It was originally intended for an
elective President of a free people, and with a principal view of casting
a mite into the even scale of *Federal Democracy.*

We hope it will safely arrive at its destined place, and that its quality
will prove to be such as may not disappoint the wishes of those who
made it.

To that Infinite Being who governs the Universe we ardently pray
that your life and health may long be preserved—that your usefulness
may be still continued—that your administration may be no less pleasant to yourself than it is grateful to us and to the nation at large that the
blessing of generations yet unborn may come upon you.

In behalf of ourselves and our fellow citizens of Cheshire, we send
you the tribute of profound respect.

Samuel Harrison Smith: "At Stelle's"

Often referred to as Jefferson's newspaper, the Intelligencer *barely noticed
the delivery of the cheese and the "Wall of Separation" letter. Here, more
than one year after the cheese arrived in Washington, the editor reported
that the cheese, which was served at a local gathering of ladies and gentlemen at Stelle's Hotel, still needed time to age before it would be "excellent."*

National Intelligencer (District of Columbia), 8 July 1803

We omitted to notice, in our last, that the President had furnished the
last company at Stelle's with a supply of the Mammoth Cheese, which was
also distributed among the ladies and gentlemen who waited upon him in
the morning. Good judges are of opinion that it has greatly improved, and
that it only requires time to be an excellent cheese. It is in a state of the best
preservation.

LAMPOONING JEFFERSON AND HIS CHEESE

Anonymous: "The Great Cheese"

*This biblical treatment of the making of the great cheese for presentation to
the president must have greatly amused the anti-Jefferson readers of the*
Gazette.

Hampshire Gazette (Northampton, Mass.), 30 September 1801

And Jacknips said unto the Cheshireites, behold the Lord hath put in a Ruler over us, who is a man after our own hearts.

Now, let us gather together our Curd, and carry it into the valley of Elisha, unto his wine press, and there make a Great Cheese, that we may offer a thank offering unto that great man.

Now these sayings pleased the Cheshireites, so they did according as Jacknips had commanded.

And they said unto Darias the son of Daniel the prophet, make us a great hoop, four feet diameter and 18 inches high, and Darius did as he was commanded, and Asahel and Benjamin, the Blacksmiths secured it with strong iron bands, so that it could not give way.

Now the time for making this great Cheese was on the 20th day of the seventh month, when all the Jacobites assembled as one man, every man with his curd, except John the Physician, who said,

I have no curd, but I will doctor the Federalists, send them to me and I will cure their fedism.

And Jacknips said, behold Frances the wife of John the Hillite, she is a goodly woman, and is wont to make good cheese, now she shall be chief among the women.

Now when all things were ready, they put it in Elisha's press—ten days did they press it, but on the eleventh, Jacknips said unto the Cheshireites—behold now let us gather together a great multitude and move it to the great house of Daniel the prophet, there to be turned and dried.

Now Daniel lives about eight furlongs from the valley of Elisha.

So they made a great parade and mounted the great cheese on a sled, and put six horses to draw it.

And Jacknips went forward, and when he came to the inn of little Moses, he said unto Moses, behold the great cheese is coming.

And Moses said unto Freelove his wife, behold the multitude advancing—now let us kill all the first born of the lambs and he-goats, and make a great feast.

And they did so, and the people did eat meat and drink wine, the fourth part of an hin each, so they were very merry.

And Jacknips said, it shall come to pass when your children shall say unto you, what mean you by this great cheese, that ye shall answer them, saying,

It is a sacrifice unto our great ruler, because he giveth gifts unto the jacobites, and takes them from the federalists.

And Jacknips said, peradventure within two years, I shall present this great cheese as a thank offering unto our great ruler—and all the Cheshireites shall say Amen.

The Newsboys: "Addressed to the Patrons of the Evening Post"

It had long been a tradition for newspaper editors to write New Year's poems to their readers. Not only did they cover the events of the day, but they also often did so in a humorous fashion. This excerpt from one of these statements was published in New York City. By the time it was published in New York City, the cheese had long passed on its way to Washington, D.C.

New-York Evening Post (New York City), 1 January 1802

...For such strong proof of genuine merit,
Such evidence of public spirit,
His grateful country, has prepar'd
For her great head, a great reward;
A MAMMOTH CHEESE! Whose wondrous bulk
Exceeds a Butcher's greasy hulk,
Whose ample breadth, and tow'ring height,
Make Earth to groan beneath its weight;
And form'd, they say, in the same mould
Which shap'd the Giant's cheese of old.
In this fam'd Cheese, as most suppose,
No fed'ral mite can poke his nose,
To him the thick tough coast presents,
Impassable impediments,
And should he travel it all round,
No single op'ning can be found,
Nay what's more strange—by this good light!
The Cheese can't breed a fed'ral mite!
Yet democratic MAGGOTS find
An easy passage through its rind,
Which gives them entrance without pain,
And when they've pass'd it, shuts again.
While from its *energies* internal,
The mass breeds thousands at its kernel!
Nay more—but here 'tis time to stop
For fear my Pegasus might drop,
I therefore wish you all good cheer,
And from my soul a happy year!

Alexander Young and Thomas Minns: Mammoth Cheese

After the cheese's arrival in Washington, editors Young and Minns told their readers that they should expect an address from the president.

The Mercury & New-England Palladium (Boston), 12 January 1802

The *Mammoth Cheese* has made its entry at the city of *Washington,* drawn by six stout horses. We suppose the presentation of this cheese will be accompanied by an Address, which will, of course, produce an answer, replete, probably, with a great personage's *principles of government!*!

The Rev. Mr. Leland, pastor of the Baptist Society, where the cheese was made, is at *Washington,* probably for the purpose of presenting it.

The Cheese was to be presented on the first of January as a New-Year's gift.

FROM THE REPUBLICAN, OR ANTI-DEMOCRAT.

The imagination of the inhabitants of Cheshire was so much expanded by the contemplation of their performance of so Herculean a task, as the manufacture of the Mammoth Cheese, that, in penning their address to the great object of their bounty, they were scarce able to make use of that sublimity of language, which the occasion demanded. The following is the substance of their address. . . .

A GREAT New-Year's Gift.
The greatest Cheese in America,
For
The greatest Man in America.
TO WIT,
The author of the History of the greatest Beast in America.

Great Sir,

It is true we live at a *great* distance from the seat of the great national government, yet we claim the *great* right of judging for ourselves. We have a *great* attachment to the constitution, and we have, for several years past had *great* apprehensions, that the *great* features of it were not properly attended to: Our joy, of course, must have been *great,* on your election to the first *great* office in the nation, having had *great* evidence, from your *great* sentiments, that it would be your *greatest* strife and glory to turn back the government to its virgin purity. The trust is *great.* The task is *great.* But we feel a *great* consolation, that the *great* ruler of the *great* universe, who raises up *great* men to achieve *great* events, has raised up a *great* Jefferson, to defend the *great* principles of republicanism.

Sir, we have attempted to prove our *great* love to our *great* president, not in *great* words, but in mighty deeds. With this address, we send you a *great* Cheese, by the hands of the *greatest* men amongst us, as a *huge pepper-corn* of the *great* esteem we bear our *chief* magistrate. It is not the last stone in the Bastile (*we presume they mean it is not so*

great as the greatest stone in the Bastile), nor is it of any great consequence as an article of worth, but we hope it will be received as a *great*
freewill offering. This *great* Cheese, *great* sir, was not made by a *great*
lord, for his *great* majesty, nor with a view to gain *great* offices, or *great*
titles, but by the *great* personal labour of the *greatest farmers* in our
great state, without the assistance of a single slave, for an elective president of a *great* people, with the only view of casting a *huge* mite into
the *great* scale of democracy. The late return of republicanism has
greatly induced the inhabitants of Cheshire, to treat the *great* characters, who now fill the *great* offices, with *great* respect. We had, sir,
formed the vast project of putting some grand inscription on this *great*
cheese, but we were *greatly* dissuaded from this attempt, from the
great inconveniency we find in paying the *great* expense on stamped
paper. May the Almighty God *greatly* preserve your life for a long time,
as a *great* blessing to the United States, and to the world at large.

Anonymous: "Reflections of Mr. Jefferson, over the Mammoth Cheese"

*Federalist writers lampooned the Cheshire Baptists' gift of cheese for
months. Published in a periodical titled* The Port Folio, *this poem was
reprinted by Federalist editors, including by that of the* Washington Federalist. *Edited and published by Joseph Dennie,* The Port Folio *was a pro-
Federalist literary and political journal. Dennie often assumed the name
Oliver Oldschool in his writings. He was charged with seditious libel for
his antidemocratic writings but was acquitted in 1805.*

The Port Folio (Philadelphia), 20 March 1802

Ye men of Cheshire, Little did ye know,
When urg'd by love, this ponderous gift you sent,
That on this heart you struck a sick'ning blow,
And gave a thousand damning feelings vent.

In this great cheese I see myself pourtray'd,
My life and fortunes in this useless mass,
I curse the hands, by which the thing was made,
To them a cheese, to me a looking-glass.

Once I was pure—Alas! that happy hour,
E'en as the milk, from which this monster came,
Till turn'd by philosophic rennet sour,
I barter'd virtue for an empty name.

Then *press'd* by doctrines from the Gallic school,
A harden'd mass of nameless stuff I stood,
Where crude confusion mingles without rule,
And countless seeds of foul corruption bud.

E'en the round form this work of art displays,
Marks the uncertain, endless path I treat,
Where truth is lost in falsehood's dreary maze,
And vice in circles whirls the giddy head.

Delusive view! where light is cast aside,
And principles surrender'd for *mere words,*
Ah me, how lost to just and noble pride,
I am indeed become *a man of curds.*

Like to this cheese, my outside, smooth and sound,
Presents an aspect kind and lasting too;
When nought but rottenness within is found,
And all my seeming rests on nothing true.

Fair to the view, I catch admiring eyes.
The nation wonders, and the world applaud,
When spread beyond *my just and nat'ral size,*
I seem to them an earthly demigod.

But midst this shew of greatness and of ease,
Ten thousand vermin gnaw this wretched heart,
Just as they feed upon this mammoth cheese,
And I and they can never, never part.

Go, hatred Mentor, blast no more my sight,
I would forget myself, and heaven defy,
Inur'd to darkness, I detest the light,
Would be a suicide, *but dare not die.*

QUESTIONS

1. Why did politicians use the mammoth cheese incident in their anti-Jefferson rhetoric?
2. Explain what you think President Jefferson meant when he wrote the legislature should build a "wall of separation between Church & State."
3. Compare contemporary newspapers' treatment of religious matters to newspaper coverage of such issues during the early national period.

4. Would the taxation of religious groups by the government be permissible today?
5. Most Americans in the early national period expected their presidents to be very religious. Compare this with what we expect of our leaders today.

NOTES

1. Daniel L. Dreisbach, *Thomas Jefferson and the Wall of Separation between Church and State* (New York: New York University Press, 2003), 65–114.

2. Letter from a committee of the Danbury Baptists Association to Thomas Jefferson, 7 October 1801. Thomas Jefferson Papers, Library of Congress.

3. C. A. Browne, "Elder John Leland and the Mammoth Cheshire Cheese," *Agricultural History* 18 (October 1944), 145.

4. Ibid., 150.

CHAPTER 8

Nativism in the Age of Jefferson

A merica was founded on the idea that it would be a haven for the oppressed across the globe. The authors of the Declaration of Independence complained that King George III had "endeavored to prevent
the population of these States" by "obstructing the Laws of Naturalization
of Foreigners" and by "refusing to pass others to encourage their migration
hither." George Washington echoed such sentiments in a 1783 letter. "The
bosom of America is open to receive not only the Opulent and respected
Stranger, but the oppressed and persecuted of all Nations and Religions," he
wrote.[1]

With America's doors open to seekers of religious and political freedom
and economic opportunity, immigration increased after the American Revolution. During the summer of 1791, 3,000 to 4,000 Irish émigrés arrived in
Philadelphia, and they were joined by thousands of others from Scotland,
Great Britain, France, and other European countries who poured into the
nation's seaports. The U.S. Constitution established a basis for enacting
rules on how such immigrants could acquire citizenship, and in 1790, Congress passed the nation's first naturalization act.[2] While the new law limited
naturalization to "free white persons" of good character, it required only
two years of residency and the renunciation of former allegiances.[3]

Contrary to such ideals, America has at times persecuted the very immigrants its founders promised to welcome. On July 1, 1798, for example,
Harrison Gray Otis delivered his now famous "Wild Irish" speech. Claiming
"hoards of wild Irishmen" had entered the country, Otis warned, "[This]
mass of vicious and disorganizing characters who can not live peaceably at
home, and who, after unfurling the standard of rebellion in their own countries, may come hither to revolutionize ours." Otis was a nativist—someone
whose fear of foreign influence led him to favor the interests of established

American inhabitants over those of immigrants. According to Otis, the Irish were dangerous radicals who he feared would threaten the peace and prosperity of the new nation.

During the 1790s, America's ever-worsening relationship with France led to even more nativism in the new nation. During the war for America's independence, France had helped the Americans fight the British. But 1789's French Revolution caused people across Europe and America to fear that its terror would spread. After the First Republic replaced the French monarchy in 1792, France took on an increasingly expansionist policy through the acquisition of new territory and the establishment of satellite republics in the name of liberty, equality, and fraternity. Some Americans feared that the Jacobins, as the radical French Republicans were named, would invade and threaten the nation. This led to a steady deterioration of relations between America and France, culminating in the quasi-war with France, which lasted from 1798 to 1800.

Throughout this period, immigrants continued to arrive in America, leading to more nativism. Irish, Scotch, and French "Jacobin" refugees were especially hated by nativistic Americans. Some of these émigrés held beliefs thought to threaten American property and stability. Many were skilled writers and orators, while others operated printing presses and bookstores. In 1801, a distraught John Adams said, "Is there no pride in American bosoms? Can their hearts endure that Callender, Duane, Cooper and Lyon should be the most influential men in the country, all foreigners and degraded characters?"[4]

Republican émigré editors did wield mighty swords in their use of newspapers and magazines. One historian estimates that up to 20 percent of the editors who called themselves Republicans were foreigners and that 18 British and Irish radicals edited no fewer than 49 newspapers and magazines in America.[5] Such editors controlled some of the country's most widely circulating, strategically placed papers. Well-known editors Mathew Carey, William Duane, James Callender, John Binns, and Joseph Gale were all immigrants, as were a number of other lesser-known editors. Some sought to reform the system from within, while a few hoped to overthrow the "social compact" itself. In 1800, *Temple of Reason* publisher Denis Driscol, a former Roman Catholic priest tried in Ireland for equating private property with robbery, wrote that "the system" was to blame for the evils that had plagued mankind and that with a "general revolution...millions would benefit."[6]

Against such perceived threats, Federalist leaders crafted a number of counterattacks. In 1795 and 1798, Congress made it tougher for immigrants to become American citizens: The 1795 act extended the waiting period to 5 years, and the 1798 act extended it once again to 14 years. Also, in 1798,

Congress enacted the Alien Act, giving President John Adams arbitrary powers to deport foreigners deemed especially dangerous.

This chapter starts with a selection of newspaper essays illustrating how preoccupied Federalists were with the supposed threats posed by foreigners. Periods when nativistic rhetoric became especially bitter coincided with the presidential elections of 1800 and 1808; the 1801 expiration of the 1798 Alien Act; the 1802 congressional repeal of the 1798 Naturalization Act, which shortened the period of time immigrants had to wait before becoming American citizens; and the appointment by President Thomas Jefferson of Swiss-born financier Albert Gallatin to the post of secretary of the treasury.

As seen in the chapter's second section, not everyone agreed that French, Irish, and Scottish immigrants were a threat to the nation's peace and prosperity. The section starts with an excerpt from an essay written and published by John Binns in his Northumberland, Pennsylvania, newspaper, *The Republican Argus, and Weekly Advertiser.* Binns's statement reminded his readers that America's greatness rested on the contributions of political and religious refugees seeking to escape persecution in England and other places. This is followed by three newspaper pieces whose authors were unsympathetic to the anti-foreign sentiments of the Federalist press. The first responded to the Federalist diatribe against Albert Gallatin's appointment as treasury secretary; the second complained about the considerable influence wielded by the British in America; and the section's final entry considered the ludicrousness of the idea that the French could possibly wield any real power in America.

Anti-Foreign Sentiment

Burleigh: "To the People of the United States"

Nativism permeated much of the anti-Republican campaign rhetoric published in newspapers in the months leading up to the presidential election of 1800. A series of articles published under the pseudonym "Burleigh" in the Connecticut Courant, *starting on June 23, 1800, which were widely reprinted, effectively portrayed Federalist sentiment about the possibility that a Republican might be the country's next president.*

Connecticut Courant (Hartford, Conn.), 29 September 1800

Look at your houses, your parents, your wives and your children. Are you prepared to see your dwellings in flames, hoary hairs bathed in blood, female chastity violated, or children writhing on the pike and the halberd? If not, prepare for the task of protecting your Government. Look at every leading Jacobin, as at a ravening wolf, preparing to enter your peaceful fold, and glut his deadly appetite on the vitals of your country. Already do their hearts leap at the prospect. Having long brooded over these scenes of death and despair, they now wake as from a trance, and in imagination, seizing the dagger, and the musket, prepare for the work of slaughter. GREAT GOD OF COMPASSION AND JUSTICE, SHIELD MY COUNTRY FROM DESTRUCTION.

Lucius: "Where Was Gallatin during the Revolution?"

After President Jefferson appointed Swiss-born Albert Gallatin as his treasury secretary, much discussion about his lack of suitable qualifications for the post was published in Federalist newspapers. One of the most frequently asked questions about foreigners like Gallatin during this period related to their whereabouts during the American Revolution. Historians have since documented that he indeed was in America during its break with Great Britain. Lucius's reference to Duane referred to radical printer William Duane, who learned his trade in Ireland.

Gazette of the United States (Philadelphia), 21 March 1801

Where was Gallatin during the revolution? In Geneva he staid till the bloody scene was over; and where was Duane? He was too obscure to be known anywhere. It is the curse of this nation that such worthless fugitives are permitted to diffuse among the weak part of our community the contagion of their corruptive principles.

Leonidas: "The Consistent Federalist"

Leonidas sought to prod Americans to wake up. How could they, he asked, risk the nation's coffers to a foreigner? Indeed, Federalist newspapers across America entertained their readers with lampoons of Gallatin's accent. The Gazette of the United States, *for example, quoted Gallatin as saying, "For ze par wisch oituke een dzattafair oidoo mos sinzerly deman ze pardone of moi contree. It is ze political zin of wisch oi gladly take zis akelson to express mois zinzere repetans."*[7]

Columbian Centinel (Boston), 18 April 1801

It is confidently asserted, that to complete this catalogue Albert Gallatin, a Genevan, who cannot yet speak our language intelligibly, and who was Secretary to one of the Conventions of Insurgents in 1793, is to be Secretary of the Treasury, and to hold the purse strings of this Infant Nation!!! Disinterested people! You not only invited to your shores, the oppressed and the unhappy, the disorderly and discontented of all nations, but you commit to their kind care your rights and your blessings—your altars and your fire-sides—your wives and your daughters—your treasures and your government.

Anonymous: "Emigration"

After his election, President Jefferson called for relaxed citizenship require-ments. Congress responded on April 14, 1802, through its passage of the Naturalization Act of 1802. This stated that immigrants could seek and gain American citizenship after residing within its boundaries for five years. In the months before this act was passed, considerable debate con-cerning the influence of foreigners was seen in the papers. This widely reprinted statement revealed the depth of anti-foreign thinking in America in the early national period. Originally published in Boston's Columbian Centinel, *its author demanded that limits be placed on immigration.*

Jenks' Portland Gazette (Maine), 27 July 1801

The importation into the United States of so many factious, rebellious for-eigners as is daily made in the middle and southern ports, is an evil of more fatal tendency than the yellow fever to our cities, of the Hessian fly to our fields; and which our wisest and best men have foreseen and deprecated. Washington more than once warned his fellow-citizens of the danger from that quarter.—Franklin early foresaw it, and pointed to its injurious effect. Adams has borne evidence against it in the most decided manner.... [S]trong, effectual measures may be taken to stop the career of importation of hot headed, idle foreigners; and to provide for the exportation of those already amongst us. These observations have reference only to that scum and feces of the elder countries, who have no visible means of support in their native places.... Let not the comparative insignificance of their numbers lull us into fatal security; but with respect to them let us remember, that many a tempest has arisen from a cloud that seemed at first no bigger than a man's hand.

Alexander Young and Thomas Minns: "We Are at a Loss"

A more temperate reaction to President Jefferson's call for relaxed citizen-ship requirements is evident in this statement published by the editors of the New-England Palladium, *another Federalist paper.*

New-England Palladium (Boston), 22 January 1802

We are at a loss to conceive the reasons of Mr. Jefferson's anxiety for alterations in our naturalization laws. He has, as a consequence of large importations, a nominal majority of fearless men, who are the only good materials for democratic Government; and their vices and patriotism is already naturalized.

Lucius Crassus: "The Examination, Number vii"

President Thomas Jefferson's first inaugural address provoked a heated response throughout the Federalist press. For example, the New-York Evening Post *printed a series of essays written by Alexander Hamilton under the pen name Lucius Crassus. The series was titled "The Examination," and each of its entries commented on one of the points covered by Jefferson. This excerpt compared President Jefferson's statements in his 1781* Notes on Virginia *on immigration to what he said after attaining the presidency.*

New-York Evening Post (New York City), 6 January 1802

The next exceptionable feature in the Message, is the proposal to abolish all restrictions on naturalization, arising from a previous residence. In this the President is not more at variance with the concurrent maxims of all commentators on popular governments, than he is with himself. The Notes on Virginia are in direct contradiction to the Message, and furnish us with strong reasons against the policy now recommended. The passage alluded to is here presented: Speaking of the population of America, Mr. Jefferson there says, "here I will beg leave to propose a doubt. The present desire of America, is to produce rapid population, by as great *importations of foreigners* as possible. *But is this founded in good policy?*" "Are there no inconveniences to be thrown into the scale, against the advantage expected from a multiplication of numbers by the importation of foreigners? It is for the happiness of those united in society, to harmonize as much as possible, in matters which they must of necessity transact together. Civil government being the sole object of forming societies, its administration must be conducted by common consent. Every species of government has its specific principles: Ours, perhaps, are more peculiar than those of any other in the universe. *It is a composition of the freest principles of the English Constitution*, with others, derived from natural rights and reason. To these, nothing can be more opposed than the maxims of absolute monarchies. Yet from such, we are to expect the greatest number of emigrants. *They will bring with them the principles of the governments they leave, imbibed in their early youth; or if able to throw them off, it will be in exchange for an unbounded licentiousness, passing, as is usual, from one extreme to another. It would be a miracle were they to stop precisely at the point of temperate liberty. Their principles with their language, they will transmit to their children.* In proportion to their numbers, *they will share with us in the legislation.* They will infuse *into it their spirit, warp and bias its direction, and render it a heterogeneous, incoherent, distracted mass.* I may appeal to experience, during the present contest, for a verification of these conjectures; but if they be not certain in event, are they not possible, are they not probable? *Is it not safer to wait with patience for the attainment of any degree of population desired or expected?* May not our government be more homogeneous, *more peaceable, more durable?* Suppose 20 millions of republican Americans, thrown all of a sudden into France, what would be the condition of that kingdom? If it would be more turbulent, less happy, less strong, we may believe that the addition of half a million of foreigners, to our present numbers, would produce a similar effect here?" Thus wrote Mr. Jefferson in 1781—Behold the reverse of the medal. The Message of the President contains the following sentiments. "A denial of citizenship under a residence of 14 years, is a denial to a great proportion of those who ask it, & control a policy pursued from their first settlement, by many of these states, and *still believed of consequence to their prosperity.* And shall we refuse to the unhappy fugitives, from distress, *that hospitality* which the savages of the wilderness extended to our father arriving in this land? Shall oppressed humanity and no asylum on this globe? Might not the general character and capabilities of a citizen, be safely communicated to *every one* manifesting a bona fide purpose of embarking his life and fortune permanently with us?"

But if gratitude can be allowed to form an excuse for inconsistency in a public character, in *The Man of the People;* a strong plea of this sort may be urged in behalf of our President. It is certain that had the late election been decided entirely by native citizens, had foreign auxiliaries been rejected on both sides, the man who ostentatiously vaunts that the *doors of public honor and confidence have been burst open to him,* would not now have been at the head of the American nation. Such a proof then of virtuous discernment in the *oppressed fugitives,* had an imperious claim on him to a grateful return, and without supposing any very uncommon share of *self-love,* would naturally be a strong reason for a revolution in his opinions.

The pathetic and plaintive exclamations by which the sentiment is enforced, might be liable to much criticism, if we are to consider it in any other light, than as a flourish of rhetoric. It might be asked in return, does the right to *asylum* or *hospitality* carry with it the right to suffrage and sovereignty? And what indeed was the courteous reception which was given to our forefathers, by the savages of the wilderness? When did these humane and philanthropic savages exercise the policy of incorporating strangers among themselves, on their first arrival in the country? When did they admit them into their huts, to make part of their families, and when did they distinguish them by making them their sachems? Our histories and traditions have been more than apocryphal, if any thing like this kind, and gentle treatment was really lavished by the much-belied savages upon our thankless forefathers. But the remark occurs, had it all been true, prudence inclines to trace the history farther, and ask what has become of the nations of savages who exercised this policy? And who now occupies the territory which they then inhabited? Perhaps a useful lesson might be drawn from this very reflection.

But we may venture to ask what does the President really mean, by insinuating that we treat aliens coming to this country, with inhospitality? Do we not permit them quietly to land on our shores? Do we not protect them equally with our own citizens, in their persons and reputations; in the acquisition and enjoyment of property? Are not our Courts of justice open for them to seek redress of injuries? And are they not permitted peaceably to return to their own country whenever they please, and to carry with them all their effects? What then means this worse than idle declamation?

The impolicy of admitting foreigners to an immediate and unreserved participation in the right of suffrage, or in the sovereignty of a Republic, is as much a received axiom as anything in the science of politics, and is verified by the experience of all ages. Among other instances, it is known, that hardly any thing contributed more to the downfall of Rome, than her precipitate communication of the privileges of citizenship to the inhabitants of Italy at large. And how terribly was Syracuse scourged by perpetual seditions, when, after the overthrow of the tyrants, a great number of foreigners were suddenly admitted to the rights of citizenship? Not only does ancient but modern, and even domestic history furnish evidence of what may be expected from the dispositions of foreigners, when they get too early footing in a country. Who wields the scepter of France, and has erected a Despotism on the ruins of a Republic? A foreigner.—Who rules the councils of our own ill-fated, unhappy country? And who stimulates persecution on the heads of its citizens, for daring to maintain an opinion, and for exercising the right of suffrage? *A foreigner!*—Where is the virtuous pride that once distinguished Americans?—Where the indignant spirit which in defence of principle, hazarded a revolution to attain that independence now *insidiously* attacked?

An Observer: "A Likeness, in a Feature of Mr. Jefferson's Character and that of Napoleon"

The 1808 presidential election was once again marred by bitter nativistic campaigning. Indeed, New Englanders were so opposed to Jefferson's policies as manifested in the Embargo crisis that they considered seceding from the union. A rhetorical strategy used at times by anti-Republican editors was to compare Thomas Jefferson to Napoleon Bonaparte.

Federal Republican & Commercial Gazette (Baltimore, Md.), 3 August 1808

Mr. Jefferson induced the people of America to believe he was the enemy of executive influence and power; yet caused the same people to put him in possession of more power than ever was possessed by any other president of the United States.

Napoleon induced the army of France to believe he was the enemy of crowns; yet caused the same army to put him in possession of one, with more power than any other crowned head in Europe.

Mr. Jefferson told the Americans that under his administration, they would have more liberty, enjoy all the comforts of life and pay less taxes; yet he has not only deprived them of the liberty of trading to all foreign ports and places, but even from one port to another in their own country, and thereby deprived them of the comforts they did enjoy, and laid the heaviest of taxes upon them by causing their produce and shipping to rot on their hands, or to be sold for a song.

Napoleon told the people of every nation, whose territory he entered, that he came as their friend to secure them in their rights and privileges, and yet he took the lives of thousands of every nation he thus entered, deprived them of every right and privilege they enjoyed, and universally laid a military tax of many millions upon the inhabitants.

Quere. May it not have been a discovery of *this likeness* that induced the great Napoleon to create Mr. Jefferson a member of his *legion of honour,* and this creation that induced Mr. Jefferson to keep secret from congress the conduct of his great friend towards this country!

An Old Whig: "My Countrymen"

The author of this letter castigated President Jefferson for his French sympathies and also criticized James Madison, who is referred to as "our next President." Originally published in the Newburyport Herald, *it illustrated that anyone adept with a pen and sufficiently vicious could get their political essays republished by editors sympathetic to their views.*

Federal Republican & Commercial Gazette (Baltimore, Md.), 26 August 1808

How vain it is to deny, that the infernal policy of France has not deeply wormed itself into our country and its councils.—Is it not as plain as a sunbeam to every open eye in our land, that its accursed canker has for many years been preying on the vitals of our independence and peace.—Can we not behold its continual ascent, throughout the land, like the smoke of the bottomless pit. If any doubt it, let them recollect the landing [of] Genet on our shore and his subsequent conduct, with that of his successors—let them remember the aid afforded them by the men who now rule us; and the manly, patriotic and arduous struggles it cost our Washington to counteract their nefarious plots—let them view the finger of France pointed at Mr. Jefferson as the man for our President, and then let them hear this same Mr. Jefferson call the blood drunken, revolutionary Government of this nation enlightened; and see him rewarding its steady friends, such as Paine, Duane, &c. with compliments and commissions—let them hear Mr. Madison, who is to be our next President, say that "France wants money and must have it"—let him read Champagny's letter, in which war is declared for us—in short let them look into the volume of enormities and insults toward us, that might be cited, and the proofs of aid and countenance they have received from among ourselves, and if they then deny the position that the curse is not among us, we will pronounce their faith of very unusual proof.

OPPOSITION TO NATIVISM

John Binns: "Fairest Portions of Europe"

This excerpt from a long essay on the glory of American independence and the nation as a haven for the oppressed was written by John Binns. Originally used to address the community of Northumberland in a Fourth of July oration, Binns included it in the first issue of his new newspaper, The Republican Argus. *Later, in 1810, he was asked to incorporate it into another Independence Day speech. Subsequently, his 1810 oration was published in pamphlet form by Philadelphia publisher Mathew Carey. Binns, a native of Ireland, immigrated to America after a hiatus in London where he had been imprisoned several times for his radical positions on matters of public policy.*

The Republican Argus, and Weekly Advertiser (Northumberland, Pa.), 24 December 1802

Three centuries have rolled down the flood of time since the adventurous Columbus discovered the shores of the New World. Every fact in its annals is interesting; every page of its history pregnant with information, but we cannot now even sip their sweets. We must rapidly hasten to more modern times. The struggles in Great Britain in the 17th Century between the Persecutor and the Persecuted were long and sanguinary and led to the most memorable events. Many independent-minded, conscientious individuals disgusted, unsafe and unhappy in England resolved to brave the dangers of the seas, abandon the tombs of their ancestors and the friends of their youth and encounter all the hardships incident to the settlement of a new and unknown country, inhabited by untutored savages rather than remain in their native land and be compelled to submit their persons, their properties, nay their very opinions and beliefs to the caprice of Despots. They embarked and safely landed on the shores of North America. From them and from succeeding emigrants from various climes have sprung the millions of people who now inhabit the United States and who have literally "made the wilderness to blossom as the rose."

The fairest portions of Europe have, for nearly twenty years, been desolated by war, depopulated by famine and their inhabitants drinking deep of the cup of misery, while, within these United States, we have enjoyed the countless blessings of peace and plenty, every man reposing under his fig tree and vine and none to make him afraid. Those nations upon which the light of liberty had gleamed, are again enveloped in the thick darkness of despotism, whilst we, a highly-favored people, are progressing in all useful knowledge, and are rich in the enjoyment of freedom, civil, religious and political.

We are the only nation in the world who interfere not with the sacred rights of conscience—we are the only people who have established and enjoy a government founded on the equal rights of man—we are the only people who at regular and frequent periods of time by the exercise of a peaceful act of sovereignty elect our public functionaries from the highest to the lowest—and we are the only people who can produce a constitution which defines the power of all the constituted authorities; guarantees "the freedom of speech and of the press" and "the right of the people to keep and bear arms."

Abijah Adams and Ebenezer Rhoades: "Albert Gallatin"

When President Jefferson appointed Gallatin to the post of secretary of the treasury in 1801, anti-foreign sentiment marked Federalist objections to his holding this important position. Jefferson supported Gallatin not only because he was an intelligent financier, but also because of a disagreement Gallatin had with Alexander Hamilton. When Gallatin had opposed Hamilton's fiscal policies, he had incurred the former treasury secretary's

wrath. Gallatin's appointment precipitated a raft of nasty pieces in Feder-
alist prints, which were as much marked by their political objections as by
their aversion to people they considered to be foreigners. In defense of Gal-
latin, the Chronicle *sought to set newspaper readers straight.*

Independent Chronicle (Boston), 11 May 1801

The character of Mr. Gallatin is far beyond the shafts of ridicule. His great talents are not disgraced by any eccentricities of mind, or manners. The vile buffoonery which sports with ignorance, can never please where Mr. Gallatin is known. The love of liberty directed his steps to America. He was no speculator, or monopolizer, no demagogue. He loved the liberty of the law, and he attached himself to our cause, because he found us a free people. He visited every part of our Union, and is among the best judges of our resources. He has converted a large estate into an interest in our soil. He cultivates the soil he has purchased. Of our commerce he has an extensive knowledge. Without Finances, he has explained to the world his intimate acquaintance; and from his pure morals, extreme prudence, and comprehensive powers, ranks among the best and greatest men in America.

Cimon: "For the True American"

According to this writer, Great Britain sought to punish radicals, many of whom escaped to America. After the expiration of the Alien Act, this Repub-lican commented that one of the act's purposes was to aid the British in their efforts to persecute radicals.

True American (Trenton, N.J.), 2 February 1802

Never, since the creation of mankind, did the scales of delusion fall from the eyes of a deceived people, more rapidly than at present.—Thousands, who had been led, by listening to a long series of falsehood and misrepresentation, to give their support and approbation to the destructive measures of the late administration, and to oppose the election of the present Chief Magistrate, are now daily discovering, acknowledging, and abandoning their errors. They now see and confess, that the Sedition-Law was a direct violation of the letter and spirit of the Constitution; an infringement of our natural right of thinking, and expressing our thoughts; and an attempt to reduce us in to the most abject state of slavery:—That the Alien Law was inhospitable, unjust, unconstitutional, and oppressive; and intended to aid the British government in its endeavors to prevent the miserable subjects of its extortion and inhumanity, from seeking an asylum on our free and comparatively, happy shores....

James J. Wilson: "French Influence!"

Important state and national elections in the early national period at times led to an upsurge in nativistic rhetoric in the newspapers. The author of this piece sought to assure the readers of the True American *that the French had little real power in America. On the contrary, he argued, Americans ought to be more fearful of the English than of the French.*

True American (Trenton, N.J.), 28 December 1807

The story of French-influence is once more revived, to frighten the good people of these states—

We believe, however, they may rest assured that this story, like most of the stories from the same source, is totally devoid of truth—and is intended only as a cover for and an engine of what really exists, British influence.

Whence should French-influence arise?

The French have no possessions surrounding our country—no "rod, as Liston said, over our backs," as the British have—

The French have not the mastery at sea, and the power to affect our interests there–as the British have—

The French have comparatively no commerce, and therefore have not filled our cities and towns with commercial agents and political spies—as the British have—

The French have not the power of governing our courts of law by their judicial decisions—as the British have.

The French have not the advantage of the same language, by which to influence us in conversations and publications—as the British have—

In short, the French have not the opportunities nor the inducements to acquire an ascendancy in our country that the British have.

John Binns: "A Democratic Creed"

In this piece, Binns attempted to expose the hypocrisy of the Federalists who refused to own up to their ties with England. In response to this column, Joseph Robinson, the editor of Baltimore's Federal Republican, *wrote: "THE ALARM BELL. TREASON! TREASON! TREASON!....It is an old saying, 'the greatest rogue cries out rogue first'; hence the cry of British party and British faction, has been raised by a set of abandoned men in order to turn the public attention from themselves, until it was time to throw off the mask. … No American will ever belong to any other party than his country. If he did he would deserve the pillory."*

Democratic Press (Philadelphia), 5 August 1808

I believe there is not a man in America, who does not belong to a *French party*, or an English one. *I acknowledge I belong to the former.*

I believe *Bonaparte* never did, nor ever will voluntarily commit an act of violence against us.

I believe the *stripling* was sold by his brethren into Egypt, he being chosen to do a great work.

I believe *Moses* was preserved in the bulrush basket floating on the Nile, being chosen to do a great work.

I believe the stripling *David* was taken from the sheepfold, and pre-served, when he cut off the skirt of Saul's garment, being chosen to do a great work, for he had a Goliath to slay.

I believe the stripling *Napoleon*, of Corsica, was preserved at Dunkirk, at Arcole, at Lodi, Marengo, and a hundred other places, being also chosen to do a great work, for he has a Goliath yet to slay.

I believe *Simon Snyder*[8] ought to be governor.

I believe *James Madison* possesses every qualification requisite, and is fully competent to discharge the duties of president of the United States; and that *he will pursue the tide laid down* by Mr. Jefferson.

I believe the writer of this creed is *a democrat,* if he is not mistaken in the *meaning* of the word.

QUESTIONS

1. What events or developments in the early years of the nineteenth century may have precipitated an intensification of nativistic sentiment in America?
2. What nativistic themes were present in the newspapers of the early national period?
3. Considering the ideal of America being a haven for the oppressed, how would you explain the presence of nativistic thinking in the country?
4. Do you think the nativism of the early nineteenth century was inspired primarily by politics? Explain.
5. Do you think that prejudice against foreigners in the early nineteenth century is connected to nativism today? Explain.
6. Considering today's diverse mass media, are newspapers still a primary place for the transmission of nativistic rhetoric in America?

Notes

1. Moses Rischin, ed., *Immigration and the American Tradition* (Indianapolis, Ind.: Bobbs-Merrill, 1976), 43.

2. Article I, Section 8 of the Constitution empowers Congress "[t]o establish an uniform Rule of Naturalization."

3. Michael LeMay and Elliot Robert Barkan, eds., *U.S. Immigration and Naturalization Laws and Issues: A Documentary History* (Westport, Conn.: Greenwood Press, 1999), 11.

4. Walt Brown, *John Adams and the American Press: Politics and Journalism at the Birth of the Republic* (Jefferson, N.C.: McFarland and Company, 1995), 258, 272.

5. Michael Durey, "Thomas Paine's Apostles: Radical Émigrés and the Triumph of Jeffersonian Republicanism," 3rd series, *William and Mary Quarterly* 44 (October 1987): 682–683. See also Michael Durey, *Transatlantic Radicals and the Early American Republic* (Lawrence: University Press of Kansas, 1997).

6. Denis Driscol, "Man, the Author and Artificer of the Most Part of his Own Evils and Misfortunes," *Temple of Reason,* 6 December 1800.

7. *Gazette of the United States,* 7 April 1801.

8. In 1808, the Pennsylvania Jeffersonians were united behind Simon Snyder, who was running for governor against incumbent Thomas McKean. John Binns was a personal friend of Snyder and led his campaign for a party labeled the New School Democrats.

CHAPTER 9

The Tripolitan War, 1801–1805

M ost of our images of pirates and buccaneers come from storybooks and Hollywood. But if you study American history carefully, you'll learn such characters are much more than fiction. In fact, pirates have played an important role in America's history. From 1801 to 1805, America was at war on the coast of Africa in the Mediterranean with the Barbary states of Morocco, Algiers, Tripoli, and Tunisia. Called the Tripolitan War, the four-year dispute is too often overlooked in histories of America. Not only did the war mark the first time Americans fought on foreign soil, but it also produced battle heroes still famous today. Associated with the birth of the U.S. Navy and the Marines Corps, the war's battles inspired the composer of the Marines' Hymn to write its well-known opening words: "From the halls of Montezuma to the shores of Tripoli." Recently, historians have commented on the similarities between the Barbary Wars and America's twenty-first century war on terrorism.[1]

The 1801–1805 Tripolitan War started when U.S. officials refused to meet the demands of Barbary pirates who regularly stopped ships in order to demand tribute for the right to sail their seas and to offer for ransom the sailors they took into slavery. Many countries, including England, France, Spain, and Sweden, had long paid the tribute demanded. But after winning the American Revolution, America's leaders were forced to consider whether they would continue England's policy of appeasement. By 1801, America had paid the pirates nearly $2 million in tribute.

When Thomas Jefferson was sworn in as America's new president in March 1801 (see chapter 3), he was immediately faced with the same dilemma as his predecessors: Would he, or would he not, support the payment of tribute to the Barbary pirates? Jefferson had long argued against the raising of a navy, which would be necessary if the country refused to pay tribute. Plus he claimed the payment of tribute or ransom would only lead to further demands. Increasingly, this view gained support. In 1786, George Washington wrote, "Would to Heaven we had a navy to reform those enemies to mankind, or crush them into non-existence."[2] Sonnet writer David Humphreys, in "Poem on the Future Glory of the United States of America," railed against the bandits:

> Audacious miscreants, fierce, yet feeble band
> Who, impious, dare
> Insult the rights of man.

Charles Cotesworth Pinckney's now-famous statement—"Millions for defence, but not one cent for tribute"—had gained popularity, and increasingly there were calls for the raising of a navy.

Despite the growth of such sentiments, on assuming office, Jefferson sent Naval Captain William Bainbridge to the Mediterranean with money to pay off the Dey of Algiers (the ruler of that region). This plan failed to work, however. When Bainbridge arrived, the Dey demanded he sail for Constantinople with gifts for the Grand Seignior. The Dey warned that if Bainbridge didn't comply, he would declare war on the United States and would take the officers and crews of the *George Washington* into slavery. After Bainbridge refused, on June 10, 1801, Tripoli declared war against the United States. On hearing the news, the president sent a squadron of four ships under the leadership of Commodore Richard Dale to the Mediterranean to confront the enemy. On July 17, Dale's squadron unsuccessfully erected a blockade around Tripoli Harbor to hem in its corsairs.

U.S. naval forces made little headway until 1805. Meanwhile, the Barbary pirates managed to capture and imprison a number of American sailors and their officers. However, America did manage to win several inspirational victories. The first was the capture of the enemy corsair *Tripoli* by Lieutenant Andrew Sterrett and his crew of the now famous ship, the *Enterprise*. In a three-hour bloody battle, the *Tripoli* was decimated, while the Americans received no injuries. Historians conclude that the great victory was possible because Tripolitan corsairs were not skilled in gunnery or musketry, and their method of coming alongside and boarding quickly with swords did not work against the *Enterprise*'s firepower.

A second great achievement came on February 16, 1804, a few months after the USS *Philadelphia* was captured after running aground near Tripoli Harbor. To free the ship's captain and 307 crewmembers, Lieutenant Stephen Decatur led 74 volunteers into the harbor on a mission to free the *Philadelphia*'s men. Although Decatur's men were unsuccessful, they managed to burn the ship to its water line in an effort to prevent the pirates from capturing it. British Admiral Lord Nelson described the raid as "the most daring act of the age." At age 31, Decatur's subsequent promotion made him the youngest captain in the history of the American navy. In the War of 1812, he would go on to further battle glories.

A third victory, achieved on April 27, 1805, brought about the end of the war. After a long trek through the Libyan desert, a group of American Marines, accompanied by recruits from Egypt, captured the town of Derna, a strongly garrisoned seaport in Tripoli's eastern province. Although the Tripolitans mounted a counterattack in May, they were beaten back. Tripoli's leaders were so shocked by the fall of Derna that, after failing to win it back, they agreed to a peace settlement. Because its terms involved the further payment of tribute and left the enemy's ruler on his throne, it was unpopular and would take the U.S. Senate until April 1806 to ratify it.

This chapter offers insight into how the journalistic press of the early national period operated during times of war. Since today's corps of war correspondents did not yet exist, the reporters of America's early wars were its naval leaders and sailors. The news they sent in their letters and dispatches often took weeks, and at times months, to be delivered. On reaching newspaper editors, such communications were often published in their entirety, and out of such reports came thrilling stories about the exploits of some of the nation's earliest heroes. Since no photographs or live images of the war could reach home, many Americans romanticized the war's events. Newspaper accounts, pamphlets, and books played a role in amplifying the war's events, as did other published and performed works. The story of the U.S. Marines' assault on Tripoli, for example, was set to music by composer Benjamin Carr in "The Siege of Tripoli: An Historical Naval Sonata for the Piano Forte."

This chapter's first section includes letters, dispatches, and essays, whose authors believed the government should do more to stop the Barbary pirates than simply pay them tribute. The first article tells of the voyage of Captain William Bainbridge of the U.S. frigate *George Washington* who had been sent to the Mediterranean to deliver tribute to the Dey of Algiers. Also included in the story is a list of the bounty and slaves taken by the Dey's pirates during the previous two years. At Tunis, for example, they captured 11 Danish vessels and 17 Greek vessels, including cargoes and crews, and at Tripoli, 24 "sail of Swedes" were confiscated.

The section's second report, published in *Jenks' Portland Gazette*, is an excerpt from a dispatch sent home in December 1800 by James L. Cathcart, the American consul at Tripoli. In it, he warns American shippers to avoid the Mediterranean. The section's final essays, by the editors of the *American Citizen* and the *Centinel of Freedom*, opposed the continued payment of tribute.

The chapter's second section includes an essay whose authors criticized Jefferson's handling of the war. Published in 1802 by Federalists Alexander

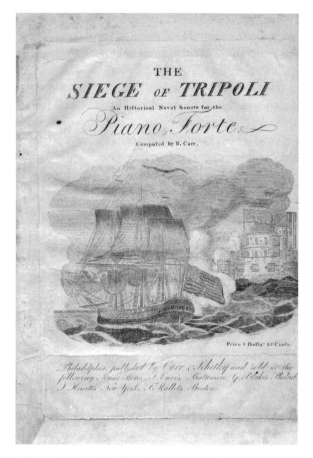

"The Siege of Tripoli." *This front cover of a piano sonata composed by Benjamin Carr ca. 1804 portrays the frigate* Constellation *attacking a Tripolitan fort. Titled "The Siege of Tripoli: An Historical Naval Sonata for the Piano Forte," it illustrates how the war captured Americans' imaginations. Courtesy of the Annenberg Rare Book and Manuscript Library, University of Pennsylvania.*

Young and Thomas Minns of Boston's *Mercury and New-England Palladium,* it criticized President Jefferson's choice of words in an address that commented on Lieutenant Sterret's famous victory over the corsair *Tripoli.*

The chapter's final section includes favorable commentary on Jefferson's handling of the war with the Barbary states. The first was published in an 1801 *Aurora* essay, whose author suggested that the war was justifiable because, at least according to him, the British were working against America behind the scenes to stir up trouble. Following this is an 1805

"New Year's Report," where editor James J. Wilson of the *True American* applauded the country's recent progress against the Barbary powers. The chapter concludes with a column published in the *National Intelligencer* that praised Jefferson's treaty with the pirates. The treaty was worked out between the leader of Tripoli, Yusuf Karamanli, and American diplomat Tobias Lear. Signed on June 4, 1805, it provided Karamanli with $60,000 for the release of Captain William Bainbridge and the crew of the USS *Philadelphia*. The treaty was signed by both parties in the main cabin of the USS *Constitution*. It was sent by Jefferson to the Senate for ratification on December 11, 1805, but it would take until well into 1806 for Congress to ratify it.

AGAINST THE PAYMENT OF TRIBUTE TO THE BARBARY POWERS

Anonymous: "Late from Algiers and Gibraltar"

This excerpt from a report sent to America from the Mediterranean must have shocked Americans and added to the growing sentiment that the nation had paid enough tribute to the Barbary powers. The account referred to the tribute Captain William Bainbridge had been ordered to deliver by the Dey of Algiers and to the consequences of what would happen if the delivery were prevented.

Connecticut Gazette (New London), 17 December 1800

Should any accident happen to the *George Washington*, in her passage to or from Constantinople, the Government of the U. States will be obliged to reimburse the Dey all damages he may sustain thereby, or his most potent Majesty will order his Corsairs to capture American vessels.

Among the presents sent to the Grand Seignior were one hundred black slaves, 50 of them females—lyons, tigers, leopards, ostritches, &c. &c. valued at several millions of dollars. Precious cargo for an American Government ship!—Captain Bainbridge was obliged to hoist the Standard of Algiers at his main-to-gallant mast head, instead of the American Pendant!...

The Algerines observed to Captain Bainbridge that he ought to consider it a great mark of the Dey's favour, to go upon his Majesty's special business to the Grand Seignior—adding, that it was an honor he would confer on very few others. There are about 2300 European Slaves in Algiers—some of them from the first families in Europe. The place appears very strong, but 6 or 8 seventy fours could batter it to pieces. The policy of the English Government is against a measure so important to the commercial world—A petty Despot of a Piratical State, with a small marine force, commands homage and respect from all the Christian world. O tempora! O mores!

James L. Cathcart: "The Barbary Powers"

This dispatch, sent just before Tripoli declared war on America, warned American shippers to stay out of the vicinity or face the consequences. It was sent by James L. Cathcart, an envoy sent by President Adams to the Mediterranean in 1799. Cathcart believed war was imminent, since nego-tiations with the Bashaw had broken down and Tripoli's navy was outfit-ting for war and nearly ready for sea.

Jenks' Portland Gazette (Maine), 20 April 1801

I had the honor to inform you in my Circular of the 12th of November 1800, that certain unjust demands having been made by the Bashaw of Tripoli upon the United States of America, which I found it my duty to repel; that said Bashaw had publickly announced in an official manner that he would declare war against the United States of America in six months, to commence from the 22nd day of October, 1800, if his demands, which he purposely made in an evasive and indeterminate manner, were not com-plied. I further informed you that it would be unsafe for our merchant ves-sels to trade in the Mediterranean, or its vicinity after the 22nd day of March, 1801, as these faithless people generally commit depredations be-fore the time or period allowed had expired.... I find it my duty to request you to take such measures as will most effectually prevent any of our vessels from trading on this sea, until you are advised officially by me or either of our Consuls at Algiers or Tunis, that this disagreeable affair is terminated, which from its nature will require much time, as it extends to making the United States tributary to Tripoli, and must first be authorized by a particu-lar act of the Legislature.

James Cheetham: "Barbary States"

Whether the new nation could afford the dollars needed to expand its naval power became a point of contention among Americans in their dis-cussions of what to do about the Barbary powers. Republican editor James Cheetham clearly favored the idea that Americans ought to pay for a navy to fight the Barbary powers rather than pay the tribute they de-manded.

American Citizen and General Advertiser (New York City), 6 June 1801

The first duty of a government is the protection of its citizens in their lawful pursuits and enterprises, whether by sea or land. This right of protection imposes a duty upon our government to protect them in the Mediterranean as well as on our coast. Nor should this protection be withheld even in these lawful pursuits, wherein the profits arising from them for the moment are not adequate to the expence of protection.... If the prosecution of our rights as a nation be attended with an expence unnecessarily and oppressively imposed upon us by others, shall we on that account abandon those rights and tamely and cowardly submit to the oppression? For the honor of our country we hope that no man in it will advocate the servile position. If the exercise of our rights by land should be attempted to be wrested from us by a foreign power, would it be right to submit lest by riding ourselves we should incur expence? No. The spirit of resistance to oppression cannot be so far forgotten in the U. States as to admit the supposition. Why then should we give up our rights in the Mediterranean on account of the expence which may attend supporting them; or refuse to chastise the oppression under which we smart from the same sordid motives? We know that so slavish a spirit does not pervade the mind of our executive. It is the desire of every man in the United States that we be freed from the shackles of the Mediterranean powers. And we hope it is reserved to Mr. Jefferson to liberate us. It would be far better for our republican cannon to thunder in the ear of the barbarians than to pay them a tribute.

Samuel Pennington and Stephen Gould: "It Is Much to Be Regretted"

By early summer in 1801, word reached the United States that the leaders of the Barbary states, having fitted out their cruisers for the capture of American vessels, had resumed their "depredations on the American commerce." According to these authors, the American government should stop paying tribute to those who were "feasting at pleasure on the spoils of our commerce."

Centinel of Freedom (Newark, N.J.), 9 June 1801

It is much to be regretted that such is the situation of America as to be obliged to pay an ignominious tribute to those Barbarians, whose only means of subsistence is plunger and rapine, which this country has sufficiently experienced. It ought not to be forgotten that under the former administration, the ruling principle in relation to France, who was our friend and benefactor, was "millions for defence but not a cent for tribute," while the Barbary Powers (for the want of a few frigates properly stationed) were either receiving tribute, or feasting at pleasure on the spoils of our commerce, taking our seamen prisoners, and subjecting them to all the horrors and sufferings which merciless barbarians could inflict, & where bleeding humanity could aid them but with a sign. WE doubt not, however, but the wisdom of our present rulers will devise means suitable to the exigency of the occasion, and honourable to the United States.

CRITICISM OF JEFFERSON'S WAR AGAINST THE BARBARY STATES

Alexander Young and Thomas Minns: "National Energies"

Even after the U.S. Navy achieved a remarkable win in a naval battle against a more heavily armed Tripolitan warship, Jefferson's Federalist critics found something to skewer him with. Commenting on the famous August 1, 1801, naval battle, editors Young and Minns criticized Jefferson's choice of words in an address that included a comment on the successful battle.

The Mercury and New-England Palladium (Boston), 15 January 1802

Lieutenant STERRET of the Navy, having captured a vessel of Tripoli, President Jefferson, in his Message, notices the fact very politely, has tendered, as usual, the homage of his respect, and offered his congratulations that the battle has convinced these pirates that the energies of this country are powerful, and are all directed to multiplying the human species.

This is doubtless very sentimental and very fine writing—unspeakably fine. With the terrible *Farmer's* leave, however, who calls it Treason to ask questions, we would make bold to enquire, whether our blowing those fellows brains out, if they have any, will really establish the proof of our multiplying, so clearly, as of our destroying energies? Some people think the latter will be our sort. It is, indeed, a new way to multiply the human species by ship's guns. It is very like giving the French liberty by the guillotine.

Admitting, however, that such are our energies, and that this is the glorious way to shew their effect, still it may be asked, whether STERRET'S battle is, in the President's sense of it, any reason for altering our Naturalization law, so that, after having made all Tripoli shake in its shoes, by the display of our multiplying energies, we ought, from the necessity and urgency of the case, to ask the assistance of their Tripoline energies to multiply the human species?

If matters are so bad, then let distressed Tripoline humanity, or barbarity, come here and find an asylum.

SUPPORT FOR JEFFERSON'S WAR AGAINST THE BARBARY STATES

A Citizen: "Barbary States"

Undoubtedly a Republican supporter of President Jefferson, this writer blamed Great Britain for America's troubles in the Mediterranean. This demonstrated a common theme in the writings of Tripoli-related newspaper correspondence: the behind-the-scenes conduct of the French and British. According to the Republicans, the British were stirring things up against them in the Mediterranean, and according to the Federalists, the French were the source of the trouble.

Aurora (Philadelphia), 10 June 1801

The commerce of the United States in the Mediterranean has been a source of jealousy and discontent to the government of Great Britain ever since the treaty of peace in '83, and it is more than probable, that the present aspect of our affairs in that quarter is the result of the foul intrigues and designs of the English government.

The celebrated work of Lord Sheffield on commerce, published immediately after the peace of '83, was aimed directly at the commerce of the United States.—It was written at a period when the English government, though just beaten by the United States, seemed to have no conception that they would ever grow so as to rival the "mother country" in arts, in science, and in commerce. It was and is the index of the mind of the government, and may be considered as uttering its thoughts. But though this "Noble Lord" speaks in the most dishonorable and contemptible manner of the United States, he exhibits some doubts of their becoming, at some future period at least, a nation that may somewhat annoy their commercial expectations and pursuit. How to avert this expected annoyance seems to have claimed the serious consideration of the author.—In a note on this subject, he has particular reference to the Mediterranean, and speaks of the best means of suppressing the American commerce in this quarter. His device is ingenious but cruel, and is highly characteristic of the English government. It consists of a method whereby the English government can be determined and merciless enemies of ours, without being apparently at war with us. It is to employ the Algerines so to harass our commerce in the Mediterranean, as to make it not worth our pursuing. His observations on this subject are sufficiently plain to be understood. The following is an extract from the work:

It is not probable the American states will have a very free trade in the Mediterranean: It will not be the interest of the great maritime power to protect them from the Barbary states. If they knew their interest, they will not encourage the Americans to be carriers. That the Barbary states are of service to the Maritime Powers is certain. If they were impressed, the little states of Italy, &c. would have much more of the carrying trade. The armed neutrality would be as hurtful to the great maritime power in the Barbary States are useful. The Americans cannot protect themselves from the latter, they cannot pretend to a navy &c.

James J. Wilson: "A New Year's Report"

Each year, around January 1, many newspaper editors published commentary on the events of the past year and forecasts about what they thought might happen in the future. In this New Year's column, Republican editor James J. Wilson briefly applauded the country's recent progress against the Barbary powers.

True American (Trenton, N.J.), 7 January 1805

Against a single Barbary power alone, are we compelled to maintain a force: its depredations and insolence did but increase with the spirit of amity and forbearance of our government, we were in self defence necessitated to substitute hostilities for tribute; and, it is grateful to our feelings to be able to recall the reader's attention to their progress....[W]ithin the last year, our defensive navy has added greatly to the dignity of our country, and its officers and seamen, by their skill and bravery, have given an idea of what they can and will do, when necessity commands their employment in such enterprises.

Samuel Harrison Smith: "Tripolitan Treaty"

Jefferson's treaty with the Barbary states, negotiated late in 1805 by diplomat Tobias Lear, had many critics. Not among them was Samuel Harrison

Smith, the author of this piece, who praised the treaty. Among the complaints of those who disliked the treaty was the payment of $60,000 to the Tripolitans. In addition, they argued that the Bashaw's throne should have been taken by force. Smith addressed such concerns in his column.

National Intelligencer (District of Columbia), 6 November 1805

Our captive countrymen have been restored to the bosom of their country, peace has been made on honorable terms.—Good men rejoice that the sword is sheathed, and the high spirited exult in the new laurels that adorn the valour of our countrymen. We have got all we wanted without shedding the blood of the innocent, without sacrificing the lives of our brave tars. We have preserved our force unbroken, ready, if necessary, to chastise the injustice of our enemies, should an indignant country bid them. For this we have paid the paltry sum of 60,000 dollars, a sum, which, divided among the people of the United States, does not exceed a cent a head. We have liberated the nation from an annual tax of near seven hundred thousand dollars. We have established with the pirates a character for justice and energy. We have taught them that we can and will command the one, if necessary, with the other.

But *unfortunately* we have not dethroned the reigning bashaw, and placed the pretender on the throne—streams of blood have not flowed in copious libations to the grim king of terrors; the helpless and the innocent have not been immolated to the false glory of military triumph; the pacific genius of republican America, whose virtue is her only true pride, has not wantonly murdered the innocent, or desolated and depopulated the fields of the unoffending, and sunk the miserable slaves of a despot still deeper in misfortunes.

Had this sanguinary scene been unfolded by the triumph of our arms, and murder, conflagration, and famine wreaked their deadly and indiscriminate vengeance on thousands and tens of thousands, history might have immortalized, but would it have approved the act? Would not its impartial award have placed it to the account of unruly passion, and regretted the absence of that magnanimity, which, always just and moderate, accomplishes its ends of means the least destructive to the happiness of others.

Besides, was it certain that the victory of Derna was the presage of triumph at Tripoli? And if it was, might not the lives of our countrymen have been lost? And for this what triumph would have atoned?

But, placing all thee considerations aside; allowing it, only for argument sake, as probable that Mr. Eaton would have vanquished every interposing obstacle, still it was proper in Mr. Lear to seize and improve the auspicious moment, and to make peace on honorable terms.

QUESTIONS

1. Aside from its slowness in reaching America, explain how war-related journalism of the early nineteenth century differs from war reports disseminated today.
2. Historians and political scientists have said that the early nineteenth-century pirates of the Mediterranean were similar to today's terrorists. Discuss such similarities and differences.
3. Do you think early nineteenth-century Americans found it frustrating to receive war-related news so slowly during the Tripolitan War of 1801–1805? Explain.
4. Discuss whether (and, if so, how) early nineteenth-century newspapers played a role in building support for a stronger American naval force.
5. This chapter discusses several songs written about the Tripolitan War. Can you think of any more recent popular songs that were written about war?
6. Why do you believe some Americans in 1801 thought the British might have been behind the troubles America was having in the Mediterranean?

NOTES

1. Richard Leiby, "Historians Say Terrorists Are Modern-day Pirates," *Washington Post*, 21 October 2001.

2. Letter from George Washington to the Marquis de LaFayette, Mount Vernon, 15 August 1786.

CHAPTER 10

The Louisiana Purchase, 1803

In 1789, New England author Jedidiah Morse made a startling prediction about the future of America. He wrote, "We cannot but anticipate the period, as not far distance, when the AMERICAN EMPIRE will comprehend millions of souls, west of the Mississippi.... [T]he Mississippi was never designed as the boundary of the American Empire."[1] Less than two decades later, Morse's prophecy was realized. In early 1803, President Thomas Jefferson sent James Monroe and Robert R. Livingston to France with orders to acquire the port of New Orleans. Unexpectedly, Napoleon decided to sell not only the port, but also all of Louisiana to the United States. Considered one of the American nation's greatest triumphs, the country more than doubled in size when its leaders purchased the Louisiana Territory for $15 million. But while many Americans lauded the deal, others were extremely critical of it.

Tensions between the United States, Spain, France, and England concerning who would ultimately own the Louisiana Territory were long standing. All four countries at one time or another had sought to dispossess the Native Americans of their hold on this vast land. Chief Tattooed Serpent, leader of the Natchez Indians, spoke of this with wonderment. About the French, he asked, "Why did the French come into our country? We did not go to seek them; they asked for land of us."[2] A temporary answer to the question of who would own Louisiana came in 1762 when France ceded New Orleans and Louisiana west of the Mississippi to Spain.

Aggravating the situation were the thousands of farmers who moved west from the eastern coastal states to the lands between the Appalachians and the Mississippi River in the waning years of the eighteenth century. In growing numbers, they used the Spanish port of New Orleans for the exportation of their produce. In 1800, Spain secretly agreed to return

Louisiana to France, and although the deal was not formally announced until 1802, rumors circulated for several years that Spain would return Louisiana. When the deal was announced, some considered it within the rights of America to claim Louisiana. In addressing Congress, Charles Brockden Brown said, "Louisiana is ours, even if to make it so, we should be obliged to treat its present inhabitants as vassals."[3] Many Americans agreed with him.

Congress considered the deal with Spain and France to be in violation of an agreement between the United States and Spain, and debates broke out about what should be done. A further complication arose on October 16, 1802, when New Orleans acting intendant Juan Ventura Morales published an order stating that Americans were henceforth barred from selling their goods through the city's wharves and warehouses. In response, a New Orleans gentleman wrote a friend at Natchez of his concerns:

> Yesterday the Intendant issued orders, not only for shutting the port of New-Orleans against American vessels coming with cargoes to sell, which was expected; but even totally to prevent the deposit—a step that must produce infinite embarrassment, as well as much loss to many of the citizens of the United States. Two boats that arrived from above yesterday, with flour, were not allowed to land it; consequently cotton, &c. coming from Natchez will be in the same predicament.[4]

When word of the shutting of the port reached Washington, Americans were enraged. Some newspaper editors questioned President Jefferson's handling of the situation, calling for a strong show of force. Meanwhile, Jefferson continued his policy of quiet diplomacy. On January 11, 1803, the U.S. Senate received a message from the president nominating Robert L. Livingston and James Monroe to go to France to negotiate.[5] Some Federalists attacked this plan. William Coleman, editor of the *New-York Evening Post*, wrote, "The appointment of an Envoy Extraordinary, at this time, and under present circumstances, is in every respect the weakest measure that ever disgraced the administration of any country."[6] Tensions heightened in February when Napolean ordered his forces to sail from Saint Dominique to New Orleans. A few weeks later, he canceled this move, and on April 11, French diplomats told Livingston that France was willing to sell all of the Louisiana Territory to the United States for $15 million.

News of the treaty did not reach America until late June, and efforts to ratify it commenced immediately. On August 19, it was learned in Washington that Napolean had ratified the agreement on May 22.[7] President Jefferson called a special session of Congress for October 17, 1803, to meet the six-month deadline for ratification. On the second day of debate in the Senate, the treaty was approved by a vote of 24 to 7. Shortly after, the House of

"Thomas Jefferson as the Prairie Dog." The title of this etching with watercolor, James Akin's earliest-known cartoon, is "The prairie dog sickened at the sting of the hornet or a diplomatic puppet exhibiting his deceptions." The point is to lampoon Jefferson's 1804 covert negotiations for the purchase of West Florida from Spain. Jefferson, as a scrawny dog, after being stung by a hornet with Napoleon's head, coughs up "Two Million" in gold coins. This amount was sought from Congress by Jefferson as a secret appropriation for the purchase. On the right dances a man with orders from French minister Talleyrand in his pocket and maps of East and West Florida in his hand. He says, "A gull for the People." Courtesy of the Library of Congress.

Representatives gave its approval with a vote of 90 to 25. On October 31, 1803, President Jefferson signed the congressional bill that authorized the largest real estate deal in history.[8]

This chapter begins with essays published in response to the Spanish government's 1802 closing of the Port of New Orleans to American shippers. While many Americans hoped that the government would send federal troops to reopen the port and then to negotiate, not everyone agreed that this would be the best course of action. The first author in this section was more restrained than those following. He questioned whether England's interest in the Mississippi ought to be of more concern to Americans rather than those of the Spanish and French. While this author called for action, he suggested that America might offer to purchase the area. The final articles included in the section called for military intervention first, with diplomacy following.

The chapter's final sections focus on Americans' reactions to the purchase. The first of these includes examples of the many laudatory statements published in the wake of the announcement of the acquisition of Louisiana. The first interviews between American and French diplomats took place on April 11. At that time, Barbé-Marbois, appointed by Napoleon to take care of the negotiations for the sale, met with Livingston. A day later, James Monroe arrived in France, and in less than three weeks, the treaty was drawn up and signed in Paris. The signing ceremony took place on May 3, but it would take two months for this news to reach America.

When word of the signing was finally received, there was much rejoicing. But not everyone, as is evident in the chapter's final section, was happy about the purchase. Among the complaints of the purchase's critics were its large price tag, the territory's remoteness, a lack of specifics about its resources, and the fear that it would come to overshadow the east in political power. In addition, some critics raised concerns about whether the government's purchase of the territory from France was in line with the U.S. Constitution.

COMMENTARY ON THE CLOSURE OF THE PORT OF NEW ORLEANS

William Carlton: "The Mississippi"

As the shocking news of the closure of the port of New Orleans spread, much discussion as to what should be done about it was published in the newspapers. Register *editor William Carlton here presaged what eventually happened: He proposed that the government consider making an offer to purchase the rights to navigate the Mississippi River.*

Salem Register (Massachusetts), 3 January 1803

The Mississippi is a subject of serious concern to the United States, but it is variously represented both in Europe and America. With some, the shutting of it is an act of Spanish policy, conformably to their general conduct in their American colonies. With others, France has the direction of this business for some political ends. But there are some who see no greater advantages to any European nation, than might arise to the English, if they were in possession of Louisiana. It connects itself with their colonies in Canada, and opens a free communication to their subjects with the ocean, either by the St. Lawrence or the gulph of Mexico. That unless we can navigate the Mississippi, we must injure if not lose the interior States, is not to be doubted. That vigorous measures are to be pursued, is evident.... Congress have immediately interested themselves in this affair, and we trust will act with the perseverance and fidelity it deserves. It has been suggested that if Louisiana is at the disposal of the first consul of France, and he is inclined to sell it to England, to assist the finances of his country, it may not be amiss for the United States to make some generous offers, and so come into possession of the whole navigation of the Mississippi.

Anonymous: "Interesting Account of the Projects of France Respecting Louisiana"

Many Americans were so antagonistic to the French that the idea that the French would possess New Orleans was untenable. The writer of this statement was emphatic: United States officials must act vigorously against the closure of the Port of New Orleans.

New-York Evening Post (New York City), 28 January 1803

The government *must not* hesitate. The western people will not be trifled with. They will not bear that injuries to their dearest rights should excite no emotion in that government whose claim to their regard is founded on the *equality and efficacy* of its protection. There never was a time when this government might gain the hearts of that important portion of its citizens more effectually than now. To let the opportunity pass unimproved, will be a deadly wound to its popularity. It will probably be followed by some immediate act of rebellion. The loss of the affections of the western states will be the certain consequence. And what unexpirable evils will ensue, should the French be enabled, by this delay, to take possession?

Their warlike bands, far different from the wretched Militia of Spain, in spirit as in numbers, will be marked by their skillful eyes, fortified with diligence, supplied with artillery, and magazines, and manned with their veteran soldiers. Their chief town, besides a little army in its walls, will be compassed by forts and bulwarks. The banks of the river will be lined with trenches and cannon, and the empire of the Mississippi, unless regained by some great, sudden, and strenuous effort, will be lost to us forever.

Pericles: "For the Evening Post"

Writing under the name Pericles, Alexander Hamilton did not entirely rule out negotiation as the way to solve the Louisiana problem. But he favored a quick show of military support, followed by negotiation.

New-York Evening Post (New York City), 8 February 1803

Since the question of independence, none has occurred more deeply interesting to the United States than the cession of Louisiana to France.

This event threatens the early dismemberment of a large portion of the country, more immediately, the safety of all the Southern States; and remotely, the independence of the whole Union. This is the portentous aspect which the affair presents to all men of sound and reflecting minds, of whatever party; and it is not to be concealed, that the only question which now offers itself, is how the evil is to be averted?

The strict right to resort at once to war, if it should be deemed expedient, cannot be doubted. A manifest and great danger to the nation; the nature of the cession to France, extending to ancient limits without respect to our rights by treaty; the direct infraction of an important article of the treaty itself, in withholding the deposit of New Orleans; either of these affords justifiable cause of war, and that they would authorize immediate hostilities, is not to be questioned by the most scrupulous mind.

The whole is then a question of expediency. Two courses only present: First, to negotiate, and endeavor to purchase; and if this fails, to go to war. Secondly, to seize at once on the Floridas and New Orleans, and then negotiate. A strong objection offers itself to the first. There is not the most distant probability that the ambitious and aggrandizing views of Buonaparte will commute the territory for money. Its acquisition is of immense importance to France, and has long been an object of her extreme solicitude. The attempt, therefore, to purchase, in the first instance, will certainly fail; and in the end, war must be resorted to, under all the accumulation of difficulties caused by a previous and strongly fortified possession of the country by our adversary.

The second plan is, therefore, evidently the best. First, because effectual; the acquisition easy; the preservation afterwards easy. The evils of a war with France at this time are certainly not very formidable; her fleet crippled and powerless; her treasury empty; her resources almost dried up; in short, gasping for breath after a tremendous conflict, which, though it left her victorious, left her nearly exhausted under her extraordinary exertions. On the other hand, we might count with certainty on the aid of Great Britain with her powerful navy.

Secondly, this plan is preferable, because it affords us the only chance of avoiding a long-continued war. When we have once taken possession the business will present itself to France in a new aspect. She will then have to weigh the immense difficulties, if not the utter impracticability, of wresting it from us. In this posture of affairs she will naturally conclude it is her interest to bargain. Now it may become expedient to terminate hostilities by a purchase, and a cheaper one may reasonably be expected. To secure the better prospect of final success, the following auxiliary measures ought to be adopted. The army should be increased to ten thousand men, for the purpose of preservation of the conquest. Preparations for increasing our naval force should be made. The militia should be classed, and effectual provision made for raising, on an emergency, forty thousand men. Negotiations should be pushed with Great Britain, to induce her to hold herself in readiness to co-operate fully with us, at a moment's warning. This plan should be adopted and proclaimed before the departure of our envoy. Such measures would astonish and disconcert Buonaparte himself; our envoy would be enabled to speak and treat with effect, and all Europe would be taught to respect us. These ideas have been long entertained by the writer, but he has never given himself the trouble to commit them to the public, because he despaired of their being adopted. They are now thrown out with very little hope of their producing any change in the conduct of the Administration, yet with the encouragement that there is a strong current of public feeling in favor of decisive measures. If the President would adopt this course, he might yet retrieve his character, induce the best part of the community to look favorably upon his political career, exalt himself in the eyes of Europe, save the country, and secure a permanent fame. But, for this, alas! Jefferson is not destined.

Americanus: "For the *Washington Federalist*"

This strident critic of the president's policy of negotiation mocked those who expressed concerns that sending troops might lead to bloodshed. To act quickly, it was asserted, would prevent the bloodshed that could result if America dawdled.

Washington Federalist (District of Columbia), 21 February 1803

Among the many powerful motives, which ought to influence our government immediately to possess itself of New-Orleans, even that of humanity ought to have irresistible force. In every human probability, we have at this time the happy opportunity of obtaining that place without the loss of an American life, without shedding one drop of blood. Only send to New Orleans a respectable force, such as would be a sufficient apology, there can be no doubt but that the Spaniards would immediately yield up the place.

Can it be believed they would be so weak, so foolish as to make a resistance, which, they must know would be useless, in order to retain its possession, it must in a very little time, be surrendered. So far from this, we have every reason to believe, that the inhabitants of that place and of Louisiana, would much sooner be under the dominion of the United States than of France—and also that the Spanish government itself, if it was left free from restraint, would much rather have us for their neighbours than the French.

If then all this dread of the calamities of war—this horror at the idea of shedding human blood, and the slaughter of the human race, expressed by the opposers of this measure, are *real*—If they are any thing more than the whining cant of philosophical cowardice—if they are the genuine effusions of pure benevolence and sacred compassion, and not the cold sweats—the timid shrieks of a weak, imbecile, pusillanimous government, we conjure them by the *sacred name of humanity* as well as by the motives of Justice, Public Honor and Public Interest, to seize on the present moment, this precious, this golden opportunity, which once lost, is lost forever.

Already are the French troops embarking—already they are perhaps even on the ocean.—Delay is ruin.—Let them once land—let them once obtain possession—what expence of blood, what expence of treasure, will it not cost us to wrest from them, what not invites, solicits our acceptance.

Let us not lose a moment.—the idea of securing our rights by negociation is contemptible—it is false and deceptive. To act on such an idea is dangerous—is destructive.

Let us nobly assert our rights first: Let us first repossess ourselves of those rights of which we have wantonly been despoiled: Then negotiate and welcome for their preservation. But let us even then negotiate with our arms in our hands, that if we fail in the Cabinet, we may succeed in the Field.

In Favor of the Purchase of the Louisiana Territory

Abijah Adams and Ebenezer Rhoades: "Louisiana Ceded to the United States"

The Independent Chronicle *was one of the first newspapers to break the news of the treaty. As friends of Jefferson, the editors hoped the article would shore up his reputation.*

Independent Chronicle (Boston), 30 June 1803

Thus our former anticipations have not only been realized, but exceeded; and thus the wise, seasonable and politic negociation of the President, approved and confirmed by Congress, has gloriously terminated to the immortal honor of the friends of peace and good government, and to the utter disappointment of the factions and turbulent throughout the Union...We shall now only say, that we hope this highly brilliant event will contribute to unite the candid and honest of every party, in an increasing confidence in the wisdom of that administration, whose greatest pleasure centres in the unbiased and enlightened, of every description; and in the peace, liberty and safety of this favored country.

William Coleman: "Purchase of Louisiana"

Although Federalists were usually at odds with President Jefferson and other Republicans over matters related to Louisiana, not all were critics of the purchase. Here a staunch Federalist praised the deal but reminded his readers that they shouldn't give the president too much of the credit for the treaty.

New-York Evening Post (New York City), 5 July 1803

At length the business of New-Orleans has terminated favourably to this country. Instead of being obliged to rely any longer on the force of treaties, for a place of deposit, the jurisdiction of the territory is now transferred to our hands and in future the navigation of the Mississippi will be ours unmolested. This, it will be allowed, is an important acquisition; nor, indeed, as territory, but as being essential to the peace and prosperity of our Western country, and as opening a free and valuable market to our commercial states. This purchase has been made during the period of Mr. Jefferson's presidency, and will, no doubt, give credit to his administration. Every man, however, possessed of the least candour and reflection will readily acknowledge that the acquisition has been solely owing to…unexpected circumstances, and not to any wise or vigorous measures on the part of the American government.

Samuel Harrison Smith: "The Cession of Louisiana"

A point often expressed by those who approved of the purchase, such as this author, was that it helped the nation avoid war. A second argument used in its favor was the size and richness of the territory, which would benefit the United States.

National Intelligencer (District of Columbia), 8 July 1803

By the cession of Louisiana, we shall preserve peace, and acquire a territory of great extent, fertility, and local importance. However great the latter object may be, the former is of inestimable value, and it is principally in relation to it that the importance of the cession is to be estimated. A nation, whose population is doubled in twenty-four years, whose resources increase with still greater rapidity, and which enjoys a free government, only requires peace to elevate her in a few years above the storms which with so little intermission, agitate the European world.

National confidence has hitherto extended our administration in all their leading ventures. This great event adds powerful reasons for its continuance. Great as were the hopes of patriotism, they have been more than realized. We have secured our rights by pacific means: truth and reason have been more powerful than the sword.

Abijah Adams and Ebenezer Rhoades: "What Strange Oddities"

The authors of this piece commented on the irony in Federalists' complaints about the purchase. When the port was shut by the Spanish, they cried for war; however, Federalists then complained about the purchase of the land they formerly said America should go to war over.

Independent Chronicle (Boston), 11 July 1803

What strange oddities the Tory Federalists are!–Ross AND Morris, with the whole Essex Junto; a few weeks since were holding up the importance of New Orleans; even desirous of involving the country in a War; probably at the expence fifty millions of dollars, and a hundred thousand lives.–But now we have obtained it [Louisiana] by an amicable Negociation, this immense and opulent Territory is nothing more to them [the Federalists] than a "*whistle!*" Fifteen thousand Kentuckians were to be armed to invade it, but as Monroe and Livingston have obtained the acquisition without the 'loan of a pistol,' the Tories are dissatisfied!!–A hopeful set truly!!!

Samuel Harrison Smith: "Americans!"

A ceremony at New Orleans on December 20, 1803, marked the official transfer of ownership of the territory from France to America. This led to a new round of newspaper editorializing.

National Intelligencer (District of Columbia), 30 January 1804

The event, for which we have all looked with so much solicitude, is at length realized. LOUISIANA is part of the union.–The acquisition is great and glorious in itself; but still greater and more glorious are the means by which it is obtained. In them are developed the energy and justice of a republican government, and its perfect competency; with the least practicable injury to others, to redress the wrongs and to secure the rights of the nation it protects. Never have mankind contemplated so vast and important an accession of empire by means so pacific and just, and never, perhaps, has there been a change of government so agreeable to the subjects of it. May the example go forth to the world, and teach rulers the superiority of right to violence!

To the firm and temperate conduct of the legislature, to the enlightened and energetic measures of the Executive, and to the commanding and supporting sentiment of the nation, we owe this splendid era in the annals of our country.–The virtues and talents of those who produced it will receive the admiration of posterity; ours they already possess.

This, fellow-citizens, is an appropriate occasion for joy. Cold must be the heart, that is not animated by the completion of this event. Every doubt has vanished; the country is ours. Our brethren in the west are exulting in the new ties that unite them to us.—LET US TOO REJOICE, that we are free, that we are happy, and that this great event promises to make them as free and happy as ourselves.

Anonymous: "Pax Bello Potior"

After the official ceding of Louisiana to America on December 20, 1803, celebrations were held across the nation. One of these parties was held at Stelle's Hotel in Washington, D.C. These stanzas are from a Latin ode performed at the party, accompanied by instruments in a round of merry toasts and songs.

National Intelligencer (District of Columbia), 30 January 1804

To Jefferson, belov'd of Heav'n,
May golden Peace be ever given,
And when Death at last shall come,
To lay him in the silent tomb,

May weeping Angels gather near,
And Laurels strew around his bier,
And waft him, on the wings of Love,
To everlasting Peace above.

OPPOSITION TO THE PURCHASE

Fabricius: "Louisiana Bought but Not Yet Paid For. Who Pays for It?"

One of the first complaints about the acquisition of Louisiana was that it was kept secret by the U.S. Senate, but it didn't take long for a host of other arguments to be raised by the Federalist press. Here, Fabricius worried that a country so vast would be broken into many states and that the interests of the people of the Northeast would be threatened. Fabricius also wondered how the purchase would be paid for.

Columbian Centinel (Boston), 13 July 1803

At length we hear *Louisiana* is bought. For what? To secure the right of deposit. Better assert our old Treaty right as derived from *Spain*, than buy new rights:—Especially to buy them with the millions that are wanted to provide ships and troops to secure them—especially too, let it be added, by giving those millions to the only government that has rendered or that will make that right and all our rights unsafe.

We are to give money of which we have too little for land of which we already have too much.—We expose our want of spirit, and aggravate our want of strength.

There ought to be some balance in the Union; as before hinted, this unexplored empire, of the size of four or five European kingdoms will...drain our people away from the pursuit of a better husbandry, and from manufacturers and commerce.

Can an Empire so unwieldy, so nearly uncivilized, that will for a century or two require such heavy charge, and contribute so little towards defraying any part of it, will it be, can it be subject to *one* Government?—And if it should, will that Government be republican? Does it not threaten to sever, and, if not to sever, to subjugate the Union?

Will not these new mountaineer states claim power and resist taxes? Give us Representatives in Congress, who will have power over the men of the east; slaves over free whites, but do not lay direct taxes in the same proportion. Will not this be their language, as it ever has been that of *Virginia?*

A momentous crisis is at hand. Ever since 1789, the consumers who pay most are from *Pennsylvania,* eastward. The inhabitants who will cost most to the United States Treasury, and those who live West from *Pennsylvania.* Ours are the burdens, theirs the benefits.

Benjamin Russell: "Fifteen Millions"

This critic of the treaty bemoaned the great sum of money spent on the territory, thinking that Americans would realize that the purchase was a mistake.

Columbian Centinel (Boston), 10 August 1803

It is not quite certain,...that the payment of fifteen millions of Dollars to France for the restoration of our rights will be thought wise by the American People when they have had time to consider it;—they will easily perceive that France could not keep New-Orleans and must have been glad to cede it to the U.S. that it might not fall into the hands of the English;—they will see that THE ADDITION OF LOUISIANA IS ONLY A PRETENCE FOR DRAWING AN IMMENSE SUM OF MONEY FROM US which can only be viewed as a contribution to support a power already too great for the safety and liberty of the civilized world.... If, happily for mankind, France should be beaten she cannot in future, deprive us of our rights on the Mississippi, and on the other hand if England falls what good will accrue to us from having assisted France to subdue her by contributing fifteen millions of our dollars? May not the time come when this whole transaction will be considered as no less ruinous than infamous? When we shall not only regret that we have aided the French to destroy those who in defending themselves effectually defend us—but when we shall also wish for this money with other means to defend ourselves?—It is well remembered that the people of Holland expressed great joy at the Treaty of 1794 by which they were bound to pay 100 millions of guilders to France for the conquest of Liberty—many thoughtless persons in this country partook of that joy—but what do all men now think of that event?

Alexander Young and Thomas Minns: "Louisiana"

Some critics complained that little was known about the land encompassed by the purchase. Furthermore, what was known was not all good. These critics focused on the difficulties of access to a large portion of the territory.

Mercury and New-England Palladium (Boston), 16 August 1803

The greatest objection to this country, is the difficulty of access to it. There is no river of any consequence, or port or harbour for ships and vessels, to the west, from the mouth of the *Mississippi* to the cape, where the west boundary of *Louisiana* commences; consequently, the only way to and from the ocean, must be through the channel of Mississippi, up as far as the river Rouge, or Red river, and thence up along that river to the high land to the *Appalusa* country, or *Necatoches,* where the first high land fit for extensive settlement is to be found.... This will ever be a great objection to that country, and it is not improbable, that when the First Consul of France and his counselors, came to be acquainted with the difficulty of colonizing this country, and its remote situation from the ocean, that he became more readily disposed to give it up to America.

There is another circumstance attending to this country, not very generally known, which is, that the whole of the lands on the west side of the Mississippi, except for a slip of one plantation deep, opposite part of *New-Orleans,* and the settlement at *Point Coupee,* is a low sunken country, almost as far up as the Ohio; [a] great part of it is covered for near four months of the year, with water from twenty to thirty feet deep, and extending nearly thirty miles back from the edge of the river—while, on the contrary, except here and there a few low places, is a high bold country....

It appears to me, therefore, that the river Mississippi is admirably calculated to form a barrier or boundary of the American empire; and the immense tract of land newly acquired, may long remain a waste, which will prevent any other nation from approaching the United States in that quarter, and may, by a judicious arrangement with the southern Indians, be allotted to them for hunting grounds, in lieu of the countries they now possess in the heart of the U. States.

QUESTIONS

1. Should the president have sent forces to New Orleans when the port was closed by the Spanish, or was diplomacy the best course of action? Explain.
2. Why do you think the Federalists opposed the Louisiana Purchase after so vigorously arguing that Jefferson ought to send troops to acquire New Orleans just a few months before?
3. Explain all the ways you believe the Louisiana Purchase changed America.
4. Consider the role of the newspaper in the Louisiana controversy. Did the time lag between events and the eventual publication about them in the newspapers reduce the impact of the stories published?
5. The era of Manifest Destiny—that is, the idea that the United States had the right and duty to expand on the North American continent—had not yet begun when America purchased Louisiana. Do you think the purchase and the publicity it received in the nation's newspapers could have helped spark this later movement? Explain.

NOTES

1. Jedidiah Morse, *The American Geography; or View of the Present Situation of the United States of America* (Elizabethtown, N.J., 1789; reprint ed., New York: Arno, 1970), 469.

2. Antoine Simon Le Page du Pratz, *Histoire de la Louisiane* (Paris, Chez de Bure, L'aîné..., laveuve Delaguette..., Lambert..., 1758), 1:203.

3. *An Address to the Government of the United States on the Cession of Louisiana to the French* (Philadelphia: J. Conrad & Co., 1803), 48, 52, 56.

4. *Natchez Herald* (Mississippi), 28 October 1802.

5. *Annals of Congress,* Senate, 7th Congress, 2nd Session, 22–23; *Senate Executive Journal,* 11 January 1803, 431.

6. William Coleman, *New-York Evening Post,* 8 February 1803.

7. Samuel Harrison Smith, *National Intelligencer,* 19 August 1803.

8. *Statutes at Large,* vol. 2, 8th Congress, 1st session, 245.

CHAPTER 11

Marbury v. Madison, 1801–1803

Imagine a United States Supreme Court without the power to decide whether laws enacted by Congress are legal under the Constitution. This situation actually existed in America during the first 15 years of the Court's existence, a period when its legitimacy was so dubious that some called for its elimination. But all this changed on February 24, 1803, when Chief Justice John Marshall announced that the Court was not bound by an act of Congress "repugnant to the Constitution."[1] Legal historians agree that *Marbury v. Madison* is the most important decision ever issued by the Supreme Court. In one fell swoop, the Court was transformed from a weak to a strong body through its assumption of the function of judicial review. This function gives the Court the power to decide whether acts of Congress or other branches of government are permissible under the Constitution. At the time, the decision's importance was not recognized. Ultimately, however, the Court's role as the nation's final arbiter of constitutional interpretation was accepted by most Americans.[2]

The situation that led to *Marbury v. Madison* began in the aftermath of the bitterly fought presidential election of 1800–1801 (see chapter 3). For 12 years, the emerging Federalist political party held sway over the nation through its control of the presidency and both houses of Congress. When it became clear by the end of December 1800 that the old leaders were losing control of both the presidency and Congress, they were in despair. The only branch of government the Federalists could still control was the federal judiciary, and President Adams and other members of his party attempted in their last weeks and days in office to shore up their power there.

Step one was the nomination of John Marshall to the vacant post of chief justice of the Supreme Court. Years later, President Adams wrote, "The proudest act of my life was the gift of John Marshall to the people of the United States."[3] Adams selected Marshall because he knew the appointment would make life a little more difficult for Jefferson and the Republicans. Marshall's appointment was for life, meaning Jefferson and his party would be saddled with him for years to come, something they found contemptible. Jefferson and his friends viewed the new chief justice as a "subtly calculating enemy of the people."[4]

Another step taken by the Federalists to keep their grip on the nation's judiciary was the passage of the Judiciary Act of 1801. Enacted on February 24, the bill essentially redrafted the nation's 1789 Judiciary Act by granting the federal judiciary tighter control over the states. Its measures included the elimination of one of the justices of the Supreme Court, the division of the union into 16 judicial districts with 6 circuits, and the creation of 16 new circuit judge positions. In addition, the act gave sitting presidents the power to appoint as many new justices of the peace for the District of Columbia as was deemed necessary. These measures clashed with the principles of incoming Democrats, who had campaigned for stronger states and constitutional liberties.

The new judiciary act would be repealed by Congress a few days after Thomas Jefferson's inauguration, but in the meantime, the Federalists had many new offices to fill. In the weeks following the 1801 bill's passage, President Adams issued a flurry of new appointments, including several in the last hours of his presidency. Called the midnight appointments, President Adams worked right up until the clock struck 12:00 on March 3, the night before President Jefferson was sworn into office. All Adams's appointees were Federalists whose principles were in strict opposition to the new president and his party.[5]

William Marbury was one of the beneficiaries of President Adams's last-minute appointments. Adams appointed him justice of the peace for the District of Columbia, but through a series of flukes, he and several other last-minute appointees failed to receive their commission papers before President Jefferson's inauguration took place. Once Jefferson was in office, it was too late, and Marbury and the others started legal proceedings. The first step in the process was a request that the Supreme Court issue an order (writ of mandamus) requiring Secretary of State James Madison to hand over the commission papers. When Chief Justice Marshall ordered Madison to deliver the documents, he refused to do so.

Little happened until January 31, 1803, when Marbury and the other plaintiffs in the case asked the U.S. Senate for help. A senator who was sympathetic to their plight introduced a motion on the Senate floor, calling on its secretary to produce the original senatorial nominations affirming the appointments of Marbury and the others. When the motion was defeated,

Marshall's Court began reviewing the case. A few weeks later, on February 24, Chief Justice Marshall ruled that, although Marbury and the others had a right to their commissions, the Court lacked the authority to order the secretary of state to deliver them. In seeming to deny its own authority, the Court was in fact radically enlarging it: Marshall's opinion in effect traded the Court's relatively minor power of forcing the delivery of commissions for the vastly greater power of nullifying congressional acts.

Compared to many of the other events of the day and considering the *Marbury* decision's ultimate importance, newspaper writers paid scant attention to it and the events surrounding it.[6] Few newspapers, for example, commented on Adams's appointment of John Marshall to the position of chief justice. One who did was James Callender, publisher of Virginia's *Richmond Examiner.* Upon Marshall's assumption of the role of chief justice, Callender wrote, "The very sound of this man's name is an insult upon truth and justice."[7] On the other hand, the editor of the *National Intelligencer* simply stated, "The President of the U.S. has nominated John Marshall Chief Justice of the United States."[8] And when the Supreme Court began hearing arguments in the *Marbury* case in mid-February 1803, few newspaper reports and little commentary were published about it.

What little material was published in the newspapers on *Marbury*, however, gives insight into the emergence of differing views on the proper roles of the federal court system and the U.S. Supreme Court in the governance of America. Federalists were concerned that, unless the reach of the federal court system was extended further into the states people would start to think of themselves first as citizens of the states and second as citizens of the United States. They worried that the states, would develop their own state courts in opposition to the federal system, leading to the undermining of the Constitution. Republicans, on the other hand, were in favor of the idea that people in the nation's territories and states should have considerable power to run their own affairs, without much interference from the federal government.

The chapter's first section includes reports and essays published in support of a stronger federal judiciary and of Marbury's case. The first in this series was published in the District of Columbia's *Washington Federalist,* one of only a handful of newspapers whose editors published material on these matters. "A Citizen" strongly supported a more powerful federal judiciary. He asserted that the nation's founders intended to create a judiciary much stronger than had yet been instituted and that Congress ought to provide it with more resources, including more judges and justices.

The two additional newspaper essays in this section also came out in the *Washington Federalist.* Written by the *Federalist's* editor, William A. Rind, the first responds to a *National Intelligencer* piece that chastised the plaintiffs in

Marbury v. Madison in their attempts to get the U.S. Senate to surrender its records in the case. The final piece in the section comments on Marshall's now famous opinion in the *Marbury* case.

The chapter's second section includes reports and essays published in newspapers that favored how President Jefferson was handling the events surrounding the midnight appointments and William Marbury's efforts to acquire the commission President Adams had awarded him. Three were published in the nation's capital by the *National Intelligencer*, which strongly supported the Jefferson administration's position on the *Marbury* case. Other Republican supporters of the disposition of this case included the *True American* and the *Courier*. The last of this group, a piece published in the *Courier*, was part of a series of heated columns on the events and issues surrounding *Marbury v. Madison*. In the piece included here, the author considered whether the judiciary should serve as a check on the federal legislature.

In Favor of a Powerful Federal Judiciary and in Support of William Marbury's Complaint

A Citizen: "Federal Judiciary"

This argument for an expanded federal judiciary was published the day before Congress passed the Judiciary Act of 1801. According to its author, the federal government would never wield the influence intended by the founders of the nation unless Congress provided it with the resources to extend its reach into the states.

Washington Federalist (District of Columbia), 26 January 1801

Of all governments, the judiciary is that part, which most affects the happiness of the people, comes the nearest to their hearts and interests, and can most improve or corrupt the qualities of the government. Nothing has more contributed to correct, improve, and preserve the British Government, than its excellent judiciary; the exercise of which is carried into all parts of the country, and held up before the eyes of the people. It is a ruinous economy which is exerted so as to defeat a due administration of any of the powers of the government; and the most ruinous, if it defeat a due administration of justice. If any thing can establish the government of the United States in the minds of the people, confirm its authority, and make its beneficial influence felt, it must be multiplying Courts, in which the administration of justice, under the laws of the United States, may be commodiously conducted in all parts of the Union, and the authority of those laws visibly exercised & impressed on the minds of the citizens.

The administration of federal laws in the state courts would effect the purpose of bringing the authority of the Federal Government to the feelings of the citizens. Whether the suspicions of rivalship or hostility between the Governments of individual states, and the United States, be so well founded, as to render a resort to the state courts hopeless and improper, can now be more decisively ascertained, than when the Federal Judiciary was organized. Then, an exercise of federal judicial power by the State Courts might reasonably be viewed as a proper measure. But we see now, in some state governments, hostility to the government of the United States, in important principles and measures, openly avowed; we see some important federal acts violently condemned, as unconstitutional, tyrannical and pernicious; we see the friends of the Federal Government, as explained by an upright intelligent and patriotic administration, denounced, as enemies to liberty, proscribed as objects of detestation, and excluded from state offices, and we see enmity to this government considered as a qualification for state favor, and a recommendation to state patronage and appointment. With such a spirit prevailing in state administration, to vest in state courts the administration of the Federal Judiciary, would be to defeat and destroy it. A useful and correct administration of justice could not be expected from such a measure, and the powers of the government, would be perverted to its own destruction.

William Alexander Rind: "The Petition of William Marbury"

A few days after the Intelligencer's *editor chastised* Marbury v. Madison *plaintiffs for petitioning the U.S. Senate for a certificate from the Executive Journal, the* Washington Federalist *vigorously responded.*

Washington Federalist (District of Columbia), 4 February 1803

A paragraph appeared in Smith's *National Intelligencer*…respecting certain proceedings in the Senate of the United States, upon the Petition of William Marbury…contained such a singular assemblage of strange, and, to us, improbable things, that we have been induced to obtain a true statement of the facts; & likewise as correct a sketch of the Debates in the Senate, on the Petition, as the nature of the case permits; not having been present ourselves to take notes of the arguments as they were delivered.

We now present them to the public, as a specimen of the anxious solicitude of our good Democrats, to preserve inviolate the rights of individuals *(of a particular sect),* and shall leave Mr. Smith's extraordinary paragraph, with all its falsehoods, its wisdom and its wit, as a banquet to regale his own sagacious mind; and to meet its merited execration from the *discerning,* the candid and the *good.*

We shall not pretend that Mr. Smith has been guilty of a contempt of Court; nor that his arrogance may produce a few weeks' restraint of his personal liberty; his brother Jacobin and fellow slanderer of Courts, Billy Duane, having experience upon such subjects, may possibly hint to him something useful upon this occasion.

The Supreme Court of the United States, may take Mr. Smith's advice upon this and other matters respecting their duty, next week, unless peradventure the shield of the Executive, the use of which, we are told, Mr. Smith boasts of, should prove so broad, & so impenetrable, that the little gentleman may, with safety, repose behind it!!!

William Alexander Rind: "The Opinion of the Supreme Court"

In this laudatory statement on Marshall's opinion in Marbury v. Madison, *Rind wrote of the Court's "wisdom, impartiality and independence." Such a position on the proper role of the Court was clearly at odds with that of Jefferson, who favored limitations on its powers.*

Washington Federalist **(District of Columbia),** **14 March 1803**

The opinion of the Supreme Court, on the motion for a Mandamus, delivered by the Chief Justice last term, cannot fail of attracting the attention and admiration of our readers. The important principles resulting from the peculiar structure of our government, which are there examined and settled—the ability with which these principles are investigated—the strength and reason with which they are supported, and the perspicuous, yet nervous stile [*sic*] in which they are delivered, must excite in every American, an honest pride, at seeing their courts of Judicature, those guardians of their property, lives and reputation, supplied with such talents, and animated with so laudable a zeal for the rights and liberties of the citizen.

There have not been wanting men, even on the floor of Congress, base enough to make the most unwarranted insinuations against the Justices of the Supreme Court. They have called this application for a Mandamus, *their* measure—instigated & supported by them as an hostile attack upon the Executive, to gratify party spirit, and to increase their own powers. Let such men read this opinion and blush, if the power of blushing still remains with them. It will remain as a monument of the wisdom, impartiality and independence of the Supreme Court, long after the names of its petty revilers shall have sunk into oblivion.

OPPOSITION TO A STRENGTHENED JUDICIARY AND TO WILLIAM MARBURY'S COMPLAINT

Samuel Harrison Smith: "At the Close of Mr. Adams's Administration"

Since many Americans were not familiar with how patronage worked, at least according to the newly installed Democratic Republican Party, Samuel Harrison Smith used this column to explain it. Only judicial appointments made before the election could not be revoked, according to Smith.

National Intelligencer **(District of Columbia), 23 March 1801**

At the close of Mr. Adams's administration, even after his successor was appointed, a long list of nominations to office was made by him. In all these instances he named men opposed in political opinion to the national will, as unequivocally declared by his removal, and the appointment of a successor of different sentiments. These appointments were of two descriptions. The first consisted of…the judges; the second consisted of offices held…[at] the pleasure of the President. The first, from their nature, are beyond the reach of revocation; the second are entirely at the disposition of the executive magistrate. As most of them are the organs of the President, whereby certain executive duties are performed, it seems to be an object of indispensable necessity that they should enjoy his confidence. How far citizens of the character nominated by Mr. Adams, when the manner in which they were appointed is considered, can have this qualification, admits of great doubt. It is evident that in some instances they cannot possess it.

There are other cases, in which removals are made from the misconduct of particular officers. This cause applies in several instances to marshals and attorneys, whose partial exercise of power, particularly in the designation of jurors, has had a pernicious tendency to render subservient to unworthy political purposes the administration of justice.

The effect of such changes on the federal judiciary will probably be in the highest degree favourable to the impartial administration of justice.

For as almost all the judges are men of certain political tenets, an undue influence of the political opinions upon the exercise of their judicial functions, will, in a degree, be prevented by the offices of attorney and marshal being held by persons of different political principles. Each being thus a check on the partialities of the other, both descriptions of citizens will be protected.

Samuel Harrison Smith: "A Letter from Washington"

Jefferson's critics complained that he was in violation of the law in his refusal to award the commissions given out by President Adams before Adams left office. President Jefferson, claimed Smith, would be the last person to abuse the law, even if his party pressured him to do so.

National Intelligencer **(District of Columbia), 3 April 1801**

A letter from Washington, published in the Philadelphia *Gazette* of the 25th ult. merits notice. . . .

This solitary complainer states, that Mr. Jefferson has departed from his professions. That a violent party had prevailed on him, to act a violent part; that he had illegally withheld Justices commissions from persons, for whom they had been made out by Mr. Adams; that he had made improper appointments in their stead; and that he had delayed making his appointments, during the fitting of the Senate, at which the friends of both the present and the past administration were alarmed.

All these charges are recited, that it might be seen, how far disappointment and chagrin could push themselves. Attention is due to the charge of illegally withholding the commissions.—In the opinion of those who know Mr. Jefferson, he would be the last person who would commit, or defend a violation of the law. As President, he is authorized to nominate, and with the consent of the Senate, to appoint "Ambassadors, Consuls, Judges, and other offices"; and he has a power of appointing many officers without that consent. He is to fill up all vacancies which may happen during their recess, "*by granting commissions.*" These are the words of the law, granting commissions. The nomination, the Senate's advising, and a vacancy's happening, are only pre-requisites, or conditions, upon which the right of making the actual appointment devolves alone on the President.

By law, the Secretary is to make out, affix the seal, and then record all the civil commissions of the officers of the United States appointed by the President.

James J. Wilson: "The Alarm!"

Congressional debates on the repeal of the 1801 Judiciary Act were bitterly partisan. Here the editor of the True American *reacted to a* Washington Federalist *comment that praised the oratorical skills of U.S. Senator James A. Bayard during an argument against the repeal of the act on the floor of the Senate.*

True American (**Trenton, N.J.), 2 March 1801**

The attempt now making by the Federalists, in and out of congress, to excite apprehensions in the public mind that a Repeal of the Judiciary Law of last session will violate the Constitution, and produce a dissolution of the Union, deserves the serious attention of the People. The alarm was first sounded in Senate by Gouverneur Morris, a man notorious for his love of Royalty, and hatred of Republicanism: It was echoed by those who followed him on the same side of the question: And Col. Ogden went so far as to insinuate that Congress would be "stamp'd out of existence" by an armed force; and that the blood of our citizens would "flow down our streets in torrents!" This alarm has been reiterated [through] the medium of private letters, and resounded from every prostituted press in the country.

What is the foundation for this alarm?–A law was passed last session of Congress, creating sixteen new Judges, with salaries of 260 dollars a year each. This law was believed at the time of its passing, and has been found, by experience, to be *unnecessary*. The present Congress to remove so large an unnecessary burden from the backs of the people, propose to repeal the late law, and restore the Judiciary system to its former state, when it was proved by practice to be adequate to all the business brought before the Federal tribunal. And *this act*, of repealing an obnoxious law, and abolishing a useless and expensive appendage to our judicial establishment, which a former Congress created, is represented as a violation of the Constitution, and as involving a dissolution of the Union!

The fact is, if our Constitution or Union is ever endangered, it will not be by the Republicans. They have been the uniform advocates and supporters of both, when persecution and prosecution… penalties and prisons… were the sure rewards of their patriotic conduct. They too well know, and to highly appreciate, the inestimable blessings guaranteed to the nation by its present form of government, to adopt or advocate any measure which might tend, in the remotest degree, to its annihilation. And in repealing the law in question, they but exercise a constitutional power, in conformity to the rightful will of a vast majority of their constituents.

What then is the object of the Federalists in exciting this alarm?–OBSERVE:…
While they held the sword and the purse, the power and the wealth, of the

nation, in their own hands, such was their oppression and rapacity, their insolence and extravagance, that they deservedly and entirely forfeited the confidence and esteem of the great body of the American People. This esteem and confidence they despair of regaining by honest means or honorable methods. And they have no chance left of recovering their lost power, but by impeaching the motives and decrying the measures of our present rulers, in order to produce, if possible, a revolution of the popular sentiment in their own favor; or, by exciting some convulsion, when they might rise to honor, power, and riches on the ruins of their country.... Their conduct resembles that of an incendiary, who sets fire to a house to obtain plunder, and to avoid suspicion gives the first alarm.

AMERICANS! Keep a watchful eye upon such men as *Morris, Dayton, Tracey, and Bayard*.... Be not alarmed by their frothy declamation, or misled by their subtle sophistry.... Their past conduct has proved them the enemies of their country; and until a reformation if avowed and evinced, their every act and intention should be distrusted.

A Jerseyman: "For the *True American*"

Many Republicans complained of the Federalists' enactment of the Judiciary Act of 1801. According to this newspaper correspondent, his experience in watching over his state's courts compelled him to write that the new judicial positions were a waste of the nation's resources.

True American (**Trenton, N.J.**), **23 February 1802**

With respect to the expediency of repealing this law, little need be said, for every candid mind, it is presumed, will readily assent to it. That the new Courts cost between one and two hundred thousand dollars a year, is by none denied. That they are unnecessary to the administration of justice is generally believed. In the State of New-Jersey the first court under this new system, was held in Trenton; on Saturday the 2nd of May last; the three judges attended; an address was delivered to the jury; and the court adjourned, without transacting any business, or having any brought forward.—On Friday, the 2nd day of October, the court against met in Trenton; the judges attended as before; an address was delivered from the bench; and the court adjourned without having done any business, or finding any that wanted doing.—In most of the other States, it is believed, they have been equally useless.

As the question for repealing this part of the judiciary law, and restoring the courts to the condition they were in previous to its enaction, is a question of principle, it would be well for every person to divest himself of all prejudice of party or opinion, and candidly decide from known facts and common sense.

Samuel Harrison Smith: "Our Readers May Have Forgotten"

When Marbury and the other Marbury v. Madison *plaintiffs failed to get their commissions from the secretary of state, they turned to the United States Senate for help. A friendly senator thus introduced a motion, calling on the secretary of the Senate to produce the record of the action in executive session on their nominations. An angry debate followed on January 31, 1803, and the motion was defeated. Here, the* Intelligencer *argued against the motion.*

National Intelligencer **(District of Columbia),** **2 February 1803**

Our readers may have forgotten, and if so, we remind them of the fact, that certain individuals were named by Mr. Adams, in the last moments of expiring power, justices of the peace for the district of Columbia. It is said the Senate approved the nomination of these individuals; but that the then President, for what reasons [are] not understood, declined issuing their commissions. So that, when Mr. Jefferson entered upon the duties of the Presidency, he found himself under the necessity, during the recess of the Senate, of making new appointments, or of being instrumental in the giving effect to an exercise of power by his predecessor, which if it did not violate the letter, certainly did violate the spirit and the end of the Constitution. Between these alternatives, he could make no other choice, than the adoption of the former course. But for the sake of harmony he appointed the greater part of the gentlemen nominated by Mr. Adams, notwithstanding their *federal* politics—Those whom he neglected to appoint, fired with party vengeance, immediately made application to the Supreme Court (that *paramount tribunal!*) to issue a mandamus to the Secretary of State, to deliver to them their commissions.

The Supreme Court ought to have refused any instrumentality into this mediated, and we may add, party invasion of Executive functions. But they so far sustained it as to allow a rule to shew cause why a Mandamus should not issue.

Contemplating a decision at this point, the aforesaid individuals some days since addressed a Memorial to the Senate of the United States, requesting permission to obtain from the *secret Executive Journals* of that body an authenticated transcript of the proceedings on their nominations by Mr. Adams. This memorial was taken up on Monday, and rejected, Ayes 15—Noes 12—on the ground that the measure was a party measure; that it was meant as the basis of Executive culmination; that it claimed an act from the Senate, who were the great constitutional Judges of the Executive in case of impeachment, that might indelicately and improperly commit them; that it sanctioned a right of the Judiciary to which they had no legal pretensions; and that it totally abrogated that rule of the Senate which enjoined that the *Executive Journal* should be kept secret.

It would seem, from the recent attempts to disturb the harmony of the legislature, that as much effect is calculated upon from the *ghost* of judicial power, as from the *reality* of it. On the annihilation of the latter, the former appears to have risen from the tomb of the Capulets, and to have stalked into either House, alternately crying *"vengeance, vengeance"*— *"money, money."*

Aaron S. Willington: "Remarks on the Debates in Senate, on the Petition of William Marbury, and Others"

When published several weeks after Marshall's opinion was announced, the author of this essay had not yet received word of Marshall's decision. Oddly, after news reached Charleston, the Courier *did not comment on Marshall's decision. It did, however, reprint the entire opinion in a series published in late March and early April.*

Charleston Courier **(South Carolina), 8 March 1803**

"No court of law on earth (says the gentleman) can controul the legislature!" What then are there no bounds or limits to the power of the legislature? Let us suppose that the legislature (the creature of the constitution) should say we will destroy the constitution to which we owe our being; we have already violated it, lopped off none of its securities, and laid down a precedent for lopping off the rest. We will abrogate all the existing laws—put down the courts—dismiss the judges—and as we are now every day advancing in the work, we will soon amalgamate the executive, legislative and judicial powers all into one body, or into one person. Suppose the legislature were to say, and attempt to do this, is there no resource? No place of appeal? No appointed power to stop them in their work? No arbiter to decide between them and the constitution? If there is not, then we pronounce that the constitution must perish of inanity.

QUESTIONS

1. The assumptions of President Jefferson and his supporters that the non-judicial appointive positions held by Federalists ought to be theirs was a

new idea when they assumed control of the government in 1801. How do you account for this change in attitude?

2. Many have referred to Jefferson's assumption of the presidency as a revolution. To what extent do you think the controversy over presidential appointments reflects such a "revolution"?
3. Explain why newspapers failed to understand the importance of the Supreme Court's *Marbury v. Madison* decision.
4. Identify any recent disputes over presidential appointments to the federal courts that have been controversial and compare them to what happened during the Jefferson administration.
5. Describe and analyze the role of today's journalistic media in communicating information about legal matters. Compare this to the role of newspapers in disseminating legal information early in the nation's history.

Notes

1. *Marbury v. Madison,* 5 US 135 (1803).

2. Scott Douglas Gerber, "The Myth of *Marbury v. Madison* and the Origins of Judicial Review," in *Marbury versus Madison: Documents and Commentary,* ed. Mark A. Graber and Michael Perhac (Washington, D.C.: CQ Press, 2002), 1.

3. Richard A. Samuelson, "The Midnight Appointments," *White House History Journal* 7 (2001): 21.

4. Stuart Gerry Brown, *Thomas Jefferson* (New York: Washington Square Press, 1966), 185.

5. Samuelson, "Midnight Appointments."

6. Donald Odell Dewey, *Marshall versus Jefferson: The Political Background of Marbury v. Madison* (New York: Alfred A. Knopf, 1970), 14.

7. James Callender, *Richmond Examiner,* 6 February 1801.

8. Samuel Harrison Smith, *National Intelligencer,* 21 January 1801.

CHAPTER 12

Aaron Burr's Conspiracy and Arrest for Treason, 1805–1807

S oldiers from Ft. Stoddert in the Louisiana Territory arrested fugitive Aaron Burr on the morning of February 13, 1807, on a muddy road near the village of Wakefield, Alabama. A former vice president of the United States, Burr was running from authorities after standing before a federal grand jury on charges that he had conspired against the government to detach the western states and the Louisiana Territory from the Union. Although the grand jury had refused to indict him, Burr refused to return to the courtroom and fled into the countryside. After his capture in Alabama, Burr was taken to Richmond, Virginia, where he was indicted and stood trial on charges of treason. In the end, Burr was not convicted. Nevertheless, the odyssey that encompassed his travels in the West and his arrest and trial is one of the most bizarre chapters in the history of the United States.[1]

How did such a man end up being arrested for treason? Some historians claimed unbridled ambition led Burr down the path to destruction. Others disagree, arguing that his actions were so misunderstood that he was unfairly maligned. To this day, historians haven't established with certainty what it was that Burr really plotted out West. What is generally known, however, is that Burr was one of early American history's most colorful figures. Rakishly handsome, charismatic, brilliant, and exceedingly ambitious, Burr had many fans and many enemies. Among those who detested him were George Washington, Alexander Hamilton, and Thomas Jefferson.[2]

Born in 1756 to influence and wealth, Burr graduated from college and made a name for himself in the Revolutionary War before the age of 20. After the war, he became a lawyer and entered politics, serving terms as New York's attorney general, as a U.S. senator, and as a New York state assemblyman. In 1796, he was unsuccessful in his bid for the presidency, but in 1800 he ran once again (see chapter 3). After an electoral college tie, the election was put in congressional hands. After its members deadlocked in more than 30 votes, the race was eventually thrown to Thomas Jefferson, with Burr coming in second. On March 4, Burr was sworn in as the nation's vice president.

Nor surprisingly, the ambitious Burr felt isolated as vice president. The nation's framers had confined the position's duties to two primary roles: to take over as president in the event the president was indisposed and to preside over the U.S. Senate. After serving in this capacity under President George Washington from 1789 to 1797, John Adams commented, "The [vice presidency] is the most insignificant office that ever the invention of men contrived or his imagination conceived." When asked to serve in this position, some ambitious men have refused. When Daniel Webster was asked to consider serving as vice president, he responded, "I do not propose to be buried until I am really dead."[3]

To make matters worse, Jefferson shunned Burr, as did many of Burr's former allies and associates. In response, newspaper correspondents followed Burr's leadership of the Senate, wondering whether he would commit to Jefferson or embrace the Federalists. For a time, Burr's conduct was puzzling. The Washington correspondent for the *Gazette of the United States*, for example, commented on an ambiguous tie-breaking vote cast by Burr on one of Jefferson's most important goals—the repeal of the Judiciary Act of 1801 (see chapter 11). On a first vote, Burr sided with Jefferson, but on the second he moved that the bill be referred to committee, where its supporters feared it might languish. The correspondent wrote:

> Col. Burr's vote to refer the bill, for destroying the judiciary, to a select committee has greatly puzzled the Virginia party...indeed his whole conduct is incomprehensible to them. Instead of lodging and boarding (as Mr. Jefferson did when Vice-President) at an Inn, he has taken a handsome suite of rooms and lives in the style of a perfect gentleman. All invitations to drink Toddy, and play cards, at Tunnicliff's Hotel, with the Virginians, have been declined, and he is not upon terms of familiarity with any one of them. It is said he has no great personal respect for the Virginia members, and indeed from what I've seen of them they are not calculated to excite the veneration of such a gentleman as Mr. Burr.[4]

Frustrated, Burr left Washington, D.C., for New York in order to shore up his political fortunes there. If he could not manage to win the presidential election during the next race, he thought he'd run for governor of New York. But once again, he was met largely with failure, and he found himself politically isolated in both New York and Washington.

In April 1805, shortly after his term as vice president ended, Burr journeyed west beyond the Appalachian Mountains and down into Louisiana. Burr was gone until September and visited dozens of towns and friends between Pittsburgh and New Orleans. After spending the winter of 1805–1806 in Washington and Philadelphia, he returned once again to the

West. Rumors of a conspiracy led by Burr began to circulate during his first trip out West. Early in 1807, firmer evidence of a conspiracy began to emerge, and federal authorities arrested him. Finally, in a Richmond, Virginia, federal courtroom, Burr was acquitted of all charges. U.S. Supreme Court Chief Justice John Marshall, who presided, enforced the constitutional requirement that two witnesses must testify against the accused in federal treason trials. This led a few newspapers to speculate that Marshall was a "partner in Burr's treason."[5]

This chapter presents newspaper reports and commentary focusing on Burr's activities during his trips West and through the period up to when he was brought back to Virginia for trial. The first section focuses on the newspaper writings of Burr's opponents, both in the eastern and western parts of the country. Burr left on his first western expedition on April 10 and returned early the next winter. In Cincinnati, he conferred with Senators John Smith and Jonathan Dayton. From there, he visited with Andrew Jackson near Nashville, and from June 6 to 10, he met with General James Wilkinson at Fort Massac, Illinois. At the fort, Burr and Wilkinson allegedly drew up plans to conquer Mexico and the American southwest. By August, rumors of a conspiracy began to appear in the newspapers. The *United States' Gazette* piece included here was one of the first to comment on this possibility.[6]

The remaining pieces in this section followed Burr's progress on his second trip West, which started in August 1806. Early that year, on January 10, the U.S. district attorney for Kentucky had sent his first warning of a conspiracy to Jefferson. He followed this up on February 10 with a communication naming Burr as the chief conspirator. Burr met with President Jefferson on February 22, and in August, he left Philadelphia on the western trip he would not return from until after his arrest.

The chapter's second section presents pro-Burr commentary. Considering the seriousness of the charges against Burr, that he would have fewer defenders than opponents seems obvious. Most of Burr's defenders were from the West, where conditions were ripe for revolt against the federal government. As illustrated by the first newspaper piece included in this section, support for Burr was growing in Louisiana, where many felt the federal government ought to do more to help them stop their roughshod treatment by the Spanish. The borders of the Louisiana Territory were being disputed by Spanish officials, and with little help from the federal government, many Louisiana citizens talked openly of secession. Sympathetic to Burr was James M. Bradford, the editor of the *Orleans Gazette*.

The second piece in this section was written by Herman Blennerhassett under the name "Quetist." Blennerhassett was one of the few who would go on record in defense of Burr. An Irishman who had settled on an island in the Ohio River, Blennerhassett became involved with Burr in 1806. Until Burr's trial in 1807, Blennerhassett's sentiments on the unfairness of the federal government in its handling of the western territories would encourage him to stand behind Burr.

The chapter's final entry illustrates that Burr did have supporters as he stood trial in Virginia. Written and published by the editor of a Norfolk, Virginia, newspaper, in January 1807, the message is clear: Burr would not have conspired to overthrow the United States of America.

BURR'S OPPOSITION

Enos Bronson: "Queries"

Burr traveled through the West from April to late 1805. By summer, rumors that his activities were suspicious began to make their way back East. One of the first newspapers to speculate on what Burr might be up to was the Gazette, *a Federalist print.*

United States' Gazette (Philadelphia), 2 August 1805

How long will it be before we shall hear of Col. Burr being at the head of a *revolution party* on the western waters?

It is a fact that Col. Burr has formed a plan to engage the adventurous and enterprising *young men* from the Atlantick [*sic*] states to come into Louisiana?

Is it one of the inducements that an *immediate convention* will be called from the states bordering on the Ohio and Mississippi, to form a separate government?

It is another that all the publick lands are to be seized and partitioned among those states, except what is *reserved* for the warlike friends and followers of *Burr* in the revolution?

Is it part of the plan for the new states to grant these lands in *bounties* to entice inhabitants from the Atlantick states?

How soon will the forts and magazines, and all the military posts at *New Orleans* on the Mississippi be in the hands of Col. Burr's revolution party?

How soon will Col. Burr engage in the reduction of Mexico, by granting *liberty* to its inhabitants, and seizing on its treasures, aided by British ships and forces?

What difficulty can there be in completing a revolution in one summer, among the western states, with the four temptations. 1st. of all the congress land—2d. Throwing off the publick debt—3d. Seizing on their commercial revenues—4th. Spanish plunder in conjunction with the British?

Thomas Ritchie: "Principles, Not Men"

By late 1806, the newspapers were full of stories about Burr's treasonous behavior. In this piece, Thomas Ritchie asserted his belief that Burr was hatching a plot that could greatly harm the republic.

Richmond Enquirer (Virginia), 7 October 1806

Whether Col. Burr...has enlisted partisans for the accomplishments of his projects...we know not. But, that he has formed, and that he is now employed in executing, a scheme, highly injurious to the interest, the tranquillity, and the welfare of the U.S., we have the strongest ground to believe.

Col. Burr may flatter himself that his plots are covered with an impenetrable shield—he may imagine that a knowledge of his connexions and intrigues, in Philadelphia a few weeks since, with certain Spanish women and Spanish men is confined to themselves; he may, however, be informed that sufficient is known to others to discover that his "busy mind is still plotting mischief;" sufficient is known to open the eyes of the government and the country, and to place them on their guard.

From information recently received, we have been induced to believe that powerful efforts will soon be made to sever the western states from the Union, connect them with Louisiana, and form the whole into a distinct empire with Col. Burr at its head. Whether, if these treasonable efforts should succeed, the new empire will be independent, or a Viceroyalty of Bonaparte, time only will develop.

A Kentucky Gentleman: "Considerable Agitation"

This letter was sent east by a Shelbyville, Kentucky, citizen who was concerned about the anti-federal government organizing going on in his state. Since early 1805, Burr and his friends had been stirring things up in Kentucky and other places in efforts to acquire support for his expedition. By the time this was printed, authorities were poised to strike their first blow at Burr in Ohio.

Richmond Enquirer (Virginia), 5 December 1806

Our state has been in considerable agitation for some time past, owing to the arrival of colonel Burr. He has been for some time traveling secretly through the state, and appears as if he was constantly on express. There are also a number of his friends from New-York, and different parts of the United

States, traveling about in the same manner. There are many conjectures as to their intentions and business; some say that a division of the union (the Allegheny mountains to be the line) is their object; others say, that they intend an expedition against the Spaniards in Louisiana; but the more general, and I believe, the most correct opinion is, that they are planning an expedition against the Spanish mines, and provinces of Santa Fe and Mexico. This much is certain, that colonel Burr and his friends, as also many of our most influential characters here, are for whole days together shut up in close rooms, and no persons but those of their own party can tell what their conferences are about; that provisions of every description are purchasing in every part of the state, sufficient for an army of twenty thousand men. On the Ohio and Kentucky rivers a number of vessels of various descriptions are building in great haste; two brigs and several barges will be completed in a very short time.

Joseph M. Street: "Communication"

To some easterners, the people in the lands west of the Appalachians should all be suspected of unfaithfulness to the republic. This communication reported on the burning of Burr's effigy. Its author explained why this was warranted and sought to assure those in the east that the people of Kentucky strongly supported the government of the United States.

The Western World (Frankfort, Ky.), 22 January 1807

This proceeding is justifed by the ardent emotions of Patriotism felt by the people, and excited from a deep conviction, that the said Burr is a TRAITOR. This conviction is produced from the conduct of Col. Burr himself in these Western states, and even in this town—the Proclamation of the President—[and] his Message to both houses of Congress,...And we have the utmost confidence in assuring our Atlantic brethren, that the idea of a separation is spurned with indignation and horror. That our lives and our property are pledged to support the General Government of the United States, as the safeguard to our personal security, and as the only asylum for oppressed humanity.

Samuel Harrison Smith: "The Conspiracy"

Jefferson's newspaper, the National Intelligencer, *published little about the conspiracy until after Burr's arrest in February. In March, its editor penned several essays where he wrote with assurance about Burr's guilt.*

National Intelligencer (District of Columbia), 13 March 1807

The conspiracy of Burr against the peace and integrity of the union unquestionably presents one of the most interesting topics for reflection, which either have occurred, or which can occur to a free people. Having for its object the immediate, or [eventual] overthrow of our representative system, to which we are indebted for the rare felicity we enjoy, and the raising on its ruins a system of military despotism, it is by no means surprising that the national feeling has been excited to the highest pitch, and that this subject has commanded an almost exclusive attention. Compared to such effects, how insignificant the common contests of party, and even the hostile displays of foreign injustice!

But we are met on the threshold by the jaundiced eye of party, which refuses to see any thing treasonable in the schemes of conduct of Aaron Burr. We are told that he is an honorable man, and that fired by that patriotism which could not brook the degradation of his country, he was only preparing to draw his sword against the aggressions and insolence of its enemy. It is not marvellous that men, who after furiously deposing the rise of this man, suddenly changed their course, and used their boldest efforts to raise him to the highest office in the government; and who, after having failed in this attempt, enlisted under his banners to make him the governor of an important state; it is not marvellous that men, so pliant in exchanging principle for policy, should now become the apologists of him they before so strenuously supported. But the intelligence of the people cannot be imposed upon by so flimsy an artifice.

That Aaron Burr has formed a treasonable plan levelled at the destruction of every ingredient of our felicity cannot be disputed.

Samuel Harrison Smith: "This Plot…Is Crushed"

Here Smith praised federal officials' vigilance and energy in their thwarting of the conspiracy. Since this was Jefferson's newspaper, taking every opportunity to shore up the reputation of his administration was part of the editor's bailiwick.

National Intelligencer (District of Columbia), 13 March 1807

This plot, menacing as it once was, is crushed. By what means? By means honorable to the government, to the nation, and to republican principles. The promptness with which these means have been taken, and the precision with which they have been applied, have not only saved the effusion of a drop of human blood, but have altogether averted those evils which must have ensued from the extension of a conspiracy so multifarious in its object, and so dreadful in its effects, had it proved in the least degree successful.

These means are—
The vigilance and energy of the general government;

The active and energetic co-operation of the state and territorial authorities; and above all,
The virtue and intelligence of the American people.

A Kentucky Gentleman: "The Thermometer of Burrism"

*This colorful letter, printed a few days after Burr's arrest, spoke of its au-
thor's assessment of public sentiment regarding Burr and his conspirator-
ial plans. Its last line referred to the belief that Burr ought to be dragged by
a lynch mob to his death for his crimes.*

Richmond Enquirer (Virginia), 17 March 1807

You have no doubt already received the account of Col. Burr's having
surrendered himself up to the civil authority at Natchez. Col. B. and all those
supposed favorable to his view are universally detested in this country,
where the people are almost unanimous in their attachment to the Union,
and to the administration of Mr. Jefferson. They view with horror the idea of
separation from their Atlantic brethren.... The thermometer of Burrism, as
you may readily suppose, is a great many degrees below 0 here at present.
There certainly ought to be *"an union of all honest men"* to drag this traitor
and stupendous robber to the punishment he so pre-eminently deserves.

Thomas Ritchie: "Aaron Burr"

*Since the crime allegedly committed by Burr was probably committed in
the Ohio Territory, which at that time was part of Virginia, he was to be
put on trial in Richmond, Virginia. This is one of a series of articles published by Richmond newspapers throughout the proceedings.*

Richmond Enquirer (Virginia), 31 March 1807

Aaron Burr,...is now in this city; guarded as a state prisoner... .
This criminal was once the Vice President of the U. States; and a man who
ranks at all times among men of the most ascendant talents of his country.
The crime likely to be alledged against him is the foulest and most atro-
cious that can possibly disgrace the inhabitant of a free country. It is the
crime of a traitor. It is the crime of a parricide in arms against his country;
who has laboured to excite a gallant people against the very best government that ever existed; who has plotted to destroy that great ark of our political safety, our union; in fact, one who has whetted the poisoned daggers
of civil insurrection, to *"levy war"* against his country. In comparison of such

a crime, what is murder; what is the robbery that clandestinely empties my purse; or the felon that boldly prowls upon the highway, and at the same blow deals robbery and murder? If he be really guilty of treason, what is Aaron Burr compared to Eugene Aram? If upon this ground, even, he be acquired, perhaps he may still be indicted and tried by the laws of the U. States for *preparing* an expedition against Mexico; the colony of a foreign state with whom we are now at peace.

Burr's Supporters

James M. Bradford: "There Was a Happy Moment"

Like many others in New Orleans, editor James M. Bradford was frustrated that President Jefferson refused to help citizens of the Louisiana Territory who hoped to take military action against the Spanish.

Orleans Gazette (New Orleans), 28 March 1806

There was a happy moment when the government of the United States, with every plea of justice and necessity on its side, might, at a blow, have expelled the Spaniards from our shore. It required nothing but the sanction of authority, and the generous spirit of the nation, which had left far behind the nerveless soul of the Government, would have performed the business even without a reward.... If the wise counsels of Federal men had been listened to, we should in the twinkling of an eye, as it were, have the rightful possession of these territories, which form a natural and very important appendage of our own.

Querist: "To the Editor of the Ohio Gazette"

In his essays, Herman Blennerhassett laid out a rationale for a separate western country. In this extract from one of his essays, he traced the history of the western country's settlement from the American Revolution on. He argued that the revolution was fought largely for the benefit of the commercial interests of Atlantic seaboard merchants and that, in independence, the fortunes of the people of the West were not being served well by the new government.

Ohio Gazette (Marietta), 18 September 1806

If the opinion I have formed [be] well founded, that the war we have happily concluded by our independence was produced by the interests of the mercantile system on the Atlantic, I have been led, also, to suspect that the political federation of the State comprises within it, in like manner, the spirit of a commercial confederacy; the effect of which, I trust, our penetration and conduct will succeed to direct to further beneficial consequences to our country than are contemplated or regarded by its members.... But how criminal has been every system of all our Federal and Republican cabinets, as regarding this division of the Union, how masked to our citizens, we will now inquire.

A wilderness that hardly had felt the footsteps of civilized man, is pierced in the midst of a foreign war. Our adventurous citizens first encounter all the miseries of the forest, and the savage warfare of the Indians, in prospect of acquiring a patrimony for their children. Their numbers are small, but they maintain their posts, and even march against a foreign foe on their frontier, whilst their brethren are encountering him on the sea-board. After many vicissitudes of hardship and privation, they are joined in the woods by their relatives and friends, who only brought with them, out of the Revolutionary war, the scars and wounds they received in fighting for their country, depending on her gratitude for the recompense of their labors. Thus united, all strive in common against the savages, and participate in the equal prospect of indemnity from the State and the congress. In a short time they discover that those lands which owed all their worth to themselves are ceded to the Union. Indian titles are set up, and extinguished by some trinkets and some spirits, and the real conquerors of the country, are either confined to the corn fields they had planted, or left to pine unknown in some more distant retreats in the wilderness. Such has been the fortune of our adventurers of the country generally, for twenty years, from Pittsburgh to the Mississippi, particularly in Kentucky. Such has been the retribution of our country to her children, who have shed their blood for her honor and independence!

Notwithstanding all restrictions, however, of impolicy and injustice, our country advances in population and settlement. Immense numbers of emigrants from the old States flock to our woods, and unite with us in forcing the face of our wilderness to unbend somewhat of the rigors of its savage features to take upon it the cheering smiles of agriculture. In ten or twelve years our disinterested statesmen on the Atlantic felicitate our delegates on the growing prosperity of our country; profess to them assurances of the fatherly love and protection of the Federal Government; invite them to return into the family of the Union, from which they had eloped by their emigration, so soon as they shall be entitled to readmission therein, by some years probation in passing through the purgatory of a territorial government, when they shall be honored by being permitted to contribute to State and Federal revenues, not through the coercion of an ordinance of congress, but by their own representatives; when, instead of no representative government at all, they shall be placed under two, without paying both of which, they will be neither able to protect themselves against Bonaparte or the grand Mogul, to make laws for the restraint of crimes or the security of property in the woods. Such or similar topics of comfort and admonition have been swallowed by the large ears of our representatives; such they have echoed to their constituents. The people, on their side, illy fitted, by their habits and occupations, for sounding the depths of these speculations, have innocently believed their interests, if not duly attended to, were not at least betrayed. But now they begin to inquire what mysterious complication of circumstances reduces them to the necessity of supporting two govern-ments, with two judiciaries to repress private wrongs, and enforce private rights, in a country where both are few and simple; to contribute two rev-enues to two executives, some of them non-resident among them, and all alive to their own interests; in short, to pay the wages of a double represen-tation, which has hitherto neglected or sacrificed the proper objects of its mission. When we soberly interrogate ourselves on these subjects we read-ily find a clue that will easily lead us out of the mazes of the labyrinth in which we have so long wandered. We shall then behold, in the open field of investigation, into which I perhaps have first entered, the two principal, if not the only, enemies of our rights and interests—ill-founded prejudices of commercial growth and origin in the Atlantic States, against the effects of our prosperity in the western country, and the neglect of that inquiry or in-formation hitherto by our citizens, which should enable them properly to appreciate their civil and political situation both present and to come.

William Davis: "Our Protest"

Not everyone believed that Burr was guilty of treason. The day this essay was published, the Gazette*'s editor published a statement issued by Matthew Lyon, who said he believed the anti-Burr allegations were with-out foundation. Lyon was a rabid anti-Federalist from Vermont who was persecuted under the Alien and Sedition Acts. Here editor Davis made it clear that he agreed.*

Norfolk Gazette and Publick Ledger (Virginia), 7 January 1807

Here we solemnly enter our protest against being supposed to impute to Mr. Burr the mean part of a design of putting the western country into the hands of any foreign power. His ambition and his common sense we firmly believe to be guarantees against that. What could he look for by it but dan-ger and the worst kind of infamy and eternal dishonour. But he has French and Spanish muskets and arms and he has been in close intrigue with the

Spanish embassador [*sic*]; some say even that he corrected and approved of the saucy letter which that intriguer (Yrujo) wrote to the president.—Well—all this is, as it ought to be, taken for granted by us. But the result in our mind is not that he means to transfer that country to Spain, but that he has made Yrujo instrumental to his designs, and received his aid with a private sneer, or as the vulgar saying is, with his tongue in his cheek at him. Be that as it may, the furnishing him with aid, coupled with the former tampering is to all intents and purposes an act of war on the part of Spain, and amounts in essence to a declaration of it.

QUESTIONS

1. Write a character study of Burr based on what you have read in this chapter. What do you think would have driven him West to consider the establishment of a new country?
2. What point is Blennerhassett, one of Burr's supporters, attempting to make in his "Querist" article? Evaluate his logic, exploring the appeals to reason he uses to support it.
3. From what you read here, what, if any, role did newspapers play in this crisis in the early history of the country?
4. Are republican democracies peculiarly open to activities that could lead to treasonous actions by ambitious characters like Burr? Explain.
5. The Civil War took place after people in various states across the South considered and passed resolutions leading to secession. Compare the Burr conspiracy, which might have led to the secession of the Louisiana Territory if left unchecked, to what happened in the South in the years leading up to the Civil War.

NOTES

1. V. B. Reed and J. D. Williams, eds., *The Case of Aaron Burr* (Boston: Houghton Mifflin, 1960).

2. F. Melton Buckner Jr., *Aaron Burr: Conspiracy to Treason* (New York: John Wiley, 2002), 1.

3. Quotes included on the www.vicepresidents.com Web site.

4. *Gazette of the United States,* 2 February 1802.

5. *Balance and Columbian Repository* (Albany, N.Y.), 7 July 1807.

6. Reed and Williams, *Case of Aaron Burr,* 3.

CHAPTER 13

The *Chesapeake–Leopard* Affair, 1807

Although sailing the ocean blue has been romanticized in ballads, books, and movies, a sailor's life was anything but glamorous in the early years of the American republic. In fact, the ships that roamed the world in the eighteenth and nineteenth centuries were harsh and dangerous places. Some of the threats to sailors came from the unpredictability of nature. Others came from conditions onboard British ships. Overcrowding, poor sanitation, harsh treatment—all these problems and more encouraged British sailors to desert the British navy in order to sail on American ships instead. According to naval historians, approximately 1,500 British sailors enlisted on U.S. ships by 1806. In retaliation, the British started a practice called impressment, which involved stopping and searching American ships in an effort to recapture deserters. Unfortunately, some American sailors were kidnapped along with the deserters, leading to rising tensions between America and Great Britain. One thousand American sailors had been impressed by British press-gangs by 1806.[1]

The impressments of American seamen posed quite a dilemma for America's leaders, many of whom hoped to build the nation's mercantile strength while remaining neutral in the long and bitter war that had been waged between England and France. But as the impressments continued, relations between America and England deteriorated. Amid growing tension in the spring of 1806, American sailor and First Mate John Pierce was killed when the guns of the British ship HMS *Leander* "accidentally" hit the ship he crewed on. Americans were shocked, and when Pierce's body was paraded around New York City, they called for war. The editor of Philadelphia's *American Daily Advertiser* responded,

> How much longer is the "Olive Branch" to be stained with this injustice?
> That some speedy measures may be taken to punish such unprecedented

aggressions cannot but be the hearty wish of every American—who loves his country, and who reveres the sacred laws of humanity, and of JUSTICE.[2]

The situation worsened on June 22, 1807, when another incident brought the countries to the brink of war. About 10 miles offshore near Norfolk, Virginia, the British frigate HMS *Leopard* fired on and boarded the USS *Chesapeake*. Four of the Chesapeake's men were captured, three were killed, and eighteen were injured. Seriously damaged, the *Chesapeake* limped back to port. One of the four captured men was a British deserter, while the others were American citizens in the British Navy; two had enlisted and the other had been impressed into service.

Norfolk people were stunned and outraged. According to some accounts, as word of the attack began to circulate, a few townspeople rowed out to meet vessels on their way in from the capes. Norfolk's Town Hall was too small to hold all who wanted to gather to discuss what should be done, so they met instead in one of the town's churches. Resolutions were passed, expressing horror and indignation. Immediately after the incident, William Davis, the editor of the *Norfolk Gazette and Publick Ledger* wrote, "Greatly as we have always deprecated war, conscious as we are that our country will experience infinite distress, we look upon it as degrading beneath contempt if we are to submit it to such an insult." Despite the many calls for revenge, Norfolk people didn't respond with violence. Instead, they waited to see what President Jefferson would do.

As the news spread across the country, Americans everywhere clamored for war. President Jefferson and his cabinet responded through issuance of a formal protest that demanded an apology, full restitution of the impressed sailors, and a promise of no further impressments of American seamen. In a letter to Secretary of the Treasury Albert Gallatin, the president compared the outrage over the *Chesapeake* attack to the "spirit of Lexington and Concord."[3] On July 2, 1807, Jefferson signed a decree declaring that all British vessels should leave American waters. Three days later, the president mobilized 100,000 militiamen, ordering them to enforce his decree.

But Jefferson knew the country was not yet in a position to go to war with Great Britain, a fact that the British unfortunately realized as well. In the midst of American protests, the sailors taken from the *Chesapeake* were tried in a British court in Halifax, Nova Scotia, in August 1807. All were convicted and the English deserter, Ratford, was hanged. In October, King George III issued an order to step up the impressment of British sailors, particularly those serving on American merchant ships. The British were calling the Americans' bluff and winning. Frustrated and faced with no real military option, Jefferson proclaimed a worldwide embargo of American trade in December 1807 (see chapter 15).

This chapter's first section includes reports and essays published in the days and weeks immediately after the *Chesapeake* was attacked. The first was published by the editor of the *Norfolk Gazette and Publick Ledger,* William Davis, who issued numerous reports on the incident and related events. American newspaper editors were universal in their condemnation of the British for the dastardly assault on American life and property. In addition, most advocated that, rather than taking matters into their own hands, Americans should wait for their government to provide them with leadership concerning what should be done to counteract the outrageous incident.

The final selection in the chapter's first section was published later, after the nation had an opportunity to further reflect on the events. According to the editor of the District of Columbia's *National Intelligencer,* a number of questions were raised about the attack, including who should get the blame: Was the British Ministry responsible for ordering the attack, or was the *Leopard*'s commander the culprit?

The author of the pieces in the chapter's second section criticized Jefferson's handling of the attack on the *Chesapeake,* as well as his overall handling of British impressments. In addition, the Federalist authors of this section's two essays complained that Jefferson had failed to provide Americans with information about the affair in his annual message to Congress.

IN FAVOR OF RETALIATION
AGAINST THE BRITISH

William Davis: "The *Chesapeake–Leopard* Affair"

This report from the editor of the Publick Ledger *illustrated the tenuousness of the situation in the weeks following the attack. According to Davis, although the town's people had calmed down a week or so after the attack, the arrival of four British ships caused further aggravation. Immediately following his report, the editor reprinted a letter to the mayor of Norfolk from J. E. Douglas, the captain of one of the ships.*

Norfolk Gazette and Publick Ledger (Virginia), 6 July 1807

The agitation which our town was thrown into by the recent occurrence had in some degree began to subside, and our citizens, waiting in calm expectation for the measures which our government might adopt, when on Friday, a movement of the British ships again excited it. On the afternoon of that day, the *Bellona, Triumph, Leopard,* and *Melampus,* came up from Lynhaven Bay, and anchored in Hampton Roads, in such manner, as evidently proved that they designed something serious. On Saturday a pilot-boat came up to town, the master of which reported that he had been brought to by the *Bellona* (the commodore's ship) and charged with the following letter from commodore Douglas to the Mayor of this place.

His Majesty's Ship *Bellona*, Hampton Roads, July 3, 1807.

Sir, I beg leave to represent to you that having observed in the Newspapers a resolution made by a committee on the 29th ult. prohibiting any communication between His Britannica Majesty's Consul at Norfolk, and his ships lying at anchor in Lynhaven Bay; and this being a measure extremely hostile, not only in depriving the British Consul from discharging the duties of his office, but at the same time preventing me from obtaining that information so absolutely necessary for his majesty's service. I am, therefore, determined, if this infringement is not immediately annulled, to prohibit every vessel bound either in or out of Norfolk, to proceed to their destination, until I know the pleasure of my government, or the commander in chief on this station. You must be perfectly aware that the British flag has, nor will be insulted with impunity. You must also be aware that it has been, and is still in my power to obstruct the whole trade of the Chesapeake, since the late circumstance which I desisted from, trusting that general unanimity would be restored. Respecting the circumstance of the deserters, lately apprehended from the United States frigate *Chesapeake*, in my opinion, must be decided between the two governments alone. It therefore rests with the inhabitants of Norfolk, either to engage in a war or remain on terms of peace. Agreeable to my intentions, I have proceeded to Hampton Roads with the squadron under my command, to await your answer, which I trust you will favour me with, without delay. I have the honour to be, Sir, Your obedient humble servant, J. E. DOUGLAS.

Samuel Harrison Smith: "British Outrage"

The first reports of the incident in the country's newspaper provided readers hungry for details with narratives loaded with facts. One of the earliest reports of the incident published outside the town of Norfolk was issued by the National Intelligencer. *As the Jefferson administration's newspaper, the* Intelligencer *had long supported the president's cautious policy of neutrality. But in this piece, it's clear that the president knew that the country would not tolerate restraint much longer. Thus, editor Smith wrote that the country would at last be united in calling for strong measures against the British.*

National Intelligencer (District of Columbia), 26 June 1807

We give the public the particulars of the following outrage on the American flag, under the influence of feelings, which, we are certain, are in unison with those entertained universally by our fellow-citizens, feelings which cannot, which ought not be suppressed. We know not, indeed, that this savage outrage has a precedent in naval annals.

On Monday last the U. States frigate, *Chesapeake,* of 33 guns, left the Capes, where there lay at anchor a British squadron consisting of three two deckers and one frigate of 38 guns. As she passed this squadron, without molestation, one of the two-deckers, the *Leopard,* put off, and went to sea before the *Chesapeake.* When the latter came up with the *Leopard,* at the distance of about three leagues from the squadron, her commander, Captain Humphries, hailed the *Chesapeake,* and said he had a dispatch to deliver from the British commander in chief (meaning admiral Berkeley of the American station). Commodore Barron, supposing it was a dispatch for Europe, shove to, when captain Humphries sent on board of her, a letter covering an order of admiral Berkeley, to take from the *Chesapeake* three men, alledged to be deserters from the *Melampus* frigate and designating them by name. Commodore Barron replied by letter that no such men, as named in admiral Berkeley's order, were on board, and added that his crew could not be mustered for any such examination by any other officers than his own. This answer was couched in terms of politeness. It was no sooner received than a broadside was discharged from the *Leopard.* The crew of the *Chesapeake* were at this time not at quarters, considering the *Leopard* a friend, and commodore Barron not contemplating the possibility of danger so immediately after leaving the Capes. No other attempt was therefore made to fight her than the discharge of a few…guns, while the *Leopard* repeated three or four more broadsides; when the *Chesapeake* struck her colors, after having three men killed and eighteen wounded.

A boat was then put off from the *Leopard* with an officer who demanded four men. Commodore Barron said he considered the *Chesapeake* as a prize to the *Leopard;*—captain of which vessel said, no—that his orders were to take out the men, which, having executed, he had nothing further to do with her. Thus dismissed, she returned to Hampton Roads, where she now lies. She received in her hull twenty two round shot, her foremast and main mast were destroyed, her mizen mast greatly injured, and her standing rigging and sails very much out.

Of the wounded, eight are considered dangerous, and two have lost an arm. Commodore Barron suffered a contusion, received from a splinter, which is not serious. No other officer is wounded, excepting midshipman Broom, and he but slightly.

Nothing evinces in more striking colours the insolence of Captain Humphries, than his immediate return, after this outrage to the Capes, where he now lies with the other ships of the squadron.

William Alexander Rind: "We Have Never Seen [Such]...Indignation"

Federalist newspapers had long been more tolerant of the British than the Republicans. But when the Leopard *attacked the* Chesapeake, *all restraint was put aside. Such an outrage should not be tolerated, according to Rind, in this comment on the "spirit of the people."*

Washington Federalist (District of Columbia), 3 July 1807

We have never, on any occasion, witnessed the spirit of the people excited to so great a degree of indignation, or such a thirst for revenge, as on hearing of the late unexampled outrage on the *Chesapeake*. All parties, ranks, and professions were unanimous in their detestation of the dastardly deed, and all cried aloud for vengeance. The accounts which we receive from every quarter tend to show that these sentiments universally prevail. The Administration may implicitly rely on the cordial support of every American citizen, in whatever manly and dignified steps they may take, to resent the insult and obtain reparation for the injury.

Washington Morton: "Considering the Present State"

People along the eastern seaboard were nervous about the possibility of additional assaults on American shipping and apparently they had every reason to be. The author of this piece described an incident that took place (a few weeks after the Chesapeake *was attacked) near Sandy Hook, a peninsula in eastern New Jersey at the entrance of New York Bay. Stories such as this added to the general hysteria, especially in the nation's eastern seaports.*

American Citizen (New York City), 20 August 1807

Considering the present state of the United States and Great Britain, I deem it my duty to make public a circumstance which occurred yesterday, about four miles from the land, and about ten miles to the southward of Sandy Hook.

While lying to and hauling the mainsail out upon the boom, the English Packet, captain John Boulderson came along, about one mile to the windward, and fired a gun without shot; in ten or twenty minutes afterwards, she fired another gun with shot, which, from my own observation, passed over our stern about 50 yards…. The boys who were on the end of the boom, employed in hauling the mainsail out over, that they could have thrown a stone to the spot where the shot struck.

As I understand the Packet called at Halifax, and therefore knew the situation of the two nations, it might have been expected that some delicacy would have been observed to our national sovereignty and to our pilots within its jurisdiction, but it appears that they are so anxious to beat us, that all occasions are thought proper and used without ceremony.

My countrymen will make their own reflections upon this subject. Some may think that only one shot fired, and that but 50 or a 100 yards off, is not very serious, and might from courtesy be passed over; while others, recollecting the fate of Pierce, who fell by a random shot, may suppose this notice not sufficiently vindictive: to both be it said that I trust the time is not distant when this and other wrongs from the same quarter will find an opportunity to be nobly redressed. I have only to add my regret that any pilot should be found to bring this ship in after having been informed of the above particulars.

Anonymous: "To the Editor of the American Citizen"

Responding to the preceding report, this letterwriter expressed the outrage of people in the city of New York. The previous year, New York City had experienced its own attack. The "Pierce" referred to was John Pierce, the American sailor killed during the HMS Leander *attack. New Yorkers were so appalled that they paraded First Mate Pierce's body around the city, calling for revenge.*

American Citizen (New York City), 20 August 1807

The wanton outrage stated by Mr. Morton is another proof of what we may expect from the British government, unless, foregoing all considerations but of our sovereignty and honor, we are resolved to right ourselves by resistance. Pierce was killed without our waters by, perhaps a random shot, but the offence consisted in firing within our jurisdiction. For that outrage we have obtained no redress, but on the contrary, upon the back of it the attack on the Chesapeake was committed; an attack which has united our citizens, and excited in all a common sentiment of the highest indignation. It certainly might have been expected, as Mr. Morton justly remarks, that under existing circumstances, the ordinary respect due to a neutral nation would have been paid to us by the commander of the packet. But the same insulting game is again played; the daring outrages of the Leander and of the Leopard are repeated by the commander of the packet. Let it not be said that murder has not been committed; it might have been committed: a cannon seems to have been well pointed, and that the shot did no execution is not the fault of capt. Boulderson. It is to be regretted that Mr. Morton, a gentlemen of intrepidity and spirit, had not with him a force which would have enabled him to chastise this fresh insult offered to our national independence and honor.

Samuel Harrison Smith: "The Responsibility for the British Outrage"

A few weeks after the incident, calmer spirits prevailed as Americans waited for answers to questions that were being raised about the incident and about who was to blame. According to the editor of the Intelligencer, *the nation's leaders were grappling with whether the incident came from the orders of the British Ministry or from the ship's commander.*

National Intelligencer (District of Columbia), 10 July 1807

We are pleased to observe the circumspection of the merchants. If they consult their own interests, or that of the country, they will for a time repress their spirit of adventure, and run as few risks as possible, until an explicit answer shall be given by the British Ministry. As yet it remains a point undetermined whether the late barbarous outrages have emanated directly from the British Cabinet, or are the acts exclusively of subordinate commanders. If they are directly authorized by the Cabinet, then we may calculate upon a scene of violence co-extensive with British power, and for another display of that perfidy so characteristic of its government. Every American vessel on the ocean will be seized and sent into some British port for adjudication, and the courts will take special care, if they do not forthwith proceed to condemnation, at any rate to keep the cases sub judice. Indeed, if the recent outrages do not emanate from the government, it is difficult to say whether they will not, notwithstanding, seize what they may consider a favorable opportunity to wreak their vengeance on this country. We know the hostility of the greater part of those who compose the British administration to our principles, and they may be Quixotic enough to imagine themselves able to crush these principles, or seriously arrest our commercial growth. They may, therefore, under some hollow pretext, refuse that satisfaction which we demand, the result of which will be war. There is indeed no small color of truth in the supposition that this outrage has flowed from the change in the British Ministry, connected with the fate the treaty has received from our government, and that without meaning or expecting war, they have virtually authorized aggressions on us, which they fancied we would tamely submit to; and that however astonished they may be with the manifestation they will soon receive of the temper of the nation, their pride may prevent them from retracting.

Everything is, and must for some time remain, uncertain. In the meantime it becomes our duty to husband all our strength. But little injury can accrue to the merchant from a suspension of his export business for a few months, compared with the incalculable evils that might befall him from its active prosecution. He is, therefore, under a double obligation to pursue this course, arising not only from a regard to his own interest, but likewise from a love of his country. In the day of danger it will want all its resources, and all its seamen. Were Congress in session, it is extremely probable that their first step would be the imposition of an embargo. What they would do, were they sitting, it is the interest and duty of the merchant to do himself. We have no doubt that the intelligence of this order of men may on this occasion, as it has on all former occasions, be relied on.

CRITICISM OF PRESIDENT JEFFERSON

William Coleman: "The *Chesapeake* and the *Leopard*"

Federalist editor William Coleman put some of the blame for the incident on the shoulders of Captain Humphreys, who he claimed should not have taken the four deserters onboard the Chesapeake. *Coleman also argued that President Jefferson's administration failed to assist the British in their earlier efforts to retrieve deserters from the Royal Navy. Still, he admitted, all of this did not justify the vicious attack.*

New-York Evening Post (New York City), 24 July 1807

We say and we once more repeat it, that the *Chesapeake*, being a national ship, was not liable to be searched for any purpose, nor to have any of her crew taken from here. This is ground that ought to be maintained at every hazard. But on the other hand, candor demands the concession, that it was in every way improper in the American commodore to enlist four deserters from the British man of war, knowing them to be such; and whether they were English subjects, or had voluntarily enlisted and received their bounty (this being a conduct long since silently permitted by us), is immaterial. And we say further that if the Administration, on being applied to by the English consul, refused to accommodate the affair, but insisted on protecting the men by placing them under the national flag, the Administration thereby became criminal, and are answerable to the people for their culpable conduct.

Such are the sentiments we hold on this subject: they have been often revised, and are believed to be correct.

The result is that our own Administration are considered as having been to blame; but not so that their misconduct justified the resort to force on the part of the English. On this point, we are ready to say that we consider the national sovereignty has been attacked, the national honor tarnished, and that ample reparations and satisfaction must be given or that war ought to be resorted to by force of arms.

William Alexander Rind: "The Message"

As the months passed, Americans waited with anticipation for official word from President Jefferson on what should be done about the incident. Surely, wrote Rind, editor of the Federalist, *President Jefferson would use his annual congressional message to provide Americans with fresh information. Unfortunately, according to Rind, Jefferson did not do so.*

Washington Federalist (District of Columbia), 31 October 1807

The public mind was never more anxious, and public expectation never ran higher, than previous to the delivery of the presidential Message.

The late attack upon our peace and sovereignty…[is a subject] on which the public feelings were particularly interested, and on which there was a general expectation of much information from the message. Every one calculated on a full and satisfactory development of these several subjects, and relied on the expectation that documents would be laid before them to enable them to judge of their situation. But it now appears that those who so calculated have reckoned without their host. It does not appear to comport with the President's views to let his trusty and obedient legislature into all the secrets of the government. They must yet be kept in darkness, that they may be the more manageable. We therefore do not find in the message so much information on the subject of either our foreign or domestic relations as we before had in the newspapers.—Of all the windy talks which, since his accession to the presidency, he has sent to Congress, this appears to be the most striking example of pompous inanity.

Why are we not told something more about the attack on the Chesapeake, than that merely she was attacked, and that he had sent to England to enquire the reason. We knew this all before. Why is not some official statement of this transaction published? Where is commodore Barron's dispatch on the occasion? The public have surely a right to expect its publication. They have now waited more than four months for it, and their patience is nearly exhausted. When Federalists administered the government, they took care that the nation should be informed of all national proceedings; but now everything is kept snug; and we are left to guess at the situation of our affairs. This does not loom well.

QUESTIONS

1. Describe how President Jefferson reacted to the impressments of Americans by the British, comparing it to how you think American officials would react to similar acts by foreign powers if they were to take place today.
2. What should the role of newspapers be in times of crisis, such as in the immediate aftermath of the *Chesapeake–Leopard* affair?
3. As discussed in this chapter, some Americans complained after the *Chesapeake–Leopard* affair that the president failed to provide them with enough information about it in his annual message to Congress. What role, if any, do you believe a president's annual message to the joint sessions of Congress should play in informing the general public about important foreign policy matters?
4. When political differences arise in America during times of national crisis, should journalists publicize views critical of the current presidential administration? Why or why not?
5. Was it proper for the United States to allow British sailors to illegally jump ship and join American crews? Why or why not?

NOTES

1. C.E.S. Dudley, "The 'Leopard' Incident, 1807," *History Today* [Great Britain] 19 (7) (1969): 468–474.

2. Zachariah Poulson, "An American Citizen," *American Daily Advertiser*, 29 April 1806.

3. Burton Spivak, *Jefferson's English Crisis: Commerce, Embargo and the Republican Revolution* (Charlottesville: University of Virginia Press, 1979), 97.

CHAPTER 14

New Jersey's Repeal of Women's Suffrage, 1807

In 1807, the New Jersey General Assembly passed an act specifying who could vote within that state's boundaries: "Free, white male citizens" at least 21 years old and worth at least 50 pounds could henceforth cast votes in electoral proceedings. In one fell swoop, women were disenfranchised. According to the state's constitution, ratified in 1776, women could vote along with anyone else, including African Americans, who met the law's requirements. Although historians have little evidence about how many women voted from 1776 until 1807, they did routinely participate in the state's electoral process. But this situation was at best an anomaly since in few areas of early American history were women considered equal to members of the opposite sex.[1]

The history of women's involvement in New Jersey politics goes back to 1702, when a woman was among the signers of a document ceding the colony to Queen Anne. The document she signed, however, excluded her and all other New Jersey women from voting. Not until 1776 would the status of New Jersey women as citizens change. That year, the state ratified a constitution that granted any landowner whose property was worth a certain amount the right to vote.

New Jersey women's hold over their right to vote was at best a tenuous one. If political leaders thought supporting the voting rights of this "petticoat band" would help them win elections, they would do so. In the election of 1800, for example, both Republicans and Federalists sought to galvanize their female supporters. Federalists who actively campaigned for the female vote included Alexander Hamilton and Senator Matthias Ogden. By December 16, 1800, the *Centinel of Freedom* printed that these campaigners had so "ingratiated themselves in the esteem of the Federal ladies of Elizabeth-

town, and in the lower part of the state, as to induce them (as it is said) to resolve on turning out to support the Federal ticket in the ensuing elections."

But these same leaders would discourage women's suffrage if they did
not think it would help them, and this is what happened in 1806. In that
year's campaign, politics demanded that women's votes be taken away. The
tide turned against women when the state's Republican Party split into two
groups—one more akin to Federalists—called the moderate Republicans,
and the second composed of the more freethinking "liberal" Republicans.
The fight between the groups was fueled by a division over where the Essex
County courthouse would be located. The northern liberals, who before
had supported female suffrage, won the courthouse fight, but in exchange,
in an effort to unite the party before the upcoming presidential election,
they promised to support the efforts of the moderate Republicans to limit
voting to men only. In the wake of all this, in 1807, the state legislature re-
considered the New Jersey constitution's suffrage clause and passed an
election law, limiting voting to taxpaying citizens who were adult white
males.

The authors of this chapter's first set of readings were not in favor of the
idea that men and women could ever be considered equal. The initial piece
is a sarcastic poem composed by an unknown writer in Newark's *Centinel of
Freedom*. It told of a woman named Briget Bearwell who argued that she and
her husband John should share all "employments, amusements and cares."
The pair, who evidently had recently had twins, could even share in the
feeding of the babies. "While I wet nurse the one, you will dry nurse the
other," she told him.

The author of the second piece, a letter, disputed the idea that it was la-
dylike for women to be rounded up and carried off to vote by the wagonful,
as had recently been done in the area of Trenton. The author of the third
and final piece in this section argued that a woman's essential nature is radically different—that is, weaker and more easily influenced—when compared
to that of men.

The second section of the chapter portrays the citizenship of women in
a less restrictive light. All articles were printed in New Jersey, where the voting rights of women, at least until 1807, may have been conducive to the
publication of newspaper material on women. The first of these was written
by a woman named Clara who wrote of a remarkable event—a July 4 gathering of a group of women bent on celebrating their equality and rights as
human beings. After opening with a paragraph in which she states her view
that this might be the first instance of such a gathering, she listed a series of
toasts raised by those who attended this unusual celebration.

The section's second article is an excerpt from a 4th of July speech that
touted the rights of women. Its author stated that men ought to accept

"Liberty. In the form of the goddess of youth, giving support to the bald eagle." Artists portraying themes of liberty often used images of women in their compositions. Published in 1796 by Edward Savage, this colored engraving portrays Liberty as a maiden in the form of the goddess Hebe. She is offering a cup to an eagle descending from the upper left. At the lower right, beyond a pedestal or altar, the town of Boston is visible, with lightning in the sky overhead. Courtesy of the Library of Congress.

women as equals and then provided a list of women who ought to be remembered for their contributions to society and culture. Among those lauded were English playwright Susannah Centlivre (ca. 1667–ca. 1773), English feminist and educationist Mary Wollstonecraft (1759–1797), and English writer Anna Leticia Barbauld (1743–1825).

The author of the third piece pondered whether or not she ought to marry. It's surprising that this made it into print, since such thoughts were undoubtedly usually kept to one's self in this era. In colonial New England, most people married. By the early nineteenth century, however, the number of unmarried women in America had increased to an unprecedented 11 percent. Marriage gradually became a less routine and more deliberate act.[2]

The following pieces are several toasts raised in honor of women voters, followed by a poem titled "Rights of Women" by an anonymous author who bemoaned society's willingness to waste women's awesome potential. The final piece in the chapter, written by Mary Meanwell on behalf of herself and her daughter Jane, offered a cogent comment on whether the growing community of Newark ought to be incorporated.

OPPOSED TO VOTING AND OTHER RIGHTS FOR WOMEN

Anonymous: "The Rights of Both Sexes"

True equality between the sexes was impossible, according to the author of this poem. For instance, how could both parents nurse their babies?

Centinel of Freedom (Newark, N.J.), 29 December 1801
IN Wollstonecraft's page Briget Bearwell was kill'd,
And her fancy with novel inventions was filled;
But Briget improved on Miss Wollstonecraft's plan,
And projected some small revolution in man.
" 'Tis plain" she exclaim'd, "that the sexes should share,
In each other's employments, amusements and cares,
I'm taught in man's duties and honors to join,
And therefore let man be partaker of mine . . ."
Henceforth, John, she cried, Our employments are common,
Be women like man, and be man like to women!
Here, take this child, John, and I'll keep his brother;
While I WET NURSE the one, you shall DRY NURSE the other.

Anonymous: "Those 'Privileged Fair' "

Republicans, who had difficulties attracting large numbers of women voters, resorted to gathering wagonloads of them to take them to the polls. Perhaps this letter could be interpreted as signaling a shift in sentiment concerning the female vote. Its Republican writer professed to being amused by the situation. Despite this, women remained politically active and parties continued to vie for their votes until 1807.

True American (Trenton, N.J.), 18 October 1802

...whole wagon loads of those 'privileged fair,' who for the lucky circumstance of being possessed of 50 pounds, and of being disengaged at the age of 21, are entitled to vote.... In some townships...they made up almost a fourth of the total votes.... [C]onsider that female delicacy and reserve are incompatible with the duties of a free elector.... Each party will of course muster all its female champions, from apprehension that its antagonists will do the same.

Anonymous: "Man is Nerv'd"

The writers of the day justified the disenfranchisement of women by emphasizing their irrationality and pliancy—qualities considered incompatible with what was needed for political judgment.

**_Genius of Liberty_ (Morristown, N.J.),
15 September 1807**

Man is nerv'd with strength complete,
Woman beautiful we meet.
Man is brave, though death be nigh,
Woman timid and will fly.
Man is great in enterprise,
Woman great in suffering lies,
Man is best abroad displayed,
Woman loveliest in shade.
Man speaks when reason's ray he sees,
Woman to persuade or please.
Man of rough unbending will,
Woman soft and tender still,
Man is bright by science grav's,
Woman by superior taste.
Man judges with facility,
Woman with sensibility.
Man severely just you meet,
Woman beams in mercy sweet!

IN FAVOR OF VOTING AND OTHER RIGHTS FOR WOMEN

Clara: "Female Festivities"

In New York, a group of married women met on July 4, 1800, to celebrate the day. Afterward, a writer named Clara wrote one of her town's newspa-

per editors, requesting that he reprint "their novel deed" and toasts. Several New Jersey Republican editors picked up the New York story, reprinting Clara's letters and the toasts.

Centinel of Freedom (Newark, N.J.), 29 July 1800; *Genius of Liberty* (Morristown, N.J.), 31 July 1800

We, wishing to acknowledge no other lords or masters but our husbands, met on the 4th of July to celebrate in our own way, the glorious and ever memorable day. This is perhaps the first instance in our country of the like meeting, and for that reason you may be induced to take notice of it in your republican sheet. I expect our toasts, if not as warm as others, will be found as patriotic as they are expressive of the genuine sentiments of our hearts. We have resolved to meet the next year on like occasion, and expect to have a considerable accession to our number. The example, for the Ladies you know, are fond of novelty, may possibly be imitated throughout the union. With all diffidence to the gentlemen, we have allowed them the precedence, conceiving that our toasts would not grow the cooler for laying a few days on the shelf. As a brother, I embrace you on behalf of the sisterhood, and am yours, &c. &c.

The Ladies' Toasts

The auspicious day that gave birth to our national independence.
Our fathers, husbands and brothers, who fought for the rights of man, and thereby secured those of the women.
The citizen and gallant soldiers who braved all dangers.—They have obtained their best reward, our love, and approbation.
Our sons, the rising generation.—May they equal their fathers in feats of love and patriotism.
Our American volunteers—May they never turn their backs in love or in battle.
Our daughters—May they have merit enough to win their hearts, and sense enough to keep them.
The female Republicans of France—May they ever have it in their power to reward the conquering heroes of their regenerate country.
A speedy downfall to all tyrants...
The graces—May the fair sex never be without them.
A free and chaste press for to instruct and delight United States.
May all national quarrels end like ours, in amity and renewing of love.
May we never forget what we owe to our persecuted friends and relatives in Europe.
May all chains be soon broken in our country but those of love.
The dear memory of the illustrious *Washington*, who led our countrymen to victory and glory.

The dear memory of all those who fell in the cause of American liberty.

May the curse of the latest generations attend those tyrants who
desolated our fields, and watered them with the blood of our best
citizens.

The infant manufacturers of our country, and may they ever preclude the
necessity of foreign importations.

May our daughters never smile on the enemies of America.

Mrs. President—May she always bias the chief magistrate the right way.

Our public functionaries—May they ever act upright.

Pure hands and sound hearts to the chiefs of departments.

May those who flight the ties of wedlock, never experience the sweets of
love.

Sentiments without coquetry, and attachment with out interest.

The rights of women—may they never be curtailed.

Piety without hypocrisy, and religious without priestcraft.

Single hearts, and silent tongues.

Anonymous: "Excerpts from a Male Citizen's Fourth of July Origin"

*Considering that women who owned property could vote, Republicans at
times appealed to them in their campaign rhetoric. At times, speeches including positive images of women were reprinted in the newspapers, such
as this one.*

Genius of Liberty (Morristown, N.J.), 7 August 1800

Our daughters are the same relations to United States as our sons; we
owe them the same duties; they have the same science, and are equally
competent to their attainments. The contrary idea originated in the same
abuse of power, as monarchy and slavery, and owes its little remaining support to stale sophistry.... Had we no examples of women breaking down
the barrier of the tyrant man, and storming the temple of fame—if we but
reflected that the effects of their degradation recoiled upon ourselves, our
own good sense would induce United States to rescue them from TAMBOUR
and FILIGREE, and the endless concerns of the TOILET, and raise them to nature and philosophy. But to confound our presumption, and forever to destroy our cobweb theories, the history of women is forever obtruding on
our unwilling eyes bold and ardent spirits, who no tyrant could tame—no
prejudice enslave. Besides the heroic daughters of antiquity, our own age
has been blessed with the deep classic erudition of a Damien—the flowery
meandering of a Rowe—the comic wit of Centlivre—the laborious patience
and republican energy of a Macauley—the dramatic genius of Moore, of

Lee, and of Inchbald—the melody and piety of Barbauld—the untaught towerings of Yeastly and Wheatly—the sprightly sallies of Dummer—the unconquerable heroism of Roland, and the invulnerable reason of Mary Wollencraft [*sic*]! Female—Citizens, follow examples so glorious; accept the station nature intended for you, and double the knowledge and happiness of mankind.

Anonymous: "On Marriage"

Most men and women married in the early years of the republic. This piece is unusual in that its author, a woman, pondered whether or not she should follow the path of least resistance to matrimony.

Centinel of Freedom (Newark, N.J.), 21 October 1800

That I hate all the doctrines by wedlock prescribed;
Its law of obedience could never suit me.
My spirit's too lofty, my thoughts are too free,
Like a haughty republic my heart with disdain,
Views the edicts of Hymen and laughs at his chain....
But round freedom's fair standard I've rallied and paid,
A vow of allegiance to die an old maid.
Long live the Republic of freedom and ease,
May its subjects live happy and so as they please.

Anonymous: "Toasts Praising the Voting Woman"

After the inauguration of Thomas Jefferson, numerous toasts were raised across the state of New Jersey praising the role women voters played in his election. The first of the toasts was raised at a celebration in Stony Hill, the second at Bloomfield, and the third at Mendham.

New-Jersey Journal (Elizabethtown, N.J.), 10 March 1801

The Republican fair; May their patriotic conduct in the late elections add an irresistible zest to their charms; and raise the female character in the estimation of every friend to his country.

New-Jersey Journal (Elizabethtown, N.J.), 24 March 1801

The fair daughters of Columbia, those who voted in behalf of Jefferson and Burr in particular.

Centinel of Freedom (Newark, N.J.), 24 March 1801
May their Republican conduct be pleasing and exemplary to their sisters of the Union.

Anonymous: "Rights of Women"

As their votes began to make a difference, signs of women's political in-volvement began to fill Republican papers. This, in turn, precipitated con-cerns about whether women's enhanced status was a good or bad thing. Here, a poet pleaded the cause of newly enlightened women, insisting that, whether men liked it or not, it would be unfair to confine educated women to the domestic sphere.

Centinel of Freedom (Newark, N.J.), 22 September 1801
The rights of Women says a female pen,
Are to do every thing as well as men;
To think, to argue, to decide, to write,
To talk undoubtedly—perhaps to fight;
(For females march to war, like brave commanders,
Not in old authors, only, but to Flanders.)
I grant this matter may be strained too far,
And maid 'gainst man is most uncivil war,
I grant, as all my worthy friends will say,
That men should rule, and women should obey,
I grant their nature and their frailty such,
Women may make too free and know too much.
But since the sex at length has been inclin'd
To cultivate that useful part, the mind;
Since they have learned to read, to write, to spell;
Since some of them have wit, and use it well;
Let us not force them back, with brow severe,
Within the pale of ignorance and fear,
Confin'd entirely by domestic arts;
Producing only children, pies and tarts;
The fav'rite fable of the tuneful nine
Implies, that Female genius is divine.

Mary Meanwell: "For the *Centinel*"

As seen here, some early nineteenth-century women followed community affairs and felt comfortable involving themselves in the spirited public de-bates that at times arose over them.

Centinel of Freedom (Newark, N.J.), 1 April 1806

To the Printer,

I and my daughter Jane, live in one of the back streets. A few days ago, in she hops from broad-street. O mamma, says she, what a fine thing: Newark is to be incorporated—ain't you glad, I'm sure I am. My child, says I, are you mad? What do you mean? Why mama, she says, I have been at Mr. Goldman's, and there was Mr. Lightfoot, Mr. Tyrannize, Mr. Regulator, and a young man whom they called Mr. Quiz, and they were all talking about a corporation, and what a fine thing it would be. La! What a fine market we are to have—streets are to be paved—lamps are to be erected, and plenty of engines purchased—Hush Jane, says I, you am far enough—you don't know a word about it: Those gentlemen at Mr. Goldman's are interested in this business, but you and I are not.—Perhaps Mr. Lightfoot expects to be mayor; Mr. Tyrannize alderman or inspector; Mr. Regulator wants the streets clean when he and his family takes the evening air; and even young Quiz, perhaps, expects to be elevated to the clerkship of the corporation, and thus be rewarded for his prolix essays, frothy sprouting, and profound nonsense.—Confound such folks!—it may suit a few big people in the heart of the town, but such common folks as you and I, my dear, and even many plain farmers, who don't like to be hoppled and chained, as were our fellow citizens in Tripoli, don't wish it, nor are we willing to pay the taxes, that will be exacted to support corporation officers. For ourselves, we are already poor enough—with a corporation, our few acres of land would be taxed double or treble what it now is. And pray what is it for? Why to make pavements and light lamps so that Miss Kitty Nicety, and master Quiz may roam the streets, without dirting her morocco's, or he soiling his jet shining suwarrows.—They won't pave our streets; no, we don't live in broad street.—They won't light our lanes; no, we don't live among quality people. But tho' we do not, nor cannot participate in the advantages resulting from a corporation, yet they will make us pay taxes, merely to accommodate the rich, who live in a particular part of the town, the very persons who ought, and who are able to do it themselves! As to fire, I like child, to see proper arrangements for its extinguishment.—But will a corporation mend our condition; no, it is the rich, who live in big houses, who will reap all advantages, with only bearing a proportion of the taxes; according to my ideas of right, as they are able, so they ought to be willing to provide for their own security; or at least not to compel others to assist them.—There are my sentiments, and as I'm a customer, please put them in your paper.

QUESTIONS

1. Today's history students are often surprised to learn that some women were allowed to vote in early America. Why do you think this information is unexpected to so many?
2. What are the primary arguments of the writers whose work is reprinted here for and against women's rights as voters and citizens more generally? How different are these arguments from those who today argue that discrimination against women is permissible?
3. Why do you think early nineteenth-century printers from New Jersey (who were usually men) would have inserted these articles in their newspapers?
4. Do you think the New Jersey newspapers that printed materials opposed to women suffrage in the early years of the nineteenth century affected the state legislature in its vote against it in 1807? Explain.
5. In one poem, the author writes, "[Wedlock's] law of obedience could never suit me. My spirit's too lofty, my thoughts are too free...." What does this tell you about marital relations in the early nineteenth century?

NOTES

1. Judith Apter Klinghoffer and Lois Elkis, " 'The Petticoat Electors': Women's Suffrage in New Jersey, 1776–1807," *Journal of the Early Republic* 12 (summer 1992): 159–193.

2. S. Mintz, "The History of Private Life," *Digital History*, http://www.digitalhistory.uh.edu/historyonline/uscourt.cfm.

CHAPTER 15

The Embargo Act, 1807–1809

merica needs free trade, wrote a young American poet in 1808 in response to President Thomas Jefferson's Embargo Act, a law that banned all foreign trade. In a poem titled "The Embargo," 13-year-old William Cullen Bryant bemoaned the sad fate of the many Americans that he argued the law was hurting. According to Bryant, sailors, farmers, and mechanics were suffering. Of the first group he wrote, "bold Sailor[s] from the ocean torn" cannot feed their "starving children." On the plight of the country's farmers, he commented, "since supporting trade is fled… cheerless hangs his head" while "debts follow debts, on taxes, taxes pour." And about laborers and craftsmen, he stated, "In vain Mechanics ply their curious art, And bootless mourn the interdicted mart."[1] Bryant called the act the "curse of the nation, source of countless woes, From whose dark womb unreckon'd misery flows." He labeled Jefferson's embargo a "Terrapin policy" that would shut the nation up in its own shell.[2]

Bryant's words reflected the feelings of many other Americans who also hated Jefferson's law. Passed by Congress on December 22, 1807, the Embargo Act especially infuriated eastern seaboard residents who depended on ocean trade for their livelihoods. Passed to counteract trade restrictions imposed by Great Britain and to help the country avoid becoming entangled in the ongoing disputes between Britain and France, the embargo was a costly failure. Historian Louis Martin Sears wrote, "The embargo shook to its foundations the entire economic structure of New England."[3] Not only did it devastate its economy, but it also led to widespread smuggling. Exports fell from $108 million in revenue in 1807, to $22 million in 1808. In addition, farm prices fell sharply, shippers suffered, harbors filled with idle ships, and nearly 30,000 sailors were thrown out of their jobs.

The history behind this crisis started just after the Revolutionary War, when Americans began to build the nation's mercantile shipping industry into a powerful player in the Atlantic community. The fledgling nation's success in the lucrative shipping trades so irritated Britain that its leaders sought to thwart American trade. To do this, they issued a series of Orders in Council to be enforced through naval action against anyone who disobeyed them. In 1793, for example, as they sought to conquer the French colony of St. Dominique, the British ordered America to restrict its trade with France. When America refused to comply, an American shipment of grain was seized by the British on its way to France. In 1807, another Order in Council was announced, this one designed to force all neutral ships to call either at British ports or be subject to searches by British authorities. Added to Americans' troubles were the impressments of thousands of American sailors by the British (see chapter 13). All this led to cries for retaliation, and the June 1807 *Chesapeake–Leopard* affair was the final straw.

By the end of 1807, many Americans realized something had to be done, but there was little consensus as to what it should be. Finally, President Thomas Jefferson and Secretary of State James Madison succeeded in convincing Congress to pass the Embargo Act over the strenuous objections of members of the Federalist Party. President Jefferson regarded the embargo as a moral alternative to war, believing economic coercion would convince Britain and France to respect America's neutral rights. He hoped Americans would cooperate with the measure out of a sense of patriotism. The Federalist Party would have supported an act designed to punish France but did not feel the same about one that also targeted Great Britain. They worried that Britain was struggling for its life and that Jefferson and his Democratic-Republican followers were tools of Napoleon Bonaparte.

The Embargo Act was in effect for 14 months, from December 11, 1807, to March 1, 1809. A few days before he left office, Jefferson replaced it with the Non-Intercourse Act, which reopened trade with all nations except Britain and France. After this second act failed, a third law—Macon's Bill No. 2—was enacted in May 1810. This act affirmed trade with all countries, but it banned trade with France and Britain unless their seizures of American ships stopped.

This chapter includes two sections: The first includes newspaper materials opposing the Embargo Act, and the second features newspaper materials supporting it. The first section begins with a *Boston Gazette* report predicting the amount of future profits that would be lost because of the embargo's trade restrictions. Not surprisingly, the most rabid anti-embargo rhetoric was published by Federalist newspapers in the heart of the nation's shipping industry: New England and America's mid-Atlantic states. Editors in Boston,

New York City, Portland (Maine, at that time a part of Massachusetts), and Baltimore predicted the worst. As time passed, it was clear their fears were warranted, since Americans lost many millions of dollars in profits.

The remaining pieces in this section illustrate the arguments against the embargo. In a *New-York Evening Post* column, William Coleman declared that the embargo would not only hurt America, but that it would also lead to starvation in the European countries whose people depended on American trade for food. Baltimore newspaper journalist Alexander Contee Hanson wrote that the embargo's devastating effects harmed not only those engaged in the "carrying trade," but America's farmers, merchants, and laborers, too. The author of the section's final piece reminded his readers that Jefferson's Embargo Act was passed in an effort to help the French against the British, a position that no Federalist would ever endorse.

The final section begins with an article, published in the *National Intelligencer,* that described the act's many advantages. The chapter's final three columns were published in Massachusetts and New York City—places known for their opposition to the embargo. The first of these, published in a New York City newspaper, supported the embargo because, as it was explained, it showed the rest of the world that America would not be intimidated. The last two pieces, published in Boston, questioned the patriotism of those who so bitterly objected to the president's embargo.

OPPOSED TO THE EMBARGO ACT

John Russell and James Cutler: "Extra"

The Boston Gazette *ran an extra edition on the economic losses that the state of Massachusetts would incur as a result of the Embargo Act. The profits—$25 per capita—earned by America through commerce during the Napoleonic War would be sacrificed. In the end, Massachusetts would bear far more than its fair share of the overall losses—$38 million—or one-fourth of the nation's total losses.*

Boston Gazette, 11 January 1808

Thus, then, Old Massachusets will lose by one year's Embargo, 38 millions being 38 times our whole State Debt. The Interest of this will be 1,980,000 dolls. a year—Boston will pay of this interest, 310,000 dolls. a year—and each town will lose 14 times the amount of its share of the present State tax, only to pay the Interest of one year's loss by embargo.

William Coleman: "In 1793 England Issued an Order"

Coleman objected to the Embargo Act because it would lead to starvation in certain European countries that were dependent on trade for their food supplies. He argued that famine, despair, and violence would be the results.

New-York Evening Post (New York City), 12 February 1808

In 1793 England issued an order to her cruisers, to stop and send into her port, all vessels laden with "corn, flour and meal," bound to France. This measure she justified, by what is called the *right of artisans;* a right acknowledged by all writers on the law of nations, as what may be resorted to in extreme cases, such as she alleged was hers at that time; that is, England, being in want to food, occasioned by various causes, and among the rest by an order which had issued from France a month before, ordering French cruisers to capture all vessels destined to English ports laden with "provisions" of any sort, stopped and fed her own people with the corn, flour and meal destined for the supply of her enemy, *paying for the cargoes so taken.*

This proceeding caused great complaint against England, and was reprobated in the most violent manner by the French party here, with our great Philosopher at their head, as an odious attempt to starve France into submission. Yes, the persons who now govern this country, and their artisans were loud and incessant in their censures, and are even so still against the English orders.

Every one knows that France does not ordinarily depend on foreign countries for a supply of food. And although by scanty harvests, she may sometimes require supplies of grain from abroad, the occurrence is rare, and by the various substitutes, which a fruitful country affords, the failure of foreign supplies is never attended with extensive calamity. This, however, is not the case in countries, which, like some parts of Europe and the different colonies in the West-Indies, are dependant upon such supplies for their food.

Here the unexpected and sudden interruption of provisions, especially when the climate does not allow the establishment of granaries and magazines, must always occasion great distress, and may be followed by the most dreadful calamity that can afflict the human race—FAMINE.

The cutting off of the supplies of a fortress, or of a besieged city, from which the women and children are allowed to depart, is but a partial measure; but the application of this mode of warfare to the whole population of a country, is without precedent, and contrary to the acknowledged laws of war.

If this inhuman practice, then, ought not to be employed between enemies, what shall we say of those who employ it between friends?

Yet, incredible as it may appear, and dishonorable as it will be considered to our national character, the ministerial writers in the National Intelligencer, in commenting upon the "strong measure" of the embargo, do not scruple to confess the malignant satisfaction with which they watch for, collect, and publish every article of intelligence of the scarcity of food in foreign countries.

The people of Ireland, of Portugal, and of Spain, are said at this moment to want food. No supplies can reach them from the North of Europe. The wants of the West-Indies, habitually dependant on foreign supplies, must be still more urgent. Should famine be produced, despair and violence will overturn law and subordination, and whether the negro or the white man will be the first victim, is impossible to foresee.

Our own country, having experienced the smiles of providence in an unusual degree, is overstocked with food and all kinds of produce. But the government, with equal inhumanity and folly, and with a wicked ingratitude to the bountiful bestower of these blessings, forbids us to dispose of them, or any portion of them to those who suffer for want of them: It obliges us to keep them wasting and rotting on our hands, and thus injuring ourselves, at the same time they are engaged in the guilty attempt to starve others.

Alexander Contee Hanson: "Embargo"

As the effects of the embargo took their toll, its critics continued to mount a campaign against it. This writer claimed the embargo had seriously harmed the country's commerce and that nearly everyone had turned against America.

Federal Republican and Commercial Gazette
(Baltimore, Md.), 11 July 1808

The more obstinate and zealous defenders of administration say that the commerce of the country was already annihilated by the French Degrees and British Orders of Council, and therefore an Embargo was indispensably necessary. But such is not the fact. These Decrees and Orders merely affected the carrying trade—the most profitable to successful enterprising merchants, most of whom were carrying on the gambling commerce upon a fictitious capital, but which did not concern the great body of the people. The French Decrees are merely nominal, as the means were wanting to enforce them, and the English Orders had a very inconsiderable effect upon that important and only permanent branch of commerce, which consists in carrying off our surplus produce, and bringing in return the exclusive productions of other countries. It is susceptible of easy demonstration, that if the Embargo had never been laid, that a most lucrative and undenied commerce would have been still left open to the country, and instead of groaning under oppressions and privations we now do, commerce would still flourish, and Europe suffer very little less than she now does. But such demonstrations are becoming totally unnecessary.

Conviction continues to flash upon the mind of the people generally, and we have no doubt that a majority of ten to one in the country are decidedly hostile to the measure.

Anonymous: "Mr. Jefferson Disgraced"

One of the chief complaints of members of the anti-Jefferson party was his affinity for the French, who they fiercely hated and feared. The author of this piece suggested that Thomas Jefferson sought to pass the Embargo Act in an effort to support the interests of France against those of Spain.

Mercury and New-England Palladium (Boston), 14 October 1808

Happily for the country, it will soon be well understood by the world that THE PEOPLE of *America*, do not support Mr. Jefferson in his gallic attachments.—Next to the direful effects of the Embargo Laws (dictated by Mr. Jefferson to pacify Bonaparte), the indecent manner in which the government papers have treated the cause of the Spanish patriots, has tended to wean the people of this country from their attachment to this hypocritical mock-Philosopher.

The people of these States have too much sincere love of liberty, and with such feelings have had too much sympathy for the cause of Spain, not to be disgusted with the contemptuous manner in which Mr. Jefferson and his partisans have treated this interesting subject. The "Contest for Government" we trust will soon be ended.—The vile instruments of the Tyrant are destroyed or driven before the Patriotic Armies of Spain, and eternal disgrace will justly attach to all those, who not immediately under controul of the Despot, had expressed an indifference to a cause SO JUST.—What then can be said of the man who, though at the head of a FREE REPUBLIC, has countenanced and supported the Despotic conduct of BONAPARTE, and has endeavored to suppress the sympathy of his fellow countrymen towards a patriotic people struggling for their National Independence? But he has his reward! Even the loss of his ill-earned popularity at home, and of his reputation abroad....

FAVORABLE COMMENTARY ON THE EMBARGO ACT

Samuel Harrison Smith: "The Embargo"

The Intelligencer's *editor strongly supported the embargo throughout the two years of its existence. He recounted the ways it would help the nation stay out of war.*

National Intelligencer (District of Columbia), 28 December 1807

We have said that the embargo gives no pretext to any foreign nation to make war on us. More may be said. It destroys the temptation to war.

Would war be directed against us on the ocean? There it would find at present but a remnant of our commerce not yet got home from distant voyages, and in a little time, none at all. On that element therefore we shall be invulnerable.

Will it assail us on the other element? There too every tempting object fails. Already our means of defence are forbidding; and the activity and efficacy given to our preparations, by the confinement of our seamen and stores to our own ports, will quickly bid defiance to all the force that can be brought against them. The only spot for which serious apprehensions have been felt is the city of New York; at once the richest and most exposed of our emporiums. But let it be remembered that its resources for defence, are in proportion to those of its commerce. Besides; the preparations already made, with others on foot and in prospect, are placing it beyond the reach of danger. Great as the stake is (much of it by the way the invader's own property), and enemy that counts all the cost of an armament giving even a chance of success, will strike the balance, against the bargain.

Such would be our situation on both elements. What would be that of an enemy, should it be the one most in condition to threaten us? With indefensible territories at our doors; all the wealth that floats on the ocean would be also exposed. There might indeed be a thousand clumsy ships of war parading on that element. But there would be many thousands laden with the commerce of the world, inviting, under a mock protection, the pursuits of our eagle eyed cruisers; swift as the wind; swarming in every sea, and finding a haunt and a home in every port.

War therefore can have no real charms for such an enemy. So far from it that the American nation in preferring an embargo to war, under circumstances demanding one of the two, or a submission to evils greater than either, gives the most signal of proofs that it delights in peace, that the sword is the last weapon it is disposed to employ, and that it allows to interest but little of its weight when put into the scale against humanity.

It is not denied that an embargo imposes on us privations. But what are those compared with its effects on those who have driven us into the measure? We shall be deprived of market for our superfluities. They will feel the want of necessaries. The profits of our labor will be diminished. The supplies that feed theirs will fail. Which of the parties will suffer most? Which will first be tired of the trial?

An embargo will not be without advantages, separate from the immediate purpose it is to answer. It forces frugality in the use of things depending on habit alone for the gratification they yield. It fosters applications of labor, which contributes to our internal sufficiency for our wants. It will extend those household manufacturers, which are particularly adapted to the present stage of our society. And it favors the introduction of particular branches of others, highly important in their nature, which will proceed of themselves when once put into motion, and moreover by attracting from abroad hands suitable for the service, will take the fewer from the cultivation of our soil.... Let the example teach the world that our firmness equals our moderation; that having resorted to a measure just in itself, and adequate to its object, we will flinch from no sacrifices which the honor and good of the nation demand from virtuous and faithful citizens. This manly spirit will ensure success, and success in this case will be our defence, and the cheapest of all defences against a repetition of wrongs which might provoke a repetition of such a remedy. With other injured nations, there may be no choice, but between disgraceful submission or war. A benignant providence has given to this a happy resource for avoiding both. It is our duty to avail ourselves of it; and particularly on the present occasion to demonstrate its efficacy.

Jacob Frank: "Our Situation"

Not all the Embargo Act's supporters were from the southern Atlantic states. A few were from the northeast, such as this New York City writer, who argued that the act should be imposed so that America would receive the respect it was due around the world.

The Public Advertiser (New York City), 8 January 1808

We are now arrived at that crisis, when the first ebullitions of feelings, excited by the suddenness of the Embargo, have subsided, and when we can with more confidence of success, make our appeals of the understandings of men. In all apprehended evils, the imagination is a powerful engine; sometimes magnifying and often distorting the objects of our fears; and our opinions are formed and governed by a species of delusion, which continues until the returning reason assumes its proper empire.

What is our situation? To ascertain this correctly, it is necessary to consider formulations, and the state of collusion with them, in which circumstances, independent of ourselves, had placed us. England, beaten out of every part of the Continent of Europe, left without a single Ally, and confined to the exercise of her remaining energies upon what is considered her *proper element,* now is compelled to direct on that element, exclusively, the whole of that spirit of domination and aggrandizement, which has at all times influenced her conduct toward the other nations of the world.—It is this spirit, then, which has led her to restrain our navigation, to impress our seamen, and to commit those acts of violence and outrage, as well against the law of nations, as against the individual rights and claims of humanity. The union of art and force, too often aided by other circumstances, have at length raised her aggressions against us to such a height that forbearance and moderation would sink into cowardice and national debasement, if they were any longer to govern our political conduct.

France (when we speak of her, we must certainly be understood as including nearly the whole continent of Europe)—France, governed by the mighty mind of one great genius, with exhaustless physical powers, seconded by a constellation of talents and warlike experience, of which the ancient or modern world has no example, and, as it is said, "having that insatiable thirst for universal empire which in various ages has been sent as a scourge to mankind.—This man, wanting only the aid of "commerce and of colonies," to perfect his plan of general dominion, and overwhelm the only power which obstructs it, *is indifferent to the rights of all who interfere with those gigantic schemes;* and needs but more powerful means, *on another element,* to inflict more wide-spread mischief."—Such are the arguments used against France, with what justice we will leave the reader to determine.

These two great contending powers then (with whose mutual aggressions on each other, we have not, and desire not to interfere); *whose infringements on our neutral and national rights* we are at length determined to oppose; and to lay aside a long exercised but abused forbearance, for the assertion and security of those immunities without which we should be unworthy of the rank we hold—must then be taught to feel as well the justice and respect to which we are entitled, as the interest they have in cultivating equally our friendship and our commerce.

With the view of effecting these desirable ends, our Executive and Legislative wisdom have happily united in imposing an Embargo on our external commerce—and that man must be lost to all manly feelings for national character—to individual candor and good sense—who can deny its necessity, or the moderation and disinterestedness of it, as a first expedient.

That it is a "desperate appliance" is naturally felt on its first shock. That mercantile credit, in many instances, should be deranged for a while. That home produce should fall in value. That privations should be felt from the want of many European and West-India necessaries; and that many of our citizens should lose their accustomed employment;—but that individual good should be sacrificed to the public or general weal, is a principle that has been always acted on, since the first establishment of civil society.

Here, then, is the whole case, as it respects our selves:—making these sacrifices to obtain what?—The safe return of our sailors and fellow citizens—of our own ships—and that immense mercantile property which is now afloat in so many parts of the world. These important accessions to our means will be in our own possession when it shall be ascertained how far the folly of the belligerent powers will relax towards us, and when the terrible privations they must suffer by the want of our produce in Europe and the West-Indies shall be felt.

Abijah Adams and Ebenezer Rhoades: "Mercantile Interests"

Adams and Rhoades were among the few Republican newspaper writers in Boston. They claimed the members of the country's mercantile class were putting their own needs over the needs of the rest of the country's population in their campaign against the embargo. In short, they questioned the former group's patriotism.

Independent Chronicle (Boston), 11 January 1808

We often hear the disinterested patriotism of the mercantile interest of the United States spoken of in the highest terms, as though the very existence of the government depended on their exertions. There are not perhaps in the community (with a few exceptions) a class of citizens disposed to make so few sacrifices for the good of the country as the merchants. If they can promote their own interests, the indignities and outrages committed on our government by the British will not trouble them.

William Gray: "Mr. Cushing"

William Gray, a prosperous Salem, Massachusetts, businessman, endured his embargo-related losses without complaint. After a fellow Federalist criticized his lack of public condemnation of the Embargo Act, he explained his position in this letter to the editor of the Gazette.

Salem Gazette (Massachusetts), 25 August 1808

I observe in your paper of Friday last, over the signature "Cuesta," a piece imputing to me base and sordid motives for approving the embargo; in consequence of that, I am compelled to declare to the public FACTS, and leave them to judge how far selfishness has influenced my opinion and conduct.

It is suggested that I set the opinions of others at defiance.

I have presumed to think for myself, and made the Constitution my guide; however mistaken I may be, my intentions are at least correct, nor do

I defy or condemn others for thinking differently; and so far from excusing the administration for submission to France, had I perceived symptoms of submission to that or any other foreign power, sooner than advocate such measures, I would devote my whole property for the support of the Independence of the United States.

When the embargo law passed, I thought it a constitutional measure, and I did not think proper to oppose it. The policy of the measure has been much questioned; yet I think the then existing circumstances rendered it prudent and necessary; as Great Britain had threatened, and had at that time passed (though not officially known to us) the orders of council of the 11th of November, 1807, authorizing the capture and condemnation of all vessels bound from the United States, that should sail for France or the countries of her allies, after orders of council were known in America; which included all Europe, except at Britain, Gibraltar, Malta and perhaps Sweden; at those places very few of those articles which we generally export, are admitted; and I think fewer still would have brought the cost and charges. Great Britain, it is said, would have permitted us, after touching there and paying duties, to go to France and the countries of her allies. Is there an independent American, who would submit to such impositions?

Bonaparte had threatened to put in operation his Berlin Decree which he had however forborne to do, so far as I know, except in one instance, of the Horizon, wrecked upon the French coast; but his severe and tyrannical decree of the 17th December last, called the Milan Decree, passed, declaring all vessels that should be spoken with by the British, liable to capture, which decree almost precluded the possibility of escape from capture or detention. After these restrictions on our commerce, had not the embargo been laid, I think a great part of our vessels, sent for the continent of Europe, would have, I think, been captured and condemned by the British (as their orders authorized condemnation), and probably the remnants would have fallen into the hands of the French. Had these events taken place, the effect upon the public mind would, I think, have produced war; this, added to the immense loss which the Americans would have sustained by capture and condemnation, must, I think, have been a greater evil than the Embargo; though that, taken separately from these considerations is a serious evil; yet, as a proof that it was necessary, I think out of seven vessels, which sailed from this district for the continent of Europe, in the month preceding the commencement of the embargo, not one ever reached her destined port in safety.

It is insinuated that I am growing rich, while others are suffering by the embargo. I have not reaped any advantage from it, that I know of, in any form whatever; those who best know me can say, whether I have benefited others, or taken advantage of their necessity. So far from reaping profit from the embargo, my estate has declined more than ten per cent in value since its operation, which I am reading to demonstrate to lay persons desirous of investigating the subject.

QUESTIONS

1. The Embargo Act, passed in an effort to keep America out of war, was a dismal failure. Identify and discuss the reasons why this was so.
2. The anti-embargo poetry of a very young William Cullen Bryant was printed in pamphlet form in Boston, where it sold well at a cost of 25 cents per copy. Discuss this, comparing his situation to that of young writers today.
3. Some of the supporters of the embargo attacked the patriotism of those who complained so loudly about it. Can you think of other times in American history when the patriotism of those who have spoken against government policies has been called into question?
4. Newspapers were important vehicles of communication during the embargo crisis. Discuss whether you believe newspaper editors helped or made things worse for America during this period.
5. If you were one of those who opposed the Embargo Act, what would you have suggested should have been done instead?

NOTES

1. William Cullen Bryant, *The Embargo, or Sketches of the Times, A Satire by a Youth of Thirteen* (Boston, Printed for the Purchasers, 1808).

2. Ibid.

3. Louis Martin Sears, *Jefferson and the Embargo* (Durham, N.C.: Duke University Press, 1927), 145.

CHAPTER 16

The Launching of the Steamboat
Clermont, 1807

With little fanfare, in the summer of 1807, Americans' ways of moving from place to place abruptly changed. On August 17, Robert Fulton, with the help of his partner Robert R. Livingston Jr., launched a steam-powered paddle-wheel boat called the *Clermont* in New York's Hudson River. Until the *Clermont's* maiden voyage, the primary sources of transportation for people around the world were sailing ships and horses. While these modes of travel were never completely abandoned, their importance would begin to diminish as technology made faster and more efficient forms of transportation possible. And the steamboat ushered in even more profound changes. The launching of the *Clermont*, in concert with other technological developments that took place in this era, would make Jefferson's vision of America as a simple, agrarian republic obsolete.

Fulton and Livingston launched the *Clermont* from its moorings on a North River dock near the state's prison after a brief trial run a few days beforehand. Accompanying Fulton on his journey were more than 30 stylishly dressed friends and relatives, all of whom he later recalled were silent and wary looking. Fulton and Livingston were so quiet about the steamboat's August 17 launch that only one newspaper, the *American Citizen*, announced the event in advance. Nevertheless, a number of largely skeptical New Yorkers were on hand to witness the occasion. In his 1913 Fulton biography, Henry W. Dickinson wrote, "The excitement was intense, the incredulity, scorn, and ridicule that had met him at every turn while 'Fulton's Folly,' for so the boat was nicknamed, was being built, gave way perforce to silence first and then to shouts of applause and congratulation."[1]

The history of the *Clermont* offers a cogent lesson on how difficult it is to recognize the importance of certain events until after they happen. Historian Allan Nevins commented on this in a 1928 book on American press opinion. About the launching of the boat, Nevins wrote, "A New Yorker who wishes to find in old files a real account of the first trial of Fulton's *Clermont* will search in vain. No report worthy of the name was written, the brief newspaper references being meager and unsatisfactory."[2] After the steamboat's successful August 17 run, however, the news spread that something rather interesting was going on down at the docks. In the days following the *Clermont's* first trip to Albany, increasing numbers of curious citizens went down to witness the boat's launchings and returns.

This chapter includes two sections of commentary on Robert Fulton and the new era of steamboats, starting with a body of favorable writing on the boat's inventor and several critical events in the early history of steamboating. The first of these consists of a letter written by Fulton to the editor of New York City's *American Citizen* after the boat's return from Albany. With a successful steamboat trip under their belts, Fulton and his partner Livingston decided to go public with their story. Following this, as illustrated by the section's next two newspaper commentaries, it would not take long for the public's initial skepticism about the steamboat to turn into wonder and appreciation. Within weeks of the *Clermont's* voyage, a regular schedule was worked out between New York and Albany, and within a few years, steamboating spread along the seacoast into the country's far interiors.

The section's fourth and fifth newspaper pieces focus on an especially momentous steamboating event that took place in 1811–1812. On October 20, 1811, the steamboat *New Orleans* left Pittsburgh for its namesake city in Louisiana. Not only was it the first steamboat that traveled down the Ohio and Mississippi rivers to the port of New Orleans, but it also became legendary because of the unusual things that happened during the trip. Other than its crew and a giant Newfoundland dog, the only passengers on the boat on its trip to New Orleans were its builder, Nicholas Roosevelt, and his wife, Lydia. Along the way, the now famous "Great Comet of 1811" was visible to the naked eye; the boat was hit by the Great Madrid earthquake of 1811; Mrs. Roosevelt delivered a baby at Louisville, and a fire broke out on deck one night as everyone slept. Finally, after stops at Cincinnati, Louisville, and Natchez, the boat arrived in New Orleans on January 12, 1812, where it was greeted by a crowd of thousands. The colorful story of the *New Orleans's* first trip has been told in a number of published accounts.[3]

The next three pieces in this section focus on the progress ushered in by Fulton's successful steamboats. The last of the three, written by the *New-York Evening Post's* William Coleman, refers to the 1815 death of Robert Fulton. How sad, Coleman wrote, that Fulton did not live to see how important his work with the steamboat would become in the field of transportation.

The final piece in this section—a brief poem on the steamboat—provides a bit of evidence as to how some members of the public responded to the invention. Even though steamboats could be dangerous, causing injuries and even the deaths of crews and passengers, the boats could also inspire a wistful romanticism.

The chapter's brief second section includes one piece of writing published in a newspaper that was critical of Fulton. As Fulton gained notoriety for his contributions, he was widely considered to be the inventor of the steamboat. But as is seen in the newspaper excerpt printed here, not everyone agreed. On August 26, 1791, Connecticut native John Fitch was granted a U.S. patent for the steamboat after having demonstrated the first successful steamboat four years earlier. In 1787, in front of the members of the U.S. Continental Congress, Fitch launched a 45-foot steamboat on the Delaware River.

Fitch died in 1798 and was generally forgotten until, after observing Fulton's success, a number of his supporters sought to re-establish interest in his contributions. In 1814, for example, Superintendent of the U.S. Patent Office Dr. William Thornton published a pamphlet in which he observed the following:

> Finding that Mr. Robert Fulton, whose genius and talents I highly respect, has by some been considered the inventor of the steamboat, I think it a duty to the memory of the late John Fitch, to set forth, with as much brevity as possible, the fallacy of this opinion; and to show, moreover, that if Mr. Fulton has any claim whatever, it is exceedingly limited.[4]

Historians generally agree today that while Fulton was not the inventor of the steamboat, he should be credited with the achievement of amassing the needed capital and public interest to make the venture a commercially viable enterprise.

FAVORABLE COMMENTARY ON STEAMBOATING

Robert Fulton: "To the Editor of the American Citizen"

Hoping to quash erroneous rumors about the Clermont's *maiden voyage, Fulton issued this brief statement to the press. The "Chancellor Livingston" referred to was his business partner, Robert R. Livingston Jr., who lived on an estate—named Clermont—located on the Hudson River between New York and Albany.*

American Citizen (New York City), 20 August 1807

Sir,

I arrived this afternoon at 4 o'clock, in the steam boat, from Albany. As the success of my experiment gives me great hope that such boats may be rendered of much importance to my country, to prevent erroneous opinions, and give some satisfaction to the friends of useful improvements, you will have the goodness to publish the following statement of facts:

I left New York on Monday at 10 o'clock and arrived at Clermont, the seat of Chancellor Livingston, at 10 o'clock on Tuesday, time 24 hours, distance 110 miles; on Wednesday I departed from the Chancellor's at 9 in the morning, and arrived at Albany at 5 in the afternoon, distance 40 miles, time 8 hours, the sum of this is 150 miles in 32 hours, equal near 5 miles an hour.

On Thursday at 9 o'clock in the morning, I left Albany, and arrived at the Chancellor's at 6 in the evening; I started from thence at 7, and arrived at New York on Friday at 4 in the afternoon; time 30 hours, space run through, 150 miles, equal 5 miles an hour. Throughout the whole way my going and returning the wind was ahead; no advantage could be drawn from my sails—the whole has, therefore, been performed by the power of the steam engine.

James Cheetham: "We Congratulate Mr. Fulton"

After the August 17 launching, Fulton granted the editor of the American Citizen *an interview. Obviously impressed with the inventor's accomplishments, these congratulatory and admiring comments must have helped stir up additional interest among New Yorkers.*

American Citizen (New York City), 22 August 1807
We congratulate Mr. Fulton and the country on his success in the Steam Boat, which cannot fail of being very advantageous. We understand that not the smallest inconvenience is felt in the boat either from heat or smoke....
[Fulton's] Ingenious Steamboat, invented with a view to the navigation of the Mississippi from New Orleans upward [will] certainly make an exceedingly valuable acquisition to the commerce of the Western States.

A New York Spectator: "The Steamboat"

Not long after the Clermont's *first successful trip, Fulton and Livingston put it into regular service between New York and Albany. As late as Octo-*

ber, great crowds continued to watch the boat's launches and returns. One of these admiring witnesses sent this letter to the Post. *Unfortunately, this particular trip was not a success. Near Tarrytown, the* Clermont *ran into a small sloop, which tore away one of her paddle wheels. The steamboat was immediately withdrawn from service and was rebuilt during the winter of 1807.*

New-York Evening Post (New York City), 2 October 1807

Among the thousands who viewed the scene permit a spectator to express his gratification at the sight, this morning, of the steamboat proceeding on her trip to Albany in a wind and swell of tide which appeared to bid defiance to every attempt to perform the voyage. The Steam Boat appeared to glide as easily and rapidly as though it were calm, and the machinery was not in the least impeded by the waves of the Hudson, the wheels moving with their usual velocity and effect. The experiment of this day removes every doubt of the practicability of the Steam Boat being able to work in rough weather.

John Scull: "Steam Boat"

In anticipation of the New Orleans's *launch for Louisiana via the Ohio and Mississippi rivers, the builder of the steamboat was sent on a trial run by its operator, Nicholas Roosevelt. This editor's report commented on its author's view that the boat seemed ready for her long trip. A few days after the launch, on October 25, the paper briefly noted, "The Steam Boat sailed from this place on Sunday last, for the Natchez."*

Pittsburgh Gazette (Pennsylvania), 18 October 1811

With pleasure we announce, that the Steam Boat lately built at this place by Mr. Roosevelt (from an experiment made on Tuesday last) fully answers the most sanguine expectations that were formed of her sailing. She is 150 feet keel, 450 tons burthen, and is built of the best materials and in the most substantial manner.–Her cabin is elegant, and the accommodations for passengers not surpassed. We are told that she is intended as a regular packet between Natchez and New Orleans.

Unidentified Correspondent: "From the *Pittsburgh Mercury*"

Commenting on the launching of the first steamboat to successfully travel down the Ohio and Mississippi rivers to New Orleans, the author of this essay argued that East Coast people ought to be better informed about the potential growth of Pittsburgh as a navigable commercial and mercantile center. The letter incorrectly stated that the boat's builder was "M. Rosevelt & Co." In fact, the boat's builder and operator was Nicholas Roosevelt.

Kentucky Gazette (Lexington), 5 November 1811

The Steam Boat built at this place by M. Rosevelt & Co. proceeded a few days ago on its first voyage. I see it noticed in the seaport papers as an object of importance; but from their remarks I perceive that they are unacquainted with the extent of the commerce that is already carried on here. If several should be fitted out (as is intended I believe) they would be of great importance to this town, and to this part of the country—of so much, that if a non-intercourse be maintained with other nations (as is expected) this town will enjoy the means of acquiring wealth to a greater extent than any sea port town on the continent.

On account of the cheapness of fuel here, steam may be applied with great advantage to a thousand purposes; might it not be well therefore to examine whether there could not be some improvement in the mode of its application.

In the boat of Mr. Rosevelt, as is usual in this country, the steam operates by filling and exhausting the two ends of the cylinder, alternately, which contains the piston; not according to the manner explained in our systems of philosophy, by expansion and condensation.

This new method has been brought to great perfection, otherwise it is in its nature much inferior to the old, because by it the contractile power of the steam is entirely lost. That power is equal to the weight of the atmosphere, or (to make the matter plain to our mill-wrights) it is equal to the power of a head of water thirty feet high, acting upon a surface the size of the piston, which may be two or three feet in diameter.

Unidentified Pittsburgh Correspondent: "Mississippi Steam Boat"

Here, the author commented on the importance of the launching of the Vesuvius, *the second steamboat built and equipped for a regular route from Pittsburgh to New Orleans. He commented on the swiftness of the boat, as well as the favorable effects it promised to have on Pittsburgh's economy.*

National Intelligencer (District of Columbia), 22 April 1814

This morning the steam boat *Vesuvius* intended as a regular trader between New Orleans and the falls of Ohio, left Pittsburgh.... The departure of the *Vesuvius* is a very important event, not only for this place but for the whole western part of the union, and its influence will be felt over the whole of the United States.—In describing it, it is not necessary to use the inflated language, which unfortunately for the credit of our trade, too often renders real facts incredible, or at least lowers their importance by the manner in which they are puffed into notice.

It does not require the ornament of metaphor to impress upon the public mind the incalculable advantage of an intercourse by water, effected in large vessels, which move with certainty and rapidity through an extent of internal navigation embracing a space almost as large as the whole continent of Europe, and comprising in it, the productions of almost every climate. This intercourse, though now only in its infancy, must in a few years, become of immense magnitude. About three years ago a steam boat, of 400 tons burthen was built here, and now navigates the Mississippi, between New Orleans and Natchez. The *Vesuvius,* which, with another boat of the same size and construction now building, is intended to form the second link in this chain of navigation, is of 480 tons burthen, carpenter's measurement. She has 160 feet keel, 28 feet 6 inches beam, and will, when loaded draw from 5 to 6 feet of water....

In order to witness and ascertain her speed, I crossed the Allegheny, and mounting a very capital horse, I endeavored to keep pace with her along the road which skirts the river. But she moved so rapidly, that after riding three miles and a half in nineteen minutes, I gave up the attempt....

The extent of the growing commerce of this town is, I believe, very inadequately understood to the eastward of the mountains. I am informed by one of the most respectable merchants of this place, that the amount of the freight only of his consignments to and from New Orleans, and the states below Pennsylvania, will be this year $60,000—and every day adds to the extent and the facilities of the business carried on through Pittsburgh.... Situated as I am at present, on the spot where the advantages which the public will reap from the introduction of steam navigation, will be very sensibly felt, it is difficult to repress the expression of feelings which arise towards the person to whom we owe it, that this mode of navigation, so often before attempted and laid aside in despair, has become practiced and its principles reduced to mathematical certainty. But it is unnecessary in giving them vent. The obligation which the nation, I had almost said the whole world, owes to him, will be freely acknowledged by history, when the envy and cupidity of his detractors will be remembered only with disgust and reprobation, &c.

Charles Holt: "Wonderful Travelling"

Newspaper accounts tracked the speed with which steamboats traversed various routes. The author of this report marveled that Fulton made the

160-mile trip from Albany to New York City in 19 hours. Compare this to the 30 hours it took Fulton to make his first 1807 trip from Albany to New York.

New York Columbian (New York City), 1 November 1814

The Steam-Boat Fulton, Captain Bunker, sailed from this place on Sunday morning last, after nine o'clock; arrived at Albany in 20 hours; remained there 7 hours; left there on Monday, after 12 o'clock; and got back here in 19 hours, before 7 o'clock this (Tuesday) morning; thus having performed a passage from New York to Albany, a distance of 160 miles, and back again, besides stopping at the different landings going and coming, in *forty-six hours*—an occurrence, we presume, never equaled in this country…. Ten or even seven years ago, nothing short of supernatural agency was supposed capable of effecting what we now see accomplished by the genius of Mr. Fulton. Since the invention of balloons no human contrivance has given to motion and conveyance such speed and certainty, with equal safety and comfort, as the establishment of *Steam-Boats;* by which a person is now carried 160 miles in one day, and brought home the next; and performs his journey in about the same time it formerly required to go to Amboy, Sandy-Hook or any distance of 20 miles and back again. So astonishing and beneficial is this truly admirable American invention.

William Coleman: "Steam-boat Navigation"

A decade after Fulton's launching of the Clermont, *editor Coleman commented on the proliferation of steamboats in the country and the great improvements they had precipitated. Had he lived, Coleman commented, Fulton would have been immensely gratified. Fulton had died in 1815 of complications from tuberculosis.*

New-York Evening Post (New York City), 20 August 1818

One of the most prominent traits of the American character, is a spirit of enterprise, which even under circumstances the most unpromising, seldom languishes, and generally rises superior to every obstacle. The truth of this remark every day's experience tends more or less to illustrate. We seldom find one of our countrymen who embarks in a project or enterprise, the practicability of which is any way demonstrable, who fails in his object for want of resolution; and frequently his ambition and unyielding perseverance enable him to wrestle with difficulties the most discouraging, and to encounter and subdue obstacles which would appall any but an American heart. To this as the primary cause, may be attributed the rapid advances our nation has made in science and the arts, in wealth and refinement, and in the improvement of our country, and the development of our national resources.

We have been induced to these remarks at the present time by the astonishing multiplication of *Steam-boats* in the United States, and the consequent improvement of our coasting and internal navigation. Aside from the commercial advantages derived from these boats, as a means of facilitating intercourse with different sections of our extensive country, the benefits they confer upon travelers, gentlemen of business or pleasure, are incalculably great. It is but about ten years, since the first boat propelled by steam, made a successful excursion upon the waters of the Hudson, from this city to Albany. And now we find them in operation from one extremity of the Union to the other—upon the whole range our sea-coast—in our numerous and spacious bays—upon every navigable stream of any importance—and on the bosom of our lakes. Scarcely a day passes, but we hear of a new launch, either at the east, the south or the west—until at length, our remotest territories, which of late were but seldom, and with the utmost difficulty visited, owing to rugged roads, and the sluggish movements of stages, are become places of easy access, and of fashionable resort. Gentlemen can now travel with ease, comfort and safety, and with a rapidity hitherto unknown in any country, from the remotest borders of the nation to any given point or territory. Even our ferries, often sources of vexation, danger and delay, are at almost every important place rendered commodious and pleasant by these boats. From this city, steam-boats are leaving and arriving from almost all directions daily. Three spacious boats are constantly plying between this place and Albany; two upon the sound, between N. York and N. London—several to different points in New-Jersey; and our harbour rendered lively by the numerous ferry boats passing and re-passing in all directions. Added to this, is the luxury of having boats in readiness at all times for pleasure excursions to the many elegant places of fashionable resort in our immediate vicinity. Several steam-boats are employed upon the St. Lawrence; and a New-Orleans paper received this morning, gives us a catalogue of TWENTY, engaged in trading at New-Orleans, upon the waters of the Mississippi! The total burthen of these boats is 3,722 tons.

Had the life of Fulton been spared, what a period of pride and exultation would the present have been to him. What a rich reward would he now have been reaping, for the disappointments be experienced, and for the toil, anxiety and suffering he was fated to endure, in combating the prejudices of the ignorant and unbelieving, and in struggling against the frowns of fortune. But by the force of native genius, and that unconquerable spirit of perseverance and enterprise of which we have been speaking, he was enabled to surmount every obstacle; and a world, too often given to ingratitude, is now enjoying the products of one of its greatest and best benefactors.

Anonymous: "The Steam-boat"

These lines, according to the editor of the Carolina Centinel, *were inspired by the arrival of "The Chancellor Livingston" at Albany, with the West Point Band onboard the* Clermont.

Carolina Centinel (New Bern, N.C.), 3 July 1819

And well, lov'd vessel, may'st thou glide,
Calm onward without wind or tide,
With steadfast and unalter'd motion,
Along the bright and starry ocean;
For in thy bosom's inmost cells,
Some self-compelling spirit dwells,
And thy majestic form is driven
Along the slumbering sea,
As on the blue expanse of heaven,
Unto eternity.

Anti-Fulton Commentary

Fernando Fairfax: "As to Fitch and His Company"

The issuer of this statement sought to set the record straight as to who should be identified as the steamboat's inventor. Although long forgotten after his 1798 death, inventor John Fitch was the first American to be awarded a U.S. patent for the steamboat in 1791. After Fulton got credit for inventing the steamboat, a number of people sought to set the record straight. This statement, part of an advertisement published in the Philadelphia Aurora, *was written by a member of Fitch's original company. By 1815, however, Fitch's 1791 patent had expired.*

Aurora (Philadelphia), 9 November 1815

As to Fitch and his Company, I may be permitted to observe, from evidence I possess of the most authentic kind, that their spirit of enterprise pushed them forward against numerous discouragements of that early time, when the power of steam itself was so little known in this country that there was not a man to be found in it to make a complete engine and the proposal of navigating by steam was regarded as a *Weird* project rather to be frowned on than encouraged by monied men whose aid alone could thoroughly establish its use. If those spirited individuals spent thousands of pounds in demonstrating their scheme without reaping the profit which its establishment would have insured but when others taking up their invention at a later and more fortunate period were enabled to realize, they are not the less entitled to the favour of an enlightened community, or to the reward of inventive genius.

QUESTIONS

1. Thinking of how little attention newspapers in the early national period paid to the earliest steamboat excursions, what role do you believe newspapers during that time played in the diffusion of technological innovation? How would you compare such a role to that of today's newspapers?
2. What geographical factors made America well suited for steam navigation?
3. What economic developments affected the adoption of steam navigation in America early in the nineteenth century?
4. What may have discouraged the success of steamboat inventor John Fitch in the late 1700s?
5. The federal government played only a peripheral role in the advancement of steam navigation in early America. Why?
6. Why do you think so many Americans were initially so skeptical of the steamboat?

NOTES

1. Henry W. Dickinson, *Robert Fulton, Engineer and Artist: His Life and Works* (New York: Books for Library Press, 1971), 217.

2. Allan Nevins, *American Press Opinion, Washington to Coolidge: A Documentary Record of Editorial Leadership and Criticism, 1785–1927* (New York: D.C. Heath, 1928), 78.

3. For example, J.H.B. Latrobe, a nephew of Nicholas and Lydia Roosevelt, gave an account of the voyage as he had heard it from them as a child. His story was published in 1871 as a document entitled "The First Steamboat Voyage on the Western Waters" by the Maryland Historical Society.

4. William Thornton, "Short Account of the Origin of Steamboats Written in 1810 and Now Committed to the Press" (Washington City: Eliot's Patent Press, 1814), 1.

CHAPTER 17

The Battle of Tippecanoe, November 7–8, 1811

Sound, sound the charge! spur, spur the steed,
And swift the fugitives pursue;
'Tis vain; rein in–your utmost speed
Could not o'ertake the recreant crew.
In lowland marsh, in dell or cave,
Each Indian sought his life to save;
Whence peering forth, with fear and ire,
He saw his Prophet's town on fire.[1]

So begins one of the sad narratives written about the Battle of Tippecanoe in western Indiana on November 7, 1811. Just before daybreak, a band of Shawnee warriors and 1,000 American soldiers met in battle. The Shawnees were led by a man called the Prophet, the brother of famous Shawnee tribal leader Tecumseh; U.S. troops were led by General William Henry Harrison. The battle took place at Prophet's Town, on the banks of the Tippecanoe Creek. Americans often associate the Battle of Tippecanoe with the ascendancy of General Harrison to the American presidency in 1840. Also important was the battle's role in the history of America's native peoples. At Tippecanoe, in the face of the relentless westward push of white settlers, they would lose their grip on the rich midwestern lands they had inhabited for thousands of years.[2]

The story of the Shawnee nation's defeat at Tippecanoe started long before the two forces met there on November 7. After the American Revolution, Native Americans were pushed out of their ancestral homes in the face of the ever-growing desire of white Americans to move to the West and to the South from the eastern seaboard. President Thomas Jefferson pursued an Indian policy that had two main ends: to guarantee the security of the

"The Tippecanoe Quick Step." This music cover is illustrated with a scene of William Henry Harrison leading his troops at the Battle of Tippecanoe in 1811. Harrison became famous for defeating his Native American opponents in the battle, and he capitalized on this success many years later as the Whig Party's presidential candidate in the election of 1840. Courtesy of the Library of Congress.

United States and to gradually "civilize" America's native peoples. To secure the first goal, his government sought to bind Indian nations to the United States through treaties. To further the government's program of "civilization," Jefferson instructed his representatives to encourage Native Americans to adopt European agricultural practices, shift to a sedentary way of life, and free up hunting grounds for further white settlement.

Native Americans were divided as to how to respond to these policies. The Shawnee chief Black Hoof embraced the "civilization program." He and many of his people settled within the state of Ohio and lived as farmers. In contrast, some native leaders took a different course, seeking to form a pan-Indian resistance movement against the United States government. Slowly, a tenuous association of Indian nations developed. The Alliance, as this association of nations was called, included the Shawnee, Canadian Iroquois, Wyandot, Mingo, Ottawa, Chickamauga, Miami, Kickapoo, Delaware, Ottawa, Ojibwe, Potawatomi, Fox, Sauk, and Mascouten. In 1787, the Alliance agreed to draw the line against the relentless push of American settlers into the Ohio River regions, and for a time it did so. But in 1795, after a bitter loss at the Battle of Fallen Timbers, the Alliance signed the Fort Greenville Treaty, thus ceding most of Ohio to the federal government.

The Alliance disintegrated in the wake of this treaty, and for a time it seemed any dreams of a general Indian movement were futile. But within a few years, news of a powerful Shawnee leader with plans for a new confederacy of Indian nations reached American officials. The man they heard about was Tecumseh, a minor chief at the time of the Fort Greenville Treaty. Tecumseh boycotted the negotiations leading to that treaty and refused to accept its provisions. He developed the idea that native people were all "children of the same parents" who owned the land in common. Any treaties negotiated by individual Indian nations, he maintained, were invalid.

Tecumseh's plans for his confederacy included the 1808 establishment of a settlement that would, in a sense, be its capital. The site for the confederacy's new town was at an old gathering place named Keth-tip-pe-cannunk, which had been razed by white settlers in 1791. Eventually, it would be called Prophet's Town, after Tecumseh's brother, the Prophet. Following this, Tecumseh spent much of his time traveling through the northern and southern regions of America, visiting the homes of many different Indian nations; because of this he would not play a major role in the Battle of Tippecanoe.[3] Throughout his travels, however, Tecumseh was adamant in his insistence that Indian people consent to an alliance. As he explained,

> The way, and the only way, to check and to stop this evil, is for all the Redmen to unite in claiming a common and equal right in the land, as it was at first and should be yet; for it was never divided, but belongs to all for the use of each. That no part has a right to sell, even to each other, much less to strangers—those who want all and will not do with less.[4]

Tecumseh's powerful words and influence over Native Americans were alarming to U.S. leaders. General Harrison commented on his leadership:

> If it were not for the vicinity of the United States, he would perhaps be the founder of an empire that would rival in glory Mexico or Peru. No difficulties deter him. For four years he has been in constant motion. You see him today on the Wabash, and in a short time hear of him on the shores of Lake Erie or Michigan, or on the banks of the Mississippi, and wherever he goes he makes an impression favorable to his purpose.[5]

Officials were also concerned about the power of the Prophet. More of a spiritual leader than a political representative, the Prophet preached on the virtues of temperance and the adherence of his people to their traditional values. Having experienced a spiritual awakening in 1805, he claimed to have supernatural powers. Groups of Indians large enough to alarm white settlers gathered around him near Greenville, Ohio. In response, Ohio's governor sent commissioners who ordered them to leave, since the place they were gathering had been ceded to the United States government in 1795's Fort Greenville Treaty.

As Indian support for Tecumseh and his brother grew, Prophet's Town became a center for the further organization of the confederacy and the training of warriors. While Tecumseh was away, the Prophet received as many as 1,000 warriors at a time, administering spiritual counsel and athletic training. White settlers in Indiana Territory feared these gatherings, and in the late summer of 1811, the governor of Indiana Territory, General William Henry Harrison, organized an army of 1,000 men. Harrison and his men knew that Tecumseh was not at Prophet's Town, as Tecumseh had left on a southern recruitment drive.

On November 6, Harrison's regiment arrived from Vincennes. After an agreement that there would be no hostilities until a meeting could be held the next day, Harrison's troops went to a campsite on a wooded hill about a mile west of Prophet's Town. Harrison warned his men of a possible surprise attack. Although Tecumseh had warned his brother not to attack until the confederacy was strong enough, the Prophet urged his men on, and they gave an order to attack just before daybreak. Sentinels were ready, and the troops fought off the attacking Indians. Two hours later, 37 American soldiers were dead, 25 were to later die of injuries, and more than 126 were wounded. Indian casualties are unknown, but their spirit was crushed.

The Prophet had told his warriors that the white soldier's bullets could not kill them. Angered by this deceitfulness, they stripped him of his power, threatening to kill him. The demoralized Indians left the village, abandoning their food and belongings. The next morning, after a sleepless night, Harrison's troops arrived in the village where they found only an aged Indian woman who had been left with a wounded chief. The army burned the town and returned to Vincennes. Three months later, Tecumseh returned to find his dreams in ashes. The confederacy would never become a reality.

This chapter illustrates that newspaper journalists do not always recognize the importance of events until they are long past. At this point in American history, although many reports concerning Indians appeared in the newspapers, there was little discussion about them. While a few white Americans looked upon Indian people with curiosity, most felt nothing but fear and distrust. Some writers implicated the British in the trouble that led to the Battle of Tippecanoe, but most of the blame for the event was placed on Tecumseh and the Prophet.

The chapter also underscores another important point about early nineteenth-century newspapers: Only rarely did they publish reports or essays whose authors were sympathetic to native peoples and their situation in the years and months leading up to the Battle of Tippecanoe. The one piece included here is a transcript of the speech given by a chief of the Wea Tribe, presented at Fort Wayne in northeast Indiana Territory on September 3, 1811.

The chapter's second section consists of newspaper reports that form a rough narrative that describes, from the perspectives of white Americans, the events leading up to and including the Battle of Tippecanoe. All include some reference to Tecumseh, the Prophet, or the Battle of Tippecanoe. The first piece in this section, published in August 1808, was sent from Indiana to Baltimore by an unidentified "Intelligent Gentleman." Especially during this period, it was common for eastern newspapers to print letters and reports on government–Indian relations.

The rest of the reports in this section were published in Indiana and Kentucky newspapers. Elihu Stout, the author of several of these pieces, was editor and publisher of the *Western Sun*, which was published at Vincennes, Indiana Territory. Stout's reports were eagerly awaited by the editors of other newspapers, who regularly reprinted them. Another editor who published frequent reports on what was happening in and around Prophet's Town was Thomas Smith, editor of Lexington's *Kentucky Gazette*.

In Defense of Native Americans

Laprusieur: "Speech of Laprusieur"

Rarely did western newspapers include reports or essays in support of Native Americans. But in the weeks leading up to the Battle of Tippecanoe, newspaper editors were eager to publish anything related to Tecumseh and the events in and around Prophet's Town. According to the Gazette's *editor, this speech was presented by Chief Laprusieur at Fort Wayne in northeast Indiana Territory on September 3. Laprusieur was a leader of the Wea branch of the Miami Indians. His tribe, which lived apart from the Miami Indians, was one of the groups who signed the 1795 Fort Greenville Treaty. In this agreement, the Weas, along with a number of other native groups, relinquished any claim they had to a huge tract of land, thereby making way for the white settlement of Ohio, Michigan, Indiana, and Illinois.*

Kentucky Gazette (Lexington), 8 October 1811

William H. Harrison, governor of the Indiana Territory, listen to what I have to say—you wish to know what I have to say. You now tell us that we are on a wrong road, a road that will lead us to destruction. You are deceived. When I was walking along, I heard you speak respecting the Shawanoe [Prophet]. You said we were of his party. I hold you and the Shawanoe both by the hand; I hold him slack. You have both told me one story; that if I would adhere to you, that my people (the women and children) would be happy.

The heart of the Miami's is good. The Great Spirit has put them in the choicest spot of ground; and we are now anxiously waiting to see which of you tells the truth.

Now, Father—For the first time, your eyes are open. When you cast them to your children, you see they are poor; some of them are even destitute of the necessaries of life. We want ammunition to support our women and children; this has compelled us to undertake our present journey.

Father—We have not yet let you go; we yet hold you by the hand: nor do we hold the hand of the Prophet with a view to injure you. I therefore now tell you that you are not correct when you supposed we joined hands with the Prophet to injure you.

Father—I listened to you a few days ago, when you pointed out to me the depredations of murder committed by the Indians on the Mississippi. I told you that I and my people had no wish to join in acts of that kind. I told you that we both loved our people, that it gives us pleasure when we see them standing round us—that we should deprive ourselves of this pleasure, if we commenced a war with each other, as a war would be the destruction of both parties.

You always told me that our great Father, the President of the United States, has placed you here for good purposes—that his heart is good toward his red children. How then does it happen that our father's heart is changed towards his red children?

Father—you have called upon us to follow the treaty of Greenville. In that treaty it is stipulated that we should give you information, if we knew of any hostile designs of a foreign power against each other. I now tell you that no information from any quarter has reached our ears....

Father—your speech has overtaken us here. We have heard it; it has not scared us; we are not afraid of what you say. We are going on to that country which has been frequented by Tecumseh; and we shall be able to know in the course of our journey whether he has told us lies or not; that all the Indians are of the same opinion that he is. But when we return we shall be able to inform you whether what Tecumseh has told us to be true or not. Now Father, you have heard what I have to say; you will hear it well, what comes from me.

Father—you have told me twice that you were very angry with me. I went to see you, with my warriors with me; when we were sitting face to face and toes to toes, you told me that the Indians on the Mississippi had struck your people; and I said nothing to you. You tell us that you sent a messenger after us; that we insulted your messenger, yourself, and our great father. This is twice you have said you was angry at us—we have looked for the cause, but can find none....

Father—you have told me you would draw a line; that your children should stand on one side, and the Prophet on the other. We, the Miamies, wish to be considered in the same light by you, as we were at the treaty of Greenville, holding fast to that treaty which united us, Miamies and Potawatamies to the U. States.

Father—listen to what I have to say; it is our request that you pay particular attention to it. We pray you not to bloody our grounds, if you can avoid it. In the first instance, let the prophet be requested, in mild terms, to comply with our wishes; and avoid, if possible, the spilling of blood. The land on the Wabash is ours. We have not placed the Prophet there; but on the contrary, we have endeavored to stop his going there. He must be considered as settling there without our leave.

Father—I must again repeat, that you said you should draw a line between your children and the Prophet. We are not pleased at this, because we think you have no reason to doubt our friendship towards you. I have not said much to you, but I think I have said enough for the present; my words are few, but my meaning great. I shall close by requesting you will pay particular attention to what I have said. This is all further, I have to say. I have said it in the presence of your messenger, the commanding officer, your people and all mine.

Blaming Tecumseh, the Prophet, and the British

An Intelligent Gentleman: "Letter...[from] Vincennes, Indiana Territory, Dated July 13"

In a letter sent east, this author commented on the peacefulness of his Indian neighbors, as well as on their new religious tendencies, including their eschewing of liquor. This was published about three years after the Prophet had begun preaching that his people should return to their traditional spiritual values.

Federal Republican and Commercial Gazette (Baltimore, Md.), 19 August 1808

Nothing of moment has recently occurred here. Our Indian neighbours appear to be peaceably disposed. The famous Prophet has fixed his headquarters on the Wabash, between this and fort Wayne. He and his adherents at present disavow having any hostile views. They have abandoned entirely the use of ardent spirits, and declare they are not ashamed to till the ground. The followers of this Prophet are certainly run made with strange notions of religion. He is to be here in a short time; we may then form a more correct opinion of his principles and views.

Elihu Stout: "Mr. Barron Returned from His Mission"

*This report referred to an important principle of Tecumseh's confederacy—
that any treaties formed with the United States government should be
agreed upon by all Indian tribes, not just one.*

Western Sun (Vincennes, Indiana Territory), 10 August 1810

Mr. Barron returned from his mission to the Shawnee Prophet on Thursday last.—He reports that the Governor's speech of which he was the bearer, was received by all the Indians assembled at the Prophet's town, with great apparent satisfaction. They positively deny, that they had any intention of going to war against the U. States—but the Prophet's brother (who appears to be the efficient character among them) acknowledged that they could never be good friends with the United States until they abandoned the idea of acquiring lands by purchase from the Indians, without the consent of all the tribes....

The Prophet's brother was to set out yesterday on a visit to the Governor, he told Mr. Barron that he would be attended by one hundred men—and the Prophet said that a much larger number would come. We understand that the Governor has sent up an express to meet them, and to request that a few men only may attend the Chiefs. This is done as well on account of the expense of supporting them as from a belief, that it would under present circumstances be improper to have so large a number in the settlement.

Elihu Stout: "The Boat"

*This report told of one of the events leading to heightened tensions between
the government and the Shawnee. The boat detained by the Prophet was on
its way to deliver the government's annuity to the Delaware, Miami, and
Potawatomi Indians in payment for lands they had previously ceded in a
treaty.*

Western Sun (Vincennes, Indiana Territory), 23 June 1811

The boat which was sent up the Wabash sometime past with the United States annuity of salt [for the Delaware, Miami, and Potawatomi] tribes of Indians, and a few barrels as a present to the Prophet, has returned without having accomplished the main object of its mission. Having proceeded as high up as the Prophet's town, they halted, in order to leave that part destined for him—the Prophet at first refus'd accepting any but detained the boat until he could have a council of his chiefs, and after detaining them two days, he seized the whole quantity sent for the different tribes agreeably to the *Orders in Council.*—What will be the consequence of this outrage upon our neutral rights by the Prophet, we are not prepared to say—but we cannot suppose our government will tamely submit to so flagrant a violation of their sovereignty.

Elihu Stout: "Indians"

As seen here, tensions were growing in the vicinity of Vincennes as rumors circulated about the whereabouts and activities of Tecumseh and the Prophet.

Western Sun (Vincennes, Indiana Territory), 27 July 1811

For some days past very considerable alarm has existed in this place and its neighborhood, occasioned by the approach of the Shawnee chief, Tecumseh, the brother of the Prophet, with a considerable number of Indians. The hostile intentions which have been unequivocally manifested by this insolent banditti, and the information which has been conveyed from various sources, as well to our governor, as to general William Clark, the Indian agent at St. Louis, that it has been determined to surprise this place, were sufficient to excite the attention of the people, and that of the Executive of the territory. By captain Wilson, whom we mentioned as having been sent some time since on a mission to the Prophet by the Governor, the former was informed that the Governor insisted upon his bringing but a small party with him in his contemplated visit to this place; with this injunction, he positively promised to comply.—He has however violated his word, and he is now within a short distance of us with a number of men which are totally unnecessary, if peace is his object, and which, but for the military preparations which the Governor has made, would be sufficient to sack and burn this town, and murder its inhabitants. Fifty-three canoes, have certainly been counted, bearing from two to ten men each, and there are besides a number that have come by foot; we cannot estimate the whole at less than 250 or 300 men—there are visible what further number may be secreted in the woods to the north of us or are coming on, we know not—at any rate, appearances are such as to require that every precaution be taken.

Since Sunday last Tecumseh has been within 70 or 80 miles of us with his band, and has not yet arrived—what can be the cause of this delay, but to tire us out, and put us off our guard? Every thing tends more fully to convince us of the propriety—nay, the absolute necessity of the defensive measures adopted by our Executive—and we feel confident that the preparations for defence made by the governor, will deter him at this time from making any attempt to put his villainous scheme into execution, or of its certain failure, should he dare to undertake it.

On Thursday last, capt. Wilson was sent up by the governor to meet Tecumseh, and to ascertain the cause of his delay, and to know when he would be down.—captain Wilson returned yesterday, and reports, that after a great deal of evasion and equivocation on the part of Tecumseh, he informed him he would be here today. He had, however, not arrived when this paper was put to press.

Elihu Stout: "The Council"

This report on a recent council involving Tecumseh and Indiana's territorial governor clearly implicated the British in the former leader's efforts to organize a pan-American Indian movement. Accompanying this report was a description of a July 31 gathering of citizens at the seminary at Vincennes for a discussion about what to do about Tecumseh and the Prophet. The group drafted a list of resolutions. The first of these stated the following: "1st. Resolved, That it is the opinion of this meeting, that the safety of the persons and property of this frontier, can never be effectually secured, but by the breaking up of the combination formed by the Shawanoe Prophet on the Wabash."

Western Sun (Vincennes, Indiana Territory), 3 August 1811

The council between the governor and the Indian chiefs closed on Wednesday evening. The celebrated Tecumseh was the principal speaker on the part of the indians. His display of talents and oratory was by no means such as we had anticipated.—In his first on Tuesday, he made an apology for taking the salt, and it was so weak a one, he might as well have held his tongue. In his last speech, he displayed indeed some art and ingenuity; but the veil under which he attempted to cover his designs, was so thin as to be seen through by all who are not wilfully blind. He gave indeed, no satisfaction on any point.—To the complaint of the governor upon the subject of the late murders, and other depredations, and the demand of the two men who had murdered capt. Cole and his party on the Missouri—he replied, that these ought all to be forgiven; that he was about to set out to visit the southern indians, for the purpose of inviting them to join the northern tribes, all of whom were now united, and under his control—that as soon as he effected the object of his journey which he expected would take him until next spring; he would then return, and he would then be willing to settle all differences with the white people; that he would send messages to all the different tribes under his control, to tell them what they were to do in his absence; but if any further murders were committed upon our people, he hoped it would be overlooked until his return. To the question asked him by the governor, whether it was the intention of the indians to do any mischief to those who have, or who shall settle in the new purchase, he replied, that that tract ought not to be settled until his return: because a number of indians would come to settle at his town this fall: that they intended to use that tract as a hunting ground, and that the white people would probably loose their cattle and hogs.

Stript of the thin disguise with which he attempted to cover his intentions, the plain English of what he said appeared to be this—"In obedience to the orders of my mother, the British, I have now succeeded in uniting the northern tribes of indians in a confederacy for the purpose of attacking the United States, and I am now on my way to stir up the southern indians; I wish you however to remain perfectly quiet until I return—do not attempt to obtain any satisfaction for the injuries you may sustain, or for such as you have already received; I am not yet quite ready to resist you—when I return, I shall be completely so, and then you may do as you please." We hope, however, the government will take swift and immediate measures for breaking up and effective arrangements for breaking up this confederacy.

Thomas Smith: "The Indians and the British"

People in the area of Lexington, Kentucky, were eager for word from Vincennes about what was happening. As stated herein by editor Smith, the unpredictability of mail delivery could lead to great frustration. But Smith had other sources who had told him that General Harrison was planning a campaign against the Shawnee at Prophet's Town.

Kentucky Gazette (Lexington), 27 August 1811

We were disappointed yesterday in receiving intelligence from the quarter of Indian disturbances.—There was no mail from Vincennes. But from another source, we are enabled to state, that Governor Harrison is preparing to commence a campaign against the hostile tribes under the influence of the Prophet.—Volunteer companies have been raised in Illinois and Indiana territories, and probably in the state of Ohio—4 or 500 U.S. troops under the command of Col. Boyd and Maj. Floyd, will march from New-Port garrison, and a number of volunteers from Lexington, will set out in a few days—the whole to proceed to Vincennes. So it seems our affairs are fast approaching to a crisis in different quarters at the same moment.

It would seem from the attitude of the Indians—the combination of the Northern and Southern tribes—the conference at Malden—the circumstances attendant on the mission of Foster—the late arrival of regular troops in Canada, that the British ministry were planning "*another expedition.*" What success they may calculate upon, is not our immediate province to enquire; but certain it is, if decided steps had not been taken by our government, our frontier settlements would have been much endangered by their allies—*the Indians.*

From the friendly course pursued by Mr. Jefferson, toward our red neighbors, and which has been followed by Mr. Madison, we had supposed the Indians would never more treat us otherwise than as brethren. But we have been mistaken—British intrigue and British gold, it seems, has had greater influence with them of late than American justice and benevolence. Be it so; but let England not hide herself any longer behind the curtain—let her appear to the world as she is, the instigator and protector of savage cruelties; and then real Americans will call into action that spirit of necessary resistance which so eminently distinguished their fathers in the wars of the revolution.

We have in our possession information which proves beyond doubt, the late disturbances to be owing to the too successful intrigues of British emissaries with the Indians.

Anonymous: "St. Louis, August 14"

Scattered throughout the published letters and reports on what was happening in the Indiana Territory were accusations against the British in Canada, who were thought to be stirring up the Native American leaders and their people against white Americans.

Kentucky Gazette (Lexington), 27 August 1811

From Prairie du Chien we learn that emissaries from Canada have and are now very busy tampering with the Indians.—Unfortunately there are no goods placed there to relieve their wants, and the Factory Store at Fort Bellevue is too remote for them, having to pass nations with whom they are often at war. Last spring members of the Scioux, &tc. came to the Prairie to procure goods, but were disappointed. Boulvin being at the Federal City, the Mackanaw traders commenced holding councils with them. They told them that "their American Father was poor, and was supplied with such goods as they sometimes received through him, from their English Father, who always remembered their wants and necessities. That the Americans were daily cheating them out of their lands, and if they did not immediately attack and drive them away they would not have a meeting place on this earth." One of these fellows cried, sobbed and shed tears as he spoke (in council!) of the conduct of the Americans. He strenuously advised them to go to Canada, where they would be amply provided with clothing, arms and ammunition, and be placed in a situation which would enable them to destroy the Americans.— We sincerely hope that the governors of these territories will be circumspect in giving licenses to these cut throats in the shape of traders; and we promise that we shall from time to time, procure the names of those Canadians who are in the habit of corrupting the Indians, so that if they should be caught within the settlements, they may be made examples of.

Thomas Smith: "Communication"

By early September, rumors had spread that hostile Native Americans were on their way to Vincennes. Indiana people were desperate for help, resulting in a call for help from Indiana Territory Governor Harrison to Kentucky Governor Scott.

Kentucky Gazette (Lexington), 3 September 1811

The Post-rider from Frankfort stated on yesterday morning, that an officer arrived at that place on Sunday evening, with a dispatch from governor Harrison to governor Scott.—He informed us it was rumoured in Frankfort as the purport of the communication, that the Indians had embodied and were proceeding to Vincennes. If a call has been made on the governor of Kentucky for assistance, it has not reached us—but should it be the case, it will no doubt be attended to with the greatest promptness by the governor, and most willingly obeyed by the citizens, who have always been ready to volunteer and march, when they were needed. And as we stated last week, a few volunteers from this neighbourhood will offer their services, whether they are called on or not.

Thomas Smith: "We Have Received No Intelligence"

Impatiently awaiting news of events on or near the Wabash, this editor once again reported with frustration on the receipt of no communication.

Kentucky Gazette (Lexington), 1 October 1811

We have received no intelligence from the Indians for several weeks. We presume nothing of importance has occurred.—Governor Harrison was to have set out from Vincennes on this day to the Wabash for the purpose of building a fort at or near the Prophet's town.

Anonymous: "From the Wabash"

By mid-October, news reached Kentucky that General Harrison had made progress in the construction of a fort near Prophet's Town. In addition, the governor of Kentucky had sent two companies of riflemen to assist in any future hostilities.

Kentucky Gazette (Lexington), 23 October 1811

We have received verbal intelligence from the expedition against the Indians.

Governor Harrison was building a fort about 40 miles on this side the Prophet's town, the Indians near the encampment—in number about 12 or 13 hundred. They manifested an extremely hostile disposition and refrained making an attack only on account of the favourable situation in which Governor Harrison had placed his forces. One of the governor's centinels had been shot at his post. In compliance with governor Harrison's request to Gen. Wells of this state, two companies of mounted riflemen have been raised and will march as volunteers to join that campaign in a few days from Jefferson county.

Contrary to our expectation, and we believe the apprehension of governor Harrison, the Indians are determined to make every resistance in their power. It was believed, that on the appearance of an armed force on the Wabash, the idle menaces of the savages, and the ridiculous views of their infatuated leader, under the influence and counsel of our good friends, the BRITISH would be awed into silence or totally abandoned. But the true situation of the business now seems different—a force equal to governor Harrison's has been collected—and the same warlike spirit prevails among the Indians as formerly. Surrounded as governor Harrison's forces are, much anxiety has been excited for the ultimate success of the expedition.

Anonymous: "St. Louis, October 12"

This correspondent advised that American officials in "one vigorous movement" should take care of those Indians who continued to keep white settlers "in a state of inquietude and alarm."

Kentucky Gazette (Lexington), 29 October 1811

We may learn from the errors of Braddock and St. Clair, that an Indian enemy is never to be despised. It is true he may never be able to drive us from the country, or obtain any final advantage, but it is in his power to inflict upon us, serious injury; he would deal death and destruction in his inroads on our frontier or at least, keep us in a state of inquietude and alarm.

One vigorous movement will be sufficient, however, to put a stop to these things for the future; and the present is the period when it should be made. To those who are not inclined to look upon this matter, with that seriousness it merits, ought to be sufficient, to recollect, that at the bottom of it, there is a powerful nation; that the instrument it uses, consists of an artful impostor who possesses an unlimited power over the superstitious minds of the Indians, and one of the bravest, and most active Indian warriors that ever appeared on this continent.

Thomas Smith: "We Have Received No Accounts"

By early November, newspaper reports predicted that hostilities would soon commence on or near the Wabash River in western Indiana Territory. Editor Smith worried that the size of Harrison's forces might be overcome by a larger Indian force well armed by the British.

Kentucky Gazette (Lexington), 5 November 1811

We have received no accounts from the Wabash, since the last statements; but we have no doubt we shall soon be informed of the commencement of hostilities. From the strength of Gov. Harrison's forces, we do not anticipate a very favourable result.—If a combination has taken place between the Northern and Southern tribes, as seems most probable, the odds are against him. The *Reporter* of Saturday last says, Governor Harrison has ascertained that the presents from the British to the Indians for the last season, were unusually great in arms, ammunition, &tc.

Editor: "The Blow Is Struck"

It appears from this report that a special edition of the Gazette *came out in response to the news that the war between the Shawnee and Governor Harrison's troops had begun. It's unclear, according to newspaper historian Clarence S. Brigham, just who the editor of the* Gazette *was at this time. The paper was started by Joseph Charless in 1807.*[6]

Louisville Gazette, and Western Advertiser (Kentucky), 16 November 1811

We stop the press to announce the [important] intelligence brought by Dr. J. M. Scott, who arrived this evening directly from Vincennes. This gentleman has politely favoured us with the following particulars of a Battle between the troops under Gov. Harrison and the Indians. Capt. Dubois of Vincennes, arrived at that place express from the Governor; states, that on the 7th inst. the Prophet and his party consisting of about

700 Indians, after professing friendship on the sixth in the evening, that they would the next morning come into the camp of Gov. Harrison with a white flag, and take him by the hand in friendship, made an attack on the army about 4 o'clock in the morning of the 7th, and continue the battle until 6, when they were put to flight. There were left dead on the ground about fifty or sixty Indians, with some wounded. It is supposed they suffered considerably in their wounded; but the number is not known, as the Indians are in the habit of carrying them off, together with as many of their dead as possible.

The Governor sustained an injury as report says, of about one hundred and twenty. Some say there were 160 or 70 killed and wounded.... That the Prophet's town was burnt on the morning of the 8th inst.

Thomas Smith: "British-Savage War!—From the Wabash"

It took more than a week for the people of Lexington, Kentucky, to receive news of the Battle of Tippecanoe. Editor Smith put much of the blame for the battle on the British—and not just on their Canadian agents, but on the English Cabinet itself.

Kentucky Gazette (Lexington), 19 November 1811

We have alternately indulged the hope that our differences with the Indians would have been amicably terminated; and again from various circumstances, such as the conferences of the Indians with our good friends the British, at Malden, the presents there made to them, and the intrigues which the British have uniformly had with them whenever any hostile attitude was taken by that government towards us, together with other *facts*—we have believed that war would ensue. Well, war we now have; and when we consider that the blow is struck in the western woods at the same moment that Great Britain is sweeping our vessels off the ocean, and her minister is making demands which he knows cannot possibly be indulged or acceded to—we cannot but consider these events as proceedings from one common source—the English Cabinet. Such has been her career from the beginning of the Revolution to this day; she has always been the first to "light the savage fires—the Indians are but her tools—her allies—her agents. We hope therefore to witness no more "protracted moderation" against such "inflexible hostility." Will Timothy Pickering's friends yet continue to repeat with him that Great Britain has done us "no essential injury?"

QUESTIONS

1. What were President Jefferson's plans for Native Americans, and how did they react? Do you think they were justified in responding in the ways they did?
2. Native American people had no newspapers of their own during this time—their first was the *Cherokee Phoenix*, started in 1827. How do you think they communicated across great expanses of territory in the years leading up to Tippecanoe?
3. The Shawnee, led by Tecumseh, believed the earth belonged to everyone and that to sell it would be like trying to sell the air, the clouds, or the ocean. Compare this to the position of white Americans on the environment during this period.
4. The Shawnees believed that no treaties with the United States government should be ratified unless all Indian nations agreed. Do you think they were justified in this stance? Why or why not?
5. Historians often depend heavily on newspaper accounts in their reevaluations of history. Considering the one-sided nature of newspaper reporting on the events leading up to and after the Battle of Tippecanoe, should books and articles on this topic be trusted to tell the whole story with no bias against Native Americans?

NOTES

1. Composed by an unknown author after the Battle of Tippecanoe.

2. Howard Zinn, *A People's History of the United States* (New York: Harper & Row, 1980), 124.

3. R. David Edmunds, "Tecumseh, The Shawnee Prophet, and American History: A Reassessment," *Western Historical Quarterly* 14, no. 3 (1983): 261–276.

4. Ibid., 126.

5. Quoted in Reed Beard, *Battle of Tippecanoe* (Chicago: Hammond Press, 1911).

6. Clarence S. Brigham, *History and Bibliography of American Newspapers: 1690–1820* (Worcester, Mass.: American Antiquarian Society, 1947), 1:171.

CHAPTER 18

The Declaration of the War of 1812

On June 18, 1812, the United States declared war against Great Britain. In what is often called America's second revolution, the countries were locked in a series of battles for more than two years, which led to few gains on either side. It was one of the most unpopular wars in American history; when its treaty was signed on December 24, 1814, diplomats agreed that the countries should return to the situations they were in before the start of hostilities.

How did America end up in this war? The origins of the War of 1812 go back to the period just after the American Revolution. After winning its freedom from Great Britain, the nation's fledgling entrepreneurs worked to develop a strong mercantile industry. But as the years passed, the growing presence of American ships in the Atlantic led to disputes with the British. One of the world's most powerful ocean powers, England did not tolerate competition, especially from the Americans. Further complicating matters was America's trade with the French, who were in a near-constant state of war with England.[1]

As America's shipping industry grew, it became increasingly ensnared in foreign affairs, especially in the ongoing dispute between Great Britain and France. To keep Americans out of harm's way on the high seas, President Jefferson employed a tactic that was bound to fail: He declared the United States a neutral power. This approach failed because the British refused to consider any country that traded with the French as neutral. In response, in 1805, Great Britain's courts issued an order titled the Essex decree, which declared that American ships carrying goods from the French West Indies to France were subject to seizure. Additional British measures against America heightened the growing tension.

On assuming the presidency in 1809, James Madison faced the same problems in the Atlantic as Jefferson did. The hated Embargo Act (see chapter 15) was replaced by the Non-Intercourse Act late in 1808, allowing for the resumption of all maritime trade, except with France and England. Preventing trade between America and these two countries was difficult to enforce, and in May 1810, another measure called Macon's Bill No. 2 was enacted. Unfortunately, its measures also failed to solve the problems between America and Great Britain.

Early in 1811, a group of about 20 young and vocal Democratic Republicans, who eventually would be called the War Hawks, began pressuring Congress to take stronger action against Great Britain. Representing the southern and western regions of the nation, the War Hawks were united in their outrage over the impressment of thousands of American seamen and the crippling effects of the British Orders in Council, and they were fed up with the administration's plodding diplomatic strategies. War was the only honorable way out, and from November 1811 to June 1812, they waged a campaign toward that end. The Hawks were convinced that if Great Britain realized America was serious about war, the British would come to their senses and stop harassing America's ships and sailors.

On June 18, 1812, Congress declared war against Great Britain. An address by President Madison to Congress highlighted four reasons why war against Great Britain was justifiable: the first was to retaliate against the British for their impressments of American sailors; the second was their violation of U.S. neutral rights and territorial waters; the third was their blockage of U.S. ports; and the fourth was their refusal to revoke their Orders in Council. The House supported a declaration of war by a vote of 79–49. The Senate, where action was delayed by Federalists and "Old Republican" oppositionists, voted 19–13 to support a declaration of war. The nation's southern and western states were solidly behind the vote for war, while New England, with the exception of Vermont, voted against it.

After Congress declared war against Great Britain, the deep divisions within the country became even more obvious. The news that the country was at war was a devastating blow to many Americans, especially those who made their living through the shipping industry on the eastern seaboard. New Englanders said they would not pitch in to help. Bloody riots erupted in Baltimore.[2] Fanning the flames were newspaper essays by members of both camps. Republicans tended to support the war because they had long distrusted monarchy and were outraged at the treatment of their nation by the British. Federalists, on the other hand, hated the war. Among their arguments were that the country was ill-equipped to wage war, that it couldn't afford to do so, and that the nation's shipping businesses would incur devastating losses.[3]

This chapter includes newspaper essays that debate whether the United States should go to war with Great Britain. The first series of writers strongly favored war against America's former colonial ruler. The first piece in this section is an essay published in Kentucky, a region where support for war against the British ran high. According to Thomas Smith, the editor of Lexington's *Kentucky Gazette,* the people of his community watched the proceedings of Congress's 12th Session with anticipation. "The eyes of the world are fixed on this body," he wrote. Kentucky's own Henry Clay had opened Congress's proceedings on November 4, 1811. The next day, President Madison sent a message to Congress, urging its members to consider what should be done about the outrageous British assaults against United States sovereignty. As one of Congress's War Hawks, Speaker Clay would help lead the nation to its declaration of war the following June.

The section's next two entries were published in the *National Intelligencer,* which had long been a supporter of the Jefferson and Madison administrations' measures against the British. The author of the first, a poem published in April, argued that Americans had been patient enough and that stronger measures were needed unless they were willing to sit back and be enslaved by the British. This message was stated even more stridently in a column written by the paper's editor, Joseph Gales Jr., who argued that the nation's leaders had tried to negotiate but that the time for such tactics was over.

The rest of the newspaper pieces in this section were published in the days and weeks after Congress declared war on Great Britain on June 18. The first was printed in *Niles' Weekly Register.* Its author, Hezekiah Niles, had just started the *Register,* which became well known in the areas of politics and economic policy. Niles, a native of Jeffries' Ford, Pennsylvania, had previously edited Baltimore's *Evening Post.* Strongly behind the war effort, he argued that if any other country had kidnapped America's seamen, the people would have easily voted for war. He wrote that he was convinced that America—a young, rich nation—was capable of winning the war.

Immediately after Congress declared war against the British, concerns rose about whether Americans would unite in support of it. William Tuttle, in a *Centinel of Freedom* column, expressed hope that Americans' differences would be set aside for the good of the country. He hoped that New Englanders, some of whom apparently preferred disunion to war, would put aside their personal interests for the good of the nation.

The remaining entries in the pro-war section of the chapter were published in Kentucky, where people were ecstatic when they heard that Congress had issued a declaration of war against the British. Word of this reached Lexington, Kentucky, about June 26. When the editor of the *Recorder* heard the news, he stopped his press to print an extra edition. The next day, he headed his regular column with the statement "WAR!" A few days later, Lexington-area people celebrated the war with a barbeque and numerous patriotic toasts.

Throughout the weeks and months following the declaration of war, Kentucky's newspapers published many news reports and commentaries in support of it. On July 14, *Kentucky Gazette* editor Thomas Smith, aiming directly at the Federalist enemies of the Madison administration, wrote that anyone who now criticized the government should be considered a traitor. A week later, Smith included words for a new version of "Yankee Doodle," a popular Revolutionary War–era song. A month later, Smith announced he was enlisting in the Kentucky volunteers and was to leave soon for Canada. As he explained to his readers, his choice to join Kentucky's troops was motivated by a strong desire to serve his country:

> In becoming a Volunteer, to serve my country was my only object: I could not expect distinction by the act, for I sought no commission; I could not expect fame for I occupy the station of a private soldier; I but participated in the feelings of the times, and claim no merit which is not common to all my companions.[4]

The final piece in this section was written by a woman, Hortensia, who suggested that the women in her community could do a number of important things to support the war right at home. While women were to some degree involved in public affairs in this period, it was still unusual for them to write for the newspapers (see chapter 14).

The authors of the entries in the chapter's second section were uniformly fervent in their antagonism to war with Great Britain. Opposition to "Mr. Madison's War" was largely centered in the country's New England and northern mid-Atlantic states. In the months leading up to and following Congress's June 18 declaration of war, the anti-war cries coming from the newspapers published in those areas of the country were heard loud and clear. The first in this series was published in May by Benjamin Russell in his Boston newspaper, the *Columbian Centinel*. Russell would become known as one of the war's strongest editorial critics.

Alexander Contee Hanson's June 20 column, published in Baltimore's *Federal Republican & Commercial Gazette,* helped trigger a series of bloody riots. Hanson's piece indicted everyone he considered responsible for what he considered a horrendous mistake, and he promised he would not stop until he had won over public opinion against the war. His stridency so irritated supporters of Madison that they formed a mob, which destroyed his newspaper office. Five weeks later, after boldly continuing his diatribe, the mob attacked Hanson and left him for dead. The editor then moved his paper to Georgetown in the District of Columbia where he published it unmolested. The riots continued for weeks, resulting in the deaths of several people and permanent recognition of Baltimore as a "mobtown."

Not all anti-war cities deteriorated into violence. In Salem, Massachusetts, for example, townspeople gathered and issued protest resolutions that were forwarded to Washington, D.C. A report on these proceedings was printed by Thomas C. Cushing in the *Salem Gazette*. Meanwhile in Boston, the editors of the *Gazette*, John Russell and James Cutler, wrote that they felt it their duty to proclaim the war as simply a ruse to help out the French, and that if a vote were taken, the city of Boston would easily reverse Congress's decision.

Another outspoken newspaper critic whose writings are included here is Federalist William Coleman, editor of the *New-York Evening Post*. On June 20 he called the declaration of war "madness." A little over a week later, on June 29, he published a letter from a writer named "Hamilton" who agreed to obey the "letter of the law" but stated that he would not give up his right to speak out against the war.

In Favor of War against Great Britain

Thomas Smith: "XIIth Congress"

What should Congress do to try to stop the British from seizing American property and sailors on the high seas? Thomas Smith speculated on this, indicating he would probably support a declaration of war if it came to that.

Kentucky Gazette (Lexington), 26 November 1811

The eyes of the world are fixed on this body; and the American people await in anxious solicitude its discussions.

So soon as the President's energetic speech came out—the British minister resident in this country offered reparation for the attack on the *Chesapeake*, which happened more than four years ago!!

What means this procedure?—To moderate the proceedings of Congress—And will this *moderate* Congress? Will this atonement satisfy that body for the seizure of that property and the impressment of our citizens by the British?–for the power they have assumed over American vessels that they will remain the right to search them?–and for the murders that government has lately instigated on the Wabash? We trust and believe not. But if it does, the American character *must* and *will* sink to the lowest pit of degradation.

Anonymous: "Farewell to Peace"

This poem was written several months before war was declared on June 18. Its author indicated a willingness to surrender to the inevitability of the coming war.

National Intelligencer (District of Columbia), 14 April 1812

I have woo'd thee, meek-eyd PEACE,
To *thee* have tun'd the vocal shell;
Now, the darling strain must cease–
Harsher notes the Clarion swell;

Then fare thee well! For 'till that hour
That sees my country's wrongs redress'd,
Disgrace would be thy baneful dower,
If still I clasp'd thee to my breast;

As yet, so beauteous is thy reign,
So sweet thy Amaranthine bowers,
That like the Cygnet's dying strain,
It soothes–yet grieves the parting hours;

But fare thee well! My country calls–
'Twere basest Treason now to shrink;
I haste to guard her sacred walls–
Link'd with her fate, to swim, or sink.

Our COUNTRY CALLS–freemen, AWAKE!
Rise like the Lion from his lair!
Through Comets glare, and Earthquakes shake,
What men *can do,* that bravely DARE!

Tell the proud Tyrant of the waves,
That *this* is FREEDOM's dear bought land;
That rather than be *England's slaves,*
We'll fight, and die upon the strand,

For here sweet LIBERTY resides,
And roves amidst our mountains wild;
Content, in humble guise abides,
And innocence, as sportive child;

Guard then these blessings from the foe;
Unfurl the standard—plant it high!
Strike, strike, one *great,* one *common blow;*
Live *free,* or in the *"last ditch die!"* ...

Joseph Gales Jr.: "War Should Be Declared"

It's not surprising that the editor of the Intelligencer *supported a declaration of war. The newspaper had long been a supporter of the leaders of the Republican administrations that had been in power since Thomas Jefferson assumed the presidency in 1801.*

National Intelligencer (District of Columbia), 14 April 1812

The final step ought to be taken, and that step is WAR. *By what course of measures we have reached the present crisis, is not now a question for patriots and freemen to discuss.* It exists: and it is by open and manly war only that we can get through it with honor and advantage to the country. Our wrongs have been great; our cause is just; and if we are decided and firm, success is inevitable.

Let war therefore be forthwith proclaimed against England. With her there can be no motive for delay. Any further discussion, any new attempt at negotiation, would be as fruitless as it would be dishonorable. With France we shall be at liberty to pursue the course which circumstances may require. The advance she has already made by a repeal of her decrees; the manner of its reception by the government, and the prospect which exists of an amicable accommodation, entitle her to this preference. If she acquits herself to the just claims of the United States, we shall have good cause to applaud our conduct in it, and if she fails we shall always be in time to place her on the ground of her adversary.

But it is said that we are not prepared for war, and ought therefore not to declare it. This is an idle objection, which can have weight with the timid and pusillanimous only. The fact is otherwise. Our preparations are adequate to every essential object. Do we apprehend danger to ourselves? From what quarter will it assail United States? From England, and by invasion? The idea is too absurd to merit a moment's consideration. Where are her troops? But lately she dreaded an invasion of her own dominions from her powerful and menacing neighbor. That danger, it is true, has diminished, but it has not entirely and forever disappeared. The war in the Peninsula, which lingers, requires strong armies to support it. She maintains an army in Sicily; another in India; and a strong force in Ireland, and along her own coast, and in the West Indies. Can anyone believe that, under such circumstances, the British government could be so infatuated as to send troops here for the purpose of invasion? The experience and the fortune of our Revolution, when we were comparatively in an infant state, have doubtless taught her a useful lesson that she cannot have forgotten. Since that period our population has increased threefold, whilst hers has remained almost stationary. The condition of the civilized world, too, has changed. Although Great Britain has nothing to fear as to her independence, and her military operations are rather for safety than for conquest. How we cause to dread an attack from her neighboring provinces? That apprehension is still more groundless. Seven or eight millions of people have nothing to dread from 300,000. From the moment that war is declared, the British colonies will be put on the defensive, and soon after we get in motion must sink under the pressure.

Hezekiah Niles: "War against England"

Come together during this time of crisis, urged Hezekiah Niles in this column in favor of war against England. To make his point, he told a story about an argumentative man and wife whose disputes ceased when they faced a hostile outsider together for the good of their union. Niles felt that America's regions and parties should respond like this couple.

Niles' Weekly Register (Baltimore, Md.), 20 June 1812

Let every man, solemnly, in his "closet" put this question to himself:—"Would I send another ambassador to England to crawl on his hands and knees and beg, that my countrymen may not be stolen like *African* negroes, by the accursed traders in human flesh?"

The spirit of the people is up—the proposition must come from the other side of the water. We have *retreated* to the edge of the precipice—we have used every argument and exerted every means, to repel the adversary, without striking a blow. We can retire no further. We must strike or perish. The *United States* were compelled to "unbury the tomahawk," or become *colonies*. We have solemnly determined on the former, and may God speed the cause.

War is declared—Great Britain is the enemy. What American will excite divisions among the people, and give aid and comfort to the jealous and unprincipled foe? Who will admit an *intruder?*—I once saw a man and his wife contending for the *breeches*—a person interfered with a view to injure the man. The *pair* left their *private* quarrel to repel the *general* grievance—they mauled the *foreigner,* and then resumed the "management of their own affairs in their own way." So let it be with US.

To both parties (if two parties *will* exist) we humbly recommend forbearance and temper. It is not possible for any rational man to believe that the majority of one is under *French* influence, or of the other under *British* influence. There must be, and is, bad men in both sides—but nine tenths of either have a common object in repulsing the enemy. A little time and patience with prudence, will bring about a perfect union, when the war *really* begins. The exertion of all are wanting that its duration may be short; let us not fret each other by general censures which no gentleman would particularly apply to his neighbor who happens to differ in sentiment on some minor points. By such means, in the course of a few months, our jarring opinions will settle down in peace, and every man be prepared to say, *Long live America, the asylum of freedom—sovereign, independent and happy.*

William Tuttle: "War with England"

After Congress declared war on England on June 18, this writer wrote of his hope that his countrymen would come together to serve the nation with "one voice."

Centinel of Freedom (Newark, N.J.), 23 June 1812

"Firm united let us be,
Rallying round our Liberty.—
As a band of brothers join,
Peace and safety we shall find."

The vastly interesting question which hath occupied the deliberations of Congress for several days past is now settled. That honorable body, after solemn debate and consideration, have decided that peace can no longer be maintained with G. Britain except at the expense of our invaluable rights. Therefore they have raised the arm of resistance to her encroachments—and like our fathers in '76, resolved to draw the sword, and no longer tamely to submit to man-stealing, plunder, and insult.

This solemn question having been decided on by the legitimate authorities of our country, may we not hope that the disgraceful dissentions which have sprung up in every part of our country will be banished? May we not hope that all party spirit will be sacrificed on the altar of patriotism, and all political distinctions lost in the proud name of AMERICANS!—Notwithstanding the difference of sentiment that hath prevailed on this subject, we cannot but indulge this pleasing hope. In a government like ours, different opinions are to be expected;—It is a natural consequence, where conflicting interests clash, and where every man is a politician and prides himself on the freedom of speech and of opinion. But on a question of war with any foreign nation, after it has been declared, there should be but one voice, and that voice should be in support of the government. The minority must submit to the will of the majority. Otherwise the principles of republican government are at an end.

W. W. Worsley: "At a Barbecue"

After a long report on the series of events that led to Congress's June 18 vote for war, Worsley's column included a list of toasts raised at a recent barbeque. The following toasts revealed the strong support for the war felt across Kentucky.

The Recorder (Lexington, Ky.), 1 July 1812

James Madison. Worthy of being the chief magistrate of a free people: he has prepared us for the present crisis—he has the confidence of his country.

The Twelfth Congress.—In declaring War against G. Britain, they have only [re-echoed] the sentiments of the people of Kentucky...

The Representatives of Kentucky, who voted for War against G. Britain: *they* meet the approbation of their fellow citizens.

The Volunteers of Kentucky.—They are ready to execute the late Decree of their representatives....

Thomas Smith: "The Declaration of War"

This brief comment predicted that even the Tories—that is, the Federalists— "will be silent" in the face of the recent declaration of war against England. Editor Smith was wrong, since a number of anti-Republicans, especially in New England, talked of secession from the union.

Kentucky Gazette (Lexington), 14 July 1812

The Declaration of War was received in every part of the union with the most evident marks of satisfaction—in many towns, as in Lexington, it was hailed with exultation, rejoicings, and illuminations: but one sentiment is expressed by those who love their country—all appear willing and determined to support the honor of the nation. Republicans and Federalists will unite in defence of their common rights and interests. A spirit of unanimity will undoubtedly pervade all parties—the tories will be silent, at least. "He that is not now for United States, must be against United States."

Anonymous: "War Song" [To be sung to the tune "Yankee Doodle"]

The War of 1812 has often been called America's second war for independence. For that reason, the author of this song must have thought it fitting to sing it to the tune of "Yankee Doodle," a popular American Revolutionary War–era song.

Kentucky Gazette (Lexington), 21 July 1812

The clarion loud, of war is blown,
Oppression fills its cup, sir,
The British have the gauntlet thrown,
And we have took it up, sir,
Sound the trumphet, beat the drum
Now's the time for action,
How oft we wish'd this day to come,
To crush the British faction.

Our seamen pent in floating hells,
Our trade destroyed by orders;
And westward, hear the savage yells,
Triumphing in their murders;
See the bleeding matron die,
By the savage smitten.
Her slaughter'd infants, round her lie;
'Tis all the work of Britain.

Ye gallant feds, wherever spread,
Come, and share our glories,
Your swords should cut the cobweb thread,
That links you to the tories.
Our stripes are flying over head,
'Tis no time for lagging;
For soldier foes we've steel and lead,
For traitors we have hanging.

Congress, at length, has pass'd the law,
And now the proclamation.

Requires the brave, their swords to draw,
And vindicate the nation.
Montgom'ry's ghost, the good, the brave,
Bids us avenge our quarrels,
Like men, we'll seek a glorious grave,
Or else, deck his with laurels.

Hortensia: "To the Patriotic Females of Kentucky"

Whether at the front or at home, women always served their country during times of war. The author of this piece listed a number of things the women of her community could do to help out during the crisis.

Kentucky Gazette (Lexington), 15 September 1812

Whilst our brave citizens are crowding in thousands to the standard of their country, in defence of those precious rights bequeathed to us by the fathers of our glorious revolution—in defence of that liberty which gives existence its true and only value—in defence of the homes and fire-sides, of mothers, helpless children, sisters, relations and neighbours—whilst the uplifted sword, the tomahawk and scalping knife, are undauntedly met by them in the field of death—whilst they are exposed to the bleak winds of the north in a dreary inhospitable climate—do not the swelling emotions of sympathy overflow in the bosoms of our fair country women? But when you are told that those patriotic sons of Kentucky, have hastened to the field at the first summons of duty and of danger, without cloathing, without shoes, without blankets to shelter them from the inclemency of approaching winter in the severe northern climate to which they have marched, who can forbear admiration, who can fail to be moved by the strongest compassion, at their noble suffering? Rouse fair patriots, it is with you to mitigate their sufferings.—Form subscriptions—each one of you can relieve a soldier's pains. Let the spinning wheel, the loom, knitting needles, all, be busily plied with your fair hands. Warm linsey clothes, socks, blankets, linen shirts, added to shoes, to be furnished by your fathers and brethren, will enable our brave militia, who have marched to think only of the enemy, of battle, of revenge and of victory. Hasten to make collections and deposits at convenient places for their supply. So shall the high character of our state be preserved by your aid, and the women of Kentucky, like those of Sparta, be charming in the eyes of their countrymen, and terrible to their enemies. It is pleasing to observe the progress which has been already made in this noble work. Persevere—a bright reward will be yours.

OPPOSITION TO THE WAR AGAINST GREAT BRITAIN

Benjamin Russell: "War!"

Long opposed to any Republican measure, Benjamin Russell regarded the possibility of war with a spirit of incredulity. Not just New England, but the United States more generally, would not survive the devastation such a conflict would bring, he argued.

Columbian Centinel (Boston), 20 May 1812

The universal sentiment against a British War which prevails among considerate men of all parties in this section of the Union, is accompanied by a natural, but perhaps a false security in the conviction of the impossibility of this event. With the exception of a few brawlers in the street, and of some office-holding editors, we can find none who seriously wish to promote this calamity. It is evident that under the circumstances of this country a declaration of war would be in effect a license and a bounty offered by our government to the British Fleet to scour our coasts—to sweep our remaining navigation from the ocean, to annihilate our commerce, and to drive the country, by a rapid declension, into the state of poverty and distress which attended the close of the revolutionary struggle. We are convinced of the absence of those exasperated feelings in the great body of the people which would impel them to such a conflict. We fathom the length and depth of the artificial excitement, which is attempted by men of desperate fortunes and character, and we are satisfied that, in their efforts to influence the public mind, they apply their blazing torches to a mountain of ice. Other considerations come in aid of our confidence. The proposed enemy is invulnerable, while we are on all sides open to assault.... Our red brethren forgetful of the patriotic "talks" of their "father" Jefferson would pour down upon our frontier, and our black brethren would show themselves not less enamoured with the examples of liberty taught in St. Domingo than their masters are with those derived from its mother country. New-Orleans and the Floridas would pass into the hands of the enemy. Our seaports would be under strict blockade, and the mouths of our rivers would be bridged with frigates. Besides the war would be interminable, or end in a surrender on our part of the objects of contention....

William Coleman: "The War"

*William Coleman had made his position on war with England clear for
months in the* Post: *He was decidedly opposed to it. Here he concisely and
clearly summed up his objections to Congress's June 18 vote.*

New-York Evening Post (New York City), 20 June 1812

It is now ascertained that an unconditional declaration of War against
Great Britain has passed both houses of Congress, and has become a law.

We have very little disposition to remark on this unprecedented measure
at this time; but we cannot help expressing our regret that such madness
(for we can call it nothing better) should have seized a majority of our Representatives at Washington. For the government of a country, without
armies, navies, fortification, money or credit, and in direct contradiction to
the voice of the people, to declare war against a power which is able in a few
months' time to sweep from the ocean millions of property belonging to the
people of that country, is an act of imprudence, not to say wickedness, such
as, perhaps, was never before known since civil government was established. We deplore the fate of our unfortunate fellow citizens who have
property in foreign countries and on the ocean. We had hoped they would
have been allowed an opportunity to get home their ships, money and merchandize before hostilities commenced; but this favor could not be granted!
It now remains for the people to suffer, or to make use of the constitutional
means of averting, in some measure, this dreadful calamity, by a change of
men, that there may be a change of measures.

Alexander Contee Hanson: "Thou Has Done a Deed,
Whereas Valor Will Weep"

*Starting out his anti-war article with a line from Othello, in highly in-
flammatory language, Hanson claimed the war was neither necessary nor
wise. He took on the mantle of the beleaguered patriot, duty-bound by his
profession to speak out. For this, his newspaper office was attacked and destroyed by an angry mob. He was almost killed in one of the attacks in July,
and his paper was put out of commission until August when he moved it to
the District of Columbia.*

Federal Republican & Commercial Gazette (Baltimore, Md.),
20 June 1812

Without funds, without taxes, without an army, navy, or adequate fortifications—with one hundred and fifty millions of our property in the hands of
the declared enemy, without any of his in our power, and with a vast com-

merce afloat, our rulers have promulgated a war against the clear and decided sentiments of a vast majority of the nation. As the consequences will
be soon felt, there is no need of pointing them out to the few who have not
sagacity enough to apprehend them. Instead of employing our pen in this
dreadful detail, we think it more apposite to delineate the course we are determined to pursue as long as the war shall last. We mean to represent in as
strong colors as we are capable, that it is unnecessary, inexpedient, and entered into from a partial, personal, and as we believe, motives bearing upon
their front marks of undisguised foreign influence, which cannot be mistaken. We mean to use every constitutional argument and every legal means
to render as odious and suspicious to the American people, as they deserve
to be, the patrons and contrivers of this highly impolitic and destructive war,
in the fullest persuasion that we shall be supported and ultimately applauded by nine-tenths of our countrymen, and that our silence would be
treason to them. We detest and abhor the endeavors of faction to create civil
contest through the pretext of a foreign war it has rashly and premeditately
commenced, and we shall be ready cheerfully to hazard everything most
dear, to frustrate anything leading to the prostration of civil rights, and the
establishment of a system of terror and proscription announced in the Government paper at Washington as the inevitable consequence of the measure
now proclaimed. We shall cling to the rights of freemen, both in act and
opinion, till we sink with the liberties of our country, or sink alone. We shall
hereafter, as heretofore, unravel every intrigue and imposture which has beguiled or may be put forth to circumvent our fellow-citizens into the toils of
the great earthly enemy of the human race. We are avowedly hostile to the
presidency of James Madison, and we never will breathe under the dominion, direct or derivative, of Bonaparte, let it be acknowledged when it may.
Let those who cannot openly adopt this confession, abandon us; and those
who can, we shall cherish as friends and patriots, worthy of the name.

Thomas C. Cushing: "War!"

*In Salem, Massachusetts, a busy seaport where the economy was very de-
pendent on the ocean trades, the declaration of war was announced in
solemn terms. The evening before the following letter was written, a town
meeting was held. Its members prepared this statement declaring the reasons for their opposition to the war, and it was sent to the Senate and House
of Representatives in Washington, D.C.*

Salem Gazette (Massachusetts), 23 June 1812

That your Memorialists are among that class of American Citizens to
whom a war against Great-Britain must be peculiarly calamitous—They

would not however suffer themselves to be influenced by private considerations if they could perceive that this measure was demanded by the honor or interest of their country—but they are persuaded that such a war would be unnecessary, impolitic and unjust.

The causes of the present embarrassed situation of the United States may be traced to the Decrees of France and the Edicts of England....

From a clear apprehension and careful investigation (as your Memorialists humbly trust) of the principles and effects involved in the system of war now contemplated against Great-Britain, they are compelled to suggest to their Government that in their opinion it would be fraught with incalculable evils—endangering the union and prosperity of these States....

John Russell and James Cutler: "We Are Called Upon"

Duty called these authors to declare that, if New Englanders were asked to vote on whether the nation should go to war against Great Britain, they would overwhelmingly vote against this hated congressional act.

Boston Gazette, 25 June 1812

We are called upon, this day, by imperious duty, and by a public act of the constituted authorities, to "proclaim a deed, whereat valor will weep"—an act, totally unnecessary, inexpedient, and impolitic, and calculated, in our opinion, not to procure a redress of grievances from Great-Britain, but to aid France in her subjugation of the British Empire; and to destroy the growing wealth and influence of the New-England States. These sentiments we have no hesitancy in maintaining; and were a Convention to be called by the patriots and sages of the different States, (which we hope to God will be) we believe there would not be a voice of favor of the measures now pursuing by our government. Without funds, without taxes, without an army, navy, or adequate fortifications, with 130 millions of our property in the hands of the nation we are seeking to oppose, without any of theirs in our power, and with a vast commerce afloat on the ocean, it is madness in the extreme to resort to hostility; still, with all these circumstances staring them in the face, and against the clear and divided sentiments of a vast majority of the nation, they have had the temerity to declare War, and to appeal to the Supreme Being, whose doctrines they abuse, and to their country, whose interests and welfare they have abandoned for the rectitude of their cause. For ourselves, we can see nothing, in the act but a complete subserviency and obedience to the mandates of France; and consider our country as now basely and ignominiously sold to the tyrant and fell destroyer of the world—as being bound and covenanted to support all his measures—and at last, when impoverished like Holland, and degraded like Prussia and Austria, of becoming the final victim to his lust of power and domination.

Hamilton: "For the Evening Post"

This critic of the war promised the government support within the letter of the law. At the same time, he pledged he would not surrender his freedom of speech. To do so, he exclaimed, would make him but a slave to the government.

New-York Evening Post (New York City), 29 June 1812

That the people of this country differed widely as to the propriety of going to war at this time with Great Britain, before that war was declared; and particularly that in the Northern and Eastern States a very decided majority were extremely anxious to prevent it, will not be questioned by any one. But war is declared; and it becomes now a question what new duties this new state of things imposes, and what rights previously belonging to the citizen it takes away. No freeman will repine at the performance of duties, however arduous and even assisting, if the good of his country [demands] it. And accordingly, however he may lament the *folly,* in which the present war originated, he will clearly see that his duty demands that he should without resistance, contribute the exacted proportion of his property to the support of it. And when the constitutional authority demands his personal services, it is not less his duty to obey. When he has done this, he has done all that government has a legitimate right to require. But the right of opinion remains unimpaired. The liberty of speech and of the press cannot be affected by a declaration of war....

"*Here will I hold.*" I shall implicitly obey the laws, while they are in force—and my rulers, while they are in office. For the repeal of the former, and the ejection of the latter, I shall not only feel myself at liberty, but conscientiously, bound to speak and to write, whenever in my judgment the continuance of either is incompatible with my country's good. He is no Republican who differs from this doctrine. *He is a Slave.*

QUESTIONS

1. Do you believe the United States government was justified in its decision to declare war against Great Britain? Why or why not?
2. Although many Federalist printers wrote articles chastising President

Monroe and his administration's decision to go to war, no censorship was enforced by the government. Why not?

3. Historians often refer to the War of 1812 as the forgotten war. What could account for this?

4. Identify and discuss what made this war so unpopular in America.

5. How crucial a role did newspapers play in the war of 1812? Explain.

6. Poets and songwriters composed many pieces related to the war that were published in the newspapers. Discuss whether today's artists become involved in creating works related to international conflicts. If so, identify examples and discuss where they are published or otherwise disseminated.

Notes

1. Reginald Horsman, *Causes of the War of 1812* (Philadelphia: University of Pennsylvania Press, 1962).

2. Donald R. Hickey, "The Darker Side of Democracy: The Baltimore Riots of 1812," *Maryland History* 7 (1976): 1–19.

3. Donald R. Hickey, "Federalist Party Unity and the War of 1812," *Journal of American Studies* [Great Britain] 12 (1978): 23–39.

4. Thomas Smith, *Kentucky Gazette,* 18 August 1812.

CHAPTER 19

The Burning of Washington, D.C., August 24, 1814

O ne of the most shocking events in American history was the invasion and burning of the federal capital by British troops on August 24, 1814. After harassing Americans along the eastern seaboard for months, British military leaders ordered 4,000 militiamen to disembark at the mouth of the Patuxent River, near Benedict, Maryland, on August 19. Leading the forces were Major General Robert Ross and Rear Admiral George Cockburn. For weeks they had been chasing a flotilla of galleys, barges, and small, quick gunboats led by U.S. Commodore Joshua Barney. The flotilla had easily outmaneuvered the larger British ships in the shallow waters of the Chesapeake. On landing at Benedict, Ross ordered his men to march north. Meanwhile, Cockburn's fleet trapped and destroyed Barney's flotilla. At that point, Barney marched in the same direction as Ross's troops—toward the capital.[1]

As the enemy advanced, Washingtonians panicked. The editors of the *National Intelligencer*, Joseph Gales Jr. and William Winston Seaton, sought to reassure their readers that the *Intelligencer* would provide the most up-to-date and dependable information available. On August 20, a column titled "The Enemy" pledged to sort fact from fiction. "We shall lose no time in publishing such intelligence of the enemy's movements as may safely be relied on. In the present state of things, however, the various rumors that will be daily circulated should be received with caution," wrote the editors.

Despite the growing evidence that Washington would be attacked before Baltimore, American military leaders failed to prepare adequately for this possibility. To them, the sleepy little village of Washington had little strategic significance. Secretary of War John Armstrong refused to believe Washington was in imminent danger. "By God," Armstrong said to one of the city's militia chiefs, "they would not come with such a fleet without meaning to strike somewhere. But they certainly will not come here! What the devil will they do here? No! No! Baltimore is the place, Sir. That is of so much more consequence."[2]

At the hamlet of Bladensburg, a few miles from Washington, the British encountered American troops headed by Brigadier General William Winder. The Battle of Bladensburg would be one of the most embarrassing incidents in American military history. Referred to by some as the "Bladensburg Races," local militia ran as British troops approached, even though they outnumbered the enemy 6,000 to 4,000. The only real defense offered by local forces at Bladensburg was led by Commodore Barney's flotillamen, who unsuccessfully fired several cannons and field artillery pieces against the British.

After Bladensburg, the British proceeded to Capitol Hill, where the first of them arrived about sunset. Again, they were met by little resistance, although they were hit by a volley of sniper fire from a house along the way. The shots hit Major General Ross's horse and killed at least one soldier. As was their custom, Ross's troops retaliated by setting the structure that housed the snipers on fire. From there, the British closed in on the U.S. House and Senate buildings, the Library of Congress, and the Navy Yard, which had already been set afire by the evacuating Americans.

Near midnight, Ross and Cockburn's troops arrived at the president's house after marching in an orderly column down Pennsylvania Avenue. Along the way, enemy soldiers had stopped to reassure anxious residents that their lives and private property would be safe as long as they did not resist. On their arrival at President Madison's home, the soldiers feasted on food and wine laid out earlier for a group of American military and cabinet leaders.

The story of Mrs. Madison's last hours in the house are well known, since a letter she wrote to her sister the day before the British arrived tells of her bravery in the face of the approaching danger. She stayed in the house as long as she could, instructing servants to fill a carriage full of Cabinet papers and other valuables. Among the valuables she managed to save was a now-famous painting of George Washington.[3]

Once the British troops had dined and selected souvenirs from the house's furnishings, they set it on fire, completely gutting it. The next morning, the troops returned to the Navy Yard, where they found little left for destruction. After 26 hours in the U.S. capital, the British troops headed for Baltimore, where their attacks two weeks later inspired Francis Scott Key to write "The Star-Spangled Banner."

An interesting event in this 26-hour period was a stop by Admiral Cockburn at the offices of Gales and Seaton's *National Intelligencer*. The editors, having promised their readers they would publish the paper as long as it was safe for them to do so, had only just escaped before Cockburn's arrival. Cockburn intended to destroy the *Intelligencer's* building. Cockburn was aware of the paper's critical stance on the British and was especially infuri-

U.S. Capitol after burning by the British. This somber portrait of the Capitol after the British attempted to burn it shows fire damage to the Senate and House wings. In addition, the fire so severely damaged the colonnade in the House of Representatives that it had to be propped up with firewood to prevent its collapse. Courtesy of the Library of Congress.

ated that Gales was a native of England. After being talked out of burning the building by its adjoining occupants, Cockburn ordered his troops to destroy the office's equipment and materials, including its library.

This chapter discusses the reactions of Americans to the burning of their capital as the attacks were represented in the newspapers. Its first section presents the earliest news accounts of the destruction of Washington, along with examples of reports on the defense plans initiated as the British progressed through the area of the Potomac. After leaving Washington, the British headed to Baltimore. In response, volunteer soldiers amassed and marched to Baltimore to assist in its defense. Citizens, wondering where the British would go after attacking Baltimore, formed defense committees and battle plans.

The chapter's following sections include essays that reflect Americans' need to find someone to blame for their losses at Bladensburg and Washington. Even in a time of extreme crisis, the articles revealed, few were willing to give up old political grudges. Some blamed the British for engaging in sheer barbarism. Others faulted the Madison administration. Calls for the resignations and impeachments of government and military officials were rampant. Madison responded by asking certain officials to leave their posts. One of the more notable firings was that of Secretary of War John Armstrong, who was told to leave his post just a few days after Washington was attacked.

Two final sections include essays for and against the removal of the federal capital, either temporarily or permanently, to another location.[4] Moving the capital, some argued, would allow the government to operate more efficiently and provide government officials with more accommodations and protection. The matter was debated in the House of Representatives, where both sectional and partisan politics played a role in the divisions over the question. On the other side, this attempt to break a compromise struck in 1790 over where to locate the capital was considered extremely dangerous by some, who argued vigorously against it.

In an attempt to calm Americans' fears, Madison issued a statement assuring them that the government was operating smoothly. In addition, as a Southerner, he felt it necessary to maintain the compromise that had led to the placement of the capital on the Potomac. When a special session of Congress was called, debate commenced on whether to remove the seat of government temporarily to another location. Debates lasted until mid-October, when the attempt to move the capital was defeated.

IMMEDIATE REACTIONS TO THE ATTACKS

Baltimore's Postmaster: "Capture and Destruction of the Capital. Latest from Washington."

Unlike today's nearly instantaneous news, accounts of newsworthy events traveled very slowly in the early nineteenth century. Residents of Philadelphia, who were 126 miles from Washington, D.C., would not receive news of the capitulation of the capital until 24 hours later. This statement was extracted by Gazette *editor Enos Bronson from a letter received from Baltimore's postmaster.*

United States Gazette (Philadelphia), 26 August 1814

The enemy has taken Washington. They entered it last evening without much opposition. They marched in solid column, and appeared to take no notice of the fire of our militia—Winder is said to have retreated across the long bridge into Virginia....

William Coleman: "The City of Washington Destroyed"

News would take a day longer to reach New York City, where the earliest notices of the destruction of Washington were published on August 27.

New-York Evening Post **(New York City), 27 August 1814**

This day we have the disagreeable task of recording the capture and destruction of the city of Washington, the Capital of the United States! Six months ago, no one could have thought such an event could have possibly taken place. But this is the age of wonders!

Joseph Gales Sr.: "Distressing News"

It would take about a week for the news of the burning of Washington to reach Raleigh, the capital of North Carolina. A lot of the information circulating about the battles was incorrect, as is evident in this account. It erroneously reported that the British were led by Lord Hill and that they outnumbered American militia at Bladensburg. It was later learned that General Ross, rather than Lord Hill, led the British troops and that their numbers were not as great as first reported.

Raleigh Register, and North-Carolina Gazette **(North Carolina), 2 September 1814**

CITY OF WASHINGTON TAKEN BY THE BRITISH, and all the Public Buildings destroyed! On Wednesday the 24th at about 2 o'clock in the afternoon, the Enemy, supposed to be from 10 to 12,000 strong reached Bladensburg.... The contest was a short one, and sustained principally by the Regulars and the Baltimore and City Volunteers, the militia giving way soon after the battle commenced. Indeed, being so greatly outnumbered by a regular, veteran force, it could not have been expected that the result would have been otherwise.

Anonymous: "Virginians to Arms!"

Immediately on hearing the news from Washington, Virginia Governor James Barbour issued a proclamation calling on Virginians to ready themselves for a possible attack by the British. The essay on this call to arms by a Virginian lamented the tarnishing of America's reputation through its humiliating losses at Bladensburg and Washington. Virginians, however, could reverse such damage if they would "rush like mountain torrents to the standard of…[their] country…."

Richmond Daily Compiler **(Virginia), 27 August 1814**

The time is come, the hours of heroes is arrived—not the *eleventh,* but the *twelfth* hour—the very moment of saving or losing all that is dear to the hearts of patriots and of men.—Now, if there is in the character of Virginians that love of country, that pride of valor, that generous and noble disposition which towers above inferior considerations, and emulates the glory of serving our country as the highest prize, the richest reward of the brave, now let it be seen, now let it be displayed to the world. The eyes of the world are upon us—not our country only, but all Europe looks on to behold the contest in which we are engaged. In our national character, we're already half degraded by the disaster which has befallen Washington. The people of Europe will hear with astonishment that a band of ten thousand British, after sixty days' notice of their design, could cross the Atlantic Ocean, sail more than one hundred miles up the Chesapeake bay, deliberately land their men and march straight forward, and almost unresisted, to the destruction of the American Metropolis. Was such a thing ever heard of? Oh shame, shame! We burn with grief and rage to record in our day such a stigma on the American name.

But is there no chance or hope of redress, no expedient left to purge off this base reproach of our national character? Yes, there is one means left—Our honor as Americans is tarnished by this enterprize of the enemy, but to Virginia, perhaps, is reserved the glory of wiping off the foul stain that sullies the reputation of our Country, and wresting from that proud and haughty foe the temporary plume he has won. Hasten, brave countrymen, hasten gallant youths of Virginia—rush like mountain torrents to the standard of your country, and when the enemy approaches the Capital of your State (which he soon will) let him find it covered with the panoply of wisdom and talents, patriotism and valor. Let him come to *see* this, but never let him return to *tell* it—no, if the enemy ventures to the suburbs of Richmond, let him never be suffered to reach his ships again—he may repose *as captive* in the shade of the rear of the Capitol, but he must never, as *victor*, survey from its portico the beautiful landscape that spreads beneath the pillared majesty of its front.

No—the Capitol of Virginia is the rendezvous of the brave—the remaining hope, and henceforth, we trust, the pride and glory of the nation.

Once more, brave countrymen—the eyes of the world are upon us—the example of our ancestors, the praise of posterity, the safety of all that is valuable and dear, attracts, invites, commands us to arms! In every town, in every village, in every cabin of our land, let the Proclamation of the Governor be read, and leaving cowards only behind, let all the brave, young and old, repair to the STANDARD OF VIRGINIA.

RALLYING 'ROUND THE FLAG

Hezekiah Niles: "Weekly Address"

Many Americans reacted to the news of the burning of the capital with hatred for the British. In this essay, Weekly Register *editor Hezekiah Niles accused the British of waging war in an especially vicious way. Niles also called for the nation to put its political factional disputes aside until the war was over.*

Niles' Weekly Register (Baltimore, Md.), 10 September 1814

The hate with which we have always said Great Britain regarded us, is now exhibiting by a Goth-like war, which the late strange events in Europe enables her to carry on with extraordinary force and energy. The barriers with which civilized nations have circumscribed their military operations, are cast down by the foe; and the contest, began for unalienable rights on the sea, is becoming a struggle for liberty and property on the land. The shores of the Chesapeake are lighted by the flames of farm houses and cottages, hitherto respected in war; and the fruits of the earth are wontonly consumed by the invader's torch. Whatever of private property pleases him, he lays hold of as prize; and wickedly destroys what he cannot carry away. *Household furniture* has been a favorite object of his vengeance, and *negroes* and *tobacco* are his darling spoils! His late capture of Washington City is an honor to the valor of his soldiery; but his conduct in burning the capitol, the president's house and the public offices, is a disgrace that he will not wipe away, more easily than we shall the–something that permitted the irruption. ... The scales are falling from the eyes of our people; if the blaze of the capitol shall enlighten their mind, and remove their prejudice, so that they may see the character of our enemy as it really is–the present safety and future peace of the United States, is cheaply purchased, by the capture of *Washington* and destruction of the public buildings thereat.–The capitals of every power in Europe–*London, Stockholm* and *Constantinople,* from peculiar circumstances excepted, have fallen into the hands of their enemies; and treaties have been *dictated* at some of them at the will of the conqueror. Our capitol has also been polluted by a triumphant enemy. We ought to have prevented it–but it is a common lot–it was evacuated with precipitation–and has had no other effect than to rouse the nation to arms; and we hope, to give energy where, indeed, it was wanted.... [I]f the people do not bring forward their means to support the government they themselves have established–they must expect to fail in this contest for their homes and firesides; and prepare themselves to become "hewers of wood and drawers of water" to the spoilers of "peace, liberty, and safety." Our cause is just, and us who established civil and religious freedom in America will sustain it, if we deserve the rich heritage. Courage, then! Let every one come forward in the way that he can best serve the nation, and the end shall be glorious; though inconveniences and sufferings must be encountered. Let faction cease–let party moderate its warmth–and *political peace* be established until the *foreign war* is done. "DON'T GIVE UP THE SOIL!"

A. B.: "To the Editors"

Many Americans were embittered against Great Britain for its burning of the nation's capital, which they considered a barbaric act. Reflecting on a much earlier event in ancient Greece, this student of ancient history reflected on the irony of the burning of Washington.

National Intelligencer (District of Columbia), 30 November 1814

The city of Rhodes was once saved by a picture; when that city was besieged by Demetrius, King of Macedon, he being able to attack it only on that side where Protogenes was painting. His first intention was to burn the city; he chose rather to abandon his design than to destroy so fine a picture—this was long before the birth of our Saviour. Those people were called heathens, and were unacquainted with the covenant of grace. What think you of a nation who styles itself the bulwark of the Christian religion, and wantonly destroys the mansion-house once occupied by our late venerable Washington?

BLAMING MADISON'S ADMINISTRATION

Enos Bronson: "If the Intelligence Received... Has Failed"

Only a day after the British left Washington, proprietor Enos Bronson of the staunchly federalist paper, the United States Gazette, *placed blame on the Madison administration for the city's destruction.*

United States Gazette (Philadelphia), 26 August 1814

If the intelligence received from the southward has failed to awaken the indignation of the people against the faction that has brought war with all its train of horrible circumstances to our very capital, ravaging this late happy country to its very heart, and (to borrow a thought from one of the finest poets) like a "pestilence drawing *a close incumbent cloud of death over those domes* which but a little while gone by, were the seats of innocent cheerfulness, and the pride of our youthful state"—if it does not cleanse their eyes of that foul and corrupt humour through which their view of every object has for years been distorted—If it does not convince them who were their friends and best advisers and who their worst enemies and most pernicious betrayers—and they do not now feel as well as see that they alone who were denounced as moral traitors for opposing the declaration of war, were the faithful citizens, and those who denounced them and involved the country in a war, the consequences of which must to a great extent be ruinous, even though the end of it should not be the extinction of our independence, the real traitors both moral and political—If they do not act upon these truths, as well as perceive them by exerting every nerve to exclude as far as the laws and constitution will allow them, that faction from all or any participation in the councils of the country, then do we affirm that there is not a ray left even of a hope for the salvation of the country. Since the great reservoir of national strength, its pure patriotism, and every stream that supplies it, are poisoned and polluted to their very sources.

In such a case justice proclaims that to the obstinate and willful, no pity, beyond what Christian charity exacts, ought to be afforded to those pernicious patriots.—Yet, still a vast people will remain, who deserve a better fate, and will necessarily be involved in one common ruin with the guilty. To such a people it would be insolent to apply such a term as pity—they stand upon a dignified eminence, aloof from such a mortifying offering—But they will yet be embalmed, alas! Too late perhaps, with the grateful remembrances of their abused, betrayed country.

William Coleman: "The City of Washington Destroyed"

New York City newspaper editors began receiving news from the Potomac a few days after the nation's capital was burned. Not long after, as noted in William Coleman's column, Federalist newspaper editors began to express wonder at the turn of events. How could the city be left without defense? Coleman clearly blamed Madison's administration for what happened.

New-York Evening Post (New York City), 27 August 1814
The city of Washington, containing valuable public buildings, which have cost the nation millions of money; a large naval arsenal, cannon foundry, &c. &c.—this city, situated at such a distance from the ocean & only approachable with shipping by long, crooked and narrow rivers, on a spot selected above all others as the most secure from foreign invasion;—who could have supposed that it could so easily have been destroyed by an enemy? Is it possible, that after being two years at war, our capital, the seat of our general government should have been left so defenceless? Can it be believed that a small armament of a few ships, and from six to ten thousand troops, which came into our waters on the 17th instant, could demolish our capital on the 24th?—But such is the fact. In less than one month from the sailing of the expedition from Bermuda, the British General has fixed his H. Quarters in the heart of our nation, in the seat of our government. What shall we think of such things? Where have our men at the head of affairs

been all this time? Why have they taken no measures to defend the capital?—Were there no places on the Patuxent or Potomac, which might have been fortified?—Was there no means of defending the property of the nation?—Can men who manage in this way be fit to govern a great and free people? Let their constituents answer.

William Coleman: "The News"

The country's citizens deserved an official account of what happened in Washington, according to Coleman. Even Napoleon Bonaparte during times of war had kept his people informed with weekly bulletins. From President Madison, in contrast, the American people heard nothing. Coleman demanded that administration officials ought to resign.

New-York Evening Post (New York City), 29 August 1814

A battle was fought near the seat of government, and the capital of our country was entered by an invading force on Wednesday last; and on this day, we have not received a line officially on the subject. Where are our commanders? Why have we nothing to satisfy the public mind, in such a disastrous crisis? Our President might at least in imitation of his friend Bonaparte, have ordered a bulletin to be issued daily; but nothing of the kind appears. Not a general, colonel, or corporal has thought it his duty to inform his fellow citizens of the events which have taken place. And it is a fact, that to this hour, we know not where our army is, or whether we have any! Our President and his Secretaries are also missing, and no one knows where to look for them! Was there ever such a thing known before in a civilized nation! A country invaded—battles fought—and cities taken; and yet no official account of the movements of either friend or foe! Why do not our commanders let the public know the state of affairs of the nation?...Do our rulers wish to keep us in ignorance of the movements of the enemy?—They may depend on it, deception will do no longer. It may answer to carry an election, but it will not defend the country.—The people must know what they have to depend on—they are able and willing to defend their homes and their firesides!—and if our rulers are not able to lead the people, and are not capable of forming plans, and providing means of defence, they ought forthwith to resign their places and make room for better men.

Enos Bronson: "Cowardly...Surrender"

Throughout the Federalist prints, editors issued impassioned calls for the resignations of government officials in the wake of the surrender of the capital.

United States Gazette (Philadelphia), 31 August 1814

Every day furnishes us with some additional particulars of the cowardly or treacherous surrender of the capital of the United States, almost without resistance. A few days before the abandonment of that capital, it was solemnly announced in the National Intelligencer, that there were then within the district about *twenty thousand* effective men who were impatient for the conflict. On the very morning of the 24th, in the evening of which the city was abandoned and destroyed, the Intelligencer said: "We feel assured that the number and bravery of our men will afford complete protection to the city."—Yet, notwithstanding all these superabundant means, and all these assurances, notwithstanding the president of the United States and all his cabinet ministers were on the spot, the capital was basely given up with scarcely a show of resistance. If Hull deserved death for surrendering a paltry post upon a remote and uninhabitable frontier, what do the whole cabinet deserve for surrendering the very heart of the country to a handful of men, not amounting, as we fully believe to 3,000 in number? Beside the disgrace which has been thus tamely and pusillanimously incurred, the nation has suffered a loss of publick property to the value of from ten to fifteen millions of dollars.

One would suppose that this administration had been now sufficiently proved. They have tried to make foreign conquests and they have tried, or pretended to try, to defend their own capital, and have been found utterly incompetent to either. If this war is to terminate in any thing short of total ruin and disgrace, it must be by inducing the men at present in power voluntarily to give place to others who are competent to the task—or they must be constitutionally impeached, and driven with scorn and execration from the seats which they have dishonoured and polluted.

William Coleman: "Good Coming out of Evil"

Coleman saw good coming out of the disaster when President Madison dismissed several of his officials, including Secretary of War John Armstrong. On July 1, Armstrong assured the president the capital was not at risk. Instead, he claimed the British would attack Baltimore. Armstrong left Washington's defense in the hands of General William Winder, a lawyer and volunteer soldier wholly unqualified for the task.

New-York Evening Post (New York City), 2 September 1814

It appears that the late disgraceful disaster at Washington, has so far opened the eyes of the people, to the incapacity of the public officers, that the President has been obliged to remove U.S. Secretary of War General John Armstrong from office. And we are informed that the citizens of Philadelphia have petitioned the President to remove Gen. Bloomfield from the command of that district, and to appoint Governor Aaron Ogden to succeed him. Other removals and other appointments must take place before the people will have that confidence in their commanders which will ensure success.

Joseph Gales Sr.: "From All Accounts"

Generally a supporter of the Madison administration, Raleigh Register *editor Joseph Gales hesitated to criticize government or military officials just after the battle. But on September 9, he took a more critical stance of U.S. military officials, particularly those at Bladensburg.*

Raleigh Register, and North-Carolina Gazette (North Carolina), 9 September 1814

From all accounts we have received of the Battle at Bladensburg, we cannot help believing that all was not done that might have been done in defence of the capital of the Nation. It appears but a small portion of the American force was bro't into action; and that when a part of the undisciplined Militia gave way, and orders were given by Gen. Winder for the whole army to *retreat,* between 2 and 3,000 of the men (composed of Regulars and well trained Volunteer Companies) had not fired a gun. Strange, that when so much depended on the issue of this engagement, so little energy should have been displayed by the Commanding General to concentrate and unite the whole of the force under his control!

William Coleman: "What Ought to Be the Conduct of Federalists in the Present State of Affairs?"

It was a difficult call for Federalists after the destruction of Washington: Should they continue their scathing criticism of President Madison and his administration's handling of the war? Or, in the wake of the destruction of their capital, should they unite with their political opponents to help bring the country back to its feet?

New-York Evening Post (New York City), 26 September 1814

[Should] the Federalists...unite with their political opponents, and given an unanimous support to the measures of the administration, in defence of the country, without once permitting themselves to ask whether these measures are the best adapted to the end proposed, and without once questioning whether those who have the management of our concerns are men of sufficient capacity to extricate us from the alarming perils that surround us?...

A few weeks ago, when the enemy invaded the seat of government, and, in violation of all the laws of modern warfare, like the Goths of a barbarous age, burnt the public edifices, and the public library, and destroyed the public monuments, and when threatenings were openly given out by him that similar scenes should be acted wherever our coasts were found assailable;— at this time and under these circumstances, there was no room, no possibility for a division of sentiment among the people. A single idea engrossed us—menaced with conflagration and ruin, it was no time to enquire with whom the evil arose, or who were to blame. Self-defense, the first law of nature, animated every heart and nerved every arm. Nothing was heard but here are we and here are our homes,—shew us the enemy. And if ever such a crisis shall again arrive, a similar spirit will again shew itself. At such a moment domestic disputes and local distinctions are forgotten; we are neither all federalists nor all republicans; we are all Americans....

Before, however, I close this article, a sense of candor and justice compels me to add, that while the present war is carried on by the enemy in a manner that of late so marks and disgraces his steps, and which if not disavowed by the sovereign of Great Britain, will fix an indelible stain on the page of her history, we will unite our best efforts with those of our political opponents, to resist them in whatever quarter they may appear. At the same time we must declare that we consider it an imperious and indispensable duty to neglect no opportunity to point out to the people, in mild and decent language, all such instances of misconduct or of ignorance in our rulers, as shew them to be the authors of the present deplorable state of our unhappy country, and as prove them to be utterly incapable to conduct the affairs of a great nation.

Essex: "Character of the War"

Rather than attack the English for the brutality of their acts at Washington, D.C., this author reminded his readers that war is always brutal. Although he didn't specifically mention the destruction of Washington, there was a reference to the April 1813 Battle of York (in Toronto), where U.S. troops burned the capital of Upper Canada.

Salem Gazette (Massachusetts), 30 September 1814

Let us not listen to every idle story of the excesses of the enemy. Excesses always attend war, and that is one among the many reasons why war is to be dreaded as the greatest evil, & never resorted to but in cases of absolute necessity. Let us also remember, that our armies first carried fire and sword among our innocent neighbors, who are at this moment filled with the greatest hatred against us, for the cruel manner in which they believe we have carried on the war.

Now our Country is in a degraded ruinous condition, we are called on to rally round those, who have brought all our evils upon us. Yes.—Mr. Madison, from the ruins of the capital, deserted by him and left a prey to a

Brigade of the enemy's troops, like the raven, with his discordant voice, croaks out "Union! Union!" and many deluded people are charmed with the melodious sound!

In Support of Madison's Administration

John Bickley: "It Is a Matter of Astonishment"

The following essay commented on an event that followed on the heels of the destruction of Washington, D.C.: the president's efforts to force the removal of Secretary of War John Armstrong from his position.

Kentucky Gazette (Lexington), 19 September 1814

It is a matter of astonishment and regret to the friends of the government in this quarter of the union that the clamor of the people of the District of Columbia should have driven the secretary of war from his office.

The population of thirty thousand, to be permitted to usurp and control the concerns of eight millions of people! Are the people from Maine to Louisiana to be governed by this inconsiderable population, a great portion of whom are hostile to the government? It is ridiculous that we charge revolutionary France with the crime of being ruled by the Jacobin Society of Paris, and wink at the same thing ourselves. If it were impossible to resist the clamor of people about Washington, the seat of government should have been instantly changed; but if the clamor could have been resisted in any manner, was there ever a greater symptom of imbecility exhibited in the universe than the President has, by permitting it to derange the views of the government?

"There is something rotten in the state of Denmark."

In Favor of Moving the Federal Capital

Vivat respublica!: "The President and Congress!— to Philadelphia!"

The old debate regarding where the nation's capital should be located resurfaced shortly after the British destroyed Washington, D.C. This essayist suggested that the president and Congress should move to Philadelphia to "take refuge…in the bosom of a brave and loyal people." It was also mentioned that local boosters would help move the government's offices and guarantee military protection and ample accommodations.

United States Gazette (Philadelphia), 27 August 1814

Where is the President? We are told, in capitals, of the destruction of THE NAVY YARD, and the Conflagration of THE CAPITOL—but what is become of THE PRESIDENT?—Is his safety of no importance to the Union!

Has he retired to Montpelier, with his Cabinet Council?—There to remain, with whatever has been saved of the Publick Archives, until a Detachment of Horse may surprise them at breakfast; and transfer Monroe, and Campbell, and Armstrong, and Jones, to a conference in Lord Hill's marquee?

It is to be hoped not.—

Frederick Town, in Maryland, is the nearest place of safety; though York or Lancaster, in Pennsylvania, would be the only permanent or secure retreats, short of *this City*, or the Capital of New Jersey.

Wherever he may be—would it not be a proper step?—is it not an incumbent duty?—to invite him forthwith to take refuge in Philadelphia—in the heart of his Country—in the bosom of a brave and loyal people.

Let the City Councils immediately direct the necessary preparations for his honourable reception; and the accommodation of the approaching Session of Congress.

And let the provisional COMMITTEE OF DEFENCE, as soon as their more immediate arrangements will permit, dispatch a respectable Deputation of Citizens, to assure the President of the unshaken fidelity of the ancient Capital of the Union; and to request that he would be pleased immediately to return to the political residence of HANCOCK and ADAMS, of FRANKLIN and WASHINGTON.

John Bickley: "The Loss of the Capital"

This brief note indicated the eagerness of some Americans to move the capital to another location.

Kentucky Gazette (Lexington), 5 September 1814

If the public records have been preserved, as we suppose they have, the fall of Washington City will not be felt by the people of the United States.—Congress can convene and transact the national business at any other place just as well as it could be done at Washington. Thank God, the fall of the American capitol unlike the fall of the French capital cannot be followed by the conquest of the nation.

Brutus: "Rebellion at the Capital"

According to this author, the people of Kentucky had read with anxiety the reports from Washington. Now they wondered whether the city would descend into chaos and suggested the nation's capital ought to be moved to a safer location.

Kentucky Gazette **(Lexington), 19 September 1814**

The question now seems to be whether the vanquished people of the District of Columbia are to supercede the laws of the union, with arms in their hands, substitute a dictation of the most horrible kind, or whether the constitution and the federal compact still exists: in a word, shall the people of the district, a few infuriated individuals generally never well affected to the government, be permitted to displace its principal officer that their sovereign will and pleasure. If our situation has arrived at this extremity, it is time that not merely them, but the people of the United States generally should have some influence in the revolution which the district has commenced.

These remarks are excited by the intelligence that the Secretary of War was driven from his post, which he filled with so much more honor to himself and his country than any of his predecessors since the present war—was shamefully driven from his post by the violence of a few demagogues—men who fled from the battle of Bladensburgh—by men who were tame spectators of their own disgrace and their country's infamy. Did they expect that whilst the surrounding states were with the most abject and contemptible excuses selling themselves to everlasting dishonor by withholding assistance at such a crisis, the secretary of war was alone competent to fight their battles? Did they suppose that the magic of his station like the conjuration of the Shawnoe prophet, was to shield them from harm, and change their enemies' bullets into sand?—O shame where is thy blush!!!

Is James Madison President of the United States under the government of the people of the district of Columbia?

Then we the people of the U. States are not under the government of our own choice, but subject to the domination of the violent and usurped authority of an inflamed and cowardly mob. If Mr. Madison is under duress, the people of the west are willing I have no doubt, to march and restore him to that freedom of action which will enable him to support political right and conform to the solemn obligation she has incurred to his country.

It is time the seat of government was removed from the land of mobs and non-combatants.

Keep the Federal Capital in Washington

Joseph Gales Jr. and William Seaton: "A Very Few Words on an Interesting Subject"

Calls for removal of the seat of government to a different location were issued within a week of the burning of the capital. The proprietors of the National Intelligencer *were clearly opposed to such a move.*

National Intelligencer (District of Columbia), 5 September 1814

We have heard some indistinct suggestions buzzed abroad of a design to endeavour, in consequence of the recent events to remove the seat of government, temporarily or permanently, from this place. We cannot find language to express our abhorrence and astonishment at the suggestion of a permanent removal of the seat of government. Besides being a violation of the constitution establishing a permanent seat of government, it would be injustice so great to the people of this district, to those who have enriched the publick offices with population and laid our fortunes in the purchase of property in and about the city, as Congress cannot, dare not sanction. There is besides something of cruelty in the idea of robbing the citizens of their all, because they have already greatly suffered by the incursion of the enemy. We say coldly, and we say it more freely because we have little personal interest in property here, that such a measure as we have alluded to, would be a treacherous breach of the faith of the nation, pledged by a solemn law enacted under a constitutional provision. A temporary removal would be scarcely less objectionable. It would be kissing the rod an enemy has wielded; it would be deserting the seat of government at the dictation of an enemy!

A Federalist: "To the Hon. Timothy Pickering"

Although written by a Federalist, this letter, according to the Intelligencer, *contained views that made "good sense." From the pen of a "venerable gentleman," this writer was against the removal of the nation's capital to another location. The upcoming Hartford Convention, a project he feared, when combined with the effects of the proposed removal of the seat of government, would ruin the country.*

National Intelligencer (District of Columbia), 2 December 1814

SIR—I did believe, before the burning of the Capitol, that the country was to be saved by the Eastern Federalists; men who declare themselves of the "School of Washington and Steady Habits," but I ceased to believe so, when I heard that every federal man from the East voted for the removal of the seat of government, which I think would destroy the Union. For the correctness of this opinion, I will give you an author whose judgment and penetration no American could doubt. The great and good Washington the father of us all, when he laid the corner stone of our Capitol, told us, (I was present) "when this stone is removed, your troubles will commence, and there will then be an end of your government, and the next you will have will be seated with blood."…

Why, in the name of God, I demand of you, do you authorize or sanction measures calculated to divide and ruin our country? Suppose, for a moment, your disorganizing projects should be accomplished. Will your situation be benefited? If once the link is broken, the business is done—and we, like the mutilated countries of Europe, must be torn, divided, subdivided and swayed, by the iron rod of despotism.

QUESTIONS

1. Many Americans were opposed to the War of 1812. Discuss whether you think that the war's critics should have given more or less support to President Madison after the capital was destroyed.
2. After the nation's capital was burned by the British, some Americans argued that the nation's center of government should be moved to another place. What were their arguments? If you were one of those opposed to the relocation of the capital, what arguments would you have forwarded to dispute those who advocated changing its location?
3. The nation's newspapers undoubtedly played an important role in spreading information about this national crisis. Identify the various ways these newspapers helped (or hindered) the country.
4. When the news was first learned about the burning of the nation's capital, people in opposing political camps came together for a time. Can you think of other events in America's history that led political enemies to join in support of the nation? Discuss when and how such events happened.
5. Discuss how you think America's newspaper journalism may have been affected by the burning of Washington, D.C., or by similar national crises in our history.

NOTES

1. Much of the information in this description of the burning of Washington, D.C., is taken from Anthony Pitch, *The Burning of Washington: The British Invasion of 1814* (Annapolis, Md.: Naval Institute Press, 1998).

2. Anthony Pitch, "The Burning of Washington," *White House History* 4 (fall 1998): 6–17.

3. Letter from Dolley Madison to her sister, Anna Payne, dated 23 August 1814. For more information, see David B. Mattern, "Dolley Madison Has the Last Word: The Famous Letter," *White House History* 4 (fall 1998): 38–43.

4. Richard C. Rohrs, "Sectionalism, Political Parties, and the Attempt to Relocate the National Capital in 1814," *The Historian* 62 (spring 2000): 535.

CHAPTER 20

"Marats, Dantons, and Robespierres": The Hartford Convention, 1814–1815

The Civil War wasn't the only time the American Union was threatened. New England Federalists were so fed up with the federal government that a group of them met in Hartford, Connecticut, from December 15, 1814, to January 5, 1815, to discuss whether they ought to secede from the United States. The conventioneers had long felt that the northeast had not been treated favorably by the nation's Republican leaders, and they were infuriated by President Madison's handling of the War of 1812. In the end, the Hartford Convention was a dismal failure, its members humiliated and lampooned. Thomas Jefferson called them "Marats, Dantons, and Robespierres," likening them to several of the more terrifying protagonists of the French Revolution. John Adams was less scathing in his assessment of the convention, speaking of its protagonists as "intelligent and honest men who had lost touch with reality."[1]

Even before the War of 1812, rumors of secession had at times circulated in New England. Jefferson's Embargo Act provoked intense antagonism in the northeast, and when war was declared in 1812, some states, such as Massachusetts, refused to help. Throughout the war, calls were issued for action, especially after the humiliating defeat of American troops in Washington, D.C. (see chapter 19); the fall of Castine, Maine; and the loss of the island of Nantucket off the coast of Massachusetts. In November 1814, Massachusetts Governor Caleb Strong sent an emissary to Nova Scotia to explore the conditions for a separate peace agreement with the British.

The 26 men who met in Hartford in mid-December 1814 represented the states of Massachusetts, Connecticut, Rhode Island, New Hampshire, and Vermont. A subgroup within the convention, the Essex Junto, included the convention's most radical members. If given free reign, the convention likely would have voted for secession. The junto's members lived in the vicinity of Essex County, Massachusetts, where they wielded considerable power. Among them were George Cabot, Timothy Pickering, and Theodore Dwight. Cabot, a former U.S. senator from Massachusetts, presided at the convention. Pickering, who had held a number of important federal appointments during the Washington and Adams administrations, was an outspoken opponent of the War of 1812. Another of the leading spirits of the convention was Theodore Dwight, a former member of Congress who served as the convention's secretary. In 1833, Dwight wrote a history of the convention.[2]

In the end, the efforts of Cabot, Pickering and Dwight to force a vote for secession were restrained by the persuasive moderation of delegate Harrison Gray Otis and the convention's other less radical members. The convention's final report, issued January 5, 1815, castigated the Madison administration's handling of the war, complained about the harmful effects of embargoes, argued that the drafting of state militias into federal service was unconstitutional, and stated that the constitution gave unfair advantage to the South over New England. To help remedy such abuses, Otis and his colleagues proposed the addition of seven amendments to the U.S. Constitution.

As the convention convened, peace negotiations between Great Britain and the United States were underway at Ghent in Belgium. After the treaty was signed on December 24, it took weeks for the news to arrive in America. During the period before Americans knew the war was over, convention members continued to meet and draft their report. Although the convention failed to lead to any changes in the nation's government, historians believe it may have fostered several longer-term ramifications: The convention's unpopularity may have factored into the growing problems and eventual demise of the Federalists, and its actions may have added fuel to the growth of the idea that the concept of states' rights could serve the purposes of sectional groups.

The Hartford Convention received considerable press coverage, particularly in the areas north of Washington, D.C. This chapter includes three sections: the first two highlight the pro and con sentiments of people across America about the convention, and the third includes several retrospective newspaper pieces about the convention. The first section, which includes pro-convention essays, illustrates the sense of outrage felt by many of the instigators and supporters of the meeting over the federal government's policies and actions. The first two essays were written by Benjamin Russell, editor and publisher of Boston's *Columbian Centinel*. Russell was well known as one of the Madison administration's harshest critics, and he spared no ink in his determination to chastise the government.

"The Hartford Convention or Leap no Leap." This William Charles satire attacks the Hartford Convention and its leaders. The artist caricatures a conversation between Timothy Pickering, one of the most radical members of the group, and convention representatives from Rhode Island, Massachusetts, and Connecticut. Also portrayed is English King George III who encouraged them with the words, "O 'tis my Yankey boys! Jump in my fine fellows; plenty molasses and Codfish; plenty of goods to Smuggle; Honours, titles and Nobility into the bargain." On the left, below the cliff, is a medallion inscribed with the names of several of the war's heroes. Courtesy of the Library of Congress.

The *Boston Daily Advertiser* article was written by Nathan Hale, the nephew of the famous Revolutionary War hero of the same name. His essay captured the essence of one of the prime motivators of the convention: the growing defense problem coming out of state and federal governments' inability to agree on how to pay and supply their militiamen.[3] The author of the next piece, John Russell, clearly articulated the feeling of convention members that they were the bona fide representatives of the states that had sent them and that the people back home were depending on them. The last entry in this section, written by the anonymous Epaminondas, sought to reassure New Englanders that the Madison administration could not harm them with military action.

The chapter's anti-convention section begins with a piece published in New York City by editor Charles Holt about a month before the convention started. Rumors had predicted that a convention would be held, and Holt wondered whether all of New England would be involved.

Critics of Federalism such as Beta, who wrote for the November 11 *National Intelligencer,* looked for the reasons behind the upcoming gathering in New England. Perhaps, he speculated, the only hope for the men of Massachusetts to regain their lost power was to seek to change the Constitution through the organization of a formal convention to do so.

In the section's third essay, published in the November 21 *Intelligencer,* Hosmer wondered whether the rest of America would miss the "eastern malcontents" if they chose to secede.

The final entry in the anti-convention section, published in the December 26 *Intelligencer,* was written by a correspondent reporting from Hartford. According to this piece of correspondence, many of Hartford's citizens were not in favor of the convention.

The chapter's final section includes two newspaper columns published years after the Hartford Convention. The first was written by John Milton Niles and was published in the January 21, 1817, issue of a Hartford newspaper named *The Times.* The reputation of the city of Hartford had been so sullied by the convention, according to Niles, that it was time to call on its organizers to take their share of the blame.

Finally, a series of six letters published in the *National Intelligencer* early in 1820 began with the author's hope that the record could be set straight. As one of the conventioneers, he said he had special knowledge of what transpired there. He argued against the common belief that the convention called for the secession of New England from the Union. He mentioned that, since the country was then in a period of political calm, it was an ideal time to heal old wounds.

IN SUPPORT OF THE CONVENTION

Benjamin Russell: "One Voice for Peace"

Talk of secession circulated in New England by early 1813. In this essay, Benjamin Russell, the Centinel's *editor and a strident critic of Republican presidents and their politics, argued for a formal separation of New England from the South and the West. At this point he wasn't arguing for secession, but he threatened that "we must drag them out of it [the war]; or the chain will break." A year later, he strongly supported the Hartford Convention.*

Columbian Centinel (Boston), 13 January 1813

North of the Delaware, there is among all who do not bask or expect to bask in the Executive sunshine but one voice for Peace. South of that river, the general cry is "Open war, O peers!" There are not two hostile nations upon earth whose views of the principles and polity of a perfect commonwealth, and of men and measures, are more discordant than those of these two great divisions. There is but little of congeniality or sympathy in our notions or feelings; and this small residuum will be extinguished by this withering war....

The sentiment is hourly extending, and in these North States will soon be universal, that we are in a condition no better in relation to the South than that of a conquered people. We have been compelled without the least necessity or occasion to renounce our habits, occupations, means of happiness, and subsistence. We are plunged into a war, without a sense of enmity, or a perception of sufficient provocation; and obliged to fight the battles of a Cabal which, under the sickening affectation of republican equality, aims at trampling into the dust the weight, influence, and power of Commerce and her dependencies. We, whose soil was the hotbed and whose ships were the nursery of Sailors, are insulted with the hypocrisy of a devotedness to Sailors' rights, and the arrogance of a pretended skill in maritime jurisprudence, by those whose country furnishes no navigation beyond the size of a ferryboat or an Indian canoe. We have no more interest in waging this sort of war, at this period and under these circumstances, at the command of Virginia, than Holland in accelerating her ruin by uniting her destiny to France. ... The consequences of this state of things must then be, either that the Southern States must drag the Northern States farther into the war, or we must drag them out of it; or the chain will break. This will be the "imposing attitude" of the next year. We must no longer be deafened by senseless clamors about a separation of the States. It is an event we do not desire, not because we have derived advantages from the compact, but because we cannot foresee or limit the dangers or effects of revolution. But the States are separated in fact, when one section assumes an imposing attitude, and with high hand perseveres in measures fatal to the interests and repugnant to the opinions of another section, by dint of a geographical majority.

Benjamin Russell: "The Spirit of 1776: The Crisis"

By late 1814, many New Englanders were so exasperated by the war and the events surrounding it that they began to call for radical initiatives. Here, Russell argued that nothing short of rising up against the government would stop the "utter destruction" of the country.

Columbian Centinel (Boston), 10 September 1814

What, then, shall we do to be saved? One thing only: The people must rise in their majesty—PROTECT THEMSELVES, and compel their unworthy servants to obey their will. Love to the Constitution which has been so shamefully abused will pressure Mr. Madison in his chair until his term expires; but he ought to be compelled to use his power to save the country from utter destruction. He ought to be compelled to dismiss his whole corps of incompetent or corrupt Ministers, and replace them with men of fortitude and love of country. In any other country but this, the state of things which exists here would activate the author of the mischief, or disgrace his advisers. In England, in much less perilous times, the King has been obliged to dismiss his favorite Ministers, and appoint others more agreeable to his people. And shall we, in a free government, submit to accumulating wretchedness two years more, because Mr. Madison is to be so long President? GOD forbid.—The subjects of despotic governments, in which the head of the despot must expiate his criminal abandonment of his country's interest, would wag their heads at us. But let us not lose our invaluable Constitution, because our present rulers are not fit to execute it. Let us officer and man the ship anew, and then see whether she will weather the storm. How shall this be done? is the question.— Let our Legislature, when assembled, choose Commissioners, and invite the neighboring States to do the same. Let these Delegates proceed to Washington, or wherever else Mr. Madison is to be found—and tell him, that he ought to change his Ministers and his measures;—that he must abandon the invasion of Canada—to say conquest would be ridiculous;—that he ought to show to the nation with whom we are at War, that those men who made that War when Bonaparte was making his last attempt to subjugate England through Russia, are not in power;—that he must, if necessary, recall some of his present obnoxious Envoys, and appoint others;—and that he must make one fair and honest attempt to obtain Peace without cunning or equivocation. If he will do...not, the country will rise, as one man, to finish the War, then, and not til then, just and necessary. If he will not do this, but will continue to prefer his party for his country, these Delegates should be empowered to adjust terms of union with other States, and to make a Peace for themselves. Self-preservation the great law of nature, requires this, and it is worse than idle to expect any other course. The union is already dissolved, practically.—The government now cannot protect the several States, if it would....

Nathan Hale: "To the Cry of Disunion"

A few weeks before the convention started its proceedings, Nathan Hale sought to set the record straight: The responsibility for the broken "bond of union" in the nation should be placed at the hands of the president and his minions. As is indicated here, at the heart of the problem was the disagreement between many of these states and the federal government over who should pay and supply soldiers.

Boston Daily Advertiser, 1 December 1814

To the cry of disunion and separation of the States, there is a very plain and obvious answer. The states are already separated—the bond of union is already broken—broken by you [the president], and the shortsighted, selfish politicians, who compose your councils . . . .

As we are now going on, we shall certainly be brought to irretrievable ruin. If the New England States determine to pay no money, and send forth no men, while the war continues, until their own defence is provided for, they may save themselves. This arrangement may do while the war lasts. But is the war to be eternal? Are the New England states, who are now unquestionably absolved from all obligations to the United States, to continue the war, if they can make peace?

The war is the most pressing and obvious evil; but all who hope for a radical cure, and a restoration to former vigour, must prepare for more thorough changes than peace can effect.

It was to take care of our commercial rights, as you say, that you made the war. Would it be unreasonable for us to take care of them ourselves in making a peace? The Convention cannot do a more popular act, not only in New England, but throughout the Atlantic states, than to make a peace for the good of the whole.

There may be some tender-nerved gentlemen who may be startled at these propositions. And there are, probably some grown up people who, in the language of the nursery, are afraid of pokers. Such gentlemen must comfort themselves with the reflection, that if the people find their able, and honorable, and wise men, unwilling to lead the way to a peaceable and lawful remedy of evils, they will undertake to do this work for themselves, and may not, while heated by the case know when they have pursued far enough to accomplish their object.

The Convention must report to their constituents on the subjects of peace and war. And if they find that war is to continue, it is to be hoped they will recommend, and that the States will adopt the recommendation, THAT NO MEN, OR MONEY, SHALL BE PERMITTED TO GO OUT OF NEW-ENGLAND UNTIL THE MILITIA EXPENSES ALREADY INCURRED ARE REIMBURSED, NOR UNTIL THE MOST AMPLE PROVISION IS MADE FOR THE DEFENCE OF THE NEW-ENGLAND STATES DURING THE CONTINUANCE OF THE WAR. They will be justified before God and man, for so doing.

John Russell: "New England Convention"

This brief report from Boston reinforced the idea that the public was depending on the body at Hartford to fix the nation's "calamities" through the use of any means necessary.

Boston Gazette, 15 December 1814

The Delegates chosen from the new-England States, to meet at Hartford (Conn.) communicate their important session this day. The hope of millions rest on their decisions, and that hope, we are assured, will not prove illusory, combining, as this august body does, men, who have not only the wisdom and talent to discern the cause of our national calamities; but spirit and fortitude enough to point out their remedy.

"Peacefully, if we can—Forcibly, if we must."

Epaminondas: "For the Columbian Centinel: Address to the Delegates of the New-England Convention"

In the midst of the convention, Epaminondas attempted to bolster its delegates with the thought that they had nothing to fear from the threats of military coercion from an administration so incompetent that it had failed miserably in all its initiatives in the current war with the British.

Columbian Centinel (Boston), 21 December 1814

We have been threatened with military coercion, if we proceed to concert measures for our relief. We have been told that our gracious masters of the South have a right to our allegiance and services, and that disciplined veterans are prepared to bring us to a sense of our duty. What have we to fear from the weak and idle threats of an Administration, who have waged war for three successive campaigns, having the controls of eight millions of people, and the disposal of the whole resources of an extensive, young, and flourishing country, against a petty province with fewer inhabitants then those of a single county of New England, and have not gained a single foot of territory within the enemy's lines, no, not even in the wildest regions of the Canadian forests? What have we to fear from rulers, who with the whole military force of the country at their command, after three months' warning, suffered four thousand of the enemy to enter our capital, destroy many millions of public property, and chase the august head of the nation and his secretaries from the seat of government? What have we to fear from men, who, with the treasures of the nation at their control, have not been able to procure money to keep the machine of government in motion, have suffered their armies to go unpaid, public works to stop, public creditors to invoke in vain the faith of the nation, and have finally acknowledge the government to be in a state of absolute bankruptcy?

Compare this wretched imbecility with the effectual exertions of the Washington of New-England, who, in less than forty hours, called to the defence of the capital of his State twenty thousand men—and in three days concentrated the whole population of the Commonwealth on the coast to repel the invading foe? Then say, if we have need to hide our faces at the menaces of our Southern masters. As well might the hun of the forest tremble at the threats of the humble threat of a mole-hill, or Jupiter fear to be hurled from his orbit by the attraction of his revolving satellites.

We shall hereafter disclose to you our views—First, relative to our right to adopt measures for speedy relief; second, the expediency of such measures; Third, their nature, and the mode of carrying them into effect.

VIEWS AGAINST THE CONVENTION

Charles Holt: "British Alarmists"

Rumors circulating through the Union about the possibility of a meeting in Hartford were rampant in the months beforehand. Prominent Democratic editor Charles Holt asked whether all of New England's states would send delegates.

The Columbian (New York City), 7 November 1814

The...convention at Hartford is talked of with seeming formality and seriousness by the Boston alarmists and dreamers of treason. They appear to forget that they are possibly calculating without their host. Although Massachusetts and Connecticut have appointed delegates, it is to be seen whether New Hampshire, Vermont, and Rhode Island will join them in the *brimborion* of seditions, menace and impotent blustering. And if the Jacobin assembly should meet,...the mountainous labor of the illustrious congregation would undoubtedly issue in a result equal in magnitude and effect to the resolutions of the late federal convention at Albany—in a very harmless conclusion to support the laws and government of this country, and save all...[from] another puff of what is commonly called *Boston smoke.*

Beta: "To the Editor"

According to Beta, the motives behind certain Federalists' plans for a convention lay in their desperation to regain political power.

National Intelligencer (District of Columbia), 11 November 1814

Gentlemen,

In looking over the Journals of the Old Congress, a day or two ago, at page 112, of the first volume (in the year 1775), I was perfectly astonished at the contrast between the conduct of the state of Massachu-setts *then,* and *now*. In 1775, she *solicited the* ADVICE and DIRECTION *of Congress;* in 1814, she puts herself forward to *dictate* to the U. States! What is the cause of this alteration? I know not; unless it be, what is openly avowed in a late "Boston Gazette," that there is no hope of cer-tain men in that commonwealth getting into power without *a change of the constitution!* But would the change really answer the purpose? And where would the doctrine lead to? Were it possible for Massachusetts to set up a new form of government upon such an unhallowed pretext, another minority would spring up, and being stimulated by an ambi-tion equally hot, might, to gratify their impatient lust of rule, frame a third constitution; and so on, without end. The ground which the "Boston Gazette" takes is that, a minority, not being able to obtain power by fair election of the people, may, to effect their object, set up new civil institutions when they please. I annex the passage in the Journals to which I allude, and ask the favor of you to print it. I do not believe it will make Harry Otis blush, or touch the sensibility of Mr. Pickering: But there are many good men in Massachusetts to whom it will, I doubt not, be gratifying. There is a fine relish of virtue and wis-dom in it, which puts to shame the silly pranks of the weak and wicked men who are, at present, misleading that commonwealth.

Hosmer: "The Eastern Malcontents"

It's wondered how New Englanders felt when they read Hosmer's piece: America wouldn't miss the "eastern malcontents" if they seceded from the union. The loss of such "little states" would pose no hardships for the richer, more enterprising people of the areas outside the rebelling states.

National Intelligencer (District of Columbia), 21 November 1814

The eastern malcontents have brought on their own crisis, and they must suffer or be reclaimed. We can meet all the imposition on the country they injure and disgrace, and we can give them the treatment which justice, honor and patriotism demand at our hands.—The eastern malcontents are worse than the enemy, for they have excited the enemy against this coun-try.—They continue to draw him on us. Let them try the world without our provisions; our raw materials; our carrying trade; our markets for their pro-duce, manufacturers, ships and fish.

The whole soil of Massachusetts proper, Connecticut and Rhode Island, is less productive than one fourth of the soil of New York. Our extensive country, full of national advantages, will draw away from that limited region, its industrious, enterprising people, attached to equal rights in religion &c. politics; manufacturers, ship-builders and farmers, who can have no share in a soil of a few million acres, subject to long winters, which makes man and beast eat up their crops. The eastern farming genius, or their young and enterprising population, operating upon the immense soil of the states south and west of Connecticut, have fields of wealth before them, instead of the little patches of poor soil which can be bought or hired by them in the old eastern settlements. The energy of this country is suppressed by keeping a million of persons upon a few millions of acres in those little states; less in extent than a quarter part of New York, Pennsylvania, Virginia, Georgia, Ohio, &c. on an average. It is this wise principle of action, the movement from the old eastern settlements, that has given us the energetic states of Maine, Vermont, Kentucky, Ohio, &c. in a great measure. It will go on. It is a duty to promote it since the eastern malcontents try to destroy us. If they risk their lives and fortunes by a vain attempt at separation, it will be specially our duty to force these movements by preventing the consumption of all eastern produce, manufacturers, fish, and the sale and employment of their ships. The virtuous people may be facilitated at the same time, in moving with every description of property, free of duty, into the state which shall not attempt to violate the constitution, or lessen the federal capacity or authority. These reflections are deemed necessary at this crisis, when unprincipled or thoughtless men seem hurrying on to civil commotion. They are offered in great deference to the understanding of an enlightened community, and its men in authority.

Anonymous: "Hartford Convention"

There was considerable interest across the nation about the proceedings in Hartford, and the slowness of mail delivery must have added to the frustration. This description of the lukewarm reaction of some of Hartford's citizens to the convention must have offered some comfort to its critics.

National Intelligencer (District of Columbia), 26 December 1814

The gentlemen who have been often named as forming this body, convened in this city on Thursday last. As their proceedings, like those of all persons "whose deeds are evil," are involved in darkness, we can inform our readers of but little respecting them. All we are yet permitted to know is, that twelve Massachusetts men, seven Connecticut men, four Rhode-Island men, and two New-Hampshire men, met in the council chamber on that day; made choice of George Cabot for the Chairman, and Theodore Dwight, the editor of the Connecticut Mirror, for their Secretary. A Capt. Dunham, late editor of the Washingtonian, applied for admission, as a representative from the state of Vermont, but was refused the honor of a sitting.

The approach of this meeting has been observed with much anxiety by the citizens of this & the neighbouring towns. A Considerable concourse of people assembled here on the day, expecting, undoubtedly, to see something. But when they found that the great men resorted in a private apartment, like beasts of prey to their den, they went their way with much chagrin and disappointment.

The expression depicted on the countenances of men, were generally that of contempt and abhorrence of the plot. Some of the lighter sort, however, appeared as much pleased as if it were the annunciation of the jubilee.

The American flag was displayed thro' the day, with the British flag beneath at half mast. Three of the meeting-house bells tolled a solemn knell, and the United States' band of music played appropriate (funeral) marches through the streets. Upon the whole, we are fully satisfied that the people generally expect nothing good from this convention.

In Retrospect

John Milton Niles: "On Hartford's Fame"

Hartford should not be heaped with all the blame for the Hartford Convention, according to the author of this piece. John Milton Niles, editor of The Times, *argued that the Boston Federalists who organized the convention should take share in the opprobrium attached to the event. Niles was a young Republican lawyer who sought, through his newspaper, to diffuse "correct political information...the support of Republican principles... and...the encouragement of TOLERATION."*

The Times (Hartford, Conn.), 21 January 1817

Many circumstances have occurred since the commencement of the late war, which have rendered the city of Hartford famous; and in the opinion of many, it would seem infamous. If there are no considerations which can destroy that association of ideas in the mind, which has connected the words "HARTFORD CONVENTION" with the ideas of treason, disunion, and all the horrors of a civil war, there are, we believe, some reasons which may be suggested, calculated to shew that this city and this State, have received *more* than their *quota* of the *honor* and *glory* which so justly belong to the "Cossack faction," for their distinguished zeal and exertions in the late war.

The citizens in general of this town and of this state, do not thank the 'Bulwark Junto' of Boston, for having inveighed some of the leaders of the federal party, and through their influence, to have made this State an *ally* in the war which they were proposing to prosecute against "Madison's War"— They do not thank them for having made Hartford the PANDEMONIUM of their councils.—They do not thank them for having dissuaded, by a delegation sent from Boston expressly for the purpose, the then Governor of the State, (now no more) from complying with the requisition of the executive, for ordering the militia into service, from which measure the State has been subjected to an expense of one hundred and fifty thousand dollars…. We could pursue this detail to a great extent, but the limits designed for this article will not admit of it. But we hope that the facts here noticed, will at least have the effect of diminishing the opprobrium, which seems to be so profusely bestowed upon this State, and upon this city.

A Convention Attendee: "Hartford Convention— Letter I"

The editors of the National Intelligencer *were persuaded in early 1820 to run a series of six letters about the Hartford Convention. This excerpt from the first letter revealed its author's hope that the record be set straight as to what happened at the convention. In short, the author argued against the common belief that the convention called for the secession of various New England states from the Union. Because the country was in a calmer political period—the Era of Good Feelings— at the time of these writings, the author considered it a suitable time to address this contentious issue.*

National Intelligencer (District of Columbia), 8 January 1820

Gentlemen:

I herewith send you an attested copy of the private journal of the convention held at Hartford during the late war….

The transcript is, therefore, with your permission to be deposited on your shelf, solely to the end, that an opportunity may be afforded to any persons at the seat of government, whose curiosity may prompt them to devote an half hour to its perusal, of becoming acquainted with the entire proceedings of that Convention, including all the motions, propositions, and resolutions which were therein offered or debated. Thus, by comparing the original report with the journal, it will conclusively appear, beyond all probability of doubt in any ingenious mind, not only that no project for a separate confederacy, or in any other mode hostile to the integrity of the Union or the success of the war, was entertained or moved in that body, but that the original report did truly contain the substance of whatever was there mediated or transcribed.

Such, however, it is well known, is not the prevailing impression in many parts of this country, concerning the genuine character of that convention. The very name is a by-word, with thousands who never read its proceedings, which, by a talismanic influence presents at once to the disturbed and irritated imagination the specters of disunion, and civil war and treason…. In a word, it is the firm persuasion of many, that the design and tendency of that Convention, was a dismemberment of the Union, and that the event of peace alone prevented the ripening of this combination to full and fatal maturity. This illusion is not confined to minds which are rendered, by prejudice or credulity, receptacles of gross and vulgar errors. In many instances it has beguiled the understanding of men, gifted with powers of discrimination, and disposed to the exercise of candor, but habitually reposing too exclusively upon partial sources of information. It is no reproach to persons of this description (which is not common to our nature), that they have not always investigated the evidence by which their judgment of the views and measures of political antagonists should be regulated. Amid wars and the dissensions which grow out of them in free states, the portraits which contending factions draw of each other are always received as likenesses, by those who are unacquainted with, the disposed to think ill of the originals…. It can hardly be supposed that the irritation produced by the conflict of opinion respecting the late war, has so entirely subsided, that a patient hearing might be expected of a vindication of the conduct of the states or individuals who approved of that measure. And no disposition is felt, at this moment, to undertake their defence, or even to disturb the opinion of those who protest against the legitimacy of all conventions of states, or against the special acts of the Hartford Convention. But as the distinction of the great parties of the nation no longer appears in a conflict of opinions and interests, but has assumed the character of mere personal competition: and, as the passions which perpetuate the contentions for civil and religious rights, in governments where these are at issue, ought not to rankle, long after their causes have ceased, in the bosoms of a people who differ only in the means of promoting a national welfare, of which all are equally entitled to partake; it is hoped that it may not be too early to attempt to rectify errors in fact, which originate in misconception, and which, without affording support to any system of political opinions, are calculated to infuse a stain upon the character of one part of the nation, and to cherish acrimonious feelings and contentions, from which no advantage, but probably discredit and injury, may result to the whole.

QUESTIONS

1. Compare the actions of the 26 members of the Hartford Convention to those involved in the Burr conspiracy (see chapter 13). Why were the conventioneers not tried for treason?
2. Although the war was extremely unpopular in Connecticut, why would the citizens of Hartford tend to resent the convention so much?
3. The Hartford Convention illustrates just how unpopular the War of 1812 was. Compare its unpopularity with that of other wars in America's history.
4. Discuss the various difficulties experienced by early Americans during this period because the news traveled so slowly. How did this compare with today's news coverage?
5. Before and during the Hartford Convention, rumors circulated about its purpose and proceedings. Describe the role newspapers play in starting and/or stopping rumors.

NOTES

1. Brother C. Edward, " 'Marats, Dantons, and Robespierres': The Hartford Convention," *American History Illustrated* 12 (1977): 10–16.

2. Theodore Dwight, *History of the Hartford Convention: With a Review of the Policy of the United States Government which Led to the War of 1812* (New York: N. & J. White; Boston: Russell, Odiorne & Co., 1833).

3. Donald R. Hickey, "New England's Defense Problem and the Genesis of the Hartford Convention," *New England Quarterly* 50 (1977): 587–604.

CHAPTER 21

The Era of Good Feelings, 1817

Historians have labeled the early national period the "Black Age of American Journalism" because the time's political volatility led its editors and writers to write with extreme viciousness.[1] Newspaper editor James Cheetham's columns were so inflammatory that he was sued more than a dozen times after immigrating to New York City from England in 1798. Cheetham was sued in 1807, for instance, by a political opponent who he had accused of cheating at a card game. Even more notorious as a scandalmonger was James Thomson Callender (see chapter 8), who infuriated Republicans when he exposed President Jefferson's affair with Sally Hemings, one of his slaves.[2] Journalism was at times so incendiary that there were occasional calls to clean it up. In an 1800 Massachusetts newspaper column titled "On Calumny," a writer in the *Newburyport Herald and Country Gazette* stated:

> There cannot exist a more odious character than the calumniator. He is the bane of society, and dissolver of all social obligations.—He sows dissention between friend and relatives, and engenders a distaste for each other that ends but with life: and, in my opinion, I cannot close this subject better than offering the following quotation from an ancient author: "That he who pretends to correct the vices of others, ought himself to be free from the imputation of blame."[3]

But despite society's distaste for the time's intense political partisanship, this trend continued until the 1816 presidential election, when a new, less politically antagonistic, mood began to overtake the country. The country's mood was changing because, as it would later become obvious, the Federalist Party was dying a self-imposed death. Their leaders' opposition to the War of 1812 (see chapter 18) and support of the Hartford Convention (see

295

chapter 20) hurt the party's reputation badly. Rufus King, a staunch Federalist who had long supported a strong central government, was the last candidate of the old party of George Washington and Alexander Hamilton who would run in a presidential election. According to historian George Dangerfield, federalism essentially ceased to exist, although it "clung, in a rather fungoid manner, to certain localities."[4] Democratic-Republican candidate James Monroe won the presidential election in a landslide victory, winning 183 of the country's 217 electoral votes.

The question addressed in this chapter is how the nation's newspaper editors and writers reacted to the altered political landscape. Considering the strong political character of America's newspapers in the period preceding the demise of the Federalist Party, one might guess that the calmer environment would become an issue for those who published them. This chapter explores whether this indeed was the case. Its first section includes newspaper reports and essays that acknowledged the changes in the environment and that, in some cases, responded by calling for changes in the editorial contents of newspapers. The second section includes statements from newspaper writers who rejected the notion that the nation's newspapers ought to put their rhetorical tools in the nation's political wars to rest. Although the Era of Good Feelings would only exist for a few years, its effects on the country's newspapers shed light on how people were affected by it.

The initial piece in the first section is the most famous newspaper piece of the period, since it's where historians' name for the period—the Era of Good Feelings—came from. A few months after James Monroe was inaugurated, he went on a jubilee tour of the country. When, in mid-July 1817, he reached the Boston area, Benjamin Russell, the stalwart Federalist editor of Boston's *Columbian Centinel*, described the event under the heading "Era of Good Feelings." Through the countryside and across the city, wrote Russell, throngs of friendly people met the president's procession. He also described how unusual it was to see people from different political camps dining together in harmony.[5] In the years to come, Russell began to soften his stance on the Republican Party. In response, several of his correspondents refused to subscribe to his paper, and slowly, its circulation declined.[6]

The *Centinel*'s report is followed by a piece written by a Hartford, Connecticut, newspaper editor ecstatic over the Republican Party's success in the fall elections. John Milton Niles enjoyed the unprecedented success of the Republicans in that state's elections. In reaction, he heralded the dawn of a new and glorious era. According to Niles, New England Republicans' sweep of Connecticut was a sweet victory. To mark the occasion, Niles included a series of essays called "Age of Improvements," in the *Times*.[7]

The next two essays include comments on the editorial adjustments editors were forced to make in light of the radical shift in the political climate. According to the editors of the Baltimore *Morning Chronicle,* allegiance to the broader interests of Americans, rather than the more narrowly defined interests of political party leaders, was an essential step for them. Editors Thomas Maund and Frederick G. Schaeffer had started the *Chronicle* the year before to provide their friend and poet Paul Allen with an editorial position. Allen had previously edited the *Federal Republican and Baltimore Telegraph* but had left that position after a disagreement with his associates.[8]

Like Baltimore's Maund and Schaeffer, Vermont editor David Watson pledged in 1820 that his newly launched newspaper would not provoke its readers by bringing up old political arguments. Instead, he wrote, his newspaper would be tied to "Americanism," with a firm commitment to the U.S. Constitution. Watson's newspaper career began in Boston in 1810, and from there he started papers in New Hampshire, Vermont, Massachusetts, and New York. Comparing his newspaper's introductory prospectuses across the years of his career reveals the shifts the political system underwent.[9]

James C. Dunn and William A. Rind Jr., the authors of the section's last essay, more specifically stated what the contents of their newly designed newspaper would become. Both of the editors had published political newspapers before they started the *National Messenger* in Georgetown in 1817. Rind was raised in a family of well-known Federalist printers and editors. His father was the rabidly Federalist publisher William A. Rind Sr., operator and editor of Georgetown's *Washington Federalist* from 1800 to 1807.

The writers of the newspaper columns included in this chapter's second section were much less inclined to give in to the idea that politics would no longer be a factor in America. It begins with several pieces from the *American Watchman,* which was published in Wilmington, Delaware. Selleck Osborn, the editor, was adamantly opposed to the idea that Federalists and Republicans could "marry." In "The Banns Forbidden," he told a tongue-in-cheek story about a religious minister having a conversation with one of his flock about the advisability of a marriage between two members of the congregation. Osborn's second piece is less humorous, but it has a similar warning about the impossibility of Federalists and Republicans successfully coming together.

In Kentucky, John Norvell was just as convinced as Osborn that Republicans and Federalists could never coexist in harmony. Two of the essays he published in his *Kentucky Gazette* speak to this idea. In the first, Norvell claimed adherents of such an idea were in a state of disillusionment. In the second, he argued that the credibility of anyone who claimed "partyism" could be avoided would be tarnished. He also claimed that those who touted their adherence to a new canon of political neutrality should not be trusted.

Acknowledging the Dawn of the Era of Good Feelings

Benjamin Russell: "Era of Good Feelings"

Here is an excerpt from the now famous "Era of Good Feelings" report published in the Centinel *in 1817. The* Centinel *was an extremely powerful Federalist newspaper in Boston at the time this was written. But within a few years of this report, it began to decline in popularity. Russell retired from journalism in 1828. Newspaper historian Joseph T. Buckingham wrote that Russell retired when he realized the old style of journalism was no longer viable.*[10]

Columbian Centinel (Boston), 12 July 1817

During the late Presidential Jubilee many persons have met at festive boards, in pleasant converse, whom party politics had long severed. We recur with pleasure to all the circumstances which attended the demonstrations of good feelings.

John Milton Niles: "A New Era"

The fall 1817 elections in Connecticut, a longtime stronghold of Federalism, brought stunning victories to members of the Republican Party. In a series of reports and essays, the editor of the Times *heralded the "new era" through announcements of their party's "Glorious Triumph!!"*

The Times (Hartford, Conn.), 23 September 1817

The 15th of September, 1817, will long remain a proud era in the annals of Connecticut—an era from whence the state will receive a new and renovated character. On that day a system of political dominion, founded in mystery and delusion, supported by falsehood and hypocrisy, and strengthened by innumerable guards, the offspring of abused power—a system which legalized political fraud, encouraged dissimulation, combined the elements of fanaticism, enveloped itself in darkness, armed itself with the terrors of superstition, and was upheld by subverting the authority of reason and common sense—on that day this system FELL, NEVER TO RISE AGAIN. How great the fall, and how many have been overwhelmed in its ruins! We compassionate the *innocent* sufferers, and recognize the superintendance of Providence in the hand of retributive justice, which has fallen so heavily on the *guilty*.

But is it true that these things are so? Is it a reality, or is it the "baseless fabric of a vision?" Yes, it is true. Connecticut federalism is no more. It has fallen, and but a wreck remains as a sad memorial of what it once was.

Thomas Martin Maund and Frederick G. Schaeffer: *"The Chronicle"*

Like that of these two editors, a common approach during the period was to announce that, amid a new calmer era, it was necessary to adhere to a new "American" party, rather than the old Federalist or Republican parties.

Morning Chronicle and Baltimore Advertiser (Maryland), 8 April 1819

The *Chronicle* makes its first entry into the public, when the storms of political vengeance have ceased to beat; when the season so happily denominated the "Era of Good Feelings" has arrived.... With regard to the politics of this paper, it becomes necessary to state, that we shall endeavor to be exclusively American...[a pledge that some might say] includes everything and means nothing.... [But] we mean by the term American, what the term American strictly imparts—an ardent attachment to our native country.

David Watson: "Since the Political Elements...Have Ceased to War"

Editor Watson's 1820 introductory prospectus was imbued with the spirit of the new political era. Among the things he promised his new readers was that he would not print material that was charged with "party spirit."

Woodstock Observer (Vermont), 11 January 1820

Since the political elements of our government have ceased to war with each other; and since those of the European world are generally marked with the same character—no political animadversions shall be admitted into our paper, tainted, in the slightest degree, with the acrimony of party. Its character shall be purely American—a supporter of the rights and liberties of the people, and the constitution upon which those rights are predicated.

James C. Dunn and W. A. Rind Jr.:
"Universal Tranquility"

With the loss of their newspaper's primary political target—the Federalists—the two proprietors of this Georgetown newspaper issued a statement explaining their newspaper's new character. Out of necessity, they were altering the paper's size, appearance, and editorial complexion so that it would stay in tune with the community's new political environment.

National Messenger and Town and City Commercial Gazette (Georgetown, District of Columbia), 27 October 1817

Universal tranquility deprives the journalist not only of the topics legitimate to the nature of his profession, but of that endless reciprocation of conflicting opinions which arise out of them. To attract public attention in storm times, and to keep it from slumbering in the dead calm of universal and domestic tranquility, are efforts of very different natures.... The current politics of the day...will hardly saturate our columns or satisfy the curiosity of the public.... It shall be our business therefore to provide articles of amusement and information in other departments of science for the perusal of our readers. In our columns will be found essays either original or selected, on moral, scientific and literary subjects; chosen pieces of poetry, occasional strictures on the drama, and notices of, and extracts from such new publications, as shall appear to be clearly deserving of that distinction; and in a word, all such selections of matter as newspapers generally communicate.

REJECTING THE IDEA OF A NEW POLITICAL ERA

Selleck Osborn: "The Banns Forbidden"

The idea that Republicans should embrace the Federalists who so adamantly opposed them in previous times was abhorrent to this Republican writer. Even though the conciliatory behavior of Republicans and Federalists toward each other might resemble a kind of marriage banns, such diametrically opposed groups could never successfully form such a union, wrote Osborn in this stab at the idea of the coupling of the two old enemies.

American Watchman (Wilmington, Del.), 9 August 1817

"Marriage is intended between American Democracy and New England Federalism.—Whoever may know of any impediment or any sufficient cause why these parties should not be joined in wedlock, let them now speak, or forever hold their peace!"

—WE FORBID THE BANNS—

"You do? Then please to shew cause."

Then, and please your reverence, the cause is morally, if not legally sufficient—it is no less than absolute and irremovable incompatibility.

"But do you not wish for the abolition of party spirit, and the restoration of general harmony?"

Certainly—all the personal spirit of party—all pistoling, cudgeling, nose-pulling, abusive, slandering party spirit (such as that of '98) is already pretty much at an end; and so much of that spirit is militated against good neighbourhood. I wish entirely extirpated; as much social harmony as your reverence pleases; but no confounding of characters—no marrying. If we grasp at too much we shall lose what we have got. If you would have the parties peaceable, do not bring them too near together. Your reverence undoubtedly knows of some who get along very well as friends and neighbors; but marry them, and they would soon quarrel. Therefore, we forbid the Banns.

Selleck Osborn: "The Question Brought Home"

Osborn wrote prolifically on the idea that Federalists, now in an enfeebled condition, ought to be greeted with friendliness by Republicans.

American Watchman (Wilmington, Del.), 13 August 1817

When a man of little or no fortune proposes to join in the business and share the profits of an opulent dealer, it is very natural for the latter to ask, "As you have confessedly no funds, what have you got to invest by way of stock, to entitle you to a share, more or less, of the avails of my establishment? Have you an uncommonly thorough acquaintance with the goods in my line, or remarkable abilities or prudence as a merchant? Have you any voucher for your uprightedness and correctness heretofore, as an employer; or of your fidelity, capacity, and sober deportment, as one employed? Can I depend upon your friendship or zeal in a case of exigency?—And finally, have you such a confidence in my integrity and ability, as to make the proposed connection desirable upon fair and honest principles, with a view to mutual benefit? I am particular on the last point."

How would the federal party—whose political connection with republicans is now a fashionable subject of conversation—how would that party answer such questions, or how could they be truly answered in its behalf? The party which so miserably misunderstood the interests and character of the people, as to forfeit their confidence in one short trial of four years, could no more be considered as having ability and prudence in the art of government, than he could be said to be a good horseman, who should be thrown from his saddle the moment after he had fairly seated himself upon it.—What voucher has Federalism in its favor, as the head of an establishment, when the concerns of a free people were confided to its management? Alas! After a bustling, dashing, random style of business, in four short years its credit was prostrated, its custom withdrawn, and itself bankrupt!—What shall be said of the deportment of Federalism, when Democracy had succeeded to the possession of the establishment? Was it not (to carry on the figure) like that of one who abjectly seeks for any employment in the service of one whom he had always professed to hate as a rival; and abuses him if he is denied; or, if employed, returns the favor with cool and ungrateful treachery.

Let the laws and law minister, which gave to the short period of federal rule the emphatic designation of the "reign of terror," show how just and prudent federalism was at the head of a concern: Let the speeches and newspapers of that party, from 1800 to 1814, shew the decorous, the faithful, the sober deportment of federalism in a subordinate capacity!

But what answer shall federalism make to the most startling question of all—Have I reason to depend upon your friendship and zeal in a trying moment? When robbers were at my door, were you on the ground? When my house was on fire, were you there? In the day of my distress, were you near me? Alas! poor federalism can only reply—"I was indeed there; but it was rather to hinder than assist you—I guided and encouraged the robbers! I fanned the flames! I mocked you in the day of your distress!!! I even endeavored by menaces and persuasions, to prevent people from lending you money, avowedly for the purpose of compelling you to give up the concern!! Now, will you not take me into partnership?"

John Norvell: "A…Gross Delusion"

Norvell questioned the sanity of anyone who, as he put it, deluded themselves into thinking that relationships between Republicans and Federalists could ever be cordial, let alone agreeable.

Kentucky Gazette (Lexington), 16 October 1817

The truth is, that never did a more gross delusion seize the minds of rational men [than the idea] that a cordial union could be effected between two parties so hostile in their feelings, so opposite in their principles…The experiment has tended to depress the republicans and give advantage to the federalists…. It has induced weak republicans to…propagate the fallacious notion, that the federalists as a party were a patriotic set of men; that between the two parties only a slight shade of difference [existed]…[I hope the Republicans will resist such efforts at] an unholy alliance [and resist politicians who come] disguised under the cloak of canting hypocrisy and smiling moderation.

John Norvell: "At the Present Day"

According to Norvell, anyone who promised that a newspaper could be free of party spirit was a hypocrite. Plenty of evidence existed, he wrote, that such people were saying one thing, yet doing another.

Kentucky Gazette (Lexington), 6 March 1819

Even at the present day, though an organized and systematic opposition to the republican cause has ceased to exist, yet it may be probably still expected, that the introductory address of an editor should contain something on this subject. As far then as partyism may still prevail, on the old grounds of division, we pledge ourselves that the Gazette shall still be, as it ever has been, found on the republican side…. We shall occupy no half way ground; we recognize not the doctrine of 'amalgamation.'…The politician who would regard the present calm in party politics, as proceeding from an oblivion or abandonment of those principles, which produced our late inflammatory discord, would be entitled to very little respect for his wisdom and penetration…. The leaders of the opposition still retain their principles…[and in some places] we find them still pursuing their old practices.

QUESTIONS

1. The Era of Good Feelings resulted when one of the nation's political parties lost its base of power so that the nation had only one political party. Do you believe nations are more democratic when two political parties exist rather than one? Why or why not?
2. Who was right: those who claimed it was the Era of Good Feelings or those who said that it was a ridiculous notion?
3. Other than political reports and articles, identify as many kinds of items published in the newspaper during the early decades of the nineteenth century as you can.
4. Describe the kinds of materials published in America's newspapers today. How much of the content of newspapers relates to politics?
5. If political parties ceased to exist today, what would American newspapers publish in place of the political news and opinion they disseminate?

NOTES

1. Frank Luther Mott, *American Journalism* (New York: Macmillan, 1962) named the early decades of the nineteenth century the "Black Age of American Journalism." W. David Sloan discusses this in "Scurrility and the Party Press, 1789–1816," *American Journalism* 5 (1988): 98–112.

2. On Cheetham, see Patricia L. Dooley, *Taking Their Political Place: Journalists and the Making of an Occupation* (Westport, Conn.: Greenwood Press, 1997), 100. On Callender, see Annette Gordon-Reed, *Thomas Jefferson and Sally Hemings: An American Controversy* (Charlottesville: University of Virginia Press, 1998).

3. "On Calumny," *Newburyport Herald and Country Gazette*, 21 February 1800.

4. George Dangerfield, *The Era of Good Feelings* (New York: Harcourt, Brace & World, 1952), 98.

5. Benjamin Russell, "Era of Good Feelings," *Columbian Centinel*, 12 July 1817.

6. Joseph T. Buckingham, *Specimens of Newspaper Literature* (Boston: Charles C. Little and James Brown, 1850), 2:96–103.

7. Jeffrey L. Pasley, "*The Tyranny of Printers*": *Newspaper Politics in the Early American Republic* (Charlottesville: University of Virginia Press, 2001), 371.

8. *Dictionary of American Biography* (New York: C. Scribner's Sons, 1928–1958), 202–203.

9. Dooley, *Taking Their Political Place*, 114–115.

10. Buckingham, *Specimens of Newspaper Literature*, 102–103.

CHAPTER 22

New York City's Wild Dogs, Mad Hogs, and Petty Criminals, 1816–1818

By contemporary standards, public health and safety conditions in New York and America's other growing cities were terrible in the early decades of the nineteenth century. City dwellers and visitors alike were increasingly confronted with public drunkenness, panhandling, and petty crime. Dogs were also a problem, especially when they ran around attacking children and other easy prey. To make matters even worse, the people of New York City were plagued by the many pigs that routinely wandered around, fouling the city's streets as they ate the garbage that piled up. After a trip to New York, Charles Dickens warned future visitors: "Take care of the pigs. Two portly sows are trotting up behind this carriage, and a select party of half a dozen gentlemen hogs have just now turned the corner.... They are the city scavengers, these pigs."[1]

Dickens was not exaggerating, and as the nation's fledgling cities grew, such conditions worsened. In 1800, Philadelphia's 72,000 citizens made it the nation's largest city. It wasn't long, however, before New York City caught up. The nation's fastest growing city, New York grew from 60,000 to 100,000 inhabitants from 1800 to 1810. Such extraordinary growth prompted a visiting senator from Massachusetts to say, "The progress of this city is...beyond calculation."[2]

Officials in the nation's growing cities slowly realized that they should institute remedies designed to make them safer and cleaner places to live. Dog owners, for example, were required to pay a $3 licensing fee, and a city-paid dogcatcher was responsible for controlling wild dogs. While such solutions were better than nothing, they were often not enough. To help out, a few newspaper editors campaigned for improved conditions in the columns of their newspapers. The fact that only a handful of the era's newspaper editors launched campaigns designed to prod authorities to clean up their towns and cities makes the work of editors like William Coleman, of the *New-York Evening Post,* and Naphtali Phillips, editor of the *National Advocate,* that much more interesting.

The chapter's first set of newspaper articles and essays focuses on the many dogs and hogs roaming the streets of New York City. All were published in the *New-York Evening Post,* a paper known by journalism historians more for its political journalism than for its broader civic campaigns. The first report described a dog attack on a young child. This is followed by a story about the growing threat of hydrophobia (rabies) posed by such wild dogs. All but a handful of the pieces in the group were written by the *Post's* editor, William Coleman. While Coleman is best known for his role as a political editor, as is seen here, he did not limit his campaigns to the political sphere.

The chapter's second section examines the problems of public drunkenness and petty crime in New York City and what ought to be done about them. In this area of concern, the *Post's* Coleman was joined by a second crusading editor, Naphtali Phillips. In the early decades of the nineteenth century, city governments and police forces did not have the resources they have today. In 1800, for example, no American city had a full-time professional police force. Instead, cities often employed policemen and marshals who did the best they could to suppress riots, maintain order, act as court officers, and arrest offenders. In 1800, New York City employed 16 day patrolmen and about 40 marshals. In 1801, John Hayes was appointed as New York City's high constable. It was his job to govern the city's small police force, and he did so for the next 50 years. In 1845, New York would be the first city in America to adopt a full-time professional police force.[3]

CRITICISM OF CITY MUNICIPAL LEADERS

William Coleman: "Dogs"

The "corporation" referred to here by Coleman was New York City's municipal government. While dog owners were to blame, he stated, the city's municipal leaders ought to take steps to remedy the situation of wild dogs on the street.

New-York Evening Post (New York City), 15 August 1816
We are desired to state, that a few days ago a large surly mastiff dog fell upon a child about 4 years old, at the corner of William and George-streets, and before he could be choked off threw [the child] down and lacerated its

face and body in a shocking manner. If citizens will keep dogs they should be compelled to confine them to their premises. They should never be suffered to run at large in cities like this, to the danger of the passengers by day and the inexpressible annoyance of those who lie languishing on beds of sickness at night. The attention of our corporation is solicited.

William Coleman: "Dogs"

Coleman's campaign against the city's wild dogs continued for years. The term "hydrophobia" used by Coleman referred to rabies, a fatal and incurable disease sometimes passed from animals to humans.

New-York Evening Post (New York City), 25 August 1818

These useless, and at the present time, dangerous animals, were more numerous in the streets yesterday, than we recollect before to have seen them. We ask again, why is this?—Are the lives of our citizens to be perpetually endangered? The hydrophobia may not have appeared in this city, although we are of a different opinion. But it is raging in our neighboring cities; and judging from the newspapers, instances of it are more numerous than we recollect to have known at any former period. Every dog now found in the street should be instantly killed.

William Coleman: "Hogs"

Coleman abhorred the hogs that roamed the city's streets and called on hog owners to take more responsibility. According to Coleman, the city's grocers were part of the problems. Grocers bought hogs when they were young, only to turn around and sell them after letting them fatten up by feeding off the garbage littering the streets.

New-York Evening Post (New York City), 25 August 1818

Since it has been found impossible either to reason or to shame the corporation into its duty in relation to this intolerable nuisance, is there not another consideration which will induce the *hog-proprietors* to keep their stock at home—or at least out of the streets? It is not uncommon to find in our shortest streets, twenty or thirty hogs. We have recently had one mad dog running through the streets; and it is impossible to say how many hogs he may have bitten. Suppose another dog should do the like, and neither the dogs nor the hogs should be confined, how long will it be before our streets will be full of mad dogs and hogs? Besides, there is another consideration.

These hogs, fattened upon the offal in the streets, after killing, it is presumed, find their way into Fly-market. And who knows but our citizens will be compelled to eat pork, partaking, in addition to the *delicious flavor* they will derive from the offal aforesaid, of the infection of hydrophobia! These are serious considerations. Really, what with the corporation, the hogs and the dogs, we are on the point of being in a hopeful way.

The public may judge as to the extent of the evil which the good people of this metropolis are suffering, in consequence of the vast number of hogs kept in the streets, from the circumstance that in the New-York Gazette, FORTY of these *agreeable street companions* were advertised to be sold at sheriff's sale, on Friday last—the property of a single Grocer in the upper part of the city. If every petty grocer keeps upon the town an equal number (and they have a right so to do), the *swinish multitude* of New-York will exceed all calculation!

F.: "Mad Dogs"

Coleman's columns on dogs struck a chord with this writer, who reported on a mad dog that threatened the people of one of New York City's neighborhoods. The corporation referred to in the letter was the agency set up to oversee the city's responsibilities. The author called on city corporation officials to establish, like they had in Washington, a corps of workers whose task it was to destroy loose animals. The author also stated that the mad dog nipped at several pigs running loose in the area. Hogs have been referred to by some as the city's earliest street cleaners.

New-York Evening Post (New York City), **27 August 1818**
I think after this, no person who regards his safety will venture out in the evening, in our streets, without being sufficiently armed, and on the look out. Late last evening, a great alarm was created in the neighborhood of Peck slip, by the appearance of a large dog, said to be mad.—He came up Dover, and passed down Pearl street to the slip, and being rather dark, disappeared. The few people stirring in that quarter ran in every direction for safety; the dog was seen to bite at two hogs as he passed down, and he had every appearance of being mad. How long the lives of our citizens are to be held in jeopardy, or how the members of our corporation can repose, while they neglect so important a duty, I know not.—What will be their feelings when they shall see a fellow citizen in the agonies of hydrophobia? Can they, as in the case of the hogs, have "divers unknown weighty reasons" for staying the annihilation of the dogs? Valuable watch-dogs may be confined to the owner's premises—Hunting dogs may be kept in the country—but above

all, let the city be cleared of the throngs "of mongrels, curs, and dogs of low degree," that infest the streets. I am informed that in Washington (albeit in much less danger from these animals than New-York), they have taken effectual measures; persons are to be employed to go the round, and hunt the streets daily, and shoot every dog which may be found.

You, Mr. Coleman, are not wont to leave any thing which regards the well-being of the city "untouched or slightly handled in discourse," and I beg you will treat this subject with the same freedom, for surely it has many urgent considerations.

William Coleman: "Alarming!"

Coleman's campaign to protect the citizens of New York from dogs and the hydrophobia he feared they would spread included this aggressive attack on city authorities. He called on citizens to take matters into their own hands, by leaving arsenic- and strychnine-laced garbage around so as to kill any dogs that ran wild. The day before this piece was published, Coleman included an instructional column on how to cure hydrophobia with a dose of a plant named alima plantago.

New-York Evening Post (New York City), 28 August 1818

Another mad dog was killed this morning in the lower part of Broadway, by a man who pursued him some distance. The most unequivocal evidences of madness were exhibited by the animal, & the side-walk was covered, several feet round the place where he fell, with a thick saliva or froth which issued from his mouth. His eyes were dreadfully distorted; his body thin and emaciated. Our informant adds, that in the course of his walk, this morning, he met more dogs than he had seen on any day before; and there can be little doubt that many of them have been bitten by the dog killed this morning. In addition to this, we can add our own testimony, that dogs have rarely been so plenty in the streets. In walking last evening, between eight and nine o'clock, from the City Hotel to the Park, we saw several dogs, some of a very large size; and the day before, near Fulton-slip, a large dog evidently in the first stages of the hydrophobia.

For God's sake, let the citizens be on their guard, and do their duty. We have appealed to the municipal authorities in vain, long enough. We have officers enough, who are paid for their services, and laws enough. But we have entirely relinquished all hopes which we may be entertained, that the citizens are to receive that attention from officers, or protection from the laws, to which they are entitled. At present there is no safety; and a prudent citizen will not walk the streets in the day, unless armed with some defensive weapon; and it is downright presumption to venture in the street at all in the evening. Indeed, it seems as though, in utter contempt for the safety and lives of our citizens, and a total disregard of official duty, as well as of all the fine feelings of humanity, the dogs are let loose upon us at this particular juncture. Perhaps, however, our police will awake from this criminal lethargy and indifference, when some dozen of our citizens, or of their immediate friends and relatives, are stretched upon the bed of torture, and writhing in all the frightful and convulsive agonies of hydrophobia!—Let these gentlemen picture to themselves this horrid spectacle! Let them fancy the affliction, the misery, the woe, which one instance of their neglect may bring into a family,—and say if the hundred tongues of conscience will not each bring in a several tale of condemnation.

In Philadelphia, it is recommended openly for the citizens to poison all dogs found in the streets. This, it is said, can easily be effected by dropping sausages poisoned with arsenic, or by enclosing a piece of *Nux Vomica* [strychnine] in a piece of meat. A piece of sponge, well greased, will be greedily swallowed by dogs, and soon terminates their lives. No danger to other animals attends this device.

K.: "Hogs Again"

The author of this 1818 letter painted a vivid picture of what it was like to live next door to a New York City house whose owners kept pigs or what it was like to simply walk the city's streets. Much to K.'s annoyance, the city's corporation would likely continue to do nothing to stop these problems.

New-York Evening Post (New York City), 10 September 1818

These disagreeable street walkers appear to be more numerous now than at any other period. Every where I go, I am more or less troubled, for I have to go out of my course (frequently off the walk), or receive from their backs what property belongs to the gutter. If I don't want to alter my course, and go up to them and strike them with my cane, or make use of my foot, they generally move nothing but their snout, and that only for the purpose of grunting; this is all I get for my trouble—after that I have to take my usual walk around them.

The very next door to where I live, there is a family…[and] connected with their dwelling there is a large yard, at the extremity of which they have two or three pens that contain, *at times,* the objects of my communication. In looking out of the back window the other day, when they were all assembled, I counted nine large, besides many small ones. If this were all, sir, it would be well—(for no one would wish to deprive poor persons from keeping hogs, if it assists them, provided they are kept up)—but this is far from being the case, for these disagreeable creatures are permitted in the morning to go out for *recreation;* if they do not get sufficient in the street to satisfy their *hoggish* appetites, they return to the gate—but *no admittance there* until night, and they are permitted by their owners to stand off and on until that time. The gate through which they have to pass is next to our house; the door of the house is next to the gate of this mansion, and during the day these hogs are continually passing and repassing the house (on the walk) or standing around the stoop, which, unfortunately, is not a high one, there being only two steps.—Every one will readily perceive our disagreeable situation; but it not only discommodes the family-persons passing through the street, must either go off the walk, be dirtied, or run down, neither of which would be very agreeable to a lady or gentleman.

To say more on this subject is useless, as nothing appears to have any influence with the honourable Corporation of our city. Though there is no reason why they should be let run at large in the streets, and though they are almost universally [acknowledged as] a nuisance, yet do our fathers of the city seem determined not to grant the wishes of the citizens to have them confined.

William Coleman: "The Dogs, the Hogs, and the *Columbian*"

For speaking out against city officials' apparent lack of concern about the dog and hog problems experienced by its residents, Coleman was criticized by the New York Columbian. *According to its editor, Coleman had a "disposition to find fault, rather than to inquire if there be any just cause of blame." In addition, Coleman was accused of making "unfounded representations calculated to render the magistrates odious." In this column, Coleman indignantly responded.*

New-York Evening Post (New York City), 2 September 1818

It is true that we have expressed ourselves with freedom, and considerable warmth, upon the subject of the armies of dogs which to this day run at large in our city, to the imminent hazard of the lives of our citizens; and also in relation to the droves of hogs which are suffered to infest our streets, maugre all decency, and to the great annoyance of all cleanly and civil people. True, we censured the tardiness of city officers; but we did not do it until a universal indignation prevailed the whole city, and the citizens were unanimous in the cry of Shame! Shame!...

Well, after preferring all the above charges against us, the writer proceeds gravely to vindicate and exculpate the police officers. Hear him:

"A law was passed some years ago, imposing a tax of three dollars on every dog kept in the city. The same law rendered every dog liable to be killed that should be running at large, and authorized the appointment of an officer to carry it into execution. In June last, a person was appointed to fill this office, then vacant by the resignation of a former incumbent. The new officer met with some difficulties in performing his duty, and the truth is, that the public feeling is generally so averse to a law of this nature, that there always will be great difficulty in executing it when the necessity for it is not apparent. The late alarm brought the subject again before the Common Council. After mature deliberation, it was thought they could make no better provision in relation to it what is made in the existing law."

And thus, because some few years ago the Corporation imposed the paltry, pitiful tax of three dollars upon this useless and dangerous animal, and have appointed an officer to execute the law, they have done all in their power, or all that was necessary and proper for the security of our citizens! "O most lame and impotent conclusion!" A tax of three dollars " 'Tis pitiful, 'tis wondrous pitiful." In some places, a tax of thirty, and in others, we believe, of fifty dollars is imposed. Yet the lives of our citizens are balanced against three dollars. Is it not mockery! Is it not insult! Why, in the present instance, on the first appearance of the hydrophobia, was not every dog ordered to be killed, and the owner of every one found in the streets, fined in the sum of one hundred dollars? The Corporation would then have deserved credit for their energy and humanity.

For ourselves, we care not a rush about the groundless and malicious charges preferred against us in the Columbian. They evidently proceeded from some one, writhing under the lash, and suffering from the stings of conscious guilt. We feel a consciousness of having discharged our duty, and we know we have the approving voice of the people.

As for the charge of endeavouring to render the magistrates "odious," we are innocent. If the license given to have our streets filled with dogs and hogs, the most dangerous and filthy of animals, will not cast odium upon them, we should despair in the undertaking.

CRITICISM OF CITY POLICE

William Coleman: "City Watch"

New York police, according to Coleman, had failed to catch or otherwise deter criminals from committing crimes in the city. This statement's last sentence revealed a possible political dimension to the problem. Coleman asked whether the new "political character of the corporation [the city government]" could be blamed for the lack of competence in the police force.

New-York Evening Post (New York City), 17 August 1816

Each successive night gives evidence of the commission of numerous crimes, and of the impunity with which they are perpetuated…. Some more efficient measures ought to be taken, without delay, by those whose immediate province it is to see that this department of the city police is strictly attended to—Hardly a night passes, without depredations upon property and outrages upon persons, and in the very heart of our city too, notwithstanding we are at the expense of employing several hundred men for the sole purpose of watching our repose—Shall we attribute the late relaxation in the police, to the new arrangement which has taken place since the political character of the corporation has changed, and the former captains of the watch, whatever their merit, have been turned out, and inexperienced men of different politics put in their places?

Naphtali Phillips: "City Police"

In the summer of 1816, the National Advocate *launched a campaign designed to prod the city police into doing a better job of handling New York's crime problem. The writer blamed the city's vagrant population and the police for the problems experienced by the city's citizens. Phillips also believed that the city's many immigrants were part of the problem. Naphtali Phillips was the* Advocate's *publisher when this piece was printed. Although he did hire professional editors, none is identifiable during the time this series was published.*

National Advocate (New York City), 19 August 1816

In a population of 100,000 souls, it is to be supposed there must be many vagrants, who, despising the "dull pursuits of civil life," resort to their wits, or rather their vices, to supply the deficiency which idleness and debauchery occasion. At this day, particularly the city of New-York is, perhaps, more exposed than any city of the world to these depredators and freebooters on society. Her contiguity to the ocean, and the general emigration of Europe, consisting of a heterogeneous mass of the discontented in the old world, the greater part of which make their debut in the U. States through this very city, introduces among us a continual succession of strange faces, who, in vulgar language, are "here today and gone tomorrow," and who, if their wants impel them to be rogues, are not, for the most part, scrupulous whose property they draw on to supply the cravings of the moment….

Nothing is more dangerous to the wellbeing of society, than a neglect which has, from long continuance, become a custom. It is like a false and vicious pronunciation; once contracted, it is more difficult to be overcome than to teach a novice a language to perfection. Such is the state of the nightly police of New-York; from long neglect and inattention, it has become so deteriorated, that it is as bad, if not worse, than none at all.

We are convinced the public will go hand and heart with us to correct and remedy this evil; and if we can direct the attention of the proper body to this subject—if we can point out the corrections and improvements necessary to be adopted, we shall not consider our labours as useless. This we shall attempt, and, we are vain enough to believe, if the remarks which we shall in future papers make on the general and nightly police of our city are attended to, that our citizens will find themselves in much more security, and our prisons and criminal courts will exhibit a more wholesome picture of the state of morality than they do at present.

Naphtali Phillips: "City Police"

In this piece in a series on the city's police, Phillips claimed that the police should do a better job of watching out for criminals during the night. Instead of trying to fix the old system, he challenged the city to create a new, more effective, one.

National Advocate (New York City), 21 August 1816

We shall not pretend to say, that if the city watch, as now organized, was strictly and rigidly attended to, and that every watchman performed, with exactitude, his tour of duty, and that each officer of the night scrupulously exerted himself to prevent neglect or remissness, that our city would, in such case, be the worst guarded city in the world; but as the reverse this is the fact, and as the neglect and inattention complained of has grown out of the old system, we would inquire whether to organize a new system, and set it in operation under rigid rules, would not be easier than to attempt to place that in a sound, regular and safe state, which, from long habit and abuse, has become corrupted and worthless? This is a question which it may not be amiss for our honourable corporation to ask themselves, provided they are satisfied that the police of the night is defective or unattended to, and that they feel an interest, which we do not for a moment doubt, in the safety of the lives and properties of its inhabitants . . . .

The system of the police of London has long been considered a disgrace to that great city, and rather calculated to encourage vice than to depress it . . .

whereas in the neighboring city of Paris such crimes are rarely heard of nor are they in any manner proportionable in any city on the continent.... Would it not, then be wholesome and beneficial to the interests of the community, that we should take a lesson, and copy from a system which has had so salutary an operation?...

William Coleman: "A Nuisance"

Public drunkenness was a problem in big cities in early America. This brief reference to this concern was just part of a number of public health and safety issues regularly complained about by Coleman.

New-York Evening Post (New York City), 17 August 1816

It has become a custom for certain fellows to lounge about the wharves at all hours of the day and night, and to commit petty thefts by sucking the liquor out of the bungs of casks, by means of a reed; (hence they have acquired the name of the reed suckers) and several of them have fallen victims to their beastly excesses; no less than four were found yesterday, either near expiring or actually dead. Don't these things show the police of the city to be very lax?

QUESTIONS

1. Several of the authors of these newspaper articles were pessimistic about the willingness of city government and police officials to work harder to alleviate these problems. Why would city officials tend to ignore newspaper writers in this period?
2. Why do you think so few newspaper editors campaigned in this period against poor conditions in their towns and cities?
3. How might regulations on the keeping of dogs and other animals within municipal boundaries be compared to those regulations in place in today's towns and cities?
4. Explain what role, if any, you think newspapers may have played in the development of regulations in towns and cities pertaining to vagrancy and public drunkenness.
5. Can you think of any public health and safety campaigns today that newspapers or other journalistic media are involved in? If so, how effective are these journalistic campaigns?

NOTES

1. Grace M. Mayer, *Once Upon a City* (New York: Macmillan, 1958), 472.

2. The New York Public Library's exhibition *Moving Uptown: Nineteenth-century Views of Manhattan,* Section I (including early views) 24 January 1998 through 28 March 1998.

3. "New York's Finest: A History of the New York Police Department," October 20, 1998–March 21, 1999. "New York City Police Department Timeline: 1801–1863." New York Historical Society: Know Where You Live, http://www.nyhistory.org/previous/police/police.html.

CHAPTER 23

The Establishment of the Second Bank of the United States, 1816

A "monster" granting special favors to a few powerful men: that is what some Americans called the nation's First Bank of the United States. Created by Congress under the guidance of Alexander Hamilton for a 20-year term starting in 1791, its purpose was to stabilize currency and stimulate trade. But from its start, it was maligned, especially by Westerners and workers. The Bank was largely a private institution, although the government did hold some of its stock. Any profits it earned went to its individual owners. In addition, the Bank was not given the power to issue a national currency. This was so irritating to Americans that its charter for renewal, which came up in 1811, wasn't granted.[1]

While many were happy when the charter of the nation's first federal bank wasn't renewed, it was gradually recognized that the country's monetary conditions were worse without it. Without a national bank, state bank operators began issuing currency in excessive amounts, fueling inflation and general monetary confusion. After the War of 1812, the nation's banking problems became so severe that the federal government stepped in to clean up the mess. In December 1815, President Madison and Secretary of the Treasury Alexander J. Dallas sent messages to Congress, urging its members to establish a second bank with the power to provide America with a uniform national currency. Congressional debate over this issue was lengthy and acrimonious. Not until late in 1816 would Congress succeed in the establishment of the Second Bank of the United States.[2]

The nation's leaders had high hopes that the Second Bank of the United States would solve the country's monetary problems, but criticism over its role and orientation erupted immediately. The Bank's critics included the operators of the various states' banks, as well as western entrepreneurs who maligned it as an instrument of an eastern-oriented federal government. Another sore point was the Bank's launching and maintenance of a national

THE GHOST of a DOLLAR or the BANKERS SURPRIZE

"The ghost of a dollar or the bankers surprize." This caricature of a Philadelphia merchant illustrates the difficulties Americans had with scarcities of specie. The merchant stands behind a counter with a small slot in it, staring at the dollar that hovers before him. He says, "Surely my eyes do not deceive me—It certainly must be a Dollar!—I declare I have not seen such a thing since I sold the last I had in my Vaults at 18 per Cent Premium—If thou art a real Dollar do drop in my till and let me hear thee Chink—As I have been sued for payment of part of my notes in Specie I must collect some to pay them for quietness sake or the game would be up at once." Courtesy of the Library of Congress.

currency. This all came to a head in 1817–1818, when the Bank ordered its branches to cease redeeming each other's notes in an effort to check inflation. Although the public reacted with extreme indignation, it would take until the mid-1820s for a more effective national currency to be instituted.

Although the period's newspapers did not totally ignore the debates that erupted over the nation's banking problems, they afforded relatively little attention to these issues. A few newspapers included the texts of congressional debates on the establishment of the second bank, and they occasionally included essays on whether a second national bank should be established. This chapter includes several essays from both sides of this question. Its first section includes two essays written in support of a second bank. Both were published in the District of Columbia's *National Intelligencer* during the period when Congress debated this question. The first of these commented that the nation's banking problems were so serious that Congress should feel compelled to take firm steps to solve them. The author of the second piece tried to shame Congress into taking steps to help save the average American from the "extortioners" who were robbing them all.

The final section of the chapter contains three essays by authors who were not convinced that a second national bank would solve the nation's banking problems. In the first, published in *Niles' Register* in the period leading up to the Second Bank of the United States' 1816 establishment, Hezekiah Niles warned that he would seriously oppose the bank if it were instituted with the proviso that it must redeem its notes with specie (coin). Niles claimed that such a situation would lead to the nation's bankruptcy once the War of 1812 was over. A few years after the Bank was chartered, Niles again wrote about the problems people were experiencing because of its national currency.

The author of the chapter's final essay discussed *McCullough v. Maryland*, the 1819 U.S. Supreme Court decision that dealt with the constitutionality of a Congress-chartered corporation and more generally with the dispersion of power between state and federal governments. Hampden, in Thomas Ritchie's *Enquirer*, in Richmond, Virginia, wrote that the rights of people were indeed threatened by this decision. Writing for the Court, Chief Justice John Marshall stated in his opinion that the chartering of a national bank by the federal government was permissible, since such power was implied in the Constitution's sections related to federal fiscal operations. One of the most important decisions issued by the Supreme Court in its history, Marshall's opinion called for the broad interpretation of the powers of the federal government.

In Favor of a National Bank

Joseph Gales Jr. and William Winston Seaton: "The National Bank"

Editors Gales and Seaton urged Congress to do something to fix the problems that were caused by the lack of federal oversight over the country's state banks. The editors commented that the bank issue was one of a small and rare number of problems largely devoid of political overtones.

National Intelligencer (District of Columbia), 15 November 1814

The popular branch of the National Legislature has at length engaged, heart and hand, in the discussion of the project of a National Bank, which is now before them. Of the ultimate fate of this proposition, we cannot speak with confidence, but incline to believe it will pass the House nearly in its present shape.

Of the necessity of some measure to provide a circulating medium, as well for the use of the government as for the convenience of individuals, there can be no doubt. It is a question totally independent of party considerations, and no honest man, of any party, one would think, can oppose that plan which he considers most efficient to this end, and believes at the same time to be compatible with the constitutional powers of Congress.

We have seen but two plans proposed: the one for an issue of Treasury Notes, under new regulations, to the amount demanded by the present exigency; the other for the establishment of a National Bank, to accomplish the same object by the agency of associated individuals. Of these two plans, every consideration of expediency appears to us to favor the adoption of the first, if it be now practicable. If not, the second plan, being the only alternative, must be resorted to.

Those in Congress who doubt the constitutional power of Congress to establish a National Bank, are not few; and, if we add to their number those who will oppose any measure for sustaining public credit, inasmuch as nothing would delight them more than to see the wheels of government stopped by national bankruptcy, we shall find a formidable phalanx in Congress arrayed against a National Bank, however organized.

There rests, then, on the shoulders of those who, with us, believe a National Bank at any time a public benefit, and at this time indispensably necessary, a high responsibility, of which they cannot divest themselves by objections to the details of a bill on this subject, to which a majority may assent. Let each Member endeavor to give that form to the bill which suits his fancy; but, when it is once moulded by the hand of a majority, we hope to see all those united in its favor who do not fall within one or the other of the classes we have before described.

It would have pleased us, and it certainly would in theory have been more correct, that the principal bank should have been established at the seat of government. The objection, that it is to be located elsewhere, and beyond the immediate supervision of the government, however strong, in our view, is not radical. Let it be established where and how it may, the whole nation, we believe, will participate in its benign and fertilizing influence.

Philo Homo: "On a National Bank"

This writer believed that the establishment of a second national bank would help not only the prosperous, but the nation's farmers, merchants, mechanics, and "honest, humble, daily laborers," too. If a bank were created, Philo Homo argued, the nation would triumph over the "exortionists" seeking to rob the citizenry.

National Intelligencer (District of Columbia), 16 December 1814

A National Bank being now a subject under the consideration of Congress, it will not be deemed presuming in a citizen to give expression to his sentiments, respecting an institution of so much consequence to the prosperity of his country. The utility of a National Bank will depend more on its organization than on the amount of capital. I shall make no objection to the amount of the capital being fifty millions, yet I think the mode and terms of the subscription might be changed for the better, viz: 10 million in specie, instead of 5 millions—34 millions in six per cent stock, by corporations and individuals, and 6 millions by the United States in six percent stock.—Limit the bank to five per cent instead of six percent on all its discounts or transactions. A bank thus constituted will have the ability to accommodate government; will be pleasing to public creditors, and will possess the distinguishing perfection of reducing interest to five per cent, and will assure to the stockholders such a profit as will enhance their stock considerably above the currency of the country.... I fondly hope that Congress will not lose sight of the interest of the great multitude, made up of farmers, merchants, mechanics, and the honest, humble, daily laborer. These classes of our citizens give numbers and wealth to our country—without their strength and industry, we should be weak and poor—without the product of their labor, many would be worthless. Reducing interest one per cent will save to each family in its yearly consumption, more than will pay the demands of government. Here is an appeal, made to the benevolence of Congress, and political wisdom sanctions the appeal. One single act will take government out of the hands of extortioners, repair the finances of the nation, restore money to its value, facilitate the industrious man in obtaining the aid of occasional loans of money on such terms as will afford him a reasonable profit from his labour, and will have the beneficial consequences of a sumptuary law, in calculating the real value and use of money, teaching the advantage and beauty of economy to all conditions of our citizens. This being done, we shall triumph over our enemy, who hopes to conquer the destruction of our national credit. This being done, party irritation will subside, opposition will be without aliment; and we shall be again a band of brothers; the struggle will then be, who shall do most for their beloved country.

QUESTIONING THE NATIONAL BANK

Hezekiah Niles: "National Bank"

Niles argued that a second bank should be established only if it were not required to redeem its notes with specie. Great Britain, he stated, was buying up specie. The country would become bankrupt, he warned, if a second bank were established with a proviso that they had to redeem its notes with specie.

Niles' Weekly Register (Baltimore, Md.), 21 January 1815
The bill to establish a national bank is still bandied about, like a shuttle-cock, between the two houses of congress, and will probably fall to the ground in its flight from one to the other. Such a bank is proper or it is inexpedient—the people think that time enough has been spent to ascertain its quality; and it is earnestly to be wished that it should either be passed or rejected. It does not become the nature of this work, or the rule of conduct that its editor has prescribed to himself, to express the general idea that prevails in the society he mixes with, as to the *talkings* and *notions* of the representatives of the people, at a time when action is so much required; much less to show how the *minority* governs.

If, however, the bank is to be established with a requisition that it *shall* redeem its notes with specie, much will the day of its institution be lamented! In the present state of affairs, it would act as a mere *collector* of the precious metals for the *British*, and certainly become bankrupt in less than *six months.*—It is an indubitable fact, that persons are employed in the United States to drain us of every specie dollar,* and I have very little doubt, if the war lasts, and this bank is constituted as proposed by the house of representatives, that silver and gold will be purchased at a *premium of 50 per cent.* How can *Great Britain* more cheaply prosecute the war, than by undermining our credit, in draining off the basis of it? Who does not believe there are many among us that would gladly co-operate to ruin the finances of the nation, and thereby compel us to make peace on *any terms,* especially, if they themselves made a profit by it?...Can it be supposed that an American congress, fearful that his lordship would not soon enough accomplish his object, shall establish an institution to consummate his plan?—Can we suspect that any voted on the bank bill with a sole view to this purpose?

If the bank has specie for its basis, its notes will soon receive the confidence of the people; and, the large sums to be collected in taxes and duties will force their circulation, if force should be required, to the necessary amount. The bank of England has not paid specie for many years, and probably never will—but a national bank here, with six millions snug on its vaults, would the very day that peace should be made, commerce payment in specie; and, by the altered state of things, be enabled to redeem all its notes with that fidelity and promptitude which has generally distinguished such institutions in this country.

*Mr. Bibb stated in the senate, a few days ago.

Hezekiah Niles: "A National Currency"

Problems with the national currency established by the Second Bank of the United States came up immediately after its charter was approved in 1816. Hezekiah Niles, a critic of federal oversight over banking and economics more generally, complained about the great amount of speculation that was robbing the average American of the benefits they ought to expect from a national currency.

Niles' Weekly Register (Baltimore, Md.), 5 September 1818

What was the great condition on which the Bank of the United States was incorporated? It was that the exchange should be equalized...that we should have what was called a "national currency"...and what has already happened? In two short years the last vestiges of a balance in favor of the people for the immense advantages bestowed to every "beelzebub in speculation" is wrestled from them with a degree of imprudence equaled only by its violation of every principle of common justice, if not of common honesty.

Hampden: "Alarming Consequences"

In 1819, the Supreme Court announced one of the most important decisions it would ever issue: McCullough v. Maryland. *In his opinion, Chief Justice John Marshall upheld the power of the federal government to establish a national bank. In fervent opposition to the Bank, Spencer Roane maligned the decision in this article under the name Hampden. Roane, a prominent Virginian and supporter of Republican administrations, wrote for the newspapers under assumed names from time to time.*

Richmond Enquirer (Virginia), 1 February 1819

Hear him for his cause. The Supreme Court of the United States is a tribunal of great and commanding authority, whose decisions, if not received as "the law and the prophets" are always entitled to the deepest attention. To the presiding justice of that court, we are always ready to pay that tribute, which his great abilities deserve, but no tribunal, however high, no abilities, however splendid, ought to canonize the opinions which are advanced. We solemnly believe the opinion of the Supreme Court in the case of the bank to be fraught with alarming consequences; the federal constitution to be misinterpreted; and the rights of the states and of the people to be threatened with danger.

QUESTIONS

1. Identify the reasons why the Second Bank of the United States was needed.
2. Discuss why so many Americans were opposed to the idea of a second national bank.
3. Describe what you think economic life in America would be like today if the federal government did not regulate privately owned banks.
4. What other events and issues preoccupied Americans during the period that the establishment of a second bank was under consideration?
5. What should be the role of newspapers in communicating information and opinions on America's banking and monetary systems?

NOTES

1. Eric Foner and John A. Garraty, eds., *Reader's Companion to American History* (New York: Houghton Mifflin, 1992).

2. Ralph C. H. Catterall, *The Second Bank of the United States* (Chicago: University of Chicago Press, 1903), 17.

CHAPTER 24

The Financial Panic and Depression of 1819

In 1819, the nation's first major economic panic hit the people of the United States, sparing neither rich nor poor. As historian Murray N. Rothbard described it, the crisis "appeared to come mysteriously from within the economic system itself."[1] While America's economy had long suffered from periodic financial instabilities, this situation was different because no particular event, leader, or act of government could be blamed for the hard times. In reality, the country's financial conditions had been deteriorating since the end of the War of 1812. After the temporary economic bubble accompanying that war, cotton prices declined severely, efforts to curb inflation failed, a congressional requirement that land purchases had to be paid for in hard currency led to further problems, and land speculation and foreign competition aggravated the situation.

Mathew Carey estimated that three million people, one-third of the country's population, were directly affected by the panic.[2] Among other things, bankruptcy increased, prices dropped, unemployment increased, foreclosures multiplied, and investments and property values plunged. In Richmond, Virginia, for example, property values fell by 50 percent. In Pennsylvania, land values per acre plunged from $150 in 1815 to $35 in 1819. Increasing numbers of people were sent to debtors' prisons, and urban poverty became so severe that it was impossible for city authorities to ignore it.

America's newspapers were filled with reports of the country's economic problems. In 1819, *Niles' Register* reported the "distress of the people has reached an alarming extent, and there is no considerate man in our large cities and towns that looks to the approaching winter, without anticipating scenes of misery such as he never before witnessed."[3] And remedies for the panic were also suggested by newspaper writers. Time and patience would cure the problems, according to one group of writers, while others called for the dismissal of those responsible for the panic with the appointment of more "honest" men. Protective tariffs, national monetary expansion, restricted bank credit, and even heightened religious devotion were among the suggestions to solve the crisis.

Although the panic was largely over by 1823, it left a lasting imprint on American history and politics. Among its effects were demands for the democratization of state constitutions, an end to restrictions on voting and officeholding, and heightened hostility toward banks (see chapter 23) and other "privileged" corporations. The panic also led to troubles within the Republican Party and aggravated the nation's growing sectional tensions.

The readings in this chapter's three sections reflect the seriousness of the depression as it spread across the nation. The country's newspapers did not yet have a clearly defined role as the official purveyor of information on financial matters, and most journalists had little experience reporting on economic panics. Examining how the period's newspapers reacted to the nation's first major economic depression offers insight into the developing role of the press.

The first group of newspaper reports and essays comments on the conditions experienced by Americans during the panic. The first writer told the story of a man who stole a horse so he could go to prison and have a place to live. The second described how the depression affected not only the rich, but also the poor. The final pieces in this section illustrated the cynicism of some who did not believe everyone in America was as destitute as they claimed. Finally, writing under the pseudonym Howard, the author of "Domestic Economy"—Mordecai Manual Noah—saw much good coming out of the financial panic of 1819. Noah was a prominent New Yorker journalist and politician who founded many newspapers. In this piece, published in New York City's *National Advocate*, Noah reminisced about old friends who lost all their money in the panic. When first married, he recalled, their situation was modest and they lived frugally. But when they became rich, they forgot their "humble and happy origin[s]." When they lost their fortune in the panic of 1819, Noah praised their return to their old, sensible ways.

Americans' fondness for trying to understand the roots of the nation's problems is seen in the newspaper materials included in the chapter's second section. In addition, these pieces illustrated just how different this depression was from earlier ones, when it was possible to blame a particular event or government leader. These authors' theories about the causes of the depression range from blaming the banks and the general effects of "overtrading" to the extravagant spending habits of well-to-do women.

The newspaper pieces included in the chapter's third section explored remedies for the panic. Neither federal nor state governments volunteered to fix the nation's economic woes. In his congressional message of 1819, President Monroe made only passing allusions to the contraction of credit and to industrial depression. Correspondingly, some Americans minimized the depression's effects, claiming only time and patience would cure financial woes. Others argued that steps should be taken to mitigate the panic's pernicious effects. Today, Americans are used to the government stepping in when major economic problems develop. But in 1819, there was little precedent for such governmental action, and authors like Theodore Dwight opined that individuals, not governments, should take responsibility for these problems.

In contrast, as evident in an essay published in newspapers such as the Philadelphia *Union,* others argued that competition from the British and other foreigners was the source of the country's economic woes. The solution, they proposed, was stronger protective tariffs. The undisputed leader in this campaign was Mathew Carey, a Philadelphia printer and leader of an organization called the Society for the Promotion of National Industry. Carey's theory of prosperity and depression was elegant in its simplicity: free trade causes depression, and protection would bring back prosperity. Led by Carey, the protectionists launched vigorous propaganda campaigns to accomplish their goals. Among their tools were meetings, the establishment of associations, memorials, and pamphlets and newspaper essays. The group started a strictly protectionist journal, *The Patron of Industry,* to help spread their ideas. They argued that Congress should take steps to deal with the 1819 emergency. In response, Congress set up a committee on manufacturers, separate from its commerce committee. Under its chair, Mr. Baldwin of Pennsylvania, three bills were submitted to Congress early in 1820. According to one author, such remedies would "cover our country with smiles in less than six months."[4]

As illustrated by a comment published in the *Louisiana Gazette,* not everyone agreed that protective tariffs would soothe the country's economic problems.

Finally, the chapter concludes with a message designed by its writer to convey the idea that people should turn to religion as the solution to the depression's devastating effects.

COMMENTARY ON THE PANIC'S EFFECTS

An Observer: "Evidence of the Hard Times"

The sad story retold here is about a man who stole a horse in hopes of going to prison so that he would finally have a roof over his head. It was originally printed in the Dutchess Observer, *in Poughkeepsie, New York.*

***Carolina Centinel* (New Bern, N.C.), 20 November 1819**

During the sitting of the Court of Common Please, in this village last week, John Daely was arraigned for horse stealing, and plead guilty; he said he stole the horse for the purpose of going to the state prison; his reason was, that the times were so hard that he could get no work, and could hit upon no other plan so ready and certain to provide him with a home and steady employment. He is a strong, healthy young man; and was to his great gratification sentenced to the state prison for eight years.

Hezekiah Niles: "The Present Dullness"

With the panic's onset, no longer could the wealthy afford the costly food and clothing they were used to. Adopting a sarcastic tone, Niles commented that instead of inviting 300 or 400 to tea, "madam" could only invite 30 or 40. Plus the curtailment of paper credit meant that grocers and purveyors of wine frequented by the wealthy were losing customers.

***Niles' Weekly Register* (Baltimore, Md.), 16 September 1820**

A large part of the present dullness of trade and "scarcity of money" is owing to a diminished consumption of costly articles for food and raiment, or for ornament and show, whether of foreign or domestic product.... A little while ago, I frequently saw the streets crowded in an evening with a bustling multitude dashing in carriages to Mrs. Anything's party. An orderly man could hardly get along for them. I have heard of three hundred persons taking tea with the wife of the servant of a bank! But "madam's husband" can't afford it any longer, or so much respects common decency that he won't allow it. So those who may afford it receive the same comparative éclat for having thirty or forty which they used to derive from having three or four hundred at their parties; and it is much better, because in a company of the former dimensions you may find a satisfaction not to be expected in the other, designed only to make a noise. It is thus also with gentlemen's dinners and suppers—ten or twenty are occasionally invited, instead of having twenty or forth frequently. The style is still maintained, but fashion does not call for its exhibition so extensively nor so often. "The top of the wheel" is still held, and that is enough.

But the general retrenchment spoken of may be proven from a multitude of facts. In the New York, Philadelphia, and Baltimore newspapers you may often see the grocers puffing their wines by saying that certain particular pipes were expressly imported for private use. Their sayings are true. The gentlemen who ordered it had found out that there was an end to paper credit when the wine arrived, and though they might have retained some money, it would look too bad to see a pipe of wine going into a bankrupt's cellar; and the fact is that our grocers hardly sell one gallon of their costly wines for ten which they used to dispose of. So also it is for every business, trade, or profession which furnishes us with luxuries, from the wine merchant to the confectioner; and if it was known that a man in an ordinary trade gave his wife a shawl which cost $500, his note would certainly be "turned down" at the bank.

Anonymous: "Hard Times"

Scolding Americans for wallowing in self-pity, this author compared the nation's "hard times" to those suffered by Europeans. This piece was originally published in a Washington, D.C. newspaper.

Carolina Centinel (New Bern, N.C.), 12 June 1819
Addressed to the American People.

"HARD TIMES!" from ev'ry quarter is the cry.
Hard times, *indeed!* The fact I do deny.
Are the times hard, when, if the truth you tell,
You must confess you live extremely well?
On best of meats and wheaten bread you dine,
And drink in plenty whiskey, ale, or wine,
Dressed as lords, move to and fro at ease,
Work when you choose, and play when e'er you please.
O, Providence! Have such a people cause
(People who own no sovereign but the laws!)
To mourn their lot, thy mercies to decry,
Because on wings of gold they cannot fly?
Ungrateful race! to whom your God hath given
The best, the choicest, richest boon of Heaven,
Turn but your eyes to Europe's distant shore,
Silence your groundless plaints, and sigh no more:
There view your fellow-man; behold his doom—
Bound to the soil or fasten'd to the loom;
By priests and nobles daily forc'd to toil.
Who of his labor make a sport and spoil,
A scanty pittance to their victims give,
And call it charity to let him live.
Your fate with his, Americans, compare!
Be thankful, and your murmurings forbear.

Howard: "Domestic Economy"

Howard's reporting method was ethnographic in that he ventured out and about his community and the surrounding countryside, observing and meeting with people in an effort to understand their financial situations. More than a dozen of his essays on "domestic economy" were published in the Advocate *during 1818 and 1819.*

National Advocate (New York City), 18 June 1819

Things changed at last—great speculations in bank stock and cotton, joined to the failure of several mercantile houses, united to undermine the fortune and prospects of my friend, and he *failed*. His splendid establishment was given up, and his wife and daughters, with tears, relinquished their luxuries and visiting acquaintance, to retire to a situation corresponding with their future prospects. With the wreck of their fortune a small store was purchased once more in Pearl-street, the seat of their former prosperity and happiness; and after I had given them time to settle themselves, to recover from the shock, and to arrange their future plans, I paid them a visit. The change was a happy one—my friend was once more behind the counter, his wife and daughters dressed simply, but neatly, were employed at their needle—health and contentment prevailed; I was received with smiles and satisfaction, and the girls assured me, that reflection had convinced them that to enjoy life, produce contentment and happiness, they must be industrious, cheerful, amiable and economical—employ their time rationally, and improve their mind judiciously, and thus qualify themselves for all those changes and mutabilities, that "flesh is heir to."

IN SEARCH OF CAUSES

Senex: "For the *New-York Daily Advertiser*"

Senex pondered the causes of the country's shrinking money supply in this essay. After defining money, along with its uses and abuses, he argued that the underlying problem was overtrading (the proliferation of speculative activities fueled by overextensions of credit). In this, he was in line with other economic experts who generally believed that economic depressions could result from overtrading.

New-York Daily Advertiser (New York City), 6 March 1819

This system['s] over-trading has been the cause of the existing commercial distress, and of the unceasing demand for money.

It may now be said that I admit that money is scarce; otherwise, why should it be in demand? To which I would beg leave to reply, that it does not necessarily follow that money is scarce, because improvident spendthrifts daring projectors, and scheming speculators, find that their expenditure has been disproportioned to their revenue; that their stock is gone, and their credit with it. Nor even when sober men, whose projects have been disproportioned to their capitals, find themselves in that unhappy situation when they have neither wherewithal to buy money, nor credit to borrow it. It may even be, notwithstanding this apparent distress that the usual quantity of money is circulating in the country; but that many want that money who have nothing to give for it.

It is contended, that this system of overtrading has not only produced the existing commercial distress, but, that it is of necessity fraught with the most serious evils. A salutary reaction has, however, already commenced, which will ultimately prove efficacious; though before the return of a sound state of things, much individual distress must be endured; great revolutions of property must ensue; and many in this proud city, now considered opulent, and whose families revel in all the fullness of luxury and of felicitous enjoyment, must be made to experience the sad extremes of want, and to realize the aggravated bitterness of penury and reproach.

Before adverting to a probable corrective of this unhappy system, it is necessary to take a comprehensive view of the subject, and in the first place to endeavour to point out its producing cause.

Although it may not be easy to suggest a corrective so palliative, or so sane, as to admit of ready adoption, yet I cannot hesitate to assert, that the ruinous system of over-trading has arisen chiefly from the following causes: The long credits at which the foreign capitalist can afford to sell his goods to us; the long credit allowed by government on duties at the custom house; the inefficient and deplorable state of our insolvent laws; and lastly, though not least, the undue facility of obtaining money on loan from the banks. This last stated *origo mali* will, doubtless, appear paradoxical to many in this city, at this time. It is not, however, Mr. Editor, deemed the less true; on the contrary, it is considered the principal cause of all our fatal embarrassments.

Thomas Ritchie: "The Times"

The panic should be blamed on the proliferation of banks in the country, along with the mismanagement of those who operated them, according to Thomas Ritchie, who originally wrote this for the Enquirer, *his newspaper in Richmond, Virginia.*

Carolina Sentinel (New Bern, N.C.), 12 June 1819

It is a melancholy (and worse, it is a disgraceful) fact, that this country, blessed beyond any that the sun ever shone upon, has been brought to this condition, principally by monied institutions; by their *multiplication & mismanagement*. Banks have sprung up like mushrooms. One state in one moment shot up forty of them; another, thirty: There is no state, which has not been cursed by them, as Egypt was by her locusts. But every new bank added to the embarrassments of the circulating medium in these two ways; it cripples the old ones, robbing them of a part of their specie, and it grew out more paper, thus increasing a circulating medium, that was already too large.

But it was the mismanagement, more than the multiplication of the banks, which has brought on the pressure; or rather it was their multiplication which principally contributed to mismanagement.

Howard: "Domestic Economy"

Evidence that the economy was in serious trouble was obvious before the panic became a widespread reality in 1819. In this piece, Howard blamed the faltering economy on three things: unwise speculations, overspending, and the extravagance of society's women.

National Advocate (New York City), 7 November 1818
I cannot avoid noticing the extreme pressure for money at present. It would be a tedious labor to inquire into the causes of this scarcity, but this I may venture to say, with safety, that a want of economy in expenditures and imprudence in speculations are the prominent ones.... Walking a few days ago in Broadway, I saw four young ladies, the daughters of a respectable gentleman of good fortune, not a great one, but a comfortable subsistence. In taking a view of their dress, their bonnets, shawls, watches, and jewels, I calculated that the cost of each amounted to $500 at least. Here was the enormous sum of $2,000 laid out in dress, a capital for a young beginner in the world—a dowry with a wife, of importance, if well managed.... How can people be so unthinkingly extravagant? I heard, with indignation and surprise, that a storekeeper in Broadway had sold a cashmere shawl to a lady for $1,100!! Have ladies lost every sense of shame? Are they so unmindful of their duty to their family and to the world as to subject a fond, complying, weak husband to such criminal extravagance to injure himself, probably injure his creditors, and, finally, to overdraw a bank?...

Look, on the contrary, at the tidy wife—she rises in the morning at an early hour, dressed plain, neat and clean—she prepares breakfast for her husband in time for him to attend business—dresses and sends her children to school—sews or knits—looks after her domestic concerns, and is, in short, the active woman—the economical wife—the attentive mother, and, withal, the polished lady—her days are passed in usefulness, and her nights in peace. Such a woman is a "crown to her husband."

In [inquiring] last week of a confectioner what he was doing with four large iced plum cakes; he made them, he said, by order of a lady for a tea party; they amounted to 50 dollars. Amazing! Eat 50 dollars worth of cake in an evening! Why it would school five poor children for a year—it would buy 50 pair of shoes for their cold and naked feet—it would pay six months' rent for two old poor and respectable persons. Would not that party be satisfied with a cup of good coffee and toast, muffins, rusk, crumpets, wafers, cheese and fish, and not swallow so much money in eatables? How very inconsiderate it is.

IN SEARCH OF REMEDIES

Theodore Dwight: "Let Every Man Examine His Own Case"

In this piece, after discussing Congress, Dwight recommended that Americans ponder whether their behavior had somehow brought about their economic woes. Famous for his political pamphlets and articles, Dwight was a leader of the Federalist Party in New England.

New-York Daily Advertiser (New York City), 20 May 1819

Troubles, indeed, are to be found; but they grow out of circumstances beyond the reach or control of the national legislature. Can Congress stop the exportation of specie, or, by any measure within their power, force it back to the country any faster than would be the case in the ordinary course of mercantile pursuits? Can Congress give credit to Banks which have lost it…. Can Congress discover and apply a remedy for the evils of a too large importation of foreign merchandise, or a too extensive and unlimited trade at home? Can Congress…teach the people of this country the necessity and value of frugality and economy…. We are fully persuaded they cannot.—These evils, and others connected with them, though they bear hardly upon us at the present time, and, of course, produce a degree of uneasiness and restiveness, cannot be relieved or removed in a moment. The causes by which they are produced are not of yesterday—they are of much longer standing, and if a remedy can be found, it must be of slow and gradual operation. Indeed, such a remedy must probably be derived more essentially from individual, than legislation exertion. Let every man examine his own case, and trace out with fidelity to himself the causes of his own embarrassments, and if a cure be practicable, the scrutiny will teach him, with almost unerring certainty, from what source it is to be obtained.

The Friends of Natural Rights: "Careyan Scheme of Government"

Many Americans were opposed to the tariff measures proposed by reformer, writer, and publisher Mathew Carey and the others who sought such relief from Congress. In addition, there was a backlash against the manufacturers who supported protectionism. These writers deprecated the manufacturers who asked for protection, arguing that a government-planned economy would result.

National Intelligencer (District of Columbia), 25 August 1821

The people of the United States being in a very unenlightened condition, very indolent and much disposed to waste their labor and their capital...the welfare of the community requires that all goods, wares, merchandise, and estates...should be granted to the government in fee simple, forever...and should be placed under the management of a Board of Trustees, to be styled the Patrons of Industry. The said Board should thereupon guarantee to the people of the United States that thenceforth neither the capital nor labor of this nation should remain for a moment idle...It is a vulgar notion that the property which a citizen possesses, actually belongs to him: for he is a mere tenant, laborer, or agent of the government, to whom all the property in the nation legitimately belongs. The government may therefore manage this property according to its own fancy, and shift capitalists and laborers from one employment to another.

Hezekiah Niles: "The Times"

Hezekiah Niles was one of the country's staunchest protectionists. But he also had faith that the country would again prosper as soon as the "speculating madmen" who had led the country into the depression were turned out of their positions. Their more prudent replacements, he asserted, would help bring the country back to what it was before the depression.

Niles' Weekly Register (Baltimore, Md.), 5 June 1819

But let us be encouraged—*we are able to bear this trial, and good will come out of it...for honest men... [will] get into fashion,*—and...our solidly bottomed chartered companies...[will] seek to do business with plain, economical and productive men, instead of speculating madmen and visionary schemers. The latter classes, in many cases allied to, or acting the part of precious scoundrels, have had their day of honor, in the vulgar estimation; it is time that the others should have theirs.... Again we say, let the productive people, the men and women entitled to enjoy the good things of this life, be encouraged—the day is near when they will triumph over the wretched races of various gamblers,—who, commanding a large portion of the circulating medium, have despised those who gave to that medium its degree of currency or value, beyond that of old rags. And this people, the sinews of every country, the true patriots of every land, will interpose and effectually resist *oppression* on well conducted banks or well-disposed individuals....

Questions

1. Describe the events and other developments that led to the economic panic and depression of 1819.
2. Not until 1819 did Americans organize to help conquer poverty, even though plenty of people were poor before then. Why do you think this kind of practice was not instituted earlier?
3. Economic historians have stated that one of the causes of the panic of 1819 was that the economic benefits of the War of 1812 had disappeared. Identify and discuss the economic benefits that come with wars and why the nation's economy sometimes goes into decline when wars end.
4. Discuss the roles of newspapers in business, banking, and economics in 1819 and compare these roles to those of today's print media.
5. Several of the authors reprinted here suggest that the roots of poverty lie in individuals and shouldn't be blamed on social institutions such as banks or government. Do you agree? Why or why not?

Notes

1. Murray N. Rothbard, *The Panic of 1819: Reactions and Policies* (Auburn, Ala.: Ludwig von Mises Institute, 2002), ii.

2. Mathew Carey, "Address to the Farmers of the United States," in *Essays in Political Economy* (Philadelphia, 1822), 417.

3. Hezekiah Niles, *Niles' Weekly Register*, 5 June 1819.

4. Samuel Rezneck, "The Depression of 1819–1822, A Social History," *American Historical Review* 39 (October 1933): 37–39.

CHAPTER 25

Poverty and Pauperism in the Early National Period, 1805–1819

Poverty was rampant in America's early national period, and the new century provided little relief. Pauperism—defined as a condition suffered by people supported financially by public relief or private charity—was especially problematic in the new nation's growing cities, straining their officials' abilities to provide for those who suffered from it. The situation faced by New York City officials after the American Revolution offers a cogent example. In 1784, when New York City's population was 12,000, about 1,000 people were on its relief rolls. During the city's 1798 yellow-fever epidemic, its Committee of Health treated more than 2,400. The city's harsh winters led to further suffering. During the especially cruel winter of 1805, Mayor DeWitt Clinton requested a legislative appropriation for the 10,000 New York City residents dependent on public charity. When President Jefferson's embargo (see chapter 15) placed new strains on New Yorkers, municipal distributions of food, firewood, cash, and jobs were carried out.[1]

Poverty and its related problems worsened after the War of 1812 (see chapter 18), not only in New York but across the nation. Between April 1, 1814, and April 1, 1815, more than one-fifth of New York City's inhabitants sought public relief. The city opened a new municipal almshouse at Bellevue, but this was not enough. Although private charities helped, the number of indigent people only seemed to grow in the next few years. Swarms of immigrants crowded the city's tenement neighborhoods, and the streets filled with beggars. The city's paupers were joined by unemployed farmworkers who migrated there each winter to draw public relief. By the end of the decade, things were little improved, and when the economic panic and depression of 1819 hit (see chapter 24), pauperism increased once again. Relief for the poor constituted the largest single annual municipal expenditure throughout the early national period.

Despite these awful conditions, many Americans continued to dream of better lives. Complicating matters, however, was the common idea that the poor had to be cured of their immorality before poverty could be eliminated. Such a theory of poverty was evident in a 1793 DeWitt Clinton speech:

> How glorious, how God-like, to step forth to the relief of...distress; to arrest the tear of sorrow; to disarm affliction of its darts; to smooth the pillow of declining age; to rescue from the fangs of vice the helpless infant, and to diffuse the most lively joys over a whole family of rational, immortal creatures.[2]

Despite the strong hold this idea had on Americans, a few forward-thinking individuals began to search for new ways to eliminate poverty and pauperism in the early decades of the nineteenth century. Their ideas grew to a great extent out of religious revivalism, which began early in the nineteenth century. In New York City, for example, voluntary and humanitarian groups were formed, including the Free School Society, Economical School, Society for the Promotion of Useful Arts, the Humane Society, Orphan Asylum Society, and the New York Hospital.

In December 1817, a number of the leaders of these organizations scheduled the first meeting of their newly formed New York Society for the Prevention of Pauperism.[3] Among the founders of the society were Thomas Eddy, John Pintard, and John Griscom, individuals whose actions came out of dissatisfaction with the way New York City leaders were dealing with the poor. Griscom declared that relief systems perpetuated, rather than eliminated, poverty because they stifled personal initiative and self-reliance. Only societies that supplied employment to the poor deserved public patronage, he argued.

Leaders in the nation's other cities followed suit in the years to come, although not all their organizations would flourish. A group of socially minded individuals in Baltimore established the Society for the Prevention of Pauperism in 1819 to prevent what they considered the causes of poverty, such as alcohol abuse and gambling. Failing in their efforts to solve these problems, the organization disbanded in 1822. In Boston, in 1835, Unitarian leader Joseph Tuckerman founded the Society for the Prevention of Pauperism.[4]

Although the period's newspapers were generally much more interested in publishing reports and columns on political matters, they did include some material on poverty and the efforts of the period's cadre of workers who wanted to eliminate it. This chapter includes two sections: one that focuses on the causes of poverty and pauperism and a second in which authors opined on how poverty and pauperism could be eliminated. The first

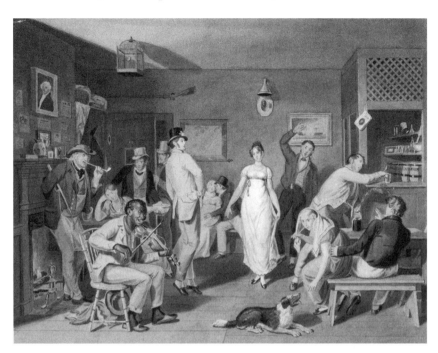

Barroom Dancing. Since overconsumption of spirits was a central cause of pauperism, according to some reformers in the early republic, this kind of portrait must have antagonized more than a few. In it, watercolorist John Lewis Krimmel shows people in a country tavern drinking and dancing while an African American man plays a fiddle. Courtesy of the Library of Congress.

writer in the first section argued that the scarcity of jobs was one cause of poverty, but he also blamed it on society's love of "spirituous liquor." The author of the section's second piece believed his standard of living was being hurt by the inflated prices charged by shoemakers. Howard, the author of this section's final essays, blamed poverty on individuals who failed to value a high level of "domestic economy."

The chapter's second section includes essays whose authors suggested what the government ought to do about poverty and pauperism. In the first, "A Mechanic" wrote that lawmakers should create a statutory remedy for the suffering of the poor. During this period, many people considered those who applied for bankruptcy to be criminals. While the U.S. Constitution granted Congress the power to pass a uniform bankruptcy law, Congress had not done so.[5] Meanwhile, some state legislatures passed harsh insolvency laws that put those convicted of this crime in prison.

The section's final three essays were published during the exceptionally cold winters of 1814 in Washington, D.C., and of 1819–1820 in Baltimore.

According to *Morning Chronicle* editor Paul Allen, the harshness of Baltimore's cold season in 1819–1820 led to the organization of the Baltimore Society for the Prevention of Pauperism. Allen, who served as the society's secretary, and its other members proposed ways to root out the causes of pauperism.[6] One of their remedies was to appoint "moral police" who would stop people from engaging in drunkenness and gambling. In response, two public meetings were convened, and a pamphlet attacking the society was published. Under the banner title "Tribunal of Liberty," the pamphlet's author warned, "Under the cover of religion and benevolence, but with little of either at heart, men now conspire to erect in our city an inquisitorial power."[7]

COMMENTARY ON THE CAUSES OF PAUPERISM

Anonymous: "For the *Watchman*"

This writer suggested that the "growing evil" of pauperism arose from a scarcity of jobs and the overconsumption of "spirituous liquors." Every good American, it was argued, should consider what should be done about these problems, which were levying a "continual and increasing tax upon [them]."

American Watchman (Wilmington, N.J.), 6 August 1817

The question, "what will be the best method of diminishing pauperism?" is an interesting one to the inhabitants of Wilmington as well as to those of Philadelphia.... I hope the attention of our citizens will be drawn to the subject, as it is one in which the feelings of humanity, as well as of pecuniary interest, are much engaged.—Certainly, if any plan can be fallen upon to diminish the number of our poor, owing to a variety of causes not strictly within their control—it is an object worthy of our close attention.

I am persuaded that much suffering is the result of real want of labor sufficient for the support of those who depend upon it—and for this reason (among others) I regret much the situation of our *Cotton and Woolen Manufacturers*. During the time that they were in brief operation, many children that are now almost entirely idle, were employed.

The question of *employment for our growing population* is a very important one; and it is desirable that some persons would undertake to examine it with the attention it merits. One fourth of the whole number of the white inhabitants in the United States are children, fit for some kind of business; and in consequence of the increase of this species of population, faster than business opens for them, there are vast numbers of children growing up without trades or occupations; in fact it is now difficult to find suitable employment for boys. The consequence of this state of things is, that those children are coming upon the community in the state of day laborers; and when to these we add the herds of young blacks that are arriving to the years of manhood without trades—we may perceive that in the course of a few years there will be a vast surplus of laborers (near our towns especially) in the United States, unless some new branches of business open to give them employment.

But certainly, in the opinion of the writer, *spirituous liquors* is by far the most fruitful evil of which we complain. The thirty millions of gallons made use of in the United States will pay the poor rates, and all the collections made use of for the relief of the poor, thrice over. And I have no doubt but there is more money expended in this town every year for whiskey and rum (and principally by laborers, including journeyman at various trades), than would maintain all the poor of the whole country.

Upon the whole, I wish it were possible to impress our citizens with the importance of the subject. Pauperism is a growing evil, a continual and increasing tax upon us, a tax upon our pockets, our time, and our thoughts; and we had the need to exert ourselves to put a stop to it if possible.

A Poor Gentleman: "On the Price of Shoes"

Rising prices for the necessities of life, including shoes, contributed to the difficulties of the nation's poor. When New York City's shoemakers joined in agreement in their refusal to lower the price of shoes and boots after Congress eliminated its taxes on them, a "poor gentleman" complained. A few days later, a shoemaker sent a letter titled "Fair Play! Hear both sides!" to the Post. *In it, he wrote that shoe and boot prices "are still comparatively low; the shoe-makers suffer, the public grumbles, and the 'Poor Gentleman' attacks them in the newspaper. Where one master has made his living for 5 years past, six have failed, or left the business for better."*

New-York Evening Post (New York City), 8 August 1816

Mr. Editor. In looking over your paper of Saturday evening, I perceived a notice to builders, of a meeting to deliberate upon the propriety of lowering the wages of mechanics employed in buildings. If this is a proper and commendable undertaking in the present critical state of business, the fall in the prices of merchandize and the extreme scarcity of money render it exceedingly proper that a corresponding reduction should be made in the wages of all our mechanics and laborers. But, sir, I hope to see this operation of retrenchment extend further: I hope to see it undertaken by shoe-makers, by whom at present a very unconscionable imposition is practiced. There is no article of clothing for which a more exorbitant price is de-manded than boots and shoes. When a tax was imposed on these articles by the United States, the price of them was advanced beyond what was suffi-cient merely to cover the tax. At the last session of Congress the tax was taken off, and we had a right to expect that boots and shoes would return to their original prices; but such a change has not yet taken place, nor is there any prospect of it. These gentlemen shoemakers, finding the tax clear gain, very unjustly continue to demand it; and the better to succeed in their extortion, they have constituted a society in which resolutions are passed regulating the price of these articles. This institution enables them to op-press the public systematically—no one will work under the established price, and the customer must go barefoot or pay just what these gentlemen are pleased to demand. If remonstrance is attempted, they whip out a card containing the prices allowed to journeymen, &c. by the shoemaker's soci-ety, and very plausibly assert "that they cannot afford to work cheaper than others." Now, Mr. Editor, are not these things provoking and oppressive?— Is not this society as completely a conspiracy as the proceedings of the milkmen, and are not the grand jurors obligated by their oath to take cog-nizance of it?

Howard: "Domestic Economy"

"Howard" contributed at least 17 essays titled "Domestic Economy" to the Advocate *through the fall of 1818 and into the waning months of 1819. Throughout, he blamed poverty and pauperism on people who failed to live up to his standards of frugality, industriousness, and self-sufficiency. Here, he inquired into the origins of the increasing number of paupers in his city, ultimately blaming women for not only their own poverty but for that of their children and husbands, too. If women were more industrious, he ar-gued, pauperism would be greatly reduced. "Howard" was really well-known New York editor and social reformer Mordecai Manual Noah.*

National Advocate (New York City), 2 October 1818

It has been frequently asked, what is the cause of this increase of pau-perism in our city? How is it that our poorhouse is not only crowded with age and decay, but even youthful mendacity? How is it that so many young women become inmates of charitable institutions, and so many of them for-eigners? And, above all, to what causes are we to attribute an increase of de-pravity, sensuality and crime? These are serious questions, which, one day, we must seriously ask ourselves. Volumes have been written on pauperism, which, though they may not fully apply to our case, yet, in principle, if not in extent, they have a close connexion. Mankind is the same all over the world, and the same remedies may be safely applied in like cases. The want of industry is the foundation of the evil, and that industry in the poor order of the community can only be promoted by example among the better educated and refined.... But the evil may increase until whole communities fall victims to its effects; and, though we tread on dangerous ground, we must pluck up courage to say, that our ladies, generally, are not sufficiently industrious, and having said so, we throw ourselves on their mercy for an indulgent hearing.... Here we have the remedy in our own hands; and never can the wife be made sensible of these facts until the husband, by a proper example, confirms them—until they both unite to promote industry, economy, content and happiness.

Howard: "Domestic Economy. 'Crib Not Thyself in Cities' "

While "Howard" revealed his appreciation for the industriousness of many of the immigrants then arriving on American shores, he warned they would add to pauperism if they stayed too long in the seaports they disembarked in. His view of such immigrants clashed with America's nativists, individuals who generally discouraged immigrants from pursuing American citizenship (see chapter 8).

National Advocate (New York City), 31 July 1819

For some time past, I have had occasion to remark the increase of emigrants in our city, and the strange faces, and still more strange habiliments, which meet our eye at every turn. Here a party of industrious Swiss, who had forsaken their mountains and valleys, their lakes and glaciers, to breathe more freely the air of liberty in the new world; the men in "russet mantle clad," with mild looks and sun burnt complexions; the women, with tight bodices, short petticoats, and hair in long and graceful plaits, holding their ruddy children by the hand....There is a party from Normandy, hardy, industrious and temperate; and those women with high caps, white ascots and stiffly starched, are from Provence, in the south of France; there goes an efficient Dutch family...here rolls an Englishman, with ruddy cheeks and a busy roast beef countenance; there's an Irishman and his five children, all with breeches and worsted stockings, feeling perfectly at home, though just landed on the soil.... Even a short residence in the city is injurious, as much money is spent in a few weeks in living and in seeing all that may be curious in a populous city than what would be required to build a comfortable cottage. Let them not lose a moment–let the farmer, with his family, shun the expensive allurements and pernicious examples of a city–let him depart for his settlement, and, with his axe, clear his land, build his cabin, plant his corn, and then his fortune has commenced; he is a proprietor of the soil–he is sovereign and independent: his wife labours, his girls work, his boys are hardy and industrious: their land produces corn–their cows furnish milk–their sheep, clothing–their forests, fuel–their hives, honey–their trees, maple sugar–they have fruits in abundance, and ample stores of provisions. What do they want? Nothing but health to labour and contentment to sweeten their fare.

COMMENTARY ON REMEDIES FOR PAUPERISM

A Mechanic: "For the *True American*"

When some early Americans could not pay their debts, they were sent to jail via their state's insolvent laws. According to this writer, such laws should be taken off the books since they led to the further impoverishment of innocent, hardworking people like storekeepers, farmers, mechanics, and laborers.

True American (Trenton, N.J.), 1 April 1805

It is hoped that the Legislature will at their next sitting take into serious consideration the present Insolvent Laws, and either amend or repeal them. As they now are, they open a wide door to villainy; and industrious and poor men, store-keepers, farmers, mechanics, and laborers, are every day defrauded of their hard earnings, under sanction of these laws by idle and knavish men. That there ought to be some provision to prevent unfortunate people from being kept in prison, no one will deny; but it ought to be so guarded as not to be taken advantage of by the indolent, extravagant, and dishonest. It is no trifling matter for men who earn their living by the strength of their bodies and the sweat of their brows, to be swindled out of the fruits of days, and weeks, and months, and years hard labor; and it is an aggravation of the wound inflicted, when the law, which ought to protect and redress honest citizens, connives at and sanctions this kind of robbery.–Let the subject receive general attention, and let those who come to the Legislature ponder well upon it, and see if some amendments cannot be made in the present system, or a more perfect one framed, which, while it would shield the victims of misfortune, and even imprudence, from the un-

merited punishment of long imprisonment, should leave roguery to the fate
it richly deserves—perpetual seclusion from the rest of the world.

Anonymous: "Relief for the Poor"

*Winter in America's northern regions always brought special challenges to
their inhabitants, but certain events, such as disasters, crop failures, and
economic panics made things worse. The winter after Washington, D.C.,
was burned by the British in 1814 proved to be an especially tough one for
the poor. In the midst of the crisis, this writer called on its citizens to discuss
ways to help those who had no means to help themselves.*

National Intelligencer (District of Columbia), 28 December 1814

I have been for several weeks past anxiously looking into your paper for
a call on the citizens to assemble, and to take into consideration the situation of the poorer class of our fellow citizens. It would be unnecessary to
state the reasons for the temporary establishment of some institutions, calculated to relieve in some degree those who have not the means of supporting themselves.

I am happy to learn that a Thespian Benevolent Society, will, in a short
time, perform in the theatre, which will answer a double purpose. 1st. It will
be an innocent amusement for those who have a dollar to spare, and it will
be a consolation to the benevolent heart to know, that that dollar will be appropriated to supply the wants of his suffering neighbor. As a month or six
weeks may elapse before any assistance can be given out of the proceeds of
the above institution; would it not be proper, that the citizens assemble to
devise means for immediate relief?

With a view to answer the objects of this communication, a meeting of the
citizens of the First and Second Wards is requested at Mr. Macleod's Hotel
Pennsylvania Avenue, on Wednesday next, 28th instant at 5 o'clock, P.M.

Paul Allen: "The Horrors, the Sufferings, the Privations"

*Its existing benevolent organizations overwhelmed with calls for charity,
the city of Baltimore established the Society for the Prevention of Pauperism
in March 1819. Editor Paul Allen was a supporter of the organization and
was influential in its formation. Winter was always a time when more
charity was needed, but an especially hard winter and the effects of the eco-*

nomic panic of 1819 (see chapter 24) gave further impetus to the society's organizers.

Morning Chronicle & Baltimore Advertiser (Maryland), 15 April 1819

We surely need not lead our readers back to the horrors, the sufferings, the privations endured by our fellow citizens during the season of cold; we will not lead back their funereal recollections to the bankruptcies of our principal houses, to the disorder of the banks, to the want of a circulating medium, to the decline of commerce, to the influx of foreign paupers, or the increase of our poor, and the exhausting drains occasioned by the collision, and we may add co-operation of so many unfortunate events on the charity of Baltimore. To those who have witnessed such scenes, we would deem the question almost superfluous, why a Society for the Prevention of Pauperism has been established in this city.

Paul Allen: "A Claimant's Rights"

Allen explained the purposes of the newly formed Boston Society for the Prevention of Pauperism. In his view, its aim was not to prevent poverty, but to prevent people from becoming "degrading object[s] of public bounty."

Morning Chronicle & Baltimore Advertiser (Maryland), 24 April 1820

It was [erroneously and uncharitably] thought that many claimants on charity had no right to such claims; that many were able by their own industry to provide the support of themselves, and of their families; that many were downright and detestable imposters, who, while they implored alms, deserved a residence in the Penitentiary; that many of this motley class did not belong to Baltimore, while they were so severely taxing the liberality of the inhabitants, that many had grown hoary in depravity and crime, and were consuming that bounty which should be applied to the relief of indigent merit; that many might be better provided for, by furnishing them with employment, than by pecuniary assistance; that many received public and private donations, not for the purpose of furnishing bread for their families, but for the indulgence of their low, sordid, selfish and criminal appetites, that many real and meritorious objects of pity in the depth of the cold season would rather suffer every privation, than to enjoy either public or private munificence in the company of such wretches.

QUESTIONS

1. Compare today's predominant views on the causes of poverty with those in the early nineteenth century.
2. Why do you think printers—most commonly men—included essays that told women they were to be responsible for the elimination of pauperism?
3. Why do you think some of the laws passed in America—such as the insolvency laws referred to by the New Jersey newspaper correspondent—were so harsh?
4. Identify at least five organizations or agencies whose job it is today to help those stricken by poverty. Do they seem driven by the same "moral reform" agendas of those organizations established early in the nineteenth century?

NOTES

1. Raymond A. Mohl, "Humanitarianism in the Preindustrial City: The New York Society for the Prevention of Pauperism, 1817–1823," *Journal of American History* 57 (December 1970): 576–599.

2. DeWitt Clinton, *An Address Delivered before Holland Lodge*, 12 December 1793 (New York: F. Childs and J. Swaine, 1859), 15.

3. Mohl, "Humanitarianism in the Preindustrial City," 582.

4. Blanche D. Coll, "The Baltimore Society for the Prevention of Pauperism, 1820–1822," *American Historical Review* 61 (October 1955): 77–87; Joel Schwartz, *Fighting Poverty with Virtue: Moral Reform and America's Urban Poor, 1825–2000* (Indianapolis: University of Indiana Press, 2000).

5. Article 1, Section 8, of the U.S. Constitution.

6. Coll, "Baltimore Society," 81.

7. [Tribunal of Liberty], *A Warning to the Citizens of Baltimore* (Baltimore, 1821).

CHAPTER 26

The Missouri Compromise, 1819–1820

The crisis seemed to come out of nowhere. By late 1819, America was poised on the threshold of what would become its most serious dispute to date over the extension of slavery into territories seeking statehood. Thomas Jefferson later wrote it was like "a fire bell in the night."[1] In hindsight, it's difficult to understand why it was so surprising, since signs of trouble over the extension of slavery into the nation's developing territories were visible for decades. In the eighteenth century, the earliest manumission societies were established, and some Americans expressed distaste for Southern manners and customs. Commenting on the ill-treatment of slaves by slaveholders in the 1770s, for example, Philip Fithian stated: "Good God, are these Christians?"[2] The American Revolution undermined the basis of slavery, but the nation's Constitution protected slavery in a variety of ways. By 1800, many states had adopted "gradual emancipation statutes," and increasingly, Americans were speaking out against slavery.

In April 1818, when the people of the Missouri Territory introduced a bill to the United States Congress asking for statehood, America was comprised of 22 states—11 that banned slavery and 11 that permitted it. The South's economy was dependent on slavery, and 200 years of living with the institution had made it an integral part of Southern life and culture. This led to bitter disputes as territories in the West and the South developed and asked for acceptance into the Union as states. But the Missouri crisis would become the most virulent to date. In an address to Congress in 1859, New York Senator William H. Seward remarked: "History tells us...that the Union reeled under the vehemence of that great debate."[3]

The story of whether Missouri would be admitted to the union as a slave or free state began with the 1803 Louisiana Purchase. Like many other

Americans captured by wanderlust, slaveholders from Virginia, North Carolina, Kentucky, and Tennessee wanted to move west into the Louisiana Territory to start new lives. But where could they settle and take their slaves with them? In 1787, slavery had been prohibited in regions north of Missouri by the Ordinance of 1787, and many states had outlawed slavery by the turn of the century. Missouri must have seemed to Southerners like a "promised land," since it already had many slaves—one-sixth of its 66,000 inhabitants—when it applied for statehood. All this forced Congress, in February 1819, to consider Missouri's future as a slave state or as a free state. No matter how the representatives answered this question, there would be an imbalance between America's free and slaveholding states. The nation was poised for a great debate.[4]

In February 1819, a bill to admit Missouri as a state was taken up by Congress. During its deliberations, James Tallmadge Jr. proposed that the following amendment be accepted:

> That the further introduction of slavery or involuntary servitude be prohibited, except for the punishment of crimes, whereof the party shall be duly convicted; and that all children of slaves, born within the said state, after the admission thereof into the Union, shall be free, but may be held to service until the age of twenty-five years.[5]

Tallmadge's amendment was a pivotal moment in the controversy, for it unleashed an acrimonious debate that reflected the deep fissures that had developed in America over the question of slavery. Salma Hale, a congressman from Keene, New Hampshire, wrote to New Hampshire Governor William Plumer: "It was a painful scene, & I hope a similar discussion will never again take place in our walls."[6] The pro-slavery members of the house were not able to prevent the adoption of the amendment. Southern strength in the Senate, however, defeated the bill.

The Missouri question was not dead, however. It came up once again in Congress's next session, after Maine, then a part of Massachusetts, applied for statehood. Through the efforts of Speaker of the House Henry Clay, who eventually became known as "the great pacificator," a compromise was reached on March 3, 1820. Clay, of Kentucky, warned Northern congressmen that, unless they changed their positions on Missouri, Southern congressmen would reject Maine's petition. To please the South, the slavery restrictions for Missouri were removed, and, to please the North the proviso that slavery was prohibited forever in Louisiana Purchase territories north from 36 30' latitude was added. Although many objected, Clay maneuvered the proposal through the House by a three-vote majority. Thus, to preserve the balance between slaveholding and free states, Missouri and Maine were granted statehood simultaneously.

As illustrated, the period's newspapers were heavily involved in the great debates that culminated in the Missouri Compromise. The chapter begins with a selection of newspaper essays published by writers who were either unopposed or adamantly in favor of the extension of slavery into Missouri. The first was written under the name "Hampden" and was published in April 1819 in the *St. Louis Enquirer,* not long after Congress had rejected the Tallmadge amendment, which would have banned slavery in the territory. Missourians were mortified during the period when the amendment was under consideration. As he introduced Hampden to his readers, the *Enquirer's* editor, Thomas Hart Benton, informed his readers that Hampden was living up to his namesake in English history who had "resisted the payment of twenty shillings, and staked his life and fortune upon the issue, because in paying it he yielded to the king the right of taking the people's money, whenever he pleased."[7]

The next two pieces were published in Virginia's *Richmond Enquirer.* The first, by an anonymous correspondent, argued that the nation's slavery problems wouldn't be solved by prohibiting slavery in Missouri. The following *Enquirer* column was written by its editor, Thomas Ritchie, who was fast becoming a leader in the country's pro-slavery faction. Ritchie strongly opposed the compromise for constitutional reasons. He and his friends argued that the Constitution guaranteed slaveholders the right to take their property wherever they wanted.

The chapter's second section includes newspaper essays whose authors opposed the Missouri Compromise. The first, written by an anti-slavery organizer, was published in November 1819, the period when Congress was considering whether to put the compromise into law. Its author, Theodore Dwight, had for years been writing against slavery for newspapers such as the *Connecticut Courant* and *Connecticut Mirror.* He established the *New-York Daily Advertiser* in 1817, and as he watched Congress consider and defeat the Tallmadge amendment, he knew the issue of slavery in Missouri was not dead. He predicted in the piece included here that, if the compromise were enacted, the slavery question would soon lead to another bitter debate among Americans.

The second of the anti-compromise writers featured here is William Coleman, editor of the *New-York Evening Post.* Coleman understood the many legal difficulties that would exist across America if the compromise were put into law. In the column included here, he expounded on two examples that he argued illustrated how unfair the compromise would be to members of America's free African American community. During and after the Revolutionary War, New York had moved in stages to ban slavery and the slave trade. In 1781, the state freed any slave who had served in the armed forces during the revolution. At the turn of the nineteenth century,

New York had a larger African American community than any other state north of the Chesapeake. The New York Manumission Society was organized in 1785, helping to establish the state as one of the strongholds in the nation's developing abolitionist movement.[8]

The final two pieces in this section were written and published by the editors of the *National Intelligencer*, who published their paper in the District of Columbia, where slavery was permitted. The editors stated they would not be opposed to the elimination of slavery in the district. Agitation against slavery in the nation's capital would become widespread, encouraged by activists who called the situation a "national shame." President Abraham Lincoln abolished slavery in the nation's capital on April 16, 1862, nine months before his Emancipation Proclamation.

The chapter's third and final section consists mainly of newspaper reports and essays published just after the compromise was enacted by Congress on March 3, 1820. The first of the reports was published by the *National Intelligencer* immediately after the late night congressional passage of the act. The editor reported on the vote, which was very close, and indicated great relief that the matter was finally settled.

The second piece in this section was published in the *Richmond Enquirer*, a paper whose editor, Thomas Ritchie, found no reason to celebrate, even though Missourians had succeeded in convincing Congress to permit slavery in their territory. Ritchie lamented that the people of the South and West were restricted by the provisions of the settlement from moving with their slaves wherever they chose.

This section's third newspaper essay was published in Boston, the heart of the growing American abolitionist movement. Its author attributed the passage of the compromise to the threats of disunion of the pro-slavery faction from the southern and western states.

The chapter's final newspaper report was published in Baltimore, ten months after the compromise was enacted. Its author, Hezekiah Niles, owner and editor of *Niles' Register*, forecast a gloomy future for America. The country, he argued, would not be able to put off the awful question forever: Would America free itself of slavery or not?

In Favor of Slavery in Missouri

Hampden: "To the People of Missouri Territory"

The Enquirer *published several essays on the Missouri question. This one was published not long after Congress rejected the Tallmadge amendment, which would have banned slavery in Missouri.*

St. Louis Enquirer (Missouri Territory), 7 April 1819

Nothing is calculated to produce feelings of deeper mortification and re-gret, than the necessity of withdrawing our confidence and esteem from those, to whom we have been accustomed to look up [to] with respect and reverence. Such were my feelings towards the house of representatives of the United States, (whom from my infancy, I have been accustomed to con-template with sentiments bordering on filial love) when I was informed that pending the bill for the admission of this territory into the union, an amend-ment was proposed, and actually carried by a small majority, to impose upon us a novel and unconstitutional condition. Fortunately for them and per-haps for us, a redeeming spirit was found in the senate. They rejected the amendment, and thereby saved congress from the foul disgrace of such an act of usurpation, and saved us from the jarring and discord incident to the necessity of maintaining our rights in defiance of such usurped authority. Since the amendment has failed in the senate, and the bill will probably pass cleansed of that blot, we shall not, I hope be called upon, for the painful ex-ercise of that republican firmness and persevering determination which I know belongs to the people of this country. Nevertheless, it behoves us to speak to the people of the union, in the indignant language of injured freemen; and tell them how much they are mistaken, in supposing that be-cause we inhabit a country once belonging to the kind of Spain, we are the poor remnant of Spanish despotism. Can it be necessary to inform the peo-ple of the United States that the great mass of our population was born in a land of liberty; that we know how to appreciate our natural and constitu-tional rights; and are at all times prepared to maintain and defend them?...

But it has been reserved for the representatives of the present congress to commit the most gross and barefaced usurpation that has yet been at-tempted. They have ingrafted on the bill for our admission into the union, a provision that the state constitution shall prohibit the further introduction of slavery; and that all children born of slaves shall be free at the age of five and twenty years. Bear in mind fellow citizens, that the question now before you is not whether slavery shall be permitted or prohibited in the future state of Missouri; but whether you will meanly abandon your rights, and suffer any earthly power to dictate the terms of your constitution. The federal constitu-tion guarantees a republican form of government to every state, and is itself the supreme law of the land. The only question then, that can arise on the presentation of a new state constitution for the approbation of Congress, are these—Is it republican? Is it consistent with the federal constitution?

Anonymous: "The Missouri Question"

This piece, from an anonymous slaveholder, warned that a restriction of slavery in Missouri would not remedy the problems anti-slavery people ar-

gued it would and that Missourians should be permitted to make up their own minds about whether they would allow slavery or not.

Richmond Enquirer (Virginia), 21 December 1819

But it is said...that humanity proscribes slavery. And how will this restriction remedy it? The evil is fastened around our necks without our consent, contrary to our most solemn protestations. How is it to be removed? Will this restriction remove it? Crowd our slaves into a smaller compass; increase their relative proportion to the whites; enlarge this kind of property in the hands of fewer masters—is this the way to encourage its abolition? But humanity prohibits their introduction into the regions west of the Mississippi! How? Will they breed one less in the existing states? Can we prohibit their propagation? Shall we assassinate their infant, as the Egyptian king wished to do the sons of Israel? You can coop more of them into a smaller compass; and is this the way to insure their better treatment? Compare a flock of 100 slaves upon one estate; placed under the hands of an overseer, removed from the eye of their master; with the same number dispersed among 100 proprietors, acquainted with their wants, touched with a sympathy and a love for them; and which is the most humanely treated? Compare the West Indian negroes with those of Virginia, and then say whether condensation or diffusion is the best calculated to advance the purposes of humanity. We would not advise the citizens of Missouri to admit slaves into their state; but, under the Constitution, they are the best judges of their own interests; and they have a right to judge.

Thomas Ritchie: "Missouri Compromise"

Ritchie foresaw trouble beyond the compromise. He stated he was convinced it would not stop Congress from future meddling in the affairs of slaveholders, something he deemed to be unconstitutional. Although Texas was part of Mexico at this time, he anticipated that if it should become part of the United States, Congress would interfere with slaveholders who might wish to settle there.

Richmond Enquirer (Virginia), 10 February 1820

But if this Compromise should be adopted, then what will become of the Florida country? Can we consent to be cooped up....Yield Texas? This is another great question.

But by what right do the representatives talk of such compromises? To bind up future generations—nay, to bind up the hands of their own successors? Will any independent representative think himself irrevocably tied up by such restrictions?

Take it as you will, we disapprove this Compromise. We had rather wait the progress of events;...preserve what is right with "an eye that never winks"—and leave the rest to god.

Opposed to the Compromise

Theodore Dwight: "Slavery"

The author of this piece, the publisher and editor of the Advertiser, *was an avid abolitionist who wrote frequently on his views that slavery was an evil system.*

New-York Daily Advertiser (New York City), 10 November 1819

The question must be brought once more into discussion—the approaching session will undoubtedly witness the struggle—and it will remain with the members from the states where slavery is not admitted, to determine, whether this eventual scourge of our country shall be confined within its present limits, or shall be permitted to spread through the almost boundless regions of our unsettled and uncultivated territory. At the present moment the free states have a decided majority. It is in their power, now, to check the progress of evil. If they fail to avail themselves of this last opportunity, the point will be settled against them for ever; and this black spot in our character will be indelibly and fatally impressed upon it. The moment then is all important, and calls loudly upon every part of the country where the evils of slavery are unknown, and where the blessings of freedom are fully enjoyed, to bestir themselves in the attempt to prevent an evil which is universally acknowledged to be great—which already scatters alarm thro' a large portion of our country, and there is too much reason to fear will first or last, call down upon us the heavy judgments of Heaven.

With these feelings and views, we most earnestly hope that the proposed meeting will be generally attended, and by its unanimity and firmness, shew to our fellow countrymen, that the subject is considered here as one of vital importance, which interests the liveliest feelings of all our citizens.—IF THIS GREAT QUESTION IS LOST, IT MUST FALL A SACRIFICE TO THE MISTAKEN VIEWS, AND UNFORTUNATE VOTES OF MEMBERS FROM STATES WHERE THE CURSE OF SLAVERY DOES NOT EXIST. IF LOST, IT ANNIHILATES AT A STROKE, THE POLITICAL INFLUENCE AND CONSIDERATION OF ALL THE STATES WHERE SLAVERY HAS BEEN

ABOLISHED, AND IS UNIVERSALLY REGARDED AS A NATIONAL SIN OF THE BLACKEST DYE. WE ARE SAFE IF WE ARE UNITED—WE SHALL BE DEGRADED AND DISGRACED IF WE ARE DIVIDED.

William Coleman: "Mr. Sergeant's Speech Concluded"

Many newspapers published or commented on the speeches of members of Congress through the months of debate on the Missouri question. In this article, Coleman commented on a speech given that evening by an anticompromise orator, adding several points of his own. In his view, the compromise would create an untenable situation for "free people of color" in America.

New-York Evening Post (New York City), 12 December 1819

We cannot conceal the satisfaction with which we have perused this masterly speech which is concluded this evening. It is clear and vigorous in its reasoning, yet temperate in its expression, and really strikes as invulnerable. We will merely mention one or two remarks in addition to those Mr. Sergeant has presented, which we think place the objectional provision in a striking point of view.

It is well known that several free people of color, both mulattoes and negroes, enlisted and served out their enlistments in the last war, and consequently became entitled to bounty lands from the United States; suppose then that some of the lands to which such persons are so entitled, shall be located in the state of Missouri. Shall it be provided in the constitution, that the owner of the soil, under a title from the government, shall not occupy it; shall he not have, hold, and enjoy his fee simple estate? What sort of realty is this? Certainly not one known to the laws of either this country or England.

Secondly. Free mulattoes are forbidden to come from another state to reside in Missouri.—And pray what is a mulatto? Who can tell me? In vain may we turn to dictionaries: the word is not to be found there. Who shall decide the question? Suppose that a man is arbitrarily called a mulatto, & as such is ousted of his freehold; removed out of the state, for which injury he appeals to the laws for redress, and the question is submitted to a jury whether he is a mulatto or not? By what criterion, we would ask, is this to be decided? Will you take one half, one fourth or one eighth blood as the rule?

Joseph Gales Jr. and William W. Seaton: "The Missouri Question"

The Missouri debate was so contentious that the editors of the Intelligencer *announced that they would not publish any further materials on it until after Congress acted. Indeed, that the District of Columbia still allowed slavery must have put the editors in a delicate position. In this piece, after repeating that they would not object to the prohibition of slavery in present or future territories or states of the nation, they stated they would not be opposed to the abolition of slavery in the District of Columbia.*

National Intelligencer (District of Columbia), 25 December 1819

We take this method of announcing to correspondents, generally, that we decline to publish any more essays on the Missouri question, or in any manner connected with it, until the subject shall have been acted on by Congress. Further contention will only serve to exasperate into enmity what is now mere difference of opinion, in which some feeling mingles. Our columns have been widely opened already to all parties on the subject, and we have temperately expressed our own opinion relative to it.

Whilst referring to our expressed opinion, we will add, that what we have already said, that we have no decided objection to the prohibition of the migration of Slaves from the present states into the territories over which Congress have exclusive jurisdiction. With regard to the District in which we ourselves reside, we should cheerfully acquiesce in such a measure, though there is not in it, that we know of, a slave who was not born in the United States, and we are quite sure there never was a slave ship fitted out from it. We wish some of the districts most intent on imposing restrictions on Missouri could say as much.

Joseph Gales Jr. and William W. Seaton: "Clarification on the Missouri Question"

The Intelligencer's *editors expounded on their view that the debate over Missouri involved much more than the proposed measure's constitutionality.*

National Intelligencer (District of Columbia), 29 January 1820

The proposition which is the subject of so much debate, reduced to a familiar phraseology, is this: whether it be expedient to impose, as a condition of the admission of the territory of Missouri into the Union, an obligation on her people to prohibit the future removal or transportation of slaves into that territory. This question divides itself into three branches: 1. The constitutionality of the measure. 2. Its conformity to the stipulations of the Treaty of 1803, by which France ceded the territory in question to the United States. 3. The expediency of the measure, as it may affect the relative condition of the persons now held in servitude in the United States, and as it may affect the relations between different parts of the Union.

The affirmative and negative of these questions are supported with equal zeal, by nearly equal numbers. In the Senate the majority is supposed to be opposed to the restriction; in the House of Representatives, though the question has not been tried decisively in any shape, it is supposed there is a majority in favor of the restriction.

An excitement appears to prevail, or rather it is painfully apprehended, in regard to this question, which would, with difficulty, be accounted for, from a general view of the points embraced by it. The truth is, and it is in vain to shut our eyes to the fact, that there are considerations of deeper interest at the bottom of this question. The balance of power vibrates; and the feelings of our politicians vibrate in sympathy. It has been surmised, we perceive by letters from this city, published in the Eastern prints, that already it is attempted to establish political distinctions by this question. We incline to think, however, that this suggestion is rather the result of gloomy foreboding, than the delineation of a reality which could not be too earnestly deprecated. Of all political tests, our federative system abhors a geographical one...

It is yet attempted to impress the public mind, in defiance of repeated contradictions, that this is a question which involves *an extension of slavery*, that is, the multiplication of slaves in our country. Once for all, no such question is presented to the consideration of Congress, or of the nation. The question concerns only the *diffusion* or the *concentration* of the slaves now in the country. There is not in the Congress of the United States a single individual who would raise his hand in favor of authorizing the introduction of slaves into the United States—or, in other words, in favor of the extension of slavery. Justice to the character of our country requires that this should be distinctly understood; and never overlooked, as it frequently is, in the newspaper discussion of what is called the Missouri Question.

After the Compromise

Joseph Gales Jr. and William W. Seaton: "The Question Settled"

Many Americans were impatient with Congress during its lengthy proceedings regarding Missouri. In this report, the Intelligencer *'s editors happily announced that Congress had finally settled the question and that they hoped for more tranquil times now that a decision had been reached.*

***National Intelligencer* (District of Columbia), 3 March 1820**

We most heartily congratulate our readers—we felicitate our fellow-citizens generally, that the Missouri question is SETTLED....

The House of Representatives sat till a late hour last night; and we have only time to state that, on the question to agree to the amendment of the Senate to strike the restriction from the Missouri bill, the vote was

Against the restriction	90
For it	86

Being a majority of four votes against the Restriction.

Other proceedings took place, which will be reported hereafter; the result of which is, that the bill for the admission of Missouri without restriction, and with the inhibition of Slavery in certain territories, wants only the signature of the President to become a law.

The bill for the admission of Maine will of course pass, without restriction, incumbrance, or amendment.

The few past days have been a trying time in Congress; but the trial has passed, and we look now only for harmony and conciliation on all sides.

Thomas Ritchie: "Missouri Question—Settled!"

Unlike the editors of the Intelligencer, *Thomas Ritchie was unwilling to congratulate his Southern readers on the settlement of the Missouri question. He did congratulate, however, the people of Missouri for having "succeeded in their wishes."*

***Richmond Enquirer* (Virginia), 7 March 1820**

The *National Intelligencer* informs us, that the Question is settled. We presume it is so. He congratulates the country upon the settlement—we regret our inability to echo back the gratulation. "Those who win, says the proverb, may laugh." The *Intelligencer* approves, we presume, of *the Compromise.* We cannot join him in the sentiment. Instead of joy, we scarcely ever recollected to have tasted of a bitterer cup. We cannot chuckle over the prospect which *this* compromise presents to our comprehension. A constitution warped from its legitimate bearings, and an immense region of territory closed for ever against the Southern and Western people—such is the "sorry sight" which rises to our view.

Strip this compromise of all its glosses and pretexts, and what is it? We do not address ourselves to the race of quibblers and sophists; but to men of plain common sense. What is this compromise?—Missouri was called upon, when she knocked at the doors of Congress, to pay the price of her admission; and this price was to strip herself of a portion of her sovereign rights: the right of choosing the fundamental rules by which she would be governed, and of changing those rules whenever the interest of her people should require the change. If this iniquitous demand is not to be obtained, what is required of Congress next? That they should make a similar surrender for all those who may hereafter inhabit a much larger extent of country; in plain language, that Congress should forever take from them the privilege of self-government, under the pretence that it is a "needful regulation" for a country in which not a single human being exists that is subject to the laws of the United States?

It is thus that a compromise is patched up—"Give us for ever the territory that is to the north of 36–1/2, with the exception of such part of Missouri as lies beyond it; let that door be for ever shut to yourselves and to your slaves; and we consent that you migrate with them to the state of Missouri. We will admit Missouri unrestricted into the Union, if you for ever cede to us the immense region of soil that lies beyond the 36–1/2, and sweeps from the Missouri to the Pacific."...

But the deed is done—The treaty is signed, sealed and delivered.... We submit. It is the duty of good citizens to hold by the sheet anchor, the law of the land, so long as it remains a law. The South and the West are wronged; they must bear up patient....

But with all our disquietude and regrets, there is intermingled one pleasurable emotion, that the high minded citizens of Missouri have succeeded in their wishes; and are about to enter the Union, "unshorn of their beams"—free, sovereign—*on an equal footing with the original states.*

Anonymous: "Extract of a Letter"

This writer sorely regretted the decision of Congress to allow slavery in Missouri, comforting those who had fought against the extension of slavery anywhere under any circumstances. To them, the compromise was a terrible sacrifice to make in order to placate those who threatened disunion.

Columbian Centinel (Boston), 8 March 1820

You will hear with equal surprise and regret, that the Friends of Freedom in the House of Representatives, have at last found themselves in a minority upon the most momentous question which has ever been discussed in Congress. *A bill has passed both Houses to admit the State of Missouri into the Union, without any restriction of the barbarous custom of Slavery!*

When they heard the *names* of the Committee of Conferees, they had their forebodings; and the committee had not been assembled but a short time before the advocates of Slavery noised it abroad, that they had agreed *among themselves* upon all the great points in controversy:—Meaning, that the all-important principle of restricting Slavery in Missouri would be abandoned by the House for the deceptive *provision* for the inhibition of Slavery in the Territories, and the boon of an early admission of Maine into the Union.—A grain of sand to the Andes. The hope, however, was alive, that the majority would stand firm on their ground. But it is now found, that the threats of the Slave-holders to *dissolve the Union,* and the violence of the Hotspurs in the South in other particulars, have had their effect; and the great principle of Freedom has been abandoned in the Temple where liberty had fondly anticipated that her Altar was firmly founded. Thus have terminated all our toils and cares; and we can only hope, the true friends of Liberty will estimate them by their value and not by their success; and bear in mind those who have sacrificed, to some unknown Deity, the great concerns of Humanity, and the vital interests of the non-Slave-holding States.

Hezekiah Niles: "Slavery and the Missouri Compromise"

After the compromise was struck, Niles reflected on the naiveté of those who lived in states and territories free of slaves. Eventually, he argued, Americans would be forced to face the question as to whether it would continue to allow slavery or not.

Niles' Register (Baltimore, Md.), 23 December 1820

It is established (so far as large majorities in both houses of Congress can establish it) that the power to check the progress of a slave population within the territories of the United States exists by the Constitution; but admitted that it was not expedient to exert that power in regard to Missouri and Arkansas. The latter depended on many considerations of no ordinary importance: the safety and feelings of the white population in several of the States appeared to be involved in it, and the rights and feelings of others were as deeply concerned in the subject at large. In this conflict of interests, among persons who possibly desired the same ultimate issue, though their views of it were diametrically opposed, a spirit of conciliation prevailed and a compromise was effected. The people of those sections of country in which there are few or no slaves or persons of color, very imperfectly appreciate the wants, necessity, or general principle of others differently situated.

Collectively, the latter deprecate slavery as severely as the former, and deprecate its increase; but individual cupidity and rashness acts against the common sentiment, in the hope that an event which everybody believes must happen, will not happen in their day. It is thus that too many of us act about death; we are sure it must come, yet we commit wrong to acquire property, just as if we should hold and enjoy it forever. That the slave population will, at some certain period, cause the most horrible catastrophe, cannot be doubted; those who possess them act defensively in behalf of all that is nearest and dearest to them, when they endeavor to acquire all the strength and influence to meet that period which they can; and hence the political and civil opposition of these to the restriction which was proposed to be laid on Missouri. They *have* the offensive population, and no feasible plan has yet been contrived to rid them of it, if they were disposed so to do. Will the people of any of the States, so much alive to humanity, pass acts to encourage emancipation by agreeing to receive the emancipated? What will they do, what can they do, to assist the people of others to relieve themselves of their unfortunate condition? It is easy to use severe terms against the practice of slavery; but let us first tell the Southern people what they can safely do to abolish it, before we condemn them wholesale.

No one can hate slavery more than I do—it is a thing opposed to every principle that operates on my mind as an individual—and in my own private circle I do much to discourage it. I am also exceedingly jealous of it, so far as it affects my political rights as a citizen of the United States, entitled to be fairly and fully represented, and no more. But I can make greater allowances for those who hold slaves in districts where they bound—where, in many cases, their emancipation might be an act of cruelty to them, and of most serious injury to the white population. Their difference of color is an insuperable barrier to their incorporation within the society; and the mixture of free blacks with slaves is detrimental to the happiness of both, the cause of uncounted crimes. Yet I think that some have urged their defensive character too far; without a proper respect for the rights and feelings of others, as applicable to an extension of the evil. But we advocated the compromise, as fixing certain points for the future government of all the parties concerned; believing that the moral and political evil of spreading slavery over Missouri and even in Arkansas was not greater than that which might have risen from restriction, though to restrict was right in itself. The harmony of the Union, and the peace and prosperity of the white population, most excited our sympathies. We did not fear the dreadful things which some silly folks might lead to the worst of calamities. We had no pleasant feeling on the Compromise, for bad was the best that could be done. Nevertheless, we hoped that the contest was at an end, and that things would settle down and adapt themselves to the agreement which necessity imposed.

Questions

1. Explain the issues behind the dispute over the extension of slavery into Missouri and, eventually, over the compromise.
2. Considering the many anti-slavery activities already underway in some parts of the country in the first two decades of the nineteenth century, discuss whether you think Americans should have been surprised when the furor arose over the extension of slavery into Missouri.
3. The debate over Missouri revealed the development of deep sectional conflicts in America. Identify and discuss any other sectional issues you can think of that existed or were emerging in the country during this period.
4. Does it appear from what you've read in this chapter that newspapers split over Missouri purely on party lines, as they had done over so many other conflicts in the early national period? Why or why not?
5. Do you think the ideas published in American newspapers during the crisis over the Missouri question led to a critical realignment of the nation on what to do about the extension of slavery or did they simply reflect sentiments that already existed in America? Explain.
6. Are you surprised that Americans permitted slavery in the nation's capital until 1862? Why or why not?

Notes

1. Letter to John Holmes from Thomas Jefferson on 22 April 1820, in *The Writings of Thomas Jefferson*, ed. Paul L. Ford (New York, G.P. Putnam's Sons, 1892–1899), 10:157.

2. Peter Kolchin, *American Slavery, 1619–1877* (New York: HarperCollins, 1994), 58.

3. *Congressional Globe*, 36th Cong., 1st sess., 911.

4. Glover Moore, *The Missouri Compromise, 1819–1821* (Gloucester, Mass.: P. Smith, 1967), 1–53.

5. Ibid., 35.

6. Ibid., 48.

7. Thomas Hart Benton, *St. Louis Enquirer*, 14 April 1819.

8. Douglas Harper, http://www.slavenorth.com/nyemancip.htm, "Emancipation in New York," Slavery in the North.

Selected Bibliography

Adams, Henry. *The United States in 1800.* Ithaca, N.Y.: Cornell University Press, 1955.

Ames, William E. *A History of the "National Intelligencer."* Chapel Hill: University of North Carolina Press, 1972.

Annals of the Congress of the United States (1789–1824). 18 vols. Washington, D.C.: Gales & Seaton, 1834–1856.

Aptheker, Herbert. *American Negro Slave Revolts.* New York: Columbia University Press, 1943.

Bowling, Kenneth R. *The Creation of Washington, D.C.: The Idea and Location of the American Capital.* Fairfax, Va.: George Mason University Press, 1991.

Brown, Richard D. *Knowledge Is Power: The Diffusion of Information in Early America, 1700–1865.* New York: Oxford University Press, 1989.

Buckner, F. Melton, Jr. *Aaron Burr: Conspiracy to Treason.* New York: John Wiley, 2002.

Chambers, William H., and Walter Burnham, eds. *The American Party Systems: Stages of Political Development.* New York: Oxford University Press, 1967.

Coles, Henry L. *The War of 1812.* Chicago: University of Chicago Press, 1966.

Cook, Timothy E. *Governing with the News: The News Media as a Political Institution.* Chicago: University of Chicago Press, 1998.

Cunningham, Nobel E. *The Jeffersonian Republicans in Power: Party Operations, 1801–1809.* Chapel Hill: University of North Carolina Press, 1963.

Dangerfield, George. *The Era of Good Feelings.* New York: Harcourt, Brace & World, 1952.

Dicken-Garcia, Hazel. *Journalistic Standards in Nineteenth-Century America.* Madison: University of Wisconsin Press, 1989.

Dooley, Patricia L. *Taking Their Political Place: Journalists and the Making of an Occupation.* Westport, Conn.: Greenwood Press, 1997.

Dreisbach, Daniel L. *Thomas Jefferson and the Wall of Separation between Church and State.* New York: New York University Press, 2003.

Durey, Michael. *Transatlantic Radicals and the Early American Republic.* Lawrence: University Press of Kansas, 1997.

Ellis, Joseph J. *Founding Brothers: The Revolutionary Generation*. New York: Alfred A. Knopf, 2000.

Evans, Sarah M. *Born for Liberty: A History of Women in America*. New York: Free Press, 1989.

Graber, Mark A., and Michael Perhac, eds. *Marbury versus Madison: Documents and Commentary*. Washington, D.C.: CQ Press, 2002.

Hamilton, Milton W. *The Country Printer: New York State*. New York: Columbia University Press, 1936.

Horsman, Reginald. *Causes of the War of 1812*. Philadelphia: University of Pennsylvania Press, 1962.

Humphrey, Carol Sue. *The Press of the Young Republic, 1783–1833*. Westport, Conn.: Greenwood Press, 1996.

Kastor, Peter J. *The Nation's Crucible: The Louisiana Purchase and the Making of America*. New Haven, Conn.: Yale University Press, 2004.

Kielbowicz, Richard. *News in the Mail: Post Office and Public Information, 1700–1860*. Westport, Conn.: Greenwood Press, 1989.

Mintz, Steven. "Policing the Pre-Civil War City." www.digitalhistory.uh.edu/history online/policing.cfm? 3 Oct. 2004. Digital History.

Moore, Glover. *The Missouri Compromise, 1819–1821*. Gloucester, Mass.: P. Smith, 1967.

Nerone, John. *The Culture of the Press in the Early Republic: Cincinnati, 1793–1848*. New York: Garland, 1989.

Parcell, Lisa Millikin, and W. David Sloan. *American Journalism: History, Principles, Practices*. Jefferson, N.C.: McFarland & Company, 2002.

Pasley, Jeffrey L. *"The Tyranny of Printers": Newspaper Politics in the Early American Republic*. Charlottesville: University of Virginia Press, 2001.

Pitch, Anthony. *The Burning of Washington: The British Invasion of 1814*. Annapolis, Md.: Naval Institute Press, 1998.

Rischin, Moses, ed. *Immigration and the American Tradition*. Indianapolis, Ind.: Bobbs-Merrill, 1976.

Rosenberg, Norman L. *Protecting the Best Men: An Interpretive History of the Law of Libel*. Chapel Hill: University of North Carolina Press, 1986.

Rothbard, Murray N. *The Panic of 1819: Reactions and Policies*. www.mises.org/rothbard/panic1819.pdf.

Sears, Louis Martin. *Jefferson and the Embargo*. Durham, N.C.: Duke University Press, 1927.

Shyrock, Richard H. *Medicine and Society in America: 1660–1860*. New York: New York University Press, 1960.

Smith, Page. *The Shaping of America: A People's History of the Young Republic*. Vol. 3. New York: McGraw-Hill, 1980.

Spivak, Burton. *Jefferson's English Crisis: Commerce, Embargo and the Republican Revolution*. Charlottesville: University of Virginia Press, 1979.

Sugden, John. *Tecumseh's Last Stand*. Norman: University of Oklahoma Press, 1990.

Zinn, Howard. *A People's History of the United States*. New York: Harper & Row, 1980.

Index

Abolitionism, and abolitionist movement, 67, 74, 349–51, 352
Adams, Abijah, 92, 119, 144–46, 210
Adams, John: election of 1800–1801, 37–38, 48; George Washington's death, 2–3; Hartford Convention, 279; Jefferson's patronage, 89, 91–92, 94; midnight appointments, 151–54, 157–58, 166; Tripolitan War, 130; U.S. capital moves to Washington, D.C., 23
African Americans, 72–82, 189
Albany Gazette, 5, 25
Alien and Sedition Acts, 38, 111, 120, 175
Allen, Paul, 297, 340, 345, 346
Allen, Phinehas, 99–100
American Citizen, 87, 91–92, 127, 182–83, 213–16
American Citizen and General Advertiser, 131
American Daily Advertiser, 177
American Mercury, 94
American Revolution, 109, 337, 349
American Watchman, 297, 300–1, 340
Armstrong, John, Secretary of War, 264, 271, 274
Aurora, The: election of 1800–1801, 39–40, 43, 47, 49; George Washington's death, 3–4, 7–8, 18–19; Jefferson's patronage, 87, 89, 94; and steamboats, 222; Tripolitan War, 128,

133; U.S. capital moves to Washington, D.C., 23–25
Austin, Mr., 86

Babcock, Elisha, 94
Bache, Benjamin Franklin, 3
Bainbridge, Captain William, 126–27, 129
Baltimore Society for the Prevention of Pauperism, 338
Banking, 317–24
Banneker, Benjamin, 74, 76
Baptists, 39, 48, 66, 68–69, 97, 99, 105
Barbary Pirates, 125–26
Barbary States, 125, 128, 130–31, 134
Barbauld, Anna Leticia, 191
Barbé-Marbois, Marquis de Francois, 140
Barney, Commodore Joshua, 261–62
Bay Psalm Book, 99
Bellona, HMS., 179–80
Benton, Thomas Hart, 351
Berkeley, Admiral George Cranfield, 181
Bickley, John, 274–75
Binns, John, 110, 118, 121
Bishop, Abraham, 100
Black Hoof (Shawnee Chief), 226
Bladensburg, Battle of, 262, 265, 272, 276
Blennerhassett, Herman, 167
Bloomfield, General, 271

Boston Daily Advertiser, 281, 285
Boston Gazette, 202–3, 247, 258, 286, 288
Boston Society for the Prevention of Pauperism, 338
Boulderson, Captain John, 182–84
Bradford, Benjamin, 39
Bradford, James M., 167, 173
Bradford, John, 39, 45
Brickell, John, 4, 10
Bronson, Enos, 168, 264, 268, 270
Brown, Charles Brockden, 138
Brown, John, 65
Bryant, William Cullen, 201
Bunker, Capt., 220
Burr, Aaron: conspiracy and trial, 165–76; election to vice presidency, 38, 40, 44, 50

Cabot, George, 280, 289
Callender, James Thomson, 110, 153, 295
Campbell, John, 87
Carey, Mathew, 110, 118, 325, 327, 334
Carlton, William, 140
Carolina Centinel, 222, 328–29, 331
Carr, Benjamin, 127
Carrier's Address, 100, 104
Cathcart, James L., 127, 130
Centinel of Freedom: Jefferson's patronage, 93; Tripolitan War, 127, 131; War of 1812, 245, 251; and women's suffrage, 189–90, 192, 194, 196–98
Centlivre, Susanah, 191
Charleston City Gazette, 27
Charleston Courier, 154, 162
Cheetham, James, 87, 91–92, 130, 216, 295
Chesapeake, USS, 178–79, 181–83, 185–86, 247
Chesapeake-Leopard Affair, 177–87, 202
Chief Tatooed Serpent, 137
Clark, General William, 233
Clay, Henry, 350
Clermont, steamboat launching, 213–222
Clinton, DeWitt, 338
Cobbett, William, 3–4, 9, 54–55, 57

Cockburn, Rear Admiral George, 261–63
Coleman, William: and *Chesapeake-Leopard* Affair, 185; Embargo Act, 203–4; Louisiana Purchase, 138, 145; and medical quackery, 56, 62; Missouri Compromise, 351, 356; New York City public health and safety, 306–7, 309, 311–12; 315; and steamboats, 214, 220; War of 1812, 247, 256, 264, 269–72
The Columbian, 287
Columbian Centinel: Era of Good Feelings, 296, 298; Hartford Convention, 280, 282–83, 286; Louisiana Purchase, 147–48; Missouri Compromise, 360; nativism, 112–13; New Haven Remonstrance, 86, 89, 91; War of 1812, 246, 255
Congregationalists, 39, 98
Connecticut Courant, 39, 42, 111, 351
Connecticut Gazette, 25, 129
Connecticut Mirror, 289, 351
Constitution, United States, 151, 153
Constitution, USS, 129
Cowper, William, 74, 76
Craik, James, 1, 3, 8
Cushing, Thomas C., 247, 257
Cutler, James, 203, 247, 258

Dale, Commodore Richard, 126
Dallas, Alexander J., 317
Danbury Baptist Association, 98, 101
Danbury Baptists, 99
Davis, William, 175, 178–79
Dayton, U.S. Sen. Jonathan, 167
Decatur, Lieutenant Stephen, 126–27

Democratic Press, 122
Democratic-Republican Party. *See* Republican Party
Dennie, Joseph (Oliver Oldschool), 100, 106–7
Denniston, David, 87, 91–92
Dey of Algiers, 126–27, 129
Dickens, Charles, 305
Douglas, Commodore J.E., 180

Driscol, Denis, 110
Duane, William: election of 1800–1801, 3, 7, 39, 43, 47, 49; Jefferson's patronage, 87, 90; *Marbury v. Madison,* 156; nativism, 110, 112; U.S. capital moves to Washington, D.C., 23–26
Dunn, James C., 297, 300
Dutchess Observer, 327
Dwight, Theodore, 280, 289, 327, 333, 351, 355

Eddy, Thomas, 338
Ellicott, Andrew, 22–23
Emancipation Proclamation, 352
Embargo Act, 178, 201–212, 244, 279
Enterprise, USS, 126
Episcopalians, 68
Era of Good Feelings, 295–304
Essex Decree of 1805, 243
Essex Junto, 279–80
Evening Post, 245

Fairfax, Fernando, 222
Fallen Timbers, Battle of, 226
Federal Republican (Baltimore), 121
Federal Republican and Baltimore Telegraph, 297
Federal Republican and Commercial Gazette, 117, 205, 231
Federalist Party: Burr Conspiracy, 166, 168; *Chesapeake-Leopard* Affair, 179, 182, 185–86; election of 1800–1801, 37–50; Embargo Act, 201–6, 210; Era of Good Feelings, 295–303; Hartford Convention, 279–86; immigrants and foreigners, 110–13, 119; Louisiana Purchase, 138, 145–47; mammoth cheese and religion, 97–108; *Marbury v. Madison,* 151–53, 160; New Haven Remonstrance, 85–95; Tripolitan War, 127–28, 132–33; War of 1812, 244, 246–47, 255–59, 268–73, 277; women's suffrage, 189–90
Fellows, Sir James, 62
Financial Panic and Depression of 1819, 325–35
First Bank of the United States, 317
Fitch, John, 215, 222

Fithian, Philip, 349
Fort Greenville, Treaty of, 226–27, 229–30
Fort Massac, 167
Fort Stoddert, 165
Frank, Jacob, 208
French Revolution, 38, 110
Freneau, Philip, 24, 27
Fulton, Robert, 213–17, 220–22
Fulton's Folly, 213

Gabriel's Slave Rebellion, 65–84
Gales Jr., Joseph: Missouri Compromise, 356–58; Second Bank of the United States, 319; War of 1812, 261–63, 272, 276
Gales Sr., Joseph, 54, 265
Gazette of the United States, 23, 39, 43, 112, 166
Genius of Liberty, 193–95
George Washington, USS, 126–27, 129
Ghent, Treaty of, 280
Goodrich, Elizur, 85, 87, 92, 99–100
Gould, Stephen, 131
Gray, William, 210
Green, Timothy, 3
Griscom, John, 338

Hale, Nathan, 281, 284
Hale, Salma, 350
Hamilton, Alexander (Pericles): Aaron Burr, 165; First Bank of the United States, 317; Louisiana Purchase, 141; nativism, 114, 119; U.S. capital moves to Washington, D.C., 22; women's suffrage, 189
Hampshire Gazette, 99, 103
Hanson, Alexander Contee, 203, 205, 246–47, 256
Harrison, General William Henry, 225, 227–29, 235, 237–40
Hartford Convention, 279–93, 295
Helms, W., 34
Hemings, Sally, 295
Holt, Charles, 219, 281, 287
Hortensia, 246, 254
Howard. *See* Noah, Mordecai Manual

Humphreys, David, 126
Humphries, Captain, 181–82, 185
Impressment, of American sailors, 177–79, 202
Independent Chronicle, 93, 95, 120, 144, 146, 210

Jackson, Andrew, 86, 167
Jacobinism, 42, 44–45
James, Captain, 67, 69
Jay, John, 37
Jefferson, Thomas: appointment of Albert Gallatin, 111–12, 119; Burr conspiracy and Aaron Burr, 165–67, 170, 172–73; *Chesapeake-Leopard* Affair, 178–79, 185–86; election to presidency, 37–49; Embargo Act, 201–3, 206; Hartford Convention, 279; immigration and citizenship requirements, 113–18; inauguration, 152, 196; Indian policies, 225–26, 236; Louisiana Purchase, 137–39, 143–45; *Marbury v. Madison,* 161; midnight appointments, 154, 157–58; Missouri Compromise, 349; patronage practices, 85–95; religion, 97–107; relocation of U.S. capital to Washington, D.C., 22; and scandal, 295; Tripolitan War, 125–27, 132–34; War of 1812, 243–44
Jeffersonian-Republican Party. *See* Republican Party
Jenks, Elizer Alley, 5, 41, 86, 88–89, 113, 127, 130
Jenks' Portland Gazette, 6, 26, 41
Jenner, Edward, 56
Journalism, black period of American, 295
Judiciary Act of 1789, 152
Judiciary Act of 1801, 152, 154, 166

Karamanli, Yusuf, 129
Kentucky Gazette: Era of Good Feelings, 297, 302; Harrison's Campaign against the Shawnee, 235–40; relocation of U.S. capitol, 274–75; and steamboats, 218; Thomas Jefferson,

39, 45–46; War of 1812, 244–47, 252–54; government–Indian relations, 229
King, Rufus, 13, 296
King George III, 109
Kittera, John Wilkes, 86, 88–89
Koss, Major General Robert, 261–62

Laprusieur, Chief, 229–30
Leander, HMS, 177, 183
Lear, Tobias, 129, 134
Leland, Elder John, 97, 99, 101, 105
L'Enfant, Charles, 22
Leopard, HMS, 178–79, 181–83, 185
Libel, 9, 55
Lincoln, Abraham, 352
Livingston, Robert R., Jr, 137–38, 140, 146, 213, 215–16, 222
Louisiana Gazette, 327
Louisiana Purchase, 137–50, 349–50
Louisville Gazette, and Western Advertiser, 239
Lyon, Matthew, 175

MacGregor, Sir James, 62
Macon's Bill No. 2, 202, 244
Madison, Dolley, 262
Madison, James: burning of Washington, D.C., 262, 270, 272, 276; Hartford Convention, 279–81; Second Bank of the United States, 317; Secretary of State, 152, 202; War of 1812, declaration of, 244–47, 252
Mammoth cheese, 97–102, 104–6
Mandamus, writ of, 156
Mann, Dr. J.M., 56, 59
Marbury, William, 152–53, 157
Marbury v. Madison, 151–63
March, Angier, 86–87
Marshall, John, 2, 151–54, 162, 167, 319, 323
Maund, Thomas Martin, 297, 299
McCullough v. Maryland, 319, 323
Medicine: bloodletting and other treatments, 1, 3–4, 8–11, 53–55, 58–59; debates on medical treatments, 3–4, 8–11, 53–64; quackery, 53–54, 56–58, 62

Melampus, HMS, 179, 181

Mercury and New-England Palladium, 101, 105, 128, 132, 149

Methodists, 66, 68

Midnight appointments, 85, 152

Minns, Thomas, 104, 113, 128, 132, 149

Mississippi River, 137, 139–41, 149

Missouri Compromise, 349–62

Mitchell, Dr. Samuel L., 62–63

Monroe, James: election to presidency, 296; governor, state of Virginia, 66; Louisiana Purchase, diplomat to France, 137–38, 140, 146; panic of 1819, 327

Morales, Juan Ventura, 138

Morning Chronicle and Baltimore Advertiser, 297, 299, 340, 346

Morris, Gouverneur, 159–60

Morse, Jedidiah, 137

Morton, Washington, 182–83

Napoleon, 116–17, 137–38, 140, 202

Natchez Indians, 137

National Advocate, 306, 313–14, 326, 330, 332, 342–43

National Intelligencer: Burr conspiracy, 170–71; *Chesapeake-Leopard* Affair, 179–80, 184; District of Columbia, governance of, 24, 29; Embargo Act, 204, 208; George Washington's tomb, 15; Hartford Convention, 282, 287–89, 291; Louisiana Purchase, 145, 147; mammoth cheese, 102; *Marbury v. Madison,* 153–55, 157–58, 161; medical reforms, 57, 63; steamboats, 218; Tripolitan Treaty, 134; War of 1812, 245, 248–49, 261–62, 268, 277

National Messenger and Town and City Commercial Gazette, 297, 300

Nativism in the early national period, 109–22

Naturalization Act of 1798, 111, 113, 117

Nelson, Admiral Lord, 126

New-England Palladium, 114

New Haven Remonstrance, 85–96

New Jersey General Assembly, 189

New-Jersey Journal, 196

New Jersey's repeal of women's suffrage, 189–99

New Orleans, 137–43, 149

New Orleans (steamboat), 214, 217

New York Columbian, 220, 311

New-York Daily Advertiser, 330, 333, 351, 355

New-York Evening Post: Chesapeake-Leopard Affair, 185; Embargo Act, 204; immigration, 114; living conditions in New York City, 306–13, 315; Louisiana Purchase, 138, 141–45; mammoth cheese, 100, 104; medicine and public health, 56, 61–62, 67–71; poverty, 341; Missouri Compromise, 351, 356; and steamboats, 214, 217, 220; War of 1812, 247, 256, 259, 265, 269–72

New York Gazette, 56

New York Manumission Society, 352

New York Society for the Prevention of Pauperism, 338

Newburyport Herald, 117

Newburyport Herald and Commercial Gazette, 58

Newburyport Herald and Country Gazette, 7, 40, 88, 295

Niles, Hezekiah, 245, 250, 266, 319, 322–23, 328, 334, 352, 361

Niles, John Milton, 282, 290, 296, 298

Niles' Register, 352, 361

Niles' Weekly Register, 245, 250, 267, 319, 322–23, 325, 334

Noah, Mordecai Manual (Howard), 326, 330, 332, 342–43

Non-Intercourse Act of 1808, 202, 244

Norfolk Gazette and Publick Ledger, 175, 178–79

Norvell, John, 297, 302

Ogden, Sen. Matthias, 189

Ohio Gazette, 173

Orleans Gazette, 167, 173

Osborn, Selleck, 297, 300–1

Otis, Harrison Gray, 109, 280, 288

Paine, Thomas, 43

Palladium, 91

Panic of 1819 (economic), 325–35
Parkhurst, Jabez, 93
The Patron of Industry, 327
Patronage, of Thomas Jefferson, 85–96
Pennington, Samuel, 93, 131
Philadelphia, USS, 126, 129
Philadelphia Gazette, 56
Phillips, Naphtali, 306, 313–14
Pickering, John, 88
Pickering, Timothy, 277, 280, 288
Pierce, First Mate John, 177, 183
Pinckney, Charles Cotesworth, 37–38, 126
Pintard, John, 338
Pittsburgh Gazette, 217
Pittsburgh Mercury, 217
Pleasants, Samuel, 39, 48
Plumer, William, 350
Porcupine's Gazette, 4, 9, 54–55, 57
The Port Folio, 100, 106
Poulson, Zachariah, 60
Poulson's *American Daily Advertiser,* 60
Poverty and pauperism, in the early national period, 337–47
Presbyterians, 68
Prophet, 226, 227–29, 230–35
Prophet's Town, 226–29, 232, 235, 240
Prosser, Gabriel, 65–66, 68
Prosser, Morten, 65
Prosser, Thomas H., 65
The Public Advertiser, 208
Public health, 53
Public health and safety, New York City, 305–16

Quakers, 39, 47–48, 66
Queen Anne, 189

Raleigh Register, and North-Carolina Gazette, 265
Rawlins, George, 1
The Recorder, 246, 252
Religious liberty (freedom), 97–99
Religious oppression, 39–40, 47–48
Republican Argus, and Weekly Advertiser, 111, 118
Republican émigré editors, 110–9
Republicanism, 101

Republican Party (Democratic-Republicans; Jeffersonian Republicans): election of 1800–1801, 37–40, 48–50; Era of Good Feelings, 296–97; George Washington's death, 3; Hartford Convention, 282; *Marbury v. Madison,* 152, 155, 157; New England, 279; New Haven Remonstrance, 85–87; panic of 1819, 326; scandals, 295; U.S. Constitution, 159–61; War of 1812, 244, 249, 255, 259; women's suffrage, 189–93, 195–97
Revolutionary War, 3, 21–22, 202
Rhoades, Ebenezer, 92, 119, 144–46, 210
Richmond Daily Compiler, 265
Richmond Enquirer: Burr conspiracy, 169–172; Missouri Compromise, 351–52, 354, 359; national banks, 319, 324; slave revolts, 71, 169, 172
Richmond Examiner, 153
Rind, Jr., William A., 297, 300
Rind, Sr., William A., 45, 153, 155–56, 182, 186, 297
Riots of 1812, Baltimore, 246–47
Ritchie, Thomas, 169, 172, 319, 331, 351–52, 354, 359
Roane, Spencer, 323
Robinson, Joseph, 121
Roman Catholics, 48
Roosevelt, Lydia, 214
Roosevelt, Nicholas, 214, 218
Rothbard, Murray N., 325
Rush, Dr. Benjamin, 54–55, 57–58
The Rush-Light, 4, 10, 53, 55, 57–58
Russell, Benjamin, 148, 246, 255, 280, 282–83, 296, 298
Russell, John, 203, 247, 258, 281, 285

Salem Gazette, 210, 247, 257, 273
Salem Register, 140
Schaeffer, Frederick G., 297, 299
Scull, John, 217
Sears, Louis Martin, 201
Seaton, William W., 261–62, 276, 319, 356–58

Second Bank of the United States, 317–24
Sedition Act, 120
Seward, William H., 349
Shaw, Mrs. Charity, 62–63
Shawnee Indians, 225–26, 232, 235
Slave revolts, 65–84
Slavery, extension of, 349–62
Slaves, captives of Barbary states, 125–27, 129, 135
Small-pox (kine-pox) 53, 56, 59–60
Smith, Samuel Harrison, 40, 48, 102, 134, 145–46, 156–58, 161, 170–71, 180, 184,
Smith, Sen. John, 167
Smith, Thomas, 229, 235, 237–40. 245–47, 252
"The Star-Spangled Banner," 262
St. Domingo (Haitian) Rebellion, 70
Sterrett, Lieutenant Andrew, 126, 128, 132
St. Louis Enquirer, 351–53
Stout, Elihu, 229, 232–34
Street, Joseph M., 170
Strong, Governor Caleb, 279
Suffrage, women's, in New Jersey, 189–99
The Sun, 99–100
Supreme Court, United States, 151–52, 156–57, 161

Tallmadge, Jr., James, 350
Tecumseh, 225, 227–28, 233–34 *Temple of Reason,* 110
Thornton, Dr. William, 215
The Times, 290, 299
Tippecanoe, Battle of, 225–41
Trenton Society for the Abolition of Slavery, 67
Tripoli (corsair), 126, 128
Tripolitan (Barbary) War, 125–36
True American: election of 1800–1801, 32–34; Gabriel's rebellion, 67, 72–74, 77, 80, 82; *Marbury v. Madison,* 154, 158, 160; nativism, 121; poverty, 344; Tripolitan War, 129, 134; women's suffrage, 193
Tuckerman, Joseph, 338

Turner, Nat, 65
Tuttle, William, 245, 251
Twyman, George, 68

Union, 327
United States' Gazette, 70, 167–68, 264, 268, 271, 275

Vesey, Denmark, 65
Vesuvius (steamboat), 219
Virginia Argus, 39, 48, 68, 83
Virginia Gazette and General Advertiser, 28
Virginia Herald, 66–67, 83
Voting rights, 189–90, 192
Vulcan, Dick, 39, 43

"Wall of separation," between church and state, 97, 99, 102
War hawks, congressional, 244
War of 1812, 70; 243–60, 261–78, 279, 325, 337
Washington Federalist: Chesapeake-Leopard Affair, 182, 186; election of 1800–1801, 39, 43, 45; Jefferson's patronage, 91; Louisiana Purchase, 143–45; *Marbury v. Madison,* 153–56, 159; tomb for George Washington, 4, 12–13
Washington, George: and Aaron Burr, 165; death of, 1–19; 55, 57; eulogies, 3–8; funeral and burial, 2–6; toasts to, 194; tomb of, 12–19; and Washington, D.C., 21–22
Washington, George, USS, 126
Washington, Martha, 4
Washington, D.C., becomes the United States Capital, 21–34
Washington, D.C., burning of during War of 1812, 261–78
Waterhouse, Dr. Benjamin, 56, 59
Watson, David, 297, 299
Webster, Daniel, 166
Webster, Noah, 56
Wellington, Aaron S., 162
The Western World, 170
Wheatley, Phillis (Phyllis), 74, 76

Wild Irish Speech, 109
Wilkinson, General James, 167
Wilson, James J., 32–34, 121, 129, 134, 159
Winchester Constellation, 43
Winder, Brigadier General William, 262, 271–72
Wollstonecraft, Mary, 191–92, 196
Woodstock Observer, 299

Worsley, W. W., 252
Wright, David, 67, 82

Yellow fever, 53, 56, 337
York, 1813 Battle of, 273
Young, Alexander, 104, 113, 128, 132, 149

Zaama (African American), 67, 72–77, 80

About the Author

PATRICIA L. DOOLEY is Associate Professor and Director of Graduate Studies at the Elliot School of Communications at the University of Wichita. Her first book, *Taking Their Political Place: Journalists and the Making of an Occupation*, released in 1997, came out in paperback form in 2000.